COMPARATIVE POLITICS

The Performance of Democracies

COMPARATIVE POLITICS

Comparative Politics is a series for students and teachers of political science
that deals with contemporary issues in comparative government and politics.
As Comparative European Politics it has produced a series of high quality books since
its foundation in 1990, but now takes on a new form and new title for the new
millennium—Comparative Politics. As the process of globalization proceeds, and as
Europe becomes ever more enmeshed in world trends and events, so it is necessary to
broaden the scope of the series. The General Editors are Max Kaase, Vice President and
Dean of Humanities and Social Sciences, International University, Bremen; and Kenneth
Newton, Professor of Comparative Politics, University of Southampton. The series
is published in association with the European Consortium for Political Research.

OTHER TITLES IN THIS SERIES

Democratic Challenges, Democratic Choices
Russell J. Dalton

Democracy Transformed?
Edited by Bruce E. Cain, Russell J. Dalton, and Susan E. Scarrow

Environmental Protest in Western Europe
Edited by Christopher Rootes

Social Movements and Networks
Edited by Mario Diani and Doug McAdam

Delegation and Accountability in Parliamentary Democracies
Edited by Kaare Strøm, Wolfgang C. Müller, and Torbjörn Bergman

The Presidentialization of Politics
Edited by Thomas Poguntke and Paul Webb

Losers' Consent
*Christopher J. Anderson, André Blais, Shaun Bowler,
Todd Donovan, and Ola Listhaug*

Elections, Parties, Democracy
Michael D. McDonald and Ian Budge

The Performance of Democracies
Political Institutions and Public Policies

EDELTRAUD ROLLER

Translated by John Bendix

UNIVERSITY PRESS

OXFORD
UNIVERSITY PRESS

Great Clarendon Street, Oxford OX2 6DP

Oxford University Press is a department of the University of Oxford.
It furthers the University's objective of excellence in research, scholarship,
and education by publishing worldwide in

Oxford New York

Auckland Cape Town Dar es Salaam Hong Kong Karachi
Kuala Lumpur Madrid Melbourne Mexico City Nairobi
New Delhi Shanghai Taipei Toronto

With offices in

Argentina Austria Brazil Chile Czech Republic France Greece
Guatemala Hungary Italy Japan Poland Portugal Singapore
South Korea Switzerland Thailand Turkey Ukraine Vietnam

Oxford is a registered trade mark of Oxford University Press
in the UK and in certain other countries

Published in the United States
by Oxford University Press Inc., New York

British Library Cataloguing in Publication Data
Data available

Library of Congress Cataloging in Publication Data
Data available

Typeset by SPI Publisher Services, Pondicherry, India
Printed in Great Britain
on acid-free paper by
Biddles Ltd., King's Lynn, Norfolk

ISBN 0-19-928642-6   978-0-19-928642-3

1 3 5 7 9 10 8 6 4 2

Acknowledgements

This book was written during my tenure as Senior Fellow at the Social Science Research Center Berlin (WZB). The project was part of the research programme of the research unit 'Institutions and Social Change' directed by Hans-Dieter Klingemann. While doing this research I benefited to a great degree from the excellent working conditions and the stimulating intellectual environment at the WZB. In particular, I am greatly indebted to Hans-Dieter Klingemann for his steady encouragement and generous support for my work.

Many other individuals have supported the project in various ways. Heiko Gothe, Jutta Horstmann, and Achim Kielhorn helped with collecting the data. Katarina Pollner provided valuable assistance in computer graphics and word-processing. I am grateful to Dieter Fuchs, Richard Hofferbert, Kenneth Newton, Manfred G. Schmidt, Kai-Uwe Schnapp, Bernhard Weßels, and Thomas Zittel for their critical comments and helpful suggestions. Konstanza Prinzessin zu Löwenstein deserves special thanks for providing resources and creating a productive atmosphere. I appreciate the interest of the series editors, Max Kaase and Kenneth Newton, in the project and the encouragement they provided. Finally, I would like to thank Dominic Byatt, Claire M. Croft, as well as Maggie Shade and Elizabeth Suffling from Oxford University Press for their professional assistance in the publication of the book.

I would like to thank the following for permission to reproduce published material: Gabriel A. Almond, G. Bingham Powell Jr., Kaare Strøm, and Russell J. Dalton (Table 2.2) and VS Verlag für Sozialwissenschaften (Figure 3.5, Tables 2.1, 2.9, 3.3, and 4.24).

E.R.

Contents

viii   *Contents*

List of Figures

List of Tables

Tables in the Appendix

1

Introduction

Is the effectiveness of western political systems declining? Are differences in institutions from one country to another associated with differences in effectiveness? Contemporary analyses of the conditions and the development of modern democracies give much attention to political effectiveness. The continuous decline of effectiveness that undermines the confidence of citizens in the democratic regime and by that it is generating stress on the persistence of these regimes was a prominent theme in various crisis theories since the 1970s. Assertions of 'ungovernability' (Crozier et al. 1995; King 1975) or the 'legitimation crisis' (Habermas 1988) in western democracies during the 1970s marked the beginning of an intense political discussion about the structural causes for the decline of effectiveness. Among other things, these theories asserted that the 'failure of the state' was due to the increasing scope of governmental responsibilities.

The issue of diminishing political effectiveness has been revived since the early 1990s, now in the context of 'globalization theories' (Beck 1998; Habermas 1998; Münch 1998; Scharpf 1998; Zürn 1998; Held et al. 1999). These theories see two different processes at work. Growing transnational interdependence on the one hand decreases the capacity of national governments to control public policies, making it increasingly difficult to realize major policy goals such as social welfare, domestic security, or environmental protection. Competition between national economies on the other hand leads to relaxing domestic environmental and social policy standards in order to attract investors, with the result that poverty spreads and environmental quality degrades. Both processes will be so compelling that national public policies and policy patterns will become more and more alike and western democracies will converge on a lower level of performance.

Globalization theories assume these processes have been at work already since the mid-1970s but have been reinforced since 1990 with the breakdown of the socialist systems in Central and Eastern Europe. In accordance with academic and public discourse, these theories assume that the 'golden age of the post-war era' (Maddison 1991: 1), characterized by continuous economic growth and a simultaneous realization of other policy goals, social policy in particular, came to an end in 1973. The 1973 Oil Crisis and the subsequent economic recession marked a turning point and inaugurated a fundamental change in the effectiveness of western democracies.

According to globalization theories, the politics of finding a 'relative equilibrium' (Zürn 1998: 13) or 'balance' (Münch 1998: 17) between inherently conflicting goals such as economic efficiency and social justice, or economic efficiency and environmental protection, characteristic of the 'golden age', will be no longer possible. They assert that 'the unavoidable economic goals' can be achieved only 'at the expense' of sacrificing effectiveness in other policy areas (Dahrendorf 1996; Habermas 1998: 69). Consequently, the 'trade-off' between policy areas will increase.

Until the rediscovery of political institutions (March and Olsen 1984) at the beginning of the 1980s, the role of political institutions for performance was neglected. But empirical evidence in the wake of the economic recession that followed the Oil Crisis in 1973 revealed that some democratic systems coped better with policy problems, while others addressed them poorly or not at all (e.g. Scharpf 1991). In the 'new institutionalist' approach these differences are explained by differences in the institutional settings of democratic nation-states and consequently it is assumed that appropriate changes to such structures would lead to improved performance.

In *Constitutional Democracies*, for example, Mueller examines the 'failures' of the US and European governments to address issues such as criminality, poverty, unemployment, and state debt (1996). He sees constitutional rules as the source of these problems and suggests corresponding constitutional reforms to improve performance in the respective policies. In the case of the USA, for example, he argues that the basic 'separation of powers' structure needs to be altered. In this context we want to point out that not only political scientists but also political practitioners take it for granted that institutions 'matter' for political performance. This can be seen when practitioners suggest fundamental reforms of political institutions in order to solve current political problems. In 1997, for example, the president of a German employers' association, Henkel (1997), suggested a reform not just of the federal political structure and the bicameral system, but also a replacement of proportional representation with a majority voting system as a way of increasing Germany's adaptivity to the new international economic conditions and increasing the country's problem-solving capacity. Comparable examples can be cited for many nations.

In discussions about the effectiveness of western democracies two facts are taken for granted: a continuous decline of effectiveness and the impact of democratic political institutions on effectiveness. In this book both theoretical assumptions are taken up and tested empirically and comparatively.

Goals, Questions, and Framework of the Study

The present study has two goals. One is to systematically address, revise, and empirically review the hypotheses put forward in various theories about the development of effectiveness in western democracies since the mid-1970s. The other is to conceptualize and empirically test the widely accepted 'neo-institutionalist' thesis that political institutions decisively influence national policy effectiveness. To pursue these goals, the study is divided into descriptive and explanatory sections.

The *descriptive* section begins with an examination and broad assessment of the development of effectiveness in western democracies from the recessionary period of the mid-1970s ushered in by the Oil Crisis through the mid-1990s. We are aiming at a comprehensive stocktaking of effectiveness in western democracies. In doing so we analyse effectiveness in major domestic policy areas—domestic security policy, economic policy, social policy, and environmental policy—and a broader 'general effectiveness' that encompasses all the policy areas studied. The question guiding this part of the research is: Has the effectiveness of western democracies declined, either in policy specific or more general terms? Further, which nations show the best and worst performance?

We also raise the contentious question of the relationship between effectiveness in different policy areas, and the development of such policy patterns over time. Is it the case that economic and social, or economic and environmental goals are incompatible or in conflict, such that realizing economic goals is only possible at the cost of realizing social and environmental goals? In that case we have trade-offs between policy areas. Or, by contrast, can the goals of economic and social policy, or of economic and environmental policy, be equally realized so that their relationship could be characterized as complementary? How have these policy patterns evolved since the mid-1970s? Is it true, as it is assumed in globalization theories, that tension between various policy goals has increased to the point that conflictual relationships have supplanted complementary ones?

Effectiveness is a criterion for evaluating political performance, and it refers to the degree to which desired goals are achieved through political action. For this reason we do not analyse activities or efforts to reach the goals—whether in the form of laws, personnel, or state outlays—but instead the actual results or outcomes in these four policy areas. The implication of this approach can be most clearly demonstrated for social policy. Rather than using output indicators that measure governmental effort, such as the degree of redistribution in the form of social expenditure, we use outcome indicators measuring the result of political action, such as the poverty rate and infant mortality. Hence, the analysis does not focus on the different means for reaching goals and how or why they change, but instead on long-term and lasting political outcomes that decisively determine people's life circumstances.

The question 'Do institutions matter?' is at the core of the second, *explanatory* section of the study. Here the focus is whether the institutional settings of democracies—majoritarian and negotiation democracies[1]—have an influence on the level, development, and structure (policy patterns) of effectiveness, and what influence they have.

We deliberately do not investigate the effect of individual structural characteristics such as the relationship between executive and legislative (parliamentarism or presidentialism) or the (federal or unitary) structure of the state but instead examine the effect of democratic institutional arrangements or institutional settings as a whole.[2] There are several reasons for this. First, as noted by Lijphart (1984, 1999a) individual structural characteristics do not occur at random in modern democracies. Instead, power-concentrating structures such as unicameralism or unitary structure occur together, much as power-dispersing structures such as bicameralism or federalism do. To characterize these two differing types of democracy, Lijphart coined the contrasting terms 'majoritarian democracies' and 'consensus democracies' (1984). Second, each individual structural characteristic may have a different effect, so that only a specific combination of features will determine the performance of a given nation (Fuchs 2000).

There is a more proximate cause for proceeding in this manner. In 1999 Lijphart published a comprehensive study of the performance of majoritarian and consensus democracies in which he concludes that in some respects—in social, environmental, and foreign aid policies and in some aspects of domestic security policy—consensus democracies are superior to and outperform majoritarian democracies (Lijphart 1999a: 293–300). This finding reflects their stronger orientation toward community and a greater social consciousness; politics in consensus democracies, he argues, is generally 'kinder and gentler' than in majoritarian democracies. At present, Lijphart's study dominates the debate on the performance of different types of democracy (e.g. Anderson 2001; Armingeon 2002; Schmidt 2002). However, his work suffers from several flaws not only in research design, but more particularly in how he conceptualizes and measures political institutions and political performance. Thus, the question of the performance of different types of democracies cannot yet be regarded as resolved. At this juncture

---

[1] For reasons presented in Chapter 3 we prefer the term 'negotiation democracy' and not 'consensus democracy' coined by Lijphart (1984, 1999a).

[2] The term 'institutional arrangement' (or 'setting') draws attention to the fact that it is not individual structural characteristics or individual political institutions that are the focus, but rather a whole set of characteristics. This collective idea is sometimes simply referred to here as 'institutions' (or as the 'political order').

I will sketch briefly the problems of his conceptualization and measurement of institutions as far as they are relevant here.

Initially, Lijphart postulated two types of democracy. Yet his empirical analysis led him to conclude that his selected set of structural characteristics in fact yielded two clusters of 'clearly separate dimensions' that he named the *executives–parties dimension* and the *federal–unitary dimension* (1999a: 2–3, also 1984). The former dimension includes five characteristics: (*a*) concentration versus dispersion of executive power, (*b*) power relations between executive and legislative, (*c*) the structure of the party system, (*d*) the electoral system, and (*e*) the interest group system. The federal–unitary dimension also covers five characteristics: (*a*) state structure (unitary versus federal), (*b*) legislatures (unicameral versus bicameral), (*c*) the flexibility of the constitution, (*d*) judicial review, and (*e*) central bank autonomy (Lijphart 1999a: 3–4). The key difference between the two dimensions is that the second refers to formal or constitutionally defined structures, while the first measures informal or empirical structures arising from the interaction between collective political actors (Fuchs 2000). As will be argued in greater detail later, the theoretical conceptualization of the informal executives–parties dimension is too imprecise—it includes not just political institutions but also a politico-economic institution in the form of pluralist or corporatist interest group systems—and there are serious flaws in the measurement of this dimension. So Lijphart's empirical finding that consensus democracies outperform majoritarian democracies, along this executives–parties dimension, needs to be put in question.

The explanatory section of our study examines the following questions concerning the level, development, and structure (or policy patterns) of political effectiveness: First, do constitutional and informal institutional settings have an effect on the level of both policy-specific and general effectiveness? Is there a set of democratic institutions that is superior in terms of effectiveness, as Lijphart asserts is the case for consensus democracies along the executives–parties dimension? Second, how do the constitutional and informal institutional settings affect the development or stability of policy-specific and general effectiveness? Is politics in negotiation democracies more strongly marked by political stability while majoritarian democracies are more able to carry out policy change? Third, do constitutional and informal institutions determine national policy patterns in such a manner that negotiation democracies produce more balanced patterns than majoritarian democracies?

A sound theoretical framework is required to conduct an empirical analysis of these descriptive and causal questions. To analyse the descriptive questions, normative criteria for effectiveness need to be specified and substantiated in such a manner that they can also be measured, and the relationship between these criteria needs to be clarified theoretically. For the causal analysis, an explanatory model is required not just to establish what influence institutional settings have on effectiveness, but to also take the most important, non-institutional factors (socio-economic modernity, political actors, and economic globalization) into account. So far, research has largely concentrated on particular aspects of these broad questions—studies focus primarily on the effectiveness in particular policy areas—so that existing theoretical approaches are too specific and insufficient to guide the empirical analyses striven after here. For this reason it is necessary to develop not just a theoretical 'Model for Evaluating the Effectiveness of Liberal Democracies' but also a theoretical 'Model for Explaining the Performance of Liberal Democracies' prior to the empirical analysis.

Contemporary crisis theories on the decline of effectiveness of western democracies on the one hand, and the hypothesis that political institutions matter for effectiveness on the other, provide the starting point and context for our study. But attempts to evaluate political systems also evoke an ancient political question: How can one identify a good political order? My study specifies criteria for evaluating performance, and tests the extent to which the different institutional settings found in democracies systematically influence performance. Yet at heart it intends to make a theoretical and empirical contribution to a basic question in political science: What constitutes a good political order?

The empirical basis for the analysis is provided by evidence from twenty-one OECD nations—Australia, Austria, Belgium, Canada, Denmark, Finland, France, Germany (up to 1991 West Germany), Great Britain, Greece, Ireland, Italy, Japan, the Netherlands, New Zealand, Norway, Portugal, Spain, Sweden, Switzerland, and the USA—from 1974 to 1995.[3]

Going Beyond the Current State of Research

This study of the performance of democracies stands in the tradition of comparative research on democracy. But effectiveness, understood as the degree to which intended goals are realized, is an object of inquiry in comparative public policy and comparative sociological research on the quality of life as well. Accordingly, theoretical and empirical instruments from these other research traditions are utilized for certain aspects of the argument. Thus, we elaborate to what extent the study goes beyond the current state of research in all three traditions.

Comparative research on democracy at its core deals with three questions: How do democratic polities (structures) function? How do polities come about? What effects do they have on politics (the political process) and on policies? The last question on the effects of democratic structures is also the most recent research question in this tradition. It has been more intensively

---

[3] Luxembourg and Iceland could not be included in the analysis due to missing data.

pursued since the 1990s under the catchword 'performance'. Recent interest is due in part to the collapse of state socialist systems in Central and Eastern Europe, for with the end of the most important alternative to democracy as a form of government, renewed attention is drawn to existing differences between democratic systems. In this context, knowledge of political perform-ance takes on great practical significance as it might help answer the question which type of democracy should be implemented (through constitutional engineering) in Central and Eastern Europe (Kaase 1995; Fuchs 1998).

Democratic theorists have long called for systematic, theoretical, and empirical evaluation of political systems (Dahl 1967), but until the 1990s only a few isolated studies devoted themselves to such evaluation. The outset of systematic theoretical and empirical analysis can be precisely dated to 1971 and the publication of two related works: Eckstein's *The Evaluation of Political Performance: Problems and Dimensions* and Gurr's *Political Per-formance: A Twelve-Nation Study* (written with McClelland). Eckstein devel-oped and justified theoretical criteria for evaluating political systems, while Gurr made a first systematic attempt to empirically translate and apply Eckstein's criteria. Almond and Powell (1978), and Powell (1982), subse-quently produced a comparable pair of studies. In the fourth section of their systems-theoretical work *Comparative Politics* (1978), Almond and Powell suggested the concept of political productivity for evaluating political sys-tems. In *Contemporary Democracies* (1982), Powell then turned some of Almond and Powell's criteria into empirical indicators. He was a pioneer in systematically investigating the effect democratic structures had on a set of criteria of performance.

The more numerous analyses that have appeared during the 1990s only partly make reference to these earlier studies of political performance. One may count Putnam's *Making Democracy Work* (1993), Weaver and Rock-man's edited volume *Do Institutions Matter?* (1993), Lijphart's revised edi-tion of *Patterns of Democracy* (1999a), whose first results were originally published in article form in 1994, and Schmidt's *Demokratietheorien* (2000a), as among the most important and influential works on the performance of democracies.

Of these, Lijphart's *Patterns of Democracy* is the most relevant precursor for our study, as he investigates the structures (from 1945 to 1995) and performance (from 1970 to 1995) of thirty-six democracies. Lijphart's work provides the primary reference point for working out the specific character-istics of our study, and for determining which aspects go beyond the current state of research. Here our focus is primarily on how he conceptualizes performance as well as on his explanatory model.

To begin with, one should note that Lijphart does not have an elaborated concept of performance. He neither uses an explicit set of criteria to select his thirty-two performance indicators, nor does he justify his choice of individual measures (Lijphart 1999*a*: chs. 15 and 16). Instead, indicators are introduced in an ad hoc fashion, and justified only with plausibility arguments. A more careful examination shows that his indicators measure quite varied dimensions. Measures of governmental effort (such as social expenditure) are mixed with characteristics of policy programmes and benefits (how woman-friendly family policies are, or how 'decommodified' social policies are) and indicators for the outcomes of political action (such as poverty rates). What these measures all have in common is that they are related to policies, but by measuring different aspects of outputs and outcomes they reflect quite different policy manifestations. Lijphart also employs indicators based on attitudes (such as how satisfied citizens are with democracy) and the behaviour of citizens (such as voter turnout rates).

Clearly, Lijphart is investigating a broad spectrum of all conceivable *effects* of democracy, and in that sense one can argue that he does not attach any specific meaning to performance itself. Instead, he uses performance as a general term for all possible or supposed effects of democracy.

For our purposes, it is crucial to determine which among the many indicators could serve as measures of effectiveness in specific policy areas. Lijphart's list of indicators contains all the relevant domestic policy areas (domestic security, economic, social, and environmental). But of the ten indicators that can be assigned to these policy areas,[4] only four—unemployment, the inflation rate, socio-economic inequality, and Palmer's measure of environmental pollution (1997)—are relatively clear measures of outcomes.

A theoretical, explanatory model exists only in rudimentary form in Lijphart's work. It consists of the executives–parties and federal–unitary dimensions and two general control variables: level of economic development and population size (Lijphart 1999*a*: 262). From an action theory perspective, collective actors such as governments are missing, for 'policy results cannot be explained directly with democratic structures' (Schmidt 2000*a*: 347). It remains unclear, as the relevant theoretical considerations are also lacking, how one is to imagine the connection between political institutions and performance. The rudimentary theoretical model also has implications for empirical analysis; the effect of the institutional variables is not controlled for other competing and potentially influencing factors. It thus remains open whether the empirical connection Lijphart asserts between the executives–parties dimension and performance in fact goes back to the

---

[4] Lijphart's indicators (1999*a*: chs. 15 and 16) of 'incarceration rate' and 'death penalty' can be assigned to domestic security policy; the indicators 'economic growth', 'inflation rate', and 'unemployment' to economic policy; the indicators 'socioeconomic inequality', 'social expenditure', and 'welfare state index'—based on Esping-Anderson's (1990) 'decommodification' index—to social policy; and the 'energy efficiency' indicator and the 'Palmer index' (1997; concern for the environment) to environmental policy.

institutions themselves or is the result of other intervening variables (Schmidt 2000*a*: 346; Armingeon 2002: 89).

In terms of performance, our study attempts to be theoretically more precise and more focused than Lijphart's *Patterns of Democracy*. We are investigating one specific dimension of performance, namely effectiveness. This can be regarded as the central dimension of performance, in addition to the question of responsiveness. Our study also is guided by a theoretical frame of reference. Using a classification of performance criteria, effectiveness is defined subsequently and with the help of a normative model of political effectiveness (one heavily based on Almond and Powell's political productivity concept) and individual subdimensions of effectiveness are theoretically determined and justified. Finally, these subdimensions are measured using pure outcome indicators.

At the same time, our study clearly goes beyond Lijphart in other respects. First, we present an independent, descriptive analysis of the effectiveness of western democracies by studying its level, development, and structure. Second, we investigate the influence of political institutions not just on the level of effectiveness but also on stability and policy patterns. We go beyond Lijphart in terms of theoretical explanation by drawing on the explanatory models suggested in three different research traditions (comparative research on democracy, comparative public policy, and the veto player approach) to develop a comprehensive model for explaining the performance of liberal democracies. In so doing, we posit the most important non-institutional explanatory factors and, using a rational choice approach, theoretically conceptualize how they work in concert with institutional factors.

The core of *comparative public policy research* is to explain how policies come about, and the central question is to what extent polities (political structures) and politics (political processes) shape them (Schmidt 1997*a*; Castles 2002). Until the 1990s, the politics aspect stood at the forefront, with the question 'Do parties matter?' guiding research (Castles 1982). In the wake of the neo-institutionalist paradigm, attention in the 1990s has been devoted more frequently to the effect political institutions have on policies. Empirical studies of the effect democratic structures have on policies now exist for all domestic policy areas investigated here, with the exception of domestic security.[5]

Comparative public policy research is organized along policy areas; or rather studies generally concentrate on one policy area. If more are analysed, then at most two closely related policy areas, as with social and economic

---

[5] Examples of studies analysing the effect of political structure characteristics include Crepaz (1996), Armingeon (1999, 2002), and Anderson (2001) for economic policy; Huber et al. (1993), Schmidt (1997*b*) and Birchfield and Crepaz (1998) for social policy; and Jänicke (1992), Vogel (1993), Crepaz (1995), Jahn (1998), and Scruggs (1999, 2003) for environmental policy.

policies. The most comprehensive investigation to date of the development of policies and the effect political institutions have on them is Castles's *Comparative Public Policy* (1998*a*). In it, he examines twenty-one nations (from 1960 to 1990) with respect to the level and development of the reach of the state ('big government') and the welfare state, as well as the development of various aspects of the labour market and the private sphere (home ownership, fertility, divorce rates). His analysis is atypical for comparative public policy research, in a sense, as he examines a broad spectrum of policies simultaneously, but it is quite typical inasmuch as it largely analyses outputs, and only secondarily outcomes. Castles's chapter on the welfare state, for example, restricts itself to an analysis of government expenditures for transfer payments, health, and education (all output measures) while outcome indicators such as poverty or infant mortality are neglected.

Few comparative public policy studies have researched the trade-offs between policy areas. There is a longer tradition of work analysing the relationship between economic and social policy (see, for example, Korpi 1985; Castles and Dowrick 1990; Kenworthy 1995; Hicks and Kenworthy 1998). Generally, such studies investigate the relationship between economic outcomes (such as levels of economic development) and socio-political outputs (such as social expenditures). More recent studies investigate the relationship between economic wealth and environmental indicators (Jänicke et al. 1996*a*). But as yet no study has investigated whether political institutions have an effect on the trade-off between policy areas or on policy patterns.

The theoretical considerations and methods developed in comparative public policy are useful to our study particularly in developing our theoretical, explanatory model and in the empirical analysis of trade-offs between policy areas. Yet our study goes beyond the current state of research in comparative public policy in three ways. For one, a broad spectrum of policy areas is taken into account at the same time. Our study, unlike Castles's broadly designed investigation, focuses on the most important domestic policy areas, and only investigates outcomes. For another, both general effectiveness and policy patterns are analysed in addition. And last, three completely new aspects are addressed: whether political institutions have an effect on the stability of effectiveness, on general effectiveness, and on the balance of policy patterns.

Comparative research on the quality of life (aspects of which are also called social indicator research) is the sociological equivalent of public policy research in political science. The objects of inquiry here are individual welfare products in various areas of life delivered by different welfare producers (Zapf 1979) or institutions (Vogel 1998). Welfare with respect to various societal goals is provided not just by the government but also by the market, associations, and by private households. The focus is not on outputs or, as they are called in this research tradition, resources, but on results or 'end products' for the individuals (Zapf 1977: 235). The main objective of this research is to provide descriptive information about the degree to which societal goals have been achieved. This can find practical use in political decision-making processes, but the findings are also meant for the enlightenment of society (Zapf 1977: 234; Carley 1981: ix). A secondary objective is to explain differences in national welfare (Zapf 1977: 234). The few existing works on this question focus on structural factors such as the specific national mix of welfare producers (Vogel 1998).

By investigating welfare produced by three different institutions, the objects of inquiry in quality of life research are broader than in comparative research on democracy or public policy, as they tend to focus only on the effectiveness of one institution, namely the government. Nevertheless, *governmental* effectiveness in the form of so-called 'policy indicators' (Carley 1981: 25) are at the centre of most comparative quality of life research as well (e.g. income distribution, crime victims). Two important reasons surely account for this. The first is that policy indicators related to political tasks and goals are open to political manipulation. The second is that it is primarily international organizations pursuing political objectives, such as the OECD (1986*a*), the EU (Eurostat 1997), or the UN (1989), including the *United Nations Development Program* (UNDP 1990), that conduct comparative research on the quality of life.

The part of this research tradition most relevant to our study lies in how outcomes are conceptualized, differentiated, and measured. Welfare is seen multidimensionally and hierarchically, with the highest, global level referring to a welfare encompassing all areas of life; a middle, area-specific level referring to welfare in individual areas of life; and the lowest, specific level referring to aspects within individual areas of life (Andrews 1981). By analogy, we differentiate between three levels of political effectiveness: (*a*) a general effectiveness encompassing all policy areas, (*b*) a policy-specific effectiveness at the level of individual policy areas, and (*c*) an effectiveness with respect to the components of a particular policy such as the prevention of poverty in the area of social policy.

Beyond such conceptual differentiations, the empirical instruments developed in quality-of-life (QOL) research are also useful to our study. The hierarchical concept of welfare necessitates aggregating specific information into composite measures, called QOL indices in this research tradition. Due to the enlightened intent inherent to this research tradition, such aggregate measures are often constructed in a clear and comprehensible manner (Zapf 1977: 235). The best known example of one such global measure is the UNDP's *Human Development Index* (1990). It incorporates three 'basic capability' measures (for health, education, and income) that allow citizens to participate in and contribute to their society. This index permits one to assess to what degree a nation deviates from normatively set minimum standards of development.

Our study of the effectiveness of democracies takes a broad view encompassing effectiveness in a variety of specific policy areas, such as comparative QOL research does. But unlike it, we focus on major domestic policy areas. But we also go beyond its current state of research. First, we analyse trade-offs between different policy areas as well as policy patterns. Second, we propose an index for measuring general political effectiveness that unlike the UNDP's well-known *Human Development Index* can also differentiate within the group of highly developed nations. Third, we make a contribution to explaining the effectiveness of public policy inasmuch as we investigate the influence of key determinants such as political institutions, socio-economic modernity, political actors, and economic globalization.

In sum, we can say that our analysis of the effectiveness of democracies addresses a question specific to the comparative study of democracy, but it also stands at the intersection of three research traditions. To conceptualize the most important independent variables—the democratic institutional settings—we turn to the findings from the comparative study of democracy; we also borrow from comparative, sociological, QOL research for the dependent variables of effectiveness; and from comparative public policy research for the explanatory model.

Organization of the Book

Our study is divided between theoretical and empirical sections, with the theoretical framework presented in Chapters 2 and 3, and the empirical analysis offered in Chapters 4 and 5. Descriptive questions about political effectiveness are examined in Chapters 2 and 4, while causal questions about the influence political institutions have on effectiveness are pursued in Chapters 3 and 5. Chapter 6 provides concluding observations. Chapters 2 through 5 each end with preliminary summaries of their most important results.

'A Model for Evaluating the Effectiveness of Liberal Democracies' is developed in Chapter 2 as part of the descriptive analysis. It includes both normative and empirical-analytic components. In the normative analysis effectiveness is demarcated from other performance criteria and five criteria for evaluating effectiveness were systematically derived and justified: (*a*) international security, (*b*) domestic security, (*c*) wealth, (*d*) socio-economic security and socio-economic equality, and (*e*) environmental protection. This 'normative model of political effectiveness' is heavily based on Almond and Powell's concept of political productivity (1978) that suggests performance criteria relevant to all political systems. All but international security are scrutinized in what follows.

The task of the 'empirical-analytic concept of political effectiveness' is to specify the normatively based effectiveness criteria in such a manner that it is possible to relate them to 'empirical referents' (Eckstein 1971: 5). The concept has two aspects: vertical and horizontal. First, the four general effectiveness criteria are 'vertically' specified into several individual components and then indicators are assigned to these components. Second, 'horizontal' relationships between different effectiveness criteria are specified. Here the most prominent propositions about trade-offs, such as between economic and social goals (efficiency vs. equality), or between economic and environmental goals (efficiency vs. environmental protection), as well as the best known concepts of compatibility between multiple conflicting goals (the growth paradigm, the sustainability concept), are brought together. A theoretical typology of political effectiveness then unifies these various theories on the relationship between specific policy areas. Finally, a concept of general political effectiveness and an index to measure this global dimension are proposed, with the global index meant as a summary QOL measure for developed industrial societies.

In Chapter 3, 'A Model for Explaining the Performance of Liberal Democracies' is suggested to answer causal questions. This model makes a claim to go beyond explaining effectiveness and be more generally applicable to explain political performance. It builds on the explanatory models found in three theoretical strands, the comparative research on democracy, comparative public policy, and the 'veto player' approach of the 'new institutionalism'. Selected characteristics of these three models, partly reformulated and partly stated more precisely, are integrated together with neglected factors into a comprehensive explanatory model. The main features of this model are as follows: At the centre stand institutions of democratic governance that according to Fuchs's (2000) concept of democratic institutional arrangements can be subdivided into the constitutionally defined 'governmental system', and the 'relationship between governing and opposition parties' based on informal rules. The most important non-institutional explanatory factors are the national level of wealth, ideological orientation of the government, and the openness of the economy that need to be controlled for in the empirical analysis. Finally, rational choice institutionalism is taken as a theoretical approach to conceptualize the causal structure of the model.

Chapter 3 also includes a discussion of the constitutional and partisan veto player indices thus far suggested for measuring these two institutions of democratic governance (Huber et al. 1993; Colomer 1996; Schmidt 1996; Lijphart 1999a; Fuchs 2000). As Lijphart's executives–parties index, designed to measure informal democratic structures, is particularly problematic, several alternative partisan veto player indices are suggested. The chapter ends with the formulation of systematic hypotheses about the effect constitutional and informal institutions of democratic governance have on the level, stability, and structure (or policy pattern) of political effectiveness.

The empirical part of our study is divided between a descriptive analysis of the 'Level, Development, and Structure of the Effectiveness of Western Democracies' (Chapter 4) and a causal analysis of the 'The Influence of Political Institutions on the Effectiveness of Western Democracies' (Chapter 5) for the period from 1974 to 1995. Both chapters are similarly structured. In Chapter 4, after describing the data base and the construction of the performance indices, comparative quantitative data is presented that delineates the level and development of policy-specific and general effectiveness across the twenty-one nations over the entire time period. The chapter concludes with a detailed empirical analysis of the trade-offs between individual policy areas and the types of political effectiveness. Chapter 5 presents a factor analysis of the various constitutional and partisan veto player indices. This is followed by a re-analysis of significant parts of Lijphart's *Patterns of Democracy* (1999*a*) with an eye to establishing to what extent his results regarding the performance of majoritarian and consensus democracies are an artifact of his executives–parties index. The chapter concludes with bivariate and multivariate regression analyses to determine the impact of political institutions on the level, stability, and structure of political effectiveness.

Chapter 6 summarizes the most important results of this investigation into the development of political effectiveness in western democracies since 1974 and the impact of political institutions. In so doing they are discussed with reference to theoretical and practical implications. Some 'common wisdom' about the decrease of effectiveness is shown to be without empirical foundation, while the question 'Do institutions matter?' can be affirmed—if with reservations. Political institutions matter, but only sometimes and only to a limited degree.

Design, Data, and Methods

At the heart of this study are two questions: How did political effectiveness develop in western democracies? Do democratic institutional settings have an influence on effectiveness, holding other competing explanatory factors constant? The hypotheses guiding the study are formulated with reference to western democracies. The specific objects of inquiry are the twenty-one aforementioned OECD nations that show many similarities with respect to social, economic, and political characteristics.

Limiting the investigation to such a relatively homogenous group of nations implies holding many competing factors constant, and the study thus follows a 'most similar systems' design (Przeworski and Teune 1970: 32). Not having to explicitly control for such factors in the empirical analysis substantially reduces a basic problem of comparative research: 'many variables, small N' (Lijphart 1971; Collier 1993). But this limitation also implies one can only detect those factors responsible for differences *within* this select group of democratic polities in the empirical analysis. It is not possible to simply generalize the results to all democracies.

The period investigated is from 1974 to 1995. It thus begins immediately after the economic recession brought about by the Oil Crisis, a generally agreed-upon turning point in the development of the performance of western industrial societies. Our investigation thereby differs from many other studies in that our time series do not begin from an arbitrary point determined by data availability or other non-theoretical criteria. Instead we use a clear reference point bearing theoretical significance. However, the related question whether 1974 was in fact a turning point cannot be answered based on the research design used here. To do so, one would have to include performance *prior* to 1974 in the analysis, but the data series for environmental policy, for example, only begins in the 1970s (see OECD 1985). Due to the absence of appropriate data, the development of effectiveness can only be properly investigated for the period after 1974.

A research design that encompasses many nations and a long time period is necessary to investigate the *general* hypotheses about the decline of effectiveness in western democracies since 1974. Such a design is also indispensable to adequately analyse the influence of political institutions. Empirical studies must be designed in such a manner that institutions even have a chance to demonstrate their influence. The 'intrinsic value' of long-standing institutions can only become evident in various spatial and temporal constellations, that is, in many different cases and at many different points in time. By the same token, investigating a longer time period ensures that situation-specific constellations are not incorrectly ascribed to the political institutions itself. In discussions of the economic and political competitiveness of nations, for example, national rankings are repeatedly based on performance indicators reported for only one or two years (see World Economic Forum 1999). Fundamental institutional reforms are then recommended on the basis of such extremely narrow, if not near-episodic, snapshots. The likelihood that situation-specific constellations are studied is considerably reduced when one uses a twenty-two-year time frame.

This period starting 1974 is also a particularly apt choice for studying the influence of political institutions. The Oil Crisis created a new set of problems, sometimes even referred to as an 'external shock', in all western democracies after 1973. All nations had to respond to this abrupt change and craft effective solutions for this new constellation. One can see particularly well which democratic institutional settings have coped successfully with these problems. Hence, to some extent the post-1973 situation constitutes a natural or quasi-experiment of the ability of national democratic institutions to address or solve problems.

Investigating the development of policy effectiveness in twenty-one nations from 1974 to 1995 is extremely challenging merely at the data level. The design calls for complete data series with comparable indicators for four policy areas, but this ideal data situation does not exist. Many indicators show gaps in the data series. Data are missing not only for individual points in time or periods, but certain nations even lack entire data series. Additionally, cross-national comparability of indicators is not always ensured. Hence it is necessary to make compromises if one wishes to conduct an empirical investigation of these important and controversial questions. To be able to make valid statements, systematic and comprehensible criteria for addressing data issues are necessary.

The strategy adopted here is to minimize problems of data availability and comparability as much as possible, and to openly indicate what choices were made and what problems remain. First, the number of countries, the time periods, and the indicators were narrowed to reduce data replacement procedures as much as possible. Moreover, the replacement procedures are documented in detail. Second, problems created by inadequate comparability between indicators were minimized by using data from international organizations (especially the OECD, also the WHO and Interpol) as well as from comparative research projects such as the *Luxembourg Income Study* (LIS). This does not ensure perfect comparability, though these institutions aim to maximize cross-national comparability. Thus we start from the assumption that we are employing the best available comparative data, a judgment supported by expert opinion.

Our study asks two general questions about the development of effectiveness and the influence of democratic institutions on effectiveness. Did effectiveness in western democracies continually decline since 1973? Is the effectiveness of public policies decisively influenced by democratic institutions? The data base includes fourteen indicators of effectiveness for twenty-one nations over twenty-two years, and additional data is used for institutional and non-institutional explanatory factors. Such a large amount of data can only be analysed with the help of quantitative, statistical methods. Of course, in a study like this, one cannot do justice to the situation and development of effectiveness in individual nations. That task is reserved to more qualitatively oriented comparative case studies.

2

A Model for Evaluating the Effectiveness of Liberal Democracies

The core of democratic theory is to develop and justify normative criteria for identifying and evaluating democracies (Sartori 1987; Dahl 1989). Yet for many years, no systematic studies for evaluating democratic systems were conducted in the empirical, comparative research on democracy. This reluctance has been attributed to the value-neutral orientation that predominated in empirical research, as value-neutrality was long regarded as incompatible with the normative character of evaluation (Dahl 1967; Fuchs 1998). The first systematic, comparative evaluation studies of democracies were conducted in the 1970s, with Dahl's *Polyarchy* (1971) the *locus classicus*. Dahl's interest lay in evaluating the quality of the *democratic structure* in 114 nations, and he asked to what extent key democratic institutions such as free and fair elections and freedom of expression existed, and how effectively they were implemented. Since then many similar assessments of democracies have been undertaken (for compilations see Foweraker and Krznaric 2000; Schmidt 2000a),[1] so one can regard the evaluation of democratic structure by now as an established branch in comparative research on democracy.

This is by no means the case for the evaluation of the performance of democratic systems; an established research tradition based on common theoretical, methodological, and empirical referents does not exist here. The issue of evaluating the quality of *democratic processes* (Fuchs 1998) only began to be addressed in the 1990s, and the lack of scholarly agreement can be seen most clearly in the criteria that are chosen to measure performance.

Most authors select their own criteria without reference to those of others, which has led to a multiplicity of extremely heterogeneous, coexisting performance criteria that have until now not been systematized in any way. Putnam (1993), for example, suggests using governmental effectiveness and responsiveness as criteria, while Weaver and Rockman instead focus on capabilities. These include a wide variety of managerial abilities governments

---

[1] Among the best known works are: Bollen (1980), Vanhanen (1984), Coppedge and Reinicke (1991), Freedom House (1990), Gurr et al. (1990), and Jaggers and Gurr (1995).

should display, such as to ensure policy stability, manage political cleavages 'to ensure that the society does not degenerate into civil war' (Weaver and Rockman 1993: 6), and have the capability to make decisions and policy. Lane and Ersson (1994), by contrast, suggest the guiding values of liberty, equality, and fraternity derived from the French Revolution, while Lijphart (1999*a*) investigates quite different effects of democracy. As a rule, performance criteria are rarely systematically derived or justified and tend to be selected arbitrarily.

Only two performance concepts have been suggested thus far that satisfy such demands for quality. One is the political productivity concept of Almond and Powell (1978) that has already been used in a number of studies (Roller 1991, 1992; Schmidt 1998*a*). The other is Fuchs's suggestion of a concept to establish criteria for democratic performance (1998). The political productivity concept was developed within a systems theory framework. It covers a list of performance criteria that could be applied to all political systems, while Fuchs's suggestion emerged in the framework of democratic theory and was meant to apply only to democratic systems.

Almond and Powell's political productivity concept is the touchstone for our study of the performance of democracies, but the concept is deficient for several normative and empirical-analytic reasons. Normatively, effectiveness is not differentiated from other performance criteria, nor is the term specified. To properly classify and more precisely define the term, it is therefore necessary first to develop an analytic scheme to classify performance criteria. This allows previously suggested performance concepts to be sorted and integrated into a superordinate, common framework. This scheme is then used to discuss Almond and Powell's political productivity concept and based on this discussion a 'normative model of political effectiveness' is derived. This model includes five criteria: (*a*) international security, (*b*) domestic security, (*c*) wealth, (*d*) socio-economic security and socio-economic equality, and (*e*) environmental protection. All four domestic policy effectiveness criteria are investigated in what follows.

These normative criteria of effectiveness must be further specified for the empirical analysis. Thus far, such an empirical-analytic basis for the concept of political effectiveness has been lacking. It will be developed here for domestic public policies. It includes a 'vertical' specification of these performance criteria through disaggregation into individual components, and these components are assigned indicators in turn. This vertical specification is based on policy-specific models for evaluating effectiveness.

Additionally, it covers 'horizontal' relationships between the different performance criteria. Almond and Powell (1978: 397) already addressed the problem of trade-offs between various performance dimensions, at least in general terms. In what follows, the most significant propositions about particular goal conflicts, as well as the compatibility between multiple conflicting goals, are discussed, and a typology of political effectiveness is then developed. I then suggest a concept of general political effectiveness and conclude the chapter with a summary of the most important characteristics of the 'Model for Evaluating the Political Effectiveness of Liberal Democracies'.

This brief overview of the argument in Chapter 2 should make clear the central role Almond and Powell's political productivity concept plays in my analysis. But the theoretical 'Model for Evaluating Political Effectiveness' developed in this chapter is more comprehensive in normative terms, and it involves an empirical-analytic level without which the normative concept would not qualify for empirical analysis.

NORMATIVE CRITERIA FOR EVALUATING POLITICAL PERFORMANCE

The following section introduces a model for evaluating the effectiveness of liberal democracies. The model is thus not applicable to all democracies or even to all political systems but only to contemporary representative democracies of a type called liberal democratic (Powell 1992; Fuchs 1998; Diamond 1999). This specification is necessary because different democracies are each characterized by dissimilar normative, fundamental values (Fuchs and Klingemann 2002). As a result, in evaluating these systems, dissimilar normative criteria need to be applied. One characteristic of liberal democracies is that popular sovereignty is implemented in a particular manner: through competitive, periodic elections in which representatives of the people (or demos) are selected as delegates to a parliament. Characteristic as well are guarantees of human rights and a legal codification of basic rights (Fuchs 1998; Diamond 1999). The mutual recognition of citizens as free and equal can be regarded as the fundamental value of liberal democracy (Fuchs 1998). We will return repeatedly to these matters.

A Classification of Performance Criteria

I begin the normative analysis by suggesting an analytic scheme for classifying performance criteria for liberal democracies. This scheme is introduced with reference to three conceptual pairs suggested in the performance literature: structure and process (Fuchs 1998), goal-oriented contrasted with general political performance (Eckstein 1971), and democratic versus systemic performance (Fuchs 1998).

Structure and process
We previously noted the difference between democratic structure and democratic process as separate objects of evaluation, and Fuchs has introduced

this differentiation more systematically into the performance literature. The structure of a democracy is 'fixed by the binding legal norms of a constitution' (Fuchs 1998: 159). It is characterized by a certain number of institutions that can also be called the minimum characteristics of a democracy. They include guaranteeing basic freedoms, a competitive party system, universal suffrage with free, equal and periodic elections, as well as the use of majority rule for making collectively binding decisions (Bobbio 1987; Dahl 1989; Fuchs 1998). The democratic process, by contrast, refers to what political actors actually do, which is guided in turn by the democratic structure (Fuchs 1998: 162).

In principle, both dimensions or levels can be evaluated. In the case of the democratic structure, the most fundamental evaluative criterion is the extent to which a liberal democracy exists at all (Fuchs 1998: 160). In the case of the democratic process, a democratic structure is a precondition, and evaluative criteria are applied to the activities of political actors and the outcomes.

The term performance is particularly suited for evaluating the political process, as its two major definitions refer precisely to the dimension of action: (*a*) 'the performance of a task or action is the *doing* of it' and (*b*) 'someone's or something's performance is how well they *do* or how successful they are' (Collins, Cobuild 1987: 1066; author's emphasis). This definition indicates the term has both descriptive and evaluative components, denoting both the doing itself and the evaluation of doing. The two components are also reflected in some political science definitions, as can be seen in the following example:

> The term performance refers to the execution and accomplishment of work and also, in a connotation relevant to us, to the manner and effectiveness with which something fulfills an intended task. That is, performance contains in its very definition an evaluative criterion, that of producing what is intended or expected. Performance, to put it redundantly, is effective to the extent that it produces what is intended. (Di Palma 1977: 7)

But political performance is more often narrowly understood in its evaluative aspect, as the following three examples from studies of performance indicate:

> Measuring political performance is, of course, inherently evaluative: a matter of saying, on some basis, that a polity is doing well or badly, to one degree or another, in absolute terms or relative to other cases. (Eckstein 1971: 8)

> What do 'good governments' do, and, by implication at least, what do they do differently from bad governments. (Aberbach and Rockman 1992: 140)

> Why do some democratic governments succeed and others fail? (Putnam 1993: 3)

This narrower definition of political performance, as the evaluation of what political actors do and the outcomes of these actions, is the one adopted here.

Goal-oriented and general political performance

Political performance, understood as the evaluation of the political process, can be separated into a goal-oriented component and a general political performance component. Eckstein first drew attention to this by distinguishing between 'political performance in regard to particular goals' and 'performance in a more general sense, regardless of the special goals of polities' (1971: 5). The first is a matter of goal-attainment, while the second is defined in a manner to promote attaining specific goals (Eckstein 1971: 19). Eckstein's subsequent analysis (1971: 20) focuses on general political performance, and he employs four exemplary criteria for it—'durability, civil order, legitimacy, decisional efficacy'—that he justifies in detail. His decision to address general political performance is programmatic. Evaluations based on goal-attainment do not make sense, he argues, as 'these depend too much on conditions over which polities often have little or no control' such as 'the consistency of goals' and 'the availability of sound technical knowledge for achieving intended effects' (Eckstein 1971: 68). Only general performance can be attributed to the polity, since that is supposed to be under the control of the political system itself (Eckstein 1971: 19, 68). Yet it is questionable whether the polity can better control general political performance than goal-oriented performance. Research on the persistence and legitimacy of political systems (e.g. Linz 1978; Lipset 1981) shows that these are extraordinarily complex phenomena not readily or simply to be steered by what political actors do. Persistence or legitimacy is certainly no easier to control than economic growth, which Eckstein (1971: 68) cites as an example of a goal-oriented performance criterion.

Weaver and Rockman's performance concept (1993: 6), developed without reference to Eckstein, is based on a similar differentiation, this time between 'specific policy objectives' and a 'capabilities' dimension, defined as 'a pattern of government influence on its environment that produces substantially similar outcomes across time and policy areas'. One finds included among these capabilities, for example, the ability to 'set and maintain priorities' or to 'target resources where they are most effective' (Weaver and Rockman 1993: 6). At heart these are 'policy management' capacities that Eckstein also refers to in his concept of general political performance. Unlike Eckstein, Weaver and Rockman suggest more criteria (ten rather than four), do not assume that a high level of capabilities ensures greater success in goal-attainment, and do not have a programmatic goal in mind when they discuss capabilities. Weaver and Rockman's intent was to contribute to the US discussion about governmental effectiveness, and at the time that discussion focused on capabilities.

If one considers these studies together, then general political performance applies to *procedural* goals whose realization promotes the attainment of specific policy goals. But one learns little about goal-oriented performance whose intent is to achieve *substantive* goals in either formulation.

By contrast, realizing substantive goals is at the centre of Pennock's political goods concept. Pennock (1966: 420) assumes that 'political systems develop their own autonomous political goals and that the attainment of these collective goals is one of their major functions, providing an important measure of their development'. It is not the collectively binding decisions (outputs) that matter, but rather the consequences of these decisions (outcomes) for the people, the society as a whole, or for other systems such as the economy or the family. Pennock is not interested in the totality of these political goals but only in 'those goals that satisfy "needs" ... human needs whose fulfillment makes the polity valuable to man, and gives it its justification' (Pennock 1966: 420). He calls these goals 'political goods'. Pennock originally suggested there were four political goods—security, welfare, justice, and freedom—but later revised this list to place democratic ideals of liberty and equality on the one side, and 'generally recognized purposes of government'—order, security, justice, and welfare—on the other (Pennock 1979: 260).

Almond and Powell's political productivity concept is based on Pennock's concept of political goods. At this juncture we only want to note that political productivity is a more comprehensive concept than that of political goods, and that political productivity is not only goal-oriented but also encompasses general political performance.

Democratic and systemic performance
Fuchs suggested a differentiation between democratic and systemic performance. He starts from the dual character of democratic systems that, like all political systems, must produce outcomes for the society such as economic growth and domestic security. (Liberal) democracy, on the other hand, is associated with certain values like liberty and equality that mandate trying to achieve these particular democratic values (Fuchs 1998: 152). Performance that is expected of a democracy as a political system is designated as 'systemic performance', while performance specifically expected of a democratic political system is called 'democratic performance'. This pair of terms thus designates two sets of performance criteria that are to be ensured either by democratic or by all political systems. A similar dichotomy has been suggested by Foweraker (2001: 205) who differentiates between dimensions considered 'intrinsic' and 'extrinsic' to democracy.

Fuchs's analysis focuses on 'the criteria for democratic performance in liberal democracies'. He identifies two different types, one of which is comprised of basic democratic values such as liberty and equality, and the other of which refers to democratic standards following from the representative form of government of liberal democracy. With respect to the representative character, Fuchs (1998: 162–3) deduces the responsiveness of the polity to the preferences of the demos as a crucial criterion. He distinguishes further between input and output responsiveness. Input refers to responsiveness to citizen preferences in the programmes of competing political actors, while output refers to converting these preferences through decisions of the ruling government.

Putnam's distinction between responsiveness and effectiveness is also at heart a concept of democratic performance. Putnam wants to evaluate 'representative government' and has two criteria to do so: 'a good democratic government not only considers the demands of its citizenry (i.e. responsive), but also acts efficaciously upon these demands (i.e. effective)' (Putnam 1993: 63). Compared with Fuchs's analytic categories, Putnam's use of 'responsive' corresponds to Fuchs's 'input responsiveness' and Putnam's 'effectiveness' is identical with Fuchs's 'output responsiveness'. But Fuchs and Putnam are among the few who specifically address democratic performance. Eckstein, Weaver and Rockman, Pennock, and Almond and Powell, all concentrate instead on systemic performance.

A scheme for classifying performance criteria for liberal democracies
The first conceptual pair of structure and process served to identify the essential characteristic of performance: an assessment of the political process. The other conceptual pairs involved differentiation within political performance. By combining these other two pairs, one can create a scheme to establish four types of performance criteria. Both goal-oriented and general political performance can be distinguished according to whether they are to be provided by a liberal democracy as a political system (systemic performance) or as a democratic system (democratic performance). Table 2.1 includes a compilation of the definitions of the four types of performance criteria together with illustrative examples and relevant authors.

In this table, effectiveness is introduced as a general criterion of assessment of goal-oriented performance. This accords with common usage, where effectiveness describes the degree to which substantive goals are realized; the denoted relationship is between an intended goal and its realization. The term effectiveness was consciously not used to designate attaining procedural goals (general performance) as Weaver and Rockman (1993) did, as it would have meant a loss of precision.

Applying the scheme to the literature on political performance reveals that research mainly deals with three of the four types of performance criteria. No previously suggested performance concept primarily deals with the procedural goals that promote substantive democratic performance. Instead studies emphasize only particular aspects, such as accountability or participation.[2]

---

[2] On accountability, see Powell (1990), Przeworski et al. (1999), and Strøm et al. (2003); on participation, see Powell (1982) as well as Jackman and Miller (1995).

TABLE 2.1. *A scheme for classifying performance criteria for liberal democracies*

	Goal-oriented performance (substantive goals)	General performance (procedural goals)
Systemic performance	Effective realization of substantive goals valid for all political systems (e.g. security, welfare) (see Pennock 1966)	Characteristics of all political processes that promote the realization of substantive goals (e.g. efficiency, stability) (see Eckstein 1971; Weaver and Rockman 1993)
Democratic performance	Effective realization of basic democratic values (liberty, equality) and democratic standards following from the representative character of liberal democracy (responsiveness) (see Fuchs 1998)	Characteristics of the democratic political process that promote the realization of substantive democratic goals (e.g. accountability, participation)

At the intersection of goal-oriented and systemic performance stands the type of performance criterion that will be examined in this study. This is the goal-oriented performance that a democratic system, like all other political systems, must produce: outcomes for the society. This criterion properly ought to be called systemic political effectiveness, but for simplicity's sake will be designated *political effectiveness*. Pennock's political goods concept is key here. In what follows, we examine in detail Almond and Powell's further articulation of their 'political productivity' concept—the starting point for our own theoretical frame of reference.

The Concept of Political Productivity

Almond and Powell's political productivity concept (1978: 391) was formulated with the intent of finding 'an outside and relatively unbiased evaluation' of political systems. Following Pennock's concept of political goods, the productivity of political systems was to be evaluated, that is, the system itself was seen as the producer of (political) goods. Almond and Powell (1978: 394), like Pennock, limited the term productivity to those political goods that are 'commonly sought by or expected of political systems' and are 'widely acknowledged as the legitimate obligation of political systems'. Unlike Pennock, who defined political goods as satisfying 'human needs' (Pennock 1966: 42), Almond and Powell took a wider view and included goods that satisfy the 'needs of the state as such', such as maintaining the political order.

Using three studies that evaluate political systems (Pennock 1966; Dahl 1971; Eckstein 1971), Almond and Powell then constructed a list of those

TABLE 2.2. *Almond and Powell's political productivity concept*

Levels of political goods	Classes of goods	Content and examples
System level	System maintenance	Regularity and predictability of processes in domestic and international politics
	System adaptation	Structural and cultural adaptability in response to environmental change and challenges
Process level	Participation in political inputs	Instrumental to domestic and foreign policy; directly produces a sense of dignity and efficacy, where met with responsiveness
	Compliance and support	Fulfillment of citizen's duty and patriotic service
	Procedural justice	Equitable procedure and equality before the law
Policy level	Security	Safety of person and property; public order, and national security
	Liberty	Freedom from regulation, protection of privacy, and respect for autonomy of other individuals, groups, and nations
	Welfare	Growth per capita; quantity and quality of health and welfare; distributive equity

Source: Almond et al. (2003: 157).

political goods about which, in their view, a consensus existed. These political goods were then assigned to Almond and Powell's three functional levels of the political system: system, process, and policy. System maintenance and system adaptation are functions at the system level, the conversion of inputs to outputs are functions at the process level, and the policy level is defined by the behaviour of the political system as it relates to other social systems and the environment (Almond and Powell 1978: 13–16). Table 2.2 summarizes the classes of goods they identify, along with elucidations, as presented in a more recent work (Almond et al. 2003: 157). Their earlier work stated that Eckstein's 1971 concept of stability and survival was reflected in the system level, Dahl's 1971 concept of participation and competition in the process level, and Pennock's 1966 concept of political goods in the policy level (Almond and Powell 1978: 393). Political goods at the system and process levels satisfy the 'needs of the state' while those at the policy level satisfy the 'needs of the citizens'.

Almond and Powell's claim to integrate various concepts suggested for evaluating political systems into a common list is laudable. Their concept of political productivity is one of the few concepts that simultaneously incorporates different types of performance. In our terms, their concept encompasses goal-oriented and general political performance, and while they define goal-oriented performance as 'policy performance', they separate general performance into 'system performance' and 'process performance'.

The differentiation into levels of political goods marks an advance over previous conceptualizations. First, the consistency of Pennock's list of policy goods is increased. Pennock had suggested four policy goods—security, welfare, justice, and liberty—but Almond and Powell (1978) see justice as a process good ('procedural justice') and removed the justice criterion from Pennock's list. Second, this move was connected with separating procedural criteria into stability-oriented 'system performance' and procedurally-oriented 'process performance', in turn giving stability-oriented performance criteria an independent, special significance.[3]

Although Almond and Powell's political productivity concept goes beyond previous concepts, it is problematic with respect to both procedural and substantive goals. In terms of the scheme for classifying performance criteria suggested above (see Table 2.1), their list of procedural goals is inconsistent. Almond and Powell wanted to develop evaluation criteria applicable to all political systems, but in the case of 'participation in political inputs' (based on Robert Dahl's *Polyarchy*), we are evidently dealing with a performance criterion that is restricted to democratic systems. In terms of concepts of general performance dealing with procedural goals, on the other hand, Almond and Powell's process level goods remain deficient. Important criteria such as 'decisional efficacy' (Eckstein 1971) or the efficient use of resources (Weaver and Rockman 1993) are lacking.

The more relevant problems relate to the substantive goals. First, the list of three policy goods—security, liberty, and welfare—is inconsistent. With liberty, specified in part as negative liberty (freedom from regulation and intrusion in private life), we evidently have a democratic criterion, as this refers to a fundamental value of liberal democracy. Second, the remaining goals of security and welfare are defined by listing specific goals (see Table 2.2) rather than presenting a general definition. This is particularly problematic in the case of welfare, as comparative research on welfare states shows that at the specific level, welfare state goals vary strongly over time and between nations (Flora and Heidenheimer 1981; Esping-Andersen 1990). Last, when one considers the current range of state responsibilities, the

---

[3] Other authors have also assigned stability criteria particular status, as a precondition of political action on the one hand and as the ultimate goal of political action on the other (Fuchs 1993; Lane and Ersson 1994).

substantive goals specified appear quite time-bound. The policy goal of protecting the environment that emerged in the mid-1960s, for example, is absent (Roller 1991).

A Normative Model of Political Effectiveness

The two systemic policy goals of security and welfare are the starting point for our normative model of political effectiveness. It is developed in four steps. First, based on the critique of Almond and Powell's productivity concept a list of political effectiveness criteria is suggested. It includes international and domestic security, wealth, socio-economic security and socio-economic equality, as well as environmental protection. Second, the derivation of and justification for these effectiveness criteria are specified. The third step addresses the question whether outcomes such as security and environmental protection that 'only in part' result from what political actors do, can be defined as political performance. The fourth step discusses the question to what extent one can interpret political effectiveness as a democratic criterion.

A list of systemic political effectiveness criteria

Almond and Powell's list of policy goods was criticized for lacking precision in defining their criteria, and for being inconsistent and incomplete. We suggest a list of systemic criteria for political effectiveness to address these lacunae. First, we specify the political goals of security and welfare Almond and Powell (1978) suggested, and then augment their list with the new goal of protecting the environment.

Almond et al. (2003) assign three features to the goal of security: safety of person and property, public order, and national security (see Table 2.2). This list completely encompasses all individual aspects of security. Yet the categories in other formulations are often combined differently, with 'safety of person and property' and 'public order' as subcategories of the abstract goal of domestic security (Powell 1966; Ritchie 1992; Kaufmann 1996). At a more general level, the distinction is made between protecting goods of individuals (e.g. person and property) and protecting collective and communal goods (e.g. public order). Collective and communal goods in particular refer to a constitutional or legal order. In the following, we use these differentiations of domestic security. With respect to the 'externally directed' dimension of security, when the protection of territorial integrity and political independence is at issue (Brockhaus 1993: 321), we speak of international security and not of 'national security' as Almond et al. do (2003). The goals of international and domestic security are addressed in two different policy areas: foreign policy and domestic security policy.

Almond et al. (2003) assign four aspects to welfare: growth per capita, quantity and quality of health, welfare, and distributive equity (see Table 2.2).

This specification evidently confines itself to the narrow sense of economic welfare and not to the broad sense of welfare encompassing all areas of an individual's life, as the term is used in QOL (or social indicators) research. Almond et al. also make the distinction between economic policy goals, such as growth per capita, and social policy goals, such as health, welfare, and distributive equity.

A comparison with the broad concept of welfare used by Flora, Alber, and Kohl, shows Almond and Powell's aspects to be particular examples of welfare rather than a systematic, comprehensive notion. For this reason, we follow Flora, Alber, and Kohl's definition and assign general goals to the economic policy and social policy dimensions of welfare. Thus, the general goal of economic policy is 'wealth', and the general goal of social policy is 'socio-economic security and socio-economic equality'. While wealth and security refer to the volume of economic goods and resources, equality refers to the distribution of these goods and resources (Flora et al. 1977: 722).

Equality itself can mean equality of result or equality of opportunity, where equality of result can range from securing a 'national minimum' to 'redistribution or leveling' (Flora et al. 1977: 722–3). Given this range of meanings and the fact that equality is a core democratic value, to what extent and in what form can this goal even be included in a list of systemic criteria of effectiveness that is valid for all political systems? More radical notions of equality, such as income equality, are parts of normatively more demanding and at the same time more contentious models of democracy, such as that of democratic socialism or the republican model (Pocock 1975; Fuchs and Klingemann 2002).

Comparative research on welfare states concludes that all political systems have in common that they develop at least a minimal welfare state. 'The essence of the welfare state', Wilensky (1975:1) writes, 'is government-protected minimum standards of income, nutrition, health, housing, and education, assured to every citizen as a political right, not as charity.' This national minimum assurance is meant to prevent citizens from starving and dying. Given the universality of this minimum welfare provision, we introduce the assurance of a national minimum in the provision of economic goods as a systemic criterion of effectiveness that can claim to be valid in all political systems. Where we make reference to socio-economic equality, then it is this securing of a national minimum that is meant.

Almond and Powell's list of policy goods is incomplete because environmental concerns have become an important part of political action since the mid-1960s, and it has led to the institutionalization of a new policy area (Vogel and Kun 1987; Hucke 1992; Jörgens 1996). The policy goal is the 'creation, preservation, or improvement of parts of the natural environment that are important for human existence and human dignity' (Schmidt 1995:

TABLE 2.3 *A normative model of political effectiveness*

Criteria of political effectiveness (political goals)	Policy areas
International security	Foreign policy
Domestic security	Domestic security policy
Wealth	Economic policy
Socio-economic security and socio-economic equality	Social policy (welfare state)
Environmental protection	Environmental policy

969). Under the rubric of environmental protection, this goal is included in the list of political goals (Roller 1991).

Table 2.3 lists the five criteria of effectiveness associated with their respective policy areas. The goals of socio-economic security and socio-economic equality that are related to social policy are not differentiated, since all welfare state benefits have this dual character (Flora et al. 1977). The list, when read from top to bottom, also reflects the historical sequence of the expansion of governmental responsibilities, an aspect we will address later.

The effectiveness criteria each represent goals, defined positively, as well as five hypotheses of the type 'the more the political goal X is realized in a nation, the higher the effectiveness of the nation's democracy' (see Fuchs 1998). With the exception of socio-economic equality, all goals refer to the volume rather than the distribution of the respective goods. At a higher level, all five criteria of effectiveness can be subsumed under the broader definition of welfare employed in sociological research on the quality of life (or social indicators research).

Derivation and justification of the effectiveness criteria
The starting point for deriving and justifying the effectiveness criteria is Pennock's definition of political goods. He notes that these involve a specific category of political goals, namely those 'that satisfy "needs" ... human needs whose fulfillment makes the polity valuable to man, and gives it its justification' (Pennock 1966: 420). Almond and Powell (1978: 394) are more general: they speak of goals 'that ... are commonly sought by or expected of political systems and that ... are widely acknowledged as the legitimate obligations of political systems.' One can derive three characteristics of political effectiveness criteria from these definitions. First, these are political goals, which is to say these goals guide what political actors do. Second, these goals converge with the needs of citizens, and third, citizens demand the government to attain these goals. Pennock's list of political goods was based on theories of political development that described the expanding of government responsibilities over time. There is high consensus among theorists regarding the historical sequence and scope of governmental tasks. Older

theories refer to security and welfare (Merriam 1962; Rostow 1971; Rose 1976), while newer surveys (Grimm 1996) add environmental protection. Based on such theories of political development one could derive political goals, for whose realization the government or the political elite takes responsibility and whose realization then can legitimately be expected. But a list of political goals derived in this fashion could only meet the first characteristic, namely that such goals guide what political actors do. To what extent the goals converge with citizen needs (second characteristic) or demands (third characteristic) would still need to be established.

Almond and Powell (1978: 395–6) focused largely on the second characteristic, needs satisfaction, and examined some of the classic studies of human needs and values (Maslow 1938; Lasswell 1960; Sigmund 1971) to establish whether the citizens' needs and values suggested by Pennock's political goods concept were reflected there. They found high congruence. One limitation, however, is that the empirical basis for drawing this conclusion was rather narrow. The available studies of values were not comparative empirical surveys of the kind that proliferated in the 1980s and 1990s. Today it is possible to demonstrate both comparatively and systematically that security, welfare, and environmental protection are among the goals most highly prized by citizens (Roller 1995; Inglehart et al. 1998). The suggested list of performance criteria thereby also fulfills the second characteristic of political goods.

Neither Pennock nor Almond and Powell mention the third characteristic, the extent to which citizens expect the government to be responsible for achieving these goals. There may be a simple reason for this: a lack, during the 1970s, of systematic, comparative survey data. But this situation has recently changed. In the *International Social Survey Program* conducted in 1996, respondents have been asked for several goals whether they prefer governmental responsibility or not. The data was gathered for twenty-three older and newer democracies (Zentralarchiv für Empirische Sozialforschung 1999). Table 2.4 lists the percentage of respondents in fourteen western democracies who favour governmental responsibility at least for the five goals where a clear link can be made to our effectiveness criteria: industrial growth and control of inflation (economic policy goals), health care and redistribution (social policy goals), and environmental protection. No items for domestic or international security were included in this survey, though one can assume a consensus that the government is responsible for ensuring such classic goals of the state.

The results of this comparative survey are ordered following the five 'families of nations' classification later used in the empirical part of our study. On average, over 90 per cent of the respondents in these fourteen countries preferred that the government should be responsible for health care

TABLE 2.4. *Citizen's attitudes towards governmental responsibility (in %)*[a]

	Industrial growth	Control of inflation	Health care	Redistribution	Environmental protection
Australia	87	81	94	52	96
Canada	75	64	94	51	93
Great Britain	93	86	99	68	95
Ireland	94	92	99	78	98
New Zealand	85	74	97	47	97
USA	66	69	85	48	89
Denmark	—	—	—	—	—
Finland	—	—	—	—	—
Norway	80	90	99	73	94
Sweden	80	86	96	71	94
Austria	75	93	98	78	—
Belgium	—	—	—	—	—
France	82	76	89	74	95
Germany[b]	64	71	97	62	96
Italy	80	93	99	75	97
The Netherlands	—	—	—	—	—
Greece	—	—	—	—	—
Portugal	—	—	—	—	—
Spain	96	92	97	90	97
Switzerland	—	—	—	—	—
Japan	75	96	90	65	94
Average	81	83	95	67	95

[a] Percentage of respondents agreeing that government definitely or probably should be responsible for the respective task (other categories: government probably or definitely should not be responsible).
[b] West Germany.

Source: International Social Survey Programme 1996 (ISSP 1985 for Austria).

and environmental protection. A mean of over 80 per cent also favoured governmental responsibility for the two economic policy goals. By comparison, the average of only 67 per cent favouring redistribution is relatively low, and it is the only area where governmental responsibility is under 60 per cent in four nations, and under 50 per cent in two of them (New Zealand and the USA). This last finding can be regarded as empirical support for the hypothesis suggested earlier that no general consensus exists in support of radical concepts of equality. It also indirectly supports our definition of equality based on a national minimum rather than on redistribution.

In conclusion, the five effectiveness criteria we derived earlier—international security, domestic security, wealth, socio-economic security and socio-economic equality, as well as environmental protection—all possess all three characteristics of a political good.

Model for Evaluating Effectiveness

Outcome accountability
The evaluation of political effectiveness is based on the outcomes of political action, or in other words on the influence political actions have on the environment of the political system, rather than on the outputs. Almond and Powell (1978: 634) justify this distinction with the simple but no less convincing assertion that 'outputs are intended to produce political goods, but the real test is in the outcome.' Yet, though there are good arguments for conceptualizing effectiveness this way, it is also the case that outcomes cannot be directly controlled by political actors (Almond and Powell 1978: 397). If outcomes only partially can be ascribed to political actors, it raises the legitimate question whether one can speak of *political* performance here at all.

This problem is nearly universally recognized in evaluation studies, and three different conclusions have been drawn from it. Eckstein (1971) provides the most radical answer in asserting that precisely because one can only control outcomes to a limited degree, one should not even attempt to analyse it. Putnam's suggestion (1993) is less radical, though it leads to the same conclusion in the end. Unlike Eckstein, Putnam (1993: 65) makes political effectiveness one of his key criteria of performance. Putnam wants to make empirical assertions about Italian regions, the units of his study, and wants be careful 'not to give governments credit (or blame) for matters beyond their control.' For this reason, his *Index of Institutional Performance* primarily measures outputs rather than outcomes. For example, the number of day care centres and local health unit expenditures, rather than, say, mortality rates, is used to measure social policy performance.

In comparative welfare state research, outputs have long been used for measuring the effects of social policies. The assumption was that expenditures were good proxies for assessing social policy outcomes in areas such as health or poverty. In the meantime, many empirical studies have questioned this 'proxy-quality' of output indicators or even refrain from using them at all (Esping-Andersen 1990; Castles and McKinlay 1997). Accordingly, we conclude that Putnam's index is only justified as a measure of political effectiveness if outputs are in fact good proxies for outcomes. If they are not, as Putnam evidently correctly concludes, then outputs cannot be used as such measures. Therefore, Putnam's already classic *Making Democracy Work* (1993) is actually not a study of performance but rather a policy output study that looks primarily at the extent to which specific means (such as the number of infrastructural facilities or the size of government expenditures) are used in resolving problems. But both Eckstein and Putnam's answers in the end lead to abandoning any attempt to analyse political effectiveness.

Yet in comparative public policy research, outcome indicators are commonly used as dependent variables. In economic policy, growth, unemployment, or inflation rates are used as a matter of course (Hibbs 1977; Alvarez et al. 1991). Research on environmental policy has investigated outcomes, such as air pollution through sulphur or nitrogen oxides emissions since the mid-1990s (Ringquist 1995; Jänicke et al. 1996*a*; Jahn 1998; Scruggs 1999). Comparative welfare state research increasingly analyses outcome measures of poverty and inequality and less often uses expenditure data (Huber et al. 1993; Korpi and Palme 1998). Some studies of the performance of political systems even use outcome indicators (Schmidt 1998*a*; Lijphart 1999*a*; Almond et al. 2003), though in some cases the self-evident use of outcome indicators may simply reflect an inadequate recognition that there is an issue here. Nevertheless, there are systematic arguments in favour of using outcomes as measures of performance. In the following, the conditions are elaborated that have to be present so that outcomes can be used as indicators for political performance. These conditions are either implicitly accepted or explicitly stated in the performance literature.

First, only those outcomes for which political actors have taken responsibility can be interpreted as political performance measures. Information on that can be found in theories of the historical development of governmental responsibilities and in the policy-specific models for evaluating effectiveness discussed later. In this context, responsibility does not mean that the government itself has to provide the benefits; in the language of public administration, the state only has a responsibility to guarantee, not to fulfill (Hoffmann-Riem 1997). So health care, for example, does not have to be provided by the government itself. Instead, the government can accept responsibility for the health of the population by passing, framing laws and regulations but can leave the actual provision of health care to independent third parties. The acceptance of responsibility, however, does not imply that actors do have full control over them. From this, authors like Eckstein or Putnam draw the radical conclusion that one cannot use outcomes at all as political performance indicators. But Lijphart (1999*a*: 261) concludes the opposite: 'the fact that governments are not in full control does not mean that they have no control at all.' From this 'partial' control a second condition can be derived, one that is explicitly formulated by Lijphart and implicitly practised in comparative public policy. At the theoretical level, when explaining outcomes, in addition to political factors, competing non-political factors need to be taken into account as well. And to the extent that other influences 'are identifiable and measurable variables, they should be controlled for in the statistical analyses' (Lijphart 1999*a*: 262). In the case of effectiveness, one such competing factor is certainly a nation's level of economic development, as achieving a whole range of policy goals often depends on the available economic resources. These non-political factors are identified in our model for explaining the performance of liberal democracies.

Keeping within these rules certainly does not eliminate all the possible problems that result from an insufficient ability to control outcomes. But one can assume that the associated problems are reduced as much as possible. No alternative exists if one does not want to completely abandon the analysis of political effectiveness.

Political effectiveness and democratic performance

Effectiveness addresses a specific criterion for evaluating liberal democracies. It refers to the linkage between the needs and policy preferences of citizens on the one hand and the behaviour, and effects of this behaviour, of political actors on the other (Powell 1982: 10). This relationship also can be described as output responsiveness, a democratic rather than a systemic performance criterion (Fuchs 1998). Therefore, it is necessary to ask to what extent political effectiveness should be seen as output responsiveness and thus be interpreted as a democratic criterion.

At first glance, many quite disparate pieces of empirical evidence speak for the notion that political effectiveness also encompasses aspects of output responsiveness. We have indicated, based on survey results, that our suggested criteria of effectiveness are of a kind not just important to citizens but also what citizens expect of governments (see Table 2.4). Additionally, one of the best substantiated findings in the research of voting behaviour is that the assessment of political effectiveness is a key determinant of voting decisions. In explanatory models, such factors are called valence issues (or policy performance), and together with position issues (or policy positions) they constitute the two subdimensions of political issues (Stokes 1963; Roller 1998). In other words, the political effectiveness we investigate—mediated through the subjective perceptions and assessments by citizens—plays an important role in choosing representatives. Finally, one of the empirically established regularities in research on political support states that the assessment of political effectiveness or performance is an important source of the legitimacy of a democracy (Lipset 1981; Fuchs 1989). Political effectiveness thus plays a decisive role for fundamental attitudes citizens develop towards democracy.

According to these findings, political effectiveness reflects important policy preferences of citizens that have considerable consequences for the political process. However, one cannot automatically conclude that a high level of political effectiveness is the same as output responsiveness. Putnam (1993) at least implicitly assumes this by treating effectiveness as the realization of citizen demands through the behaviour of the political actors.

Two essential characteristics of responsiveness speak against such an interpretation. Responsiveness first describes a direct linkage between citizen preferences and government action, and second, since it is a democratic criterion, it is characterized by an *equal* consideration of citizen demands in

governmental action (Dahl 1989; Fuchs 1998). As our research design focuses on effectiveness, we cannot say anything about these two aspects of
responsiveness. Based only on independent empirical information about
citizen policy preferences, it can be merely assumed that political effectiveness addresses such preferences. But no direct, substantive linkage is made
between citizen demands on the one hand and the behaviour and outcomes of
political actors on the other.

This statement carries that much more weight because one cannot simply
assume all goals can be equally readily realized. Conflicts or trade-offs
between goals imply that priorities need to be set, not just in what political
actors do, but also by citizens. Empirical studies of values show relative
stability in absolute preferences about basic political goals, but much greater
situation-specific variability in relative preferences (Rokeach 1973). Responsiveness thus cannot be investigated solely on the basis of empirical information about absolute preferences. Empirical information about relative citizen
preferences would be necessary, and this information would have to be
directly connected to the behaviour of political actors as part of the research
design. In addition, all but one of our systemic effectiveness criteria (socio-
economic equality) relate to the size rather than the distribution of goods.
This means our analysis does not contain sufficient information about one of
the decisive criteria for a democracy: the equal consideration of citizen
demands in the behaviour of political actors.

In sum, given that the research design focuses on political effectiveness,
nothing can be asserted about democratic performance. A different
research design, and additional information, would be necessary for making
assertions about responsiveness.[4] Nevertheless, the political effectiveness we
investigate—mediated through citizen perceptions and assessments—has
far-reaching consequences for responsiveness and thus for the democratic
performance of liberal democracies.

AN EMPIRICAL–ANALYTIC CONCEPT OF POLITICAL EFFECTIVENESS

Our normative model of political effectiveness included five general criteria.
Subsequent analysis is limited to the four domestic policy effectiveness
criteria of domestic security, wealth, socio-economic security and socio-
economic equality, as well as environmental protection. This list of abstract
goals is inadequate for an empirical analysis of political effectiveness. Instead, systematic relationships between the normative dimensions and

---

[4] To date, few studies have investigated responsiveness in the sense of the direct linkage
between citizen demands and the behaviour of political elites (Stimson et al. 1995; Brettschneider
1995). These studies limit themselves to establishing the degree to which citizen demands and
elite behaviour are in congruence; the equal consideration of citizen demands is not investigated.

empirical phenomena need to be established, with the aid of what I will call an 'empirical-analytic' concept. Only with this can one ensure that individual empirical indicators are not arbitrarily assigned to individual goals and then inappropriate generalizations are made about the respective level of effectiveness.

Therefore, we proceed as follows: First, we develop models of effectiveness specific to the four domestic policy areas, their goals differentiated 'vertically' into individual components. These components are then assigned indicators. Starting points for these models are lists of goals specifying the desired state for each policy area (Tuchtfeldt 1982: 182). The German 'magic square of economic policy' provides a catalogue of this kind by disaggregating wealth as a general goal of economic policy into its component parts (full employment, price stability, steady and adequate economic growth, and equilibrium in the balance of payments) and then assigning indicators to each component. In principle, such lists of goals could be specified for the other three policy areas, except that there is less explicit consensus and more imprecision over what they might be, as well as an absence of indicators, than is the case for economic policy.

Second, the 'horizontal' relationships between the four different effectiveness criteria are defined based on corresponding propositions. Though the conflict or compatibility between different goals is one of the basic problems in political decision-making, and though it is also at the centre of many contemporary crisis theories, whether of ungovernability, legitimation, or globalization, no independent political science research tradition has yet developed to address such goal relationships. At best, individual aspects have been analysed, if in widely separated contexts, but no comprehensive theoretical discussion or even systematic survey exists.

For that reason, following the discussion of lists of goals, we turn next to goal conflicts and examine the most important propositions thus far offered: the assumed trade-off between economic policy and social policy, and the assumed trade-off between economic policy and environmental policy. The compatibility of multiple conflicting goals is discussed with reference to concepts of economic growth and of sustainability, and the propositions are then summarized in a 'typology of political effectiveness'. The discussion concludes with a suggestion for a 'general political effectiveness' concept, as well as a global index to measure it.

Policy-specific Models for Evaluating Effectiveness

The models suggested in what follows differ from the lists of goals on which they are based in two respects. Conceptually, only those goals are selected that have the character of political goods for individuals. Components lacking this character, such as the balance of payments equilibrium in economic policy, are not considered. Empirically, the discussion focuses on those indicators for which comparative data from 1974 to 1995 is available for the twenty-one western democracies examined.

Domestic security policy
Domestic security, together with international security, counts as one of the classic tasks of the state. But it is rarely examined in public policy research, either on a national or comparative level.

The goal of domestic security has two components: the 'protection of life and property', and the 'protection of public order' (Powell 1966; Ritchie 1992; Kaufmann 1996). The few political science studies of domestic security focus on the second component, doubtless because threats to it go hand in hand with political conflict, and political violence threatens the stability of the political order (Gurr 1980; Gurr and Lichbach 1986). Due to its immediate political significance, this component also plays an important role in studies of political performance. Eckstein (1971) counts 'civil order' among the four most important performance criteria,[5] and it has been investigated in many empirical studies of performance (Gurr and McClelland 1971; Powell 1982; Lijphart 1999a). The two indicators 'riots' and 'deaths from domestic political violence' are usually employed as measures of the 'protection of public order', with the data drawn from Taylor and Jodice's influential *World Handbook of Political and Social Indicators* (1983).

The 'protection of life and property', whose object is crime prevention, is by contrast very rarely addressed in political science research. Crime has traditionally been more an object of sociological research, as well as, of course, the primary focus of the separate discipline of criminology. When comparative public policy research turns to it, then it is to examine the activities and functions of the police or judiciary system (Ritchie 1992) rather than the criminal offences that could be seen as measures of effectiveness. The few comparative studies political scientists have conducted of crime focus on violent offences like murder and robbery (Gurr 1979), which is understandable given the state's monopoly of coercive power. It is neither compelling nor entirely appropriate to limit domestic security to only these violent offences, however, as this policy has as its goal in the end to prevent and punish any and all illegal acts. The 'protection of life and property' is concerned with preventing violent offences like murder, manslaughter, and sexual assaults, but also with preventing property crimes like theft and burglary.[6]

---

[5] On the other hand, Eckstein (1971: 20) does not regard the protection of public order as a substantive political goal but rather as general political performance that promotes the achievement of specific goals (see Table 2.1).

[6] The literature on crime distinguishes between crime against persons and crime against property, as well as between violent and property crimes. These distinctions are apparently

TABLE 2.5 *A model for evaluating domestic security policy effectiveness*

Goal	Domestic security	
Components	Protection of life and property	Protection of public order
Indicators	(*a*) Violent crime (murder/manslaughter, robbery) (*b*) Property crime (burglary)	Riots, deaths from domestic political violence

Table 2.5 illustrates the two components of the domestic security policy model, with their indicators, but it is unfortunately not possible to empirically investigate the full range of this policy due to massive data limitations. We must do entirely without an analysis of the 'protection of public order' component because the available comparative data series on riots and political deaths end in 1982 (Taylor and Jodice 1983). In principle, data for the first component of 'protection of life and property' should be better. But there are substantial problems here as well due to difficulties in comparing criminal offences between countries.

The most comprehensive, longitudinal, comparative data series on the frequency of criminal offences is provided by police statistics, as they have been gathered since 1950 by the *International Criminal Police Organization* (Interpol 1977). The basic problem with this type of data is that it only contains those offences reported to the police. The frequency of reporting varies with the severity of the offence, with nation-specific police practices, and for property crimes, with how widespread theft insurance policies are (Gurr 1977, 1989; Bennett and Lynch 1990; Lynch 1995). In addition, data comparability is limited by differing national legal definitions of crime (Kalish 1988). The only way to minimize data problems in comparative empirical analyses is to restrict oneself to offences where comparability is greatest with respect to the legal definitions of the offence, and where the frequency of reporting is the highest (Gurr 1977, 1979; Kalish 1988; Lynch 1995). To judge by expert consensus, these conditions are only met for three offences: murder and manslaughter, robbery, and burglary.

In the case of murder and manslaughter, which are different forms of unlawful killing, we are dealing with the most serious criminal act, and for just this reason, also 'the most accurately recorded violent crime' (Gurr 1989: 23; Huang and Wellford 1989; Bennett and Lynch 1990). Burglary, on the other hand, is the most serious property crime because it combines robbery

functionally equivalent, as the same criminal offences are listed under the categories of personal offences and violent offences. In the following, the term violent offences (more precisely: interpersonal violent offences) is used rather than personal offences, in order to more clearly mark the greater degree of severity of these offences.

with violent entry (Gurr 1977). Robbery is defined as a particular form of theft, as the taking of property from a person accompanied by force or threat of force (Kalish 1988: 5). Robbery is thus both a property crime and a violent offence. This dual character is responsible for the fact that it is accounted differently sometimes as an offence against property (as in Gurr 1977) but more often as a crime of violence (as in Kalish 1988 or Gurr 1989).

We also classify robbery as violent crime, and this classification is justified as well for empirical reasons. A dimensional analysis of all three indicators of criminal offences in our twenty-one nations (not shown here) revealed that robbery and murder/manslaughter all loaded onto one factor, but that burglary constituted a separate factor. Validation also comes from comparative victimization studies in which representative samples of citizens were interviewed about their crime experiences (Dijk et al. 1990; Kesteren et al. 2000). Comparison of crime frequency as based on police statistics and as reported in victimization surveys shows agreement between the two data sources to be the highest for these three offences (Lynch 1995).[7]

Effectiveness in domestic security policy will therefore be based on these three indicators—murder/manslaughter and robbery for violent crime, and burglary for property crime—even though what is empirically possible limps far behind what is theoretically desirable (see Table 2.5). Based on the available data it is only possible to make assertions about a single component of domestic security, the 'protection of life and property', and even in this category, only for serious criminal offences. These are severe limitations. On the other hand, they may weigh somewhat less heavily when one considers that domestic security is very seldom investigated in comparative public policy research or in comparative research on democracy. The 'protection of life and property' is also at the centre of current discussions of the consequences of globalization, for predictions of social disintegration at heart refer exactly to these kinds of violent and illegal acts (Fuchs 1999). Finally, based on victimization surveys, one can assert that the criminal offences examined here are also the ones citizens regard as the gravest (Dijk and Kesteren 1996).

Economic policy
There is considerable agreement between authors, and national governments, over the list of economic policy goals (Kirschen et al. 1964; Hibbs 1977; Tuchtfeldt 1982; Streit 2000). Still, this agreement is primarily about

---

[7] Lynch (1995: 19–20) does not include robbery in his comparative analysis, arguing that because weapons are more often involved in the USA than in other nations in committing this crime, this offence is not directly comparable. However, for comparative purposes, the manner in which the offence is committed is less relevant than how similar the legal definition and frequency of reporting is. Both can be assumed here (Gurr 1977, 1979; Kalish 1988).

the general goals of economic policy and less about political goods for individuals.

The list of economic policy goals can be differentiated by whether they are formulated with respect to structural or procedural policies (Tuchtfeldt 1982: 179). Structural policy refers among other things to providing an infrastructure for energy, transportation, or communication. It certainly matters to citizens how extensive the transportation or communications network is, as measured by kilometres of roads or number of telephones per household, but these are not political goods in the sense used here. Rather, this is a matter of making certain means available to meet needs, and one can determine the degree to which the need has been met only by how much the infrastructure is actually used. Structural policy goals are therefore not included in the model of economic policy effectiveness.

The heart of procedural policy is the political control of the macroeconomy. A large consensus exists in Germany, for example, about the importance of the four goals of the 'magic square of economic policy'. Three goals are part of the 'short-term stability propositions' that make up German economic stabilization policy, namely full employment, price stability, and balance of payments equilibrium (Tuchtfeldt 1982: 190; Gabler 1997). Of these, the last has no direct influence on citizen wealth, though full employment and price stability do have the character of political goods. Full employment relates to the extent of involuntary unemployment, and price stability to the range of goods citizens can acquire with the financial resources available to them. Price stability is usually measured by the inflation rate, and full employment by the unemployment rate.[8] These two indicators are central to comparative public policy research (see Hibbs 1977; Scharpf 1991; Schmidt 1998*b*), and have been combined into a summary index of economic problems, significantly dubbed the *misery index*, as it captures the economic distress citizens may find themselves in.

The fourth goal of economic policy, steady and adequate economic growth, has to do with increasing total national income or product, usually measured as the sum of the monetary value of all goods and services produced in a given period (minus advance payments) (Gabler 1997).[9] Since we focus here on analysing national performance, only the domestic production of economic goods is of interest. While it is true that changes in national

___

[8] In addition, it is increasingly common to use the employment rate instead of (Scharpf 1997; Heinze et al. 1999) or in addition to (Schmidt 1998*b*; Kohl 1999) the unemployment rate, though the employment rate has an inherent normative bias. Nations like Germany with comparatively low female employment rates thereby a priori show worse economic performance if the measure is employment.

[9] The just distribution of income and wealth is often mentioned as an additional goal of economic policy (see Streit 2000), but the consensus over it as an economic goal is weak; it is more often seen as a goal of social policy.

product primarily measure the performance of a national economy, the size of that product has a direct effect on citizens' lives. This is particularly evident if one remembers that national product measures two things at once: the monetary value of the end products produced and the total income of the national economy—including wages, income, interest, rents, and profits—that represent the production costs of these end products (Samuelson and Nordhaus 1995). An increase of national product per capita therefore represents both an improvement in the provision of goods and an increase in income. National products are thus interpreted as a measure of national income, though the question here is whether it also can be interpreted as a political good. National product refers primarily to money, either in terms of the monetary value of goods or the sum of incomes. This implies that in the end it is also a means, though unlike infrastructure, it is a means of a particular kind as it is universally fungible and can satisfy many needs. Owing to this unique quality, it seems justified to regard national product as a political good and include it in the model for evaluating economic policy effectiveness. However, because the degree to which a need is satisfied, or the level of wealth, is at issue in evaluating effectiveness, it will be included in the list of goals as an absolute (level of GDP per capita) rather than as a measure of change (economic growth).

Table 2.6 summarizes these considerations in a model of economic policy effectiveness, though it is clear that the three components do not have equal weight. National income is generally regarded as the most important component, among other reasons because it is often treated as a synonym for wealth. One should more properly distinguish between a broader and a narrower meaning of the term, though, such that wealth broadly understood is the goal of economic policy, while a narrower sense of 'wealth' is identical with the national income, or could be called the level of wealth with respect to income.

The national income plays a particular role for a different reason. On the one hand, it is a dimension of performance, but it also reflects the range of financial resources that are available for realizing other policy goals, such as ensuring social security or environmental protection. We will return to this dual meaning, as an independent criterion of performance as well as the key

TABLE 2.6 *A model for evaluating economic policy effectiveness*

Goal	Wealth		
Components	National income ('wealth')	Full employment	Price stability
Indicators	Gross domestic product per capita	Unemployment rate	Inflation rate

determinant for realizing other criteria of performance, later in the model for explaining the performance of liberal democracies.

Social policy

Because improving the lives of individuals is the primary goal of social policy, the goals here are a priori political goods, unlike the goals of economic policy. The list of social policy goals varies somewhat with respect to the actual number of components, but there seems to be a consensus that health, housing, education, and income are among the most important (Wilensky 1975; Alber 1988; Roller 1992; Zimmermann 1998). When authors suggest additional components, then they do it either because they are thinking of nation-specific aspects of welfare systems or because their broader definition of social policy includes traditional goals of economic policy. Thus, Wilensky (1975: 1) includes nutrition because food stamps form one part the welfare subsidies in the USA; Zimmermann (1998) includes work as a component of social policy. We will not take the latter path, because only a few types of welfare state regimes, such as the social democratic or communist regime type, see employment policy as a part of social policy (Esping-Andersen 1990; Roller 2000). We restrict ourselves to those spheres of life where government obligates itself to provide a specified amount of goods and services to individuals.

Because there is an overlap with the model of economic policy effectiveness in defining income as a policy component, more specification is needed. The relevant conceptual distinction is between the volume of goods and their distribution, for if the primary goal of economic policy is to increase the size of the national income, then for social policy it is to equalize income. As noted in the discussion of the normative model, general consensus exists that social policy is meant to ensure a national minimum provision with goods, or in other words, to avoid poverty. Seen this way, the portion of persons living in poverty in a society suggests itself as an indicator for measuring this income dimension.

The best comparative data on the poverty rate were gathered as part of the *LIS* (Smeeding et al. 1990; Förster 1994; Burniaux et al. 1998a). They are based on micro data for households. But substantial gaps exist in the data series, with some entire countries as well as individual time points missing. Nevertheless, as poverty is the only performance dimension that refers to the distribution of political goods, and because it is accorded key importance in lists of social policy goals (Uusitalo 1985; Castles and Mitchell 1992; Korpi and Palme 1998), we have decided to use the available data and replace missing values using appropriate techniques.

The effectiveness of social policy with respect to the health component is frequently measured by infant mortality and mean life expectancy. Long comparative data series exist for both, but they differ in the extent to which

TABLE 2.7. *A model for evaluating social policy effectiveness*

Goal	Socioeconomic security and socioeconomic equality			
Components	Health	Housing	Education	Income distribution (national minimum)
Indicators	Infant mortality	Housing space and housing amenities	Degrees obtained	Poverty rate

they can be influenced by political measures. Social policy measures such as regular prenatal care, can directly affect infant mortality, while life expectancy is affected not just by policies but also by non-political factors such as nutritional habits or the consumption of alcohol and tobacco. In addition, only marginal differences in mean life expectancy exist among the group of developed industrial countries studied here. In the empirical analysis, therefore, the social policy component of health is measured only by infant mortality.

Ordinarily, housing space (average number of rooms) and housing amenities (a bath or shower, an indoor flush toilet) are used as measures of social policy effectiveness in housing (Eurostat 1997; Zimmermann 1998). For the nations and time period investigated here, however, no comparative housing data is available. The data situation for education is equally unsatisfactory. What are needed are outcome indicators for knowledge gained and for the educational qualifications of the citizenry. In the comparative research on education, these dimensions are usually measured by literacy rate and educational attainment (UNESCO; OECD 1998a). Because literacy is a matter of elementary skills, there are few differences in this rate among the nations we examine (UNDP 1990). In the case of educational attainment, measured as the proportion of the adult population that has completed various levels of education, the OECD series *Education at a Glance* has only systematically gathered data since 1989 (OECD 1992, 1998a).[10] So of the four components in the model for evaluating social policy effectiveness shown in Table 2.7, only two—health and income distribution—can be empirically investigated. Many scholars place considerable importance on education, and it is unfortunate to not have the data to be able to include an education measure in the

---

[10] School enrollment data is often used as a substitute for educational attainment, as it gives the proportion of a particular age group attending a school at a particular level of education. But the major problem is that this data encompasses 'flows' rather than 'stocks'. It leaves open how many of those who are attending a particular type of school in fact complete the relevant level of education (Barro and Lee 1993).

analysis. Some American social scientists have argued that the equal opportunity provided in the American educational system is the functional equivalent of redistribution in Europe (Heidenheimer 1981; Lipset 1996). Still, at
least poverty, an essential distributional aspect of social policy, can be
empirically investigated.

Environmental policy

The OECD (1994, 1997) has developed a list of goals for environmental
policy, though one cannot assume much consensus about its contents. Most
comparative studies of environmental policy are qualitative case studies that
investigate particular environmental policies such as clean air policy (Vogel
and Kun 1987; Kern and Bratzel 1996). In the few studies that compare a
broad spectrum of environmental policies (Jänicke et al. 1996a; Jahn 1998;
Scruggs 1999), indicator selection is not guided by explicitly formulated
theoretical concepts. Accordingly, indices of 'environmental performance'
(Jahn 1998: 111–13) or 'environmental outcomes' (Scruggs 1999: 11) mix
indicators of environmental pressures, such as emissions of harmful substances into the air, together with indicators of environmental policy measures, such as recycling rates for glass or the population served by waste water
treatment plants. It is certainly no coincidence that one of the few conceptually based comparative studies (Ricken 1995) employs a model of environmental policy effectiveness that is compatible with the OECD's list of goals.

The OECD's 'pressure—state—response' framework is the basis for the
indicators used in its *Environmental Data Compendium*. It distinguishes
between three types of environmental indicators: indicators of environmental
pressures which 'describe pressures from human activities exerting on the
environment' (OECD 1994: 10), indicators of environmental quality and of
the quality and quantity of natural resources ('state'), and indicators of
societal responses or political measures ('response'). Following this model,
the general goal of environmental protection can be divided into two components: 'protecting environmental quality' and 'protecting the quality and
quantity of natural resources'. Environmental quality can be protected by
reducing the pressures on the environment, for example, by reducing man-
made sulphur oxides emissions. The quality and quantity of natural resources can be protected by reducing the consumption (or exploitation) of
natural resources like water. In the OECD's terminology, the former measures are called 'sink-oriented', the latter 'source-oriented' (1994: 12).

The effectiveness of these two activities can be seen by measuring the 'state
of the environment and of natural resources' (OECD 1994: 11) in a given
time and place, such as by finding the concentration of pollutants like
sulphur oxides in the air. But the basic problem for comparative research is
that the condition of the water, air, soil, or other natural environments are

influenced to a considerable degree by entirely non-political factors such as the climatic conditions or the geographical location of a country. For that reason, the effectiveness of a national environmental policy cannot be established solely by the quality of environmental conditions themselves, in other words through the outcomes. Instead, it is the level and development of anthropogenic intervention in the environment that is at stake (OECD 1994: 10, Ringquist 1995: 306; Jänicke et al. 1996a: 41). Thus, in the case of clean air policy, it is not the existing concentration of air pollutants (immission) but the volume of pollutants emitted into the air by firms and citizens (emission) that is measured.

The decisive question, however, is whether this decision not measuring the quality of the environment violates our analytic and conceptual stricture against using output measures. Put differently, must we analyse outputs rather than outcomes in environmental policy? The answer is no, as anthropogenic interventions are conceptually located between outputs and outcomes. The OECD calls this intervention dimension 'pressures on the environment caused by human activities' (1994: 9), while in comparative research on environmental policy it is called impact and refers to the behaviour of the addressees of a political measure (Weidner and Knoepfel 1983: 222). Thus, it is not the actual quality of the environment that is measured but the behaviour of firms and individuals that directly influences environmental quality. Clearly such impacts are not an end product, even though the behaviour of the addressees of a policy does constitute a central subdimension of the effectiveness of this (environmental) policy.

The advantage of impacts is that they can be directly controlled by political actors and are thereby relatively clearly interpretable as political performance. The disadvantage is that these indicators largely measure flows rather than stocks. Jänicke et al. (1996a: 131) draw attention to the problem of waxing stocks despite waning flows. Though fewer pollutants may be flowing today into groundwater or into the soil (decreased flow), the growing concentration of pollutants (increased stock) means the environment continues to degrade over the longer term.

Table 2.8 summarizes the foregoing discussion and complements the model by listing six indicators. The selection of the indicators is determined by the availability of appropriate data for our countries and time period.[11] The first component 'protecting environmental quality' can be measured by five indicators (sulphur oxides, nitrogen oxides, and carbon dioxide emissions, municipal waste production, fertilizer use) with the first three aiming at air pollution. For measuring the second component only one indicator is

---

[11] All six indicators are classified by the OECD (1994: 14–15) as measures of environmental pressure. The OECD also uses more general indicators of pressure placed on the environment, such as population growth or energy consumption. We will not use them as their connection to environmental policy measures is only indirect.

TABLE 2.8. *A model for evaluating environmental policy effectiveness*

Goal	Environmental protection	
Components	Protecting environmental quality	Protecting the quality and quantity of natural resources
Indicators	Sulphur oxides, nitrogen oxides, and carbon dioxide emissions, municipal waste production, fertilizer use	Water consumption

available (water consumption). These indicators only reflect some pressures on the environment. Water pollution measures or indicators for other harmful substances in the air, for example, are entirely missing (for more on this issue, see OECD 1997). The fact, that air pollution indicators are overrepresented reflects both how relatively easy it is to measure air pollution, and that clean air programmes were among the first environmental policies to be implemented (Knoepfel and Weidner 1985). The limited set of indicators can be seen as an implicit advantage; however, since it indirectly ensures that we analyse only those environmental conditions for which governments have explicitly taken a responsibility to improve.

In sum, we have presented models for evaluating effectiveness in each of the four domestic policy areas we are investigating, and have specified appropriate indicators to measure them. A compilation of these models covering altogether fourteen performance indicators can be found in the form of a tree diagram (see Figure 2.3). More detailed specification of the indicators and their data sources can be found at the beginning of Chapter 4 (see Table 4.1).

Propositions about the Relationship between Policy Goals

After differentiating the normative criteria or policy goals 'vertically' into its components and their corresponding indicators, the 'horizontal' relationship between different policy goals is addressed in the second step. The question of relationship is important because one cannot assume that all policy goals, expressing desired goals of political action, can be realized simultaneously. In fact, policy goals may be in conflict or be compatible. The most important propositions on the relationship between policy goals are discussed later. This discussion provides the basis for our theoretical typology of political effectiveness developed in the next section.

Goal conflicts or trade-offs[12] between goals are an integral part of any decision, especially political decisions. For that reason goal conflicts as well

---

[12] 'Trade-off' has two meanings: a conflictual relation between two goals where one goal can only be attained at the cost of the other, and a balancing of goals all of which are not attainable at the same time (Webster's Dictionary). Trade-off is used here as a synonym for the term 'goal conflict'.

as propositions of compatibility between conflicting goals are often discussed in political science contexts. The most general, and thus basic, conflict in democracies is between representation and governance (Berelson et al. 1954: ch. 14; Almond and Verba 1963: 476; Lijphart 1984, 1999*a*; Shepsle 1988). The essence of democracy as a form of government is that the interests of all citizens are taken into account equally in the political decision-making process. At the same time, like all political systems, democracies must also be able to act and make decisions. According to decision-making theories, one cannot maximize both goals at the same time: inclusive representation can only come at the cost of effective governing, and vice versa (Buchanan and Tullock 1962; Sartori 1987). But this 'great legislative trade-off' (Shepsle 1988) is not investigated here. Our concern is the relationship between various policy goals, or put differently, trade-offs within the dimension of governing.

While this distinguishes general trade-offs from the trade-offs that are of interest here, a second differentiation is needed from trade-offs existing within policy areas. One of the best known is the conflict between the economic policy goals of full employment and price stability, often discussed in terms of a downward sloping Phillips curve that plots unemployment against inflation (Phillips 1958; Samuelson and Nordhaus 1995). This relationship seemed to indicate that, at least during particular time periods, governments could 'buy' low unemployment only at the cost of high inflation, and vice versa. Yet as we are interested in the overall performance of democracies, it is not the conflicts within a policy area but rather the conflicts between policy areas that interest us.

There are two key propositions about conflicting goals and two about goal compatibility. The economy is at the centre of both conflict theories, since they assert a trade-off between the goals of economic policy and social policy, as well as between the goals of economic policy and environmental policy. Such a view of conflict or contrast is enhanced by the fundamental importance economic thought places on trade-offs. 'Tradeoffs are the central study of the economist', Arthur Okun (1975: 1) writes, and ' "you can't have your cake and eat it too" is a good candidate for the fundamental theorem of economic analysis.'

The most well-known and influential propositions on the compatibility of policy goals are the concept of economic growth and the concept of sustainability. The concept of economic growth can serve to make economic policy compatible with social policy, while the concept of sustainability integrates economic, social, and environmental goals. Sustainability is a serious attempt to balance the two most important goal conflicts at the same time.

Figure 2.1 contains a graphic depiction of the four propositions. It shows that there is no separate theory of conflict as yet for domestic security goals. If discussed at all, then it is with reference to the first conflict proposition on

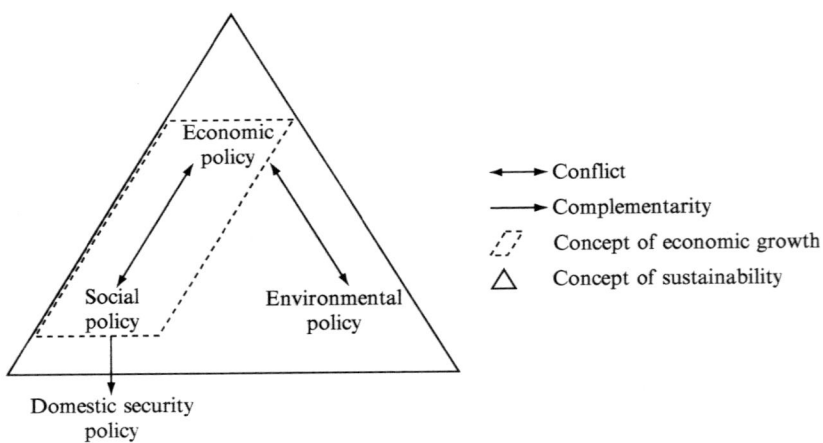

FIGURE 2.1. Propositions about goal conflict and goal compatibility

economic policy and social policy. It is often asserted that a one-sided pursuit of economic goals, particularly economic growth, without a simultaneous attempt to realize social policy goals, such as a guaranteed minimum income, will lead to an increase in crime (Gurr 1989; Lynch 1995: 24). Thus the conflict between economic policy and domestic security policy is incorporated in the proposition about the conflict between economic policy and social policy. The situation is similar with respect to the compatibility propositions. Domestic security has neither a central nor an independent status in the framework of these theories. It stands outside both of the concepts of growth and sustainability, and if it is mentioned at all, then in connection with social policy.

The two trade-off and two compatibility propositions are discussed in detail below. The discussion is limited to those characteristics most necessary for empirically analysing relations between individual effectiveness criteria, and those needed for constructing and analysing the types of political effectiveness. A scheme of goal relationships drawn from economics will be used in this discussion. It aids in differentiating between logical and empirical (or technological) goal relationships (Jöhr and Singer 1955; Gabler 1997; Streit 2000). Three logical types of goal relationship can be distinguished: (*a*) goal identity, (*b*) goal incompatibility (where the pursuit of one goal negates the attaining of another goal), and (*c*) goal compatibility (which is the precondition that multiple goals can be pursued simultaneously). Empirical goal relationships come about 'when instruments for reaching a goal are employed, and the side effects that results from them influence the attaining of other goals' (Gabler 1997). Three different forms of goal relationships can

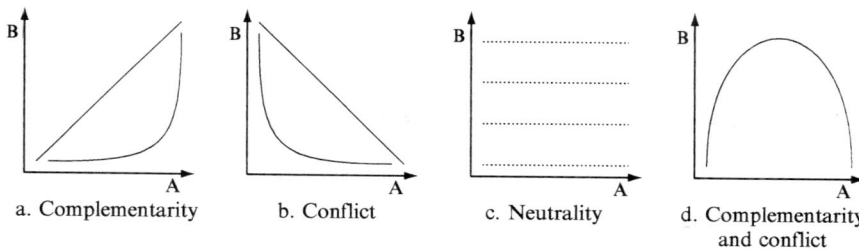

| a. Complementarity | b. Conflict | c. Neutrality | d. Complementarity and conflict |

FIGURE 2.2. Empirical relationships between goals

exist empirically: (*a*) complementarity (or harmony), in which the side effects support attaining other goals; (*b*) conflict (or competition), in which the side effects hinder pursuing other goals; and (*c*) neutrality (independence), in which the side effects leave the pursuit of other goals unchanged.

The relationship between goal A and goal B depicted in Figure 2.2[13] shows that complementary (a) and conflicting (b) goal relationships can take quite different forms—here both linear and curved—in practice. The curvilinear course of the conflictual relationship is particularly interesting, since conflict only begins at a relatively high level of goal A. Beyond a certain level of A, realizing both goals is actually incompatible (at the intersection with the x-axis). In addition to neutral relationships (c), an oft-discussed and more complex goal relationship (d) is also included. In (d), the relationship between the two goals changes depending upon the realization of goal A. At a low level of A, the goals support each other; at a high level of A, the relationship becomes conflictual. It is of course also possible to posit the opposite curvilinear relationship: first conflict and then complementarity.

The conflict between economic policy and social policy
The discussion of the first conflict proposition covers four parts. First, the conflict between economic policy and social policy has been used thus far as a shorthand for more specific goals that are presumed to be in conflict. Therefore, the theory will be defined more precisely with respect to these more specific goals. Second, with reference to the scheme of goal relationships (see Figure 2.2) we will then outline the various hypotheses on the relationship between these conflicting goals. Third, the relationship between the conflict theory and the Kuznets curve will be discussed because a dissent exists whether the Kuznets curve (Kuznets 1955, 1966), depicting the connection between economic development and income equality, is part of the conflict theory (Lindert and Williamson 1985: 342) or not. And finally, we will briefly

[13] This graphic form of representing goal relationships follows Kenworthy (1995: 42).

examine how the conflict proposition between economic policy and social policy is studied empirically.

First, the conflict between economic policy and social policy can be stated more precisely with the well-known formulation that comes in the title of Arthur Okun's book *Equality and Efficiency: The Big Tradeoff* (1975). In his view it is 'our biggest socioeconomic tradeoff' (Okun 1975: 2), as it pits the economic goal of efficiency against the political goal of equality. Put this way, it is clear that not every social policy goal hinders economic efficiency, but only those goals with respect to income distribution. Other components of social policy, such as health and education, tend to be seen as human capital investments that aid in the realization of economic goals rather than hindering them (Zimmermann 1996: 21). For that reason, at least in Germany, one speaks of the welfare state as a factor of production.

Okun's (1975: 2) definition of efficiency—'getting the most out of a given input'—is rather broad, but in the macroeconomic literature it is equated with economic growth. 'Efficiency implies that more is better' (Okun 1975: 2) and that can be best seen in the growth of the national product (Zimmermann 1996: 31). The conflict is then generally interpreted as one between economic growth and income equality, or between 'growth and distribution' (Zimmermann 1996).

Yet in the political science literature, economic efficiency is being defined more frequently and in part explicitly to expand upon its usage in this narrow, growth-oriented sense (Lindert and Williamson 1985: 343; Kenworthy 1995: 42), to include other economic goals such as full employment, price stability, investment, labour productivity, and trade balance (Kenworthy 1995: ch. 3). This broader understanding is also reflected in assertions of conflict between the goals of social policy and those of employment (Scharpf 1997, 1999; Abrams 1999; Schmidt 2000*b*) or between the goals of social policy and of national economic competitiveness (Garrett 1998).

In applying narrow and broader efficiency definitions to the policy-specific models for evaluating economic policy and social policy (see Tables 2.6 and 2.7), one can formulate two different propositions about conflict. One is comprehensive, and asserts conflict between the economic goal of wealth and the social policy component of income distribution. That is, increasing income equality will hinder realizing all three goals of economic policy—high national income, full employment, and price stability. The other is a limited proposition that only asserts a conflict between high national income and income distribution.

Second, the discussion of the connection between efficiency and equality is shaped by two contradictory hypotheses. One of these is a trade-off Hayek (1960) and Friedman (1962) argued for, also called the *economic liberal* hypothesis in the literature. This position based on neoclassical economics emphasizes the negative side effects of economic redistribution. The assumption is that reducing socio-economic differences will dampen or eliminate incentives to work that are necessary for increasing work efficiency. Moreover, higher taxes and social welfare contributions needed for redistribution will draw money away from saving and investing (Okun 1975; Kenworthy 1995: 38).[14] The other can be called the *social-democratic* hypothesis.[15] Here there is not a negation of the structural tension that exists between economic redistribution and economic efficiency; the emphasis instead is on the positive side effects socio-economic redistribution measures have on economic efficiency. These include, among other aspects, the stabilization of demand within low-income groups, the promotion of human capital, and greater motivation and cooperation at the workplace (Korpi 1985: 100; Kenworthy 1995: 4, 38). Positive side effects are assumed to outweigh the negative, with a complementary relationship existing between efficiency and equality such that increasing income equality helps promote economic efficiency. Korpi (1985) describes these two hypotheses with aqueous imagery: economic liberals see the welfare state as a 'leaky bucket' while social democrats see it as an 'irrigation system'. The 'leaky bucket' image is originally from Okun (1975: 91 et seq.) and symbolizes losses in economic efficiency; the 'irrigation system' symbolizes gains to economic efficiency with the aid of the welfare state.

There are also two less radical if less well known hypotheses, perhaps because they generally appear in empirical studies. The first, that we call the *moderate economic liberal* hypothesis, argues that socio-economic redistribution measures have both negative and positive side effects on economic efficiency, but that the negative predominates. Efficiency and equality are thereby still in conflict, but it is less harmful than in the pure economic liberal hypothesis (Kenworthy 1995: 39). More technically, the slope of the curve is flatter. The second, *independence hypothesis*, argues that there is a neutral relationship between efficiency and equality (Korpi 1985; Castles and Dowrick 1990).

The economic, and to some extent the political science literature often sees the relationship between efficiency and equality as an unalterable, almost elemental, association. This is a short-sighted view. Obviously, certain technical instruments are used to try to steer the relationship between the two goals. Accordingly, the specific means used shape the empirical form the

[14] In this context, one often reads of the 'rent-seeking society' (Buchanan et al. 1980) and of 'distributional coalitions' (Olson 1982; Weede 1984; Korpi 1985: 98). These are less propositions about the trade-off between income equality and efficiency, however, than they are arguments about the negative effects organized interests can have on economic growth.

[15] It is noteworthy that there is essentially no name given in the literature for the opposite of the trade-off between efficiency and equality. Korpi (1985), one of the few who has tried, suggests the term reformist. I think this does not go far enough, inasmuch as it does not make clear what its relation is to programmatic party positions or to general political theories. For that reason, we use the term social-democratic.

relationship between goals takes (Zimmermann 1996). This is illustrated by the different ways financial support has been provided to low-income groups. The benefits can be structured in such a manner as to provide incentives to find work, as was tried in the 'negative income tax experiment' in the USA (Blank et al. 1999). But incentives are also possible, as when benefits are provided under threat of sanctions, including curtailing them if offered work is not accepted, or limiting the total number of annual benefits will be provided, as has been done in some US states. Benefits can also be structured in the absence of such incentives or sanctions, as was long true in the German welfare state (Gebhardt and Jacobs 1997).

Against the image of almost elemental relationship also speaks that the hypotheses are grounded in differing normative convictions. This becomes particularly evident in the two more radical hypotheses. The trade-off between income equality and economic efficiency is central to economic liberalism, with the distaste for redistribution justified by the preference for liberty over equality (Korpi 1985; Kenworthy 1995). By the same token, the notion that social policy measures have beneficial side effects on economic efficiency is central to social democracy, but here it is normatively justified by a preference for equality over liberty (Esping-Andersen 1990). Thus, the discussion of the relationship between efficiency and equality touches on fundamental societal values, and thus on conceptions of a desired type of society (Kluckhohn 1962). Political actors relying on their normative preferences then will employ quite different instruments to steer this relationship—and can be seen in benefits offered to the needy, with quite different results.

Both arguments lead to the conclusion that the relationship between equality and efficiency is shaped by politics rather than being elemental. This is of some consequence for our analysis, for it only makes sense to ask about the influence of political actors and institutions if this is a relationship between goals that actually can be politically steered.

Third, most studies of the efficiency–equality conflict mention the Kuznets curve (1955, 1966) that proposes a connection between level of economic development and income equality. While some authors (Lindert and Williamson 1985: 342) regard this as a proposition of conflict, most do not assume this of Kuznets's model. Still, there is as yet no agreement just how the Kuznets curve differs from the conflict proposition.[16]

Kuznets observed that in the early phases of economic development (during the passage from agrarian to industrial society), income inequality increases, then stabilizes for a while, and then decreases again. In highly

---

[16] Among other things, the question of the causal direction (Alesina and Rodrik 1994: 467; Persson and Tabellini 1994: 601) is raised, and the fact that Kuznets investigates the level of and not the change in wealth (Persson und Tabellini 1994: 601).

developed countries, the increase took place around the turn of the nineteenth to twentieth centuries and the decrease after the end of the Second World War (Lindert and Williamson 1985: 345). Per capita income rises and falls in tandem with the increase and decrease of inequality; the curve has an upside-down U-shape (see example (d) in Figure 2.2), with the two axes levels of wealth and income inequality.

The explanation usually given for this pattern is based on economic factors associated with the shift from agrarian to industrial employment. But political factors are also cited particularly when governments take responsibility to reduce socio-economic inequality by establishing a welfare state. Kuznets's original surmise has been extended lately to argue that the pattern has reversed itself again in the wake of de-industrialization: increased levels of wealth today bring increased income inequality (Atkinson 1996: 33; Barro 1999: 9). The political concomitant is the dismantling of the welfare state since the mid-1970s that has proceeded at different speeds in most western democracies (Pierson 1999). This expanded Kuznets curve[17] is not an empirically confirmed theory but is more in the nature of a plausible argument adduced to explain increasing inequality and poverty in the USA and Great Britain since the 1970s.

Depending upon whether Kuznets's original or the expanded surmise is accurate, we thus expect to find either a positive or a negative relationship, respectively, between levels of wealth and income equality. For the immediate post-war era, Kuznets's original formulation predicts the same complementary relationship between national product and income equality as the social-democratic hypothesis, while for the time since the 1970s, the expanded surmise predicts an inverse connection, much like the economic liberal hypothesis. The difference between the Kuznets surmises and the ideological hypotheses lies in the explanatory model: The former explain the pattern with sectoral shifts in the economy and political measures, the latter focus on the side effects, negative or positive, of income equality on economic efficiency. Both approaches are relevant here because they focus on the relationship between economic policy and social policy.

Fourth, empirical analyses tend to treat measures of equality as the independent and measures of efficiency as the dependent variables. Multivariate regression analyses, including various control variables, are then undertaken to establish the effect of the social policy variables on the economic variables. Most such studies use economic growth as the indicator of efficiency, while output indicators—typically state expenditures (social expenditures or transfer payments) but sometimes also measures of tax revenue—are used to

---

[17] The expanded Kuznets curve is not identical with the 'augmented Kuznets hypothesis' (Milanovic 1994). This only emphasizes the aspect Kuznets himself noted, namely that the degree of inequality is determined not just by economic but also by political factors.

capture the social policy dimension. The results of such empirical studies are inconclusive, since all the hypotheses noted have found confirmation.[18] The reasons for this contradictory state of affairs is largely due to differences found in research designs themselves, as they vary not just with respect to the indicators used for efficiency or social policy, but also by the nations and time periods investigated. Methodological heterogeneity reigns, since one finds longitudinal as well as cross-sectional analyses and considerable variety in the control variables selected (Saunders 1986; Castles and Dowrick 1990; Atkinson 1995).

These empirical studies are insufficient relative to our own research questions, in part because income equality is often measured by governmental effort or output (social expenditure), which renders it inadequate for investigating the asserted trade-off between income equality and economic efficiency.[19] One rarely finds studies investigating the relationship between economic performance and income equality as measured by outcome (Persson and Tabellini 1994; Kenworthy 1995). Many empirical studies also implicitly assume that the efficiency–equality relationship is natural or elementary and cannot be shaped by politics. Political factors, such as the ideological orientation of political actors or even the political institutions, are neither cited as explanatory factors, nor are attempts made to measure them. Still, at least different welfare state regimes are beginning to be discussed as a factor potentially influencing the relationship between efficiency and equality (Persson and Tabellini 1994; Atkinson 1995).

The conflict between the economic policy and environmental policy
The review of the second conflict follows a similar format as for the previous, starting with a more rigorous definition of which goals are asserted to be in conflict. Then the hypotheses suggested for the connection between economic and environmental policy goals are elucidated, followed by a discussion of the so-called 'ecological Kuznets curve' (Jänicke et al. 1996*b*; Stern et al. 1996) that posits a connection between economic development and burdens placed on the environment. The discussion concludes with remarks on empirical studies of this conflict. The overall discussion is briefer than for the previous conflict, as the problem is of more recent vintage and was first triggered, many feel, by the publication of *The Limits to Growth* (Meadows et al. 1972).

---

[18] For example, the trade-off hypothesis is confirmed by Landau (1985), Pfaller and Gough (1991), Weede (1991) while Kenworthy (1995) finds complementarity. Korpi (1985) and Castles und Dowrick (1990), on the other hand, find no relationship, and Saunders (1986) reports contradictory findings.
[19] This is particularly so when social expenditure measures include growth-promoting policies such as health or education.

First, the asserted conflict focuses on the question 'environmental protection or/and economic growth?' (Wicke 1991: 495; Pearce and Warford 1993: 3). No differentiation is made within environmental goals, since it is assumed that economic growth damages all parts of the environment, with effects on environmental quality as well as on the quality and quantity of natural resources. In terms of the policy-specific models for evaluating economic policy and environmental policy (see Tables 2.6 and 2.8), there is at most a limited conflict between national income and environmental protection. In light of the recent discussion of globalization effects, this proposition has been expanded to include other economic policy goals, in particular full employment, to assert that only when environmental standards are not too high for firms—meaning not too expensive—will enough jobs be made available. So in this sense as well, a comprehensive conflict between environmental protection and economic policy is asserted, not just a conflict confined to environmental protection and national income.

Second, the debate about the relationship between environmental protection and economic growth is shaped by three hypotheses.[20] The *radical ecology* argument asserts a logical incompatibility between both goals. This position was predominant in the late 1960s and early 1970s (Pearce and Warford 1993: 10), nourished by the results of the well-known *Limits to Growth* study (Meadows et al. 1972). Continued, unregulated economic and population growth, the scenario of this study suggested, would lead to a life-threatening destruction of the environment and shortages in non-renewable resources. Only by taking the radical step of voluntarily limiting growth (or accepting zero growth rates) could one avert a catastrophe.

A *technocratic* view, by contrast, seems to have predominated since the late 1980s and early 1990s. It argues that as long as specific instruments and policies are adopted, the two goals are in principle complementary (Pearce and Warford 1993: 10). An optimal path is sought in the context of 'fixed stocks of exhaustible resources and stocks of renewable resources' (Pearce and Warford 1993: 10) that at least in German is described as 'qualitative growth' (Wicke 1991). This technocratic hypothesis on the one hand emphasizes the positive effects of a long-term producer-friendly environmental policy, as it will lead to a decline in resource use and an increase in environmental quality. On the other hand, it also emphasizes the positive effects on job creation and growth of the goods and services produced by newer environmental technology, as well as the positive effects higher environmental quality has on the attractiveness of economic locations (Wicke 1991; Spelthahn 1994).

An *economic liberal* hypothesis also has become more popular of late, its proponents arguing that environment problems can be solved through the

---

[20] Designations for the hypotheses are derived in part from Jakobeit (1997: ch. 3).

free play of market forces. Technological progress as well as the substitutability among natural resources will resolve the problems. The only perceived danger is that government bureaucrats will interfere in the marketplace and thereby distort incentives (Jakobeit 1997: ch. 3). Doing so would endanger economic growth and reduce the ability to compete, providing the basis for a conflict between economic policy and environmental policy.

Both economic liberal and radical ecology hypotheses see conflicts between the economy and the environment, unlike the technocratic view. The difference is not only that the radical ecology hypothesis sees incompatibility while the economic liberals assume compatibility in principle, but—more important—that the causal arrows run in the opposite directions. To radical ecologists, the economy produces negative side effects on the environment; to economic liberals, government environmental measures produce negative side effects on the economy.

Third, the ecological Kuznets curve describes an upside-down U-curve relationship between per capita income and the environmental conditions (see example (d) in Figure 2.2).[21] The assertion is that burdens on the environment increase until a particular level of national wealth is reached, but once reached, the burdens decrease again. One study fixes the turning point at a per capita income of $8,000 (Grossman and Krueger 1993). But other empirical analyses have shown not only that this value varies depending upon which environmental indicator is being investigated (Stern et al. 1996) but that the turning point may be higher.

Jänicke et al. (1996a) argue that one can describe the basic message of the ecological Kuznets curve with the formula 'getting rich—getting clean'. The 'ambivalent' character of wealth is thought responsible for this pattern (Shafik 1994; Ricken 1995; Jänicke et al. 1996a). On the one hand, economic growth burdens the environment because increased industrial production is accompanied by a higher emission of pollutants and a higher consumption of natural resources ('necessities'). On the other hand, a high level of wealth is also associated with greater technical, economic, and cultural resources to reduce the burdens on the environment ('possibilities'). This last also means modern environmental technology, more money, and in particular, a greater awareness or sensitivity to environmental issues (postmaterialist values) that lead to political programmes to improve environmental quality and protect natural resources. Additionally, sectoral change in the economy play a part as the service sector economy replaces the industrial economy—with beneficial spillover effects on the environment. In the first, developmental phase,

---

[21] There have been empirical investigations of the connection between economic growth and quality of the environment since the early 1990s (Shafik and Bandyopadhyay 1992; Grossman and Krueger 1993; Shafik 1994; Jänicke et al. 1996a). Only more recently has the term 'ecological Kuznets curve' found wider currency for the empirically asserted upside-down U-curve relationship (Stern et al. 1996; Roberts and Grimes 1997).

environmental burden outweighs environmental relief; in the second, relief outpaces burden. That means the first phase is characterized by a conflictual relationship between economic and environmental goals, while in the second this conflict no longer exists and both goals can be simultaneously achieved.[22]

There is strong empirical support for this model, but the question remains whether the curve itself applies to all (Grossman and Krueger 1993; Ricken 1995) or only to some components of environmental performance (Shafik and Bandyopadhyay 1992; Arrow et al. 1995; Jänicke et al. 1996*b*). Some authors believe that the ease with which an environmental problem can be resolved determines whether the development follows the shape of the Kuznets curve, or whether the damage to the environment only increases with increasing wealth (Jänicke et al. 1996*b*). The ease with which a problem can be resolved may depend on available technology and political feasibility. Jänicke, Mönch, and Binder, for example, argue that implementing an environmental policy to reduce sulphur oxides emissions (largely produced by power plants and heavy industry) was relatively easy both because a simple filter technology existed and there was little social or political opposition. But reducing waste, which demands direct intervention into industrial production, is a far more difficult problem by contrast. A more general way of conceptualizing this may be to speak of weighing the costs and benefits in implementing environmental programmes (Shafik and Bandyopadhyay 1992: 4).

The ecological Kuznets curve can be regarded as a specific example of the technocratic hypothesis, but it goes beyond this hypothesis in at least two respects. For one, it does not only look at specific instruments or policies but points to other explanatory factors such as sectoral changes in the economy or changes in societal values. For another, it implies an important modification of this hypothesis. Research indicates that the relationship captured by the ecological Kuznets curve depends upon or varies as a result of, which particular burdens on the environment are under discussion. The shape of the curve, in other words, depends entirely upon the tractability of the environmental problem not just to technological but also to political solutions.

Fourth, comparative empirical studies on the relationship between economic policy and environmental policy have been almost entirely devoted to examining the ecological Kuznets curve. As in the case of the previous conflict proposition about economic and social policies, environmental indicators are the dependent and national product is the independent variable,

---

[22] In this context it is necessary to again emphasize the difference between flows and stocks. The upside-down U-shaped curve, most agree, is only applicable to flows and not to stocks (Arrow et al. 1995; Jänicke et al. 1996*b*). Though one can continue reducing damage to the environment (flows), the size of natural resources will continue to decrease and the concentration of pollutants in the various environmental media will continue to increase (stocks).

and their connection is examined by multivariate regression analyses with control variables. Though the 'turning point' is often explained with the help of political factors (Grossman and Krueger 1993; Arrow et al. 1995), these regression analyses do not include any political factors as independent variables. Almost all the studies—Ricken (1995) is the exception—analyse a group of democratic and non-democratic systems at very different levels of economic development. It is still an open question whether the same upside-down U-shaped curve also can be found to describe the relationship between economic and environmental policies in a homogeneous group of wealthy democracies.

Growth and sustainability as propositions for making
conflicting goals compatible
In the effort to make these various goals compatible, politicians and scholars have developed various concepts for integrating policies that are meant as guidelines to political action. The two most powerful and comprehensive are economic growth and sustainability. The growth paradigm predominated politics of western democracies until the 1970s, while sustainability, conceived as an explicit alternative to growth, is now a recognized goal of many international organizations (UN, OECD, and EU) as well as national governments. Since the major function of these models is to guide political action, the development of the concepts have included not only goals and general instruments but also specific policies for realizing goals and control procedures to evaluate progress towards the goals (UN-DPCSD 1996-7; OECD 1998*b*).

In the following, we limit our discussion to the goals regarded as compatible, and then turn to the essential characteristic of these theories, namely instruments meant to lead to integration or harmonization. Since our primary interest is to unearth the relationship between individual dimensions of performance, as well as to develop a typology of political effectiveness, only the theoretical conclusions of these models are relevant. We sidestep the far more controversial question to what extent these concepts are actually capable of bringing about their intended effects.

The core of the *growth paradigm*, as critics call the growth concept (Wessels 1991), is that economic growth is the primary goal of political action. Economic growth, however, is a 'derivative' (Schröder 1971: 30) or an instrumental (Tuchtfeldt 1982: 189) goal. One expects positive effects from it on other substantive economic and social goals, including increases in citizens' material standard of living, the supply of workplaces, the more just distribution of income and wealth and a greater ease in fulfilling costly governmental tasks (Wicke 1991: 503). In the terms of our policy-specific models for evaluating effectiveness, this then refers to the economic policy components of national income and full employment (see Table 2.6), as well as all four social policy components of health, housing, education, and a national minimum with respect to income distribution (see Table 2.7). The compatibility between the most important social and economic goals is thereby ensured through a third dimension, economic growth. The mechanism is that growth of the economy produces the economic resources necessary for realizing social policy goals, and economic growth itself is based on greater productivity that in turn creates full employment.

This concept of growth is an attractively simple guide for political action, since the focus can be put entirely on realizing a single instrumental goal. Increasing economic growth appears to automatically guarantee progress in reaching all the other important economic and social policy goals. Post-war developments in western democracies, at least until the early 1970s, seemed to confirm these assumptions of the growth paradigm. Continuous economic growth coupled with the simultaneous realization of other goals, particularly in social policy, marked that 'golden age' (Maddison 1991: 1).

But two developments set in that began to question the growth paradigm as a model for political action. Critics began to argue, as environmental conditions worsened, that post-war development had focused too one-sidedly on material wealth and that had come at the cost of the environment (Meadows et al. 1972). And the Keynesian economic policies for coping with economic crises could no longer be successfully employed by the later 1970s (Scharpf 1991). Alternative concepts were sought to bring different policies into harmony, and the idea of 'sustainable development' proved itself to be the most politically popular and comprehensive.

The *sustainability concept* was popularized by the 1987 report of the *World Commission on Environment and Development* (better known as the 'Brundtland Report'). It defined 'sustainable development' as 'development that meets the needs of the present without compromising the ability of future generations to meet their own needs' (WCED 1987: 40). The original concept of dealing with natural resources in such a manner as to ensure their reproductive capacity (Maier 1999: 2) originated in forestry, but the Brundtland Report generalized and transformed it to incorporate social meanings. By now, many more specific, partially competing definitions have been suggested, and one can assume more will be formulated, given how pertinent and intensely argued the topic is. Here we only address the particular concept of sustainability that focuses on the compatibility between different policy goals, a version of the concept particularly favoured by international organizations like the OECD and the EU.[23] An OECD description (1998b: para 4), for example, states that:

---

[23] Two other concepts of sustainability also may be distinguished: sustainability as a goal of ecological development only (Zukunftskommission der Friedrich-Ebert-Stiftung 1998) and sustainability as an independent goal, respectively, for environmental policy, for social policy, and for economic policy (Elkins 1994).

Sustainable development implies a focus on welfare considerations broader than just economic growth, on equity concerns, and on the need for governments to address threats to global 'commons', such as the environment, natural resources and cohesive social systems. The emphasis is on the links between the key components of sustainability, namely the economic, social and environmental dimensions; on the need to balance these links when there are conflicts; and on ensuring that economic policy takes into account environmental and social policy concerns, and vice versa.

One can find a similar formulation in Article 2 of the EU's Amsterdam Treaty (Hinterberger et al. 1998).

It is characteristic of the sustainability concept that it claims to be more comprehensive than the growth paradigm. It focuses on welfare 'broader than just economic growth' and is explicitly about 'development' rather than 'growth'. It also explicitly addresses the conflicts between the economy and social policy, and between economy and environment, with the goal of resolving them: 'the need to balance these links when there are conflicts'. The three different goals are to be integrated, so one might speak of a new 'magic triangle' or 'triadic structure' in the form suggested by Figure 2.1. The economy is at least implicitly given priority, since it is to 'take(s) into account environmental and social policy concerns'. Policies, this document notes earlier, are to be integrated and harmonized into an 'overall economic framework' (OECD 1998*b*: para 3).

This OECD formulation is about the general integration of economic, social, and environmental issues. By contrast, the EU's Amsterdam Treaty lists specific goals such as non-inflationary growth, a high level of employment, a high degree of social protection, a high level of environmental protection, improvement in environmental quality, and improving the quality of life (Hinterberger et al. 1998: 6). In terms of our policy-specific models for evaluating effectiveness, sustainable development integrates all the components established for economic, social, and environmental policies (see Tables 2.6–2.8). As previously noted, even this comprehensive conceptualization has no place for domestic security policy.

Though the sustainability concept sets goals for future societal development, the key question is how, or by which means, the integration or harmonization of these different goals is to take place. For all three dimensions the OECD (1998*b*) provides illustrations of what integration implies in 'practical terms'. In economic development, for example, the fact that the environment is treated as a common good is seen as the main reason for environmental degradation (OECD 1998*b*: para 24–30). Economic actors can externalize environmental costs, and therefore a *laissez-faire* policy is not advisable: Costs need to be internalized either through price mechanisms or by establishing property rights. The OECD proposes a 'polluter pays' principle as an answer to this common good problem. As a general principle of environmental policy, the OECD suggests the costs and benefits of each decision should be weighed, and then a decision rule should be applied to give priority to those alternatives that maximize individual welfare (OECD 1998*b*: para 39).

The means for integrating the three goals therefore lies in coordinated political steering of these different policy areas. In all policies, the idea is to recognize potential negative side effects on other policy areas and then minimize them. Cost-benefit analysis is to be used to select programmatic alternatives and to implement the path that promises the largest societal benefits. At heart, the idea of sustainability is technocratic. It is based on the premise that conflicting goals can be made compatible by developing and implementing adequate policy programmes.

The central message of this discussion is that the political problems have become more difficult and varied since the 1970s. With the growth concept, it was still possible for politics to focus on and pursue a single goal that also functioned as a means to realize other goals. But it is no longer as easy to reconcile economic policy and social policy using simple means, and environmental issues add further potential for conflict between policies: unsurprisingly, the suggestions for making conflicting goals compatible have also grown more complex. In the case of sustainability it is a matter of simultaneously trying to maximize three conflicting goals, and trying to integrate or balance, let alone find coherence among them puts high demands on political behaviour. Decisions about individual policy areas can no longer be taken in isolation but must in each case be considered in a larger context, and this also means an end to politics organized by specific policy area. Instead, as a study published by the German Wuppertal Climate, Environment, and Energy Institute put it, a 'holistic approach' to political action is needed (Loske and Bleischwitz 1996: 24).

Though many international organizations, national governments, and political actors regard (technocratic) sustainability as a guide for political action (Maier 1999), it remains true that another solution exists in public discourse, namely the (economic) liberal notion that the best way to realize these goals lies in minimizing government intervention in the economy. This alternative is noted here for the sake of completeness but will not be discussed further.

A Theoretical Typology of Political Effectiveness

Most studies of performance analyse performance dimensions individually and sequentially (as in Lijphart 1999*a*). The few studies that investigate the structure or patterns of political performance confine their analyses to whether individual dimensions are incompatible or mutually reinforcing (Gurr and McClelland 1971: 72–9; Powell 1982: ch. 2). While our study, following the goal conflict hypotheses, also empirically investigates relationships between individual policy areas, we are concerned as well with a typology of effectiveness that encompasses all policy areas.

We start from the premise that to evaluate the general performance of a national government, or a political system, achievements in a particular policy area are less important than realizing a broad spectrum of policies or policy package. Such packages can be differentiated with respect to their pattern—simultaneous realization of different goals, above- or below-average realization of individual goals—as well as with respect to the overall or general level of performance. The following typology aims to capture the first, more qualitative dimension of policy packages, while the concept of general political effectiveness suggested in the ensuing section focuses on a quantitative description of the policy package.

The fact that public policy research is organized around individual policy areas is certainly responsible for the lack of a typology of political effectiveness that encompasses multiple policy areas. At most there have been 'narrow' typologies that cover few policy areas, such as the typology of political economy that is restricted to economic and social policies (Schmidt 1987, 2000b). If a more comprehensive policy pattern incorporating many policy areas is described, then it is usually not a typology but a description of a nation-specific policy pattern, as exemplified by the model of 'American Exceptionalism' (Lipset 1996). Though such nation-specific policy patterns can only properly be recognized through comparisons with other nations, such comparisons frequently remain implicit.

Benchmarking, an instrument developed in management studies, is finding increasing use in comparative public policy research as a means to improve national policies. It introduced another type of political effectiveness by naming the country that shows the 'best practice' (Schütz et al. 1998). Finding who is at the 'top of the class' is a method employed largely for evaluating individual policy areas, in particular in labour market and employment policies (Tronti 1998; Schmid et al. 1999). It can also be used to describe more comprehensive policy patterns. These three empirical typologies—the typology of political economy, the nation-specific policy pattern, and benchmarking—are first briefly addressed and then used to develop a comprehensive typology of political effectiveness.

Schmidt (2000b: 491), in his search for the German public policy pattern, suggested three types of political economy that could be used to describe different aspects of economic and social policy. One was Northern European welfare capitalism, another was North American market capitalism, and the West German 'middle way' was a third road between the extremes. The two extremes were shaped by different principles, a dominant social democratic ideology in Northern Europe, and a dominant centre-right, market-oriented ideology in North America (Schmidt 1987: 143).

Schmidt (1987: 143) originally argued that three characteristics made the German 'middle way' distinct. First, the goal of price stability took priority over full employment in economic policy (see the Phillips curve discussion), which was the exact opposite of the pattern in welfare capitalism. Second, social policy was characterized not only by high social expenditure (unlike in market capitalism) but also by transfer-intense social expenditures (unlike in welfare capitalism). Third, in terms of the relationship between economic policy and social policy, Germany took a relatively balanced position between the market capitalism preference for efficiency over equality, and the welfare capitalism preference for equality over efficiency. The explanation for this moderate position, Schmidt assumed, lay in part in a national ideology that mixed economic liberal thought together with conservative reformist and democratic socialist traditions. But it was also due to political institutions like the independent central bank and the federalist state structure that limit the powers of executive and legislature. Finally, he refers to the division of power within government that was marked by coalition governments and that exerts a moderating influence on parties in government who overwhelmingly supporting welfare state institutions and practices.

This typology of political economy is more extensive than what we attempt here, as it includes policy outcomes as well as policy outputs, and patterns within individual policy areas are described in addition. But in another sense, it is narrower because the patterns described are confined to social policy and economic policy. Schmidt provides two important guides for our own typology. One is that patterns of performance can, as a matter of principle, be distinguished by whether certain goals are being one-sidedly maximized at the cost of other goals, or whether there is a balance between conflicting goals. The other is that differing patterns of performance can be explained by cultural traditions or ideologies that influence not only the preferences of political actors but also the political institutional settings themselves.

Though they do not provide a typology of political effectiveness, public policy studies that describe nation-specific policy patterns are also very helpful for constructing such a typology. Inasmuch as they survey multiple policy areas, they describe a unique or exemplary type in a comprehensive typology. The description or idea of 'American Exceptionalism' is one such nation-specific policy pattern. While this concept describes particular aspects of American culture, these cultural features are reflected as well by a pattern of policy performance[24] that can be summarized as follows: above-average levels of crime, wealth, and education combined with below-average levels of welfare benefits and income equality (Lipset 1996: 26). This unbalanced policy pattern oscillating between extremes—the complete opposite of the

---

[24] Analyses of the distinctiveness of US public policy tend to focus on the particular features of its social and economic policy (King 1973; Amenta und Skocpol 1989).

German politics of the middle way—is explained with reference to the 'double-edged' character of American political culture. The basic values of individualism, promotion of meritocracy, and in particular anti-government attitudes, are responsible for a situation in which, as Lipset (1996: 18) puts it, 'we are the worst as well as the best, depending on which quality is being addressed'. For some authors, political institutions that emphasize checks and balances lead to this pattern, in particular the absence of broad social policy measures (King 1973; Amenta and Skocpol 1989).

The nation-specific policy pattern of 'American Exceptionalism' can be regarded as a more comprehensive and detailed example of the type Schmidt labels North American market capitalism. When compared to Schmidt, who confines his analysis to political economy, this example takes economic, social, and domestic security policy into account (though environmental policy is still missing), and much more minutely describes the cultural bases for the policy pattern. The nation-specific pattern of 'American Exceptionalism' and the typology of political economy overlap to the extent that cultural or ideological factors are ascribed central roles in shaping national policy patterns. For that reason, it seems sensible to base a typology of political effectiveness on political ideology. But before doing so, we should turn to the third, 'best practice' type of political effectiveness that appears to be growing in significance in contemporary political discourse.

It is certainly no coincidence that in an era of globalization and international competition, benchmarking, is increasingly employed as a means for improving national policies (Schütz et al. 1998: 24). It involves continual comparison of outcomes, processes, and methods used by market competitors, with the intent to systematically close the gap in performance with the 'best in the class' (Gabler 1997). When applied to policy analysis, it means comparing policies and ranking nations to ascertain who has the 'best' and 'worst' practices. Examining the performance of the 'best' in principle should allow one to elicit the factors behind the success, and draw appropriate lessons for improving national policy. Benchmarking is thus a comparison of performance aiming at political learning, and is thus not a simple evaluation or ranking of nations (Schütz et al. 1998). Still, it can be instructive in the analysis of patterns of political effectiveness, since nations with either best or worst practices (or effectiveness) in all the policy areas investigated can mark the end points or limits of the typology.

My discussion shows that typologies of political effectiveness are constructed either on the basis of ideological preferences or on the basis of best and worst practices. The drawback of the former, based on the assumption that ideological preferences of political actors manifest themselves in political action and corresponding policy outcomes, is that it cannot grasp a poor realization of ideologies. The drawback of the latter is that it is a formal,

TABLE 2.9 *Theoretical types of political effectiveness*

	Economic policy	Social policy	Environmental policy	Domestic security policy
Best possible case	++	++	++	++
Sustainability	+	+	+	− or − −
Sustainability and domestic security policy	+	+	+	+
Classical social democracy	+ or ++	+ or ++	− or − −	− or − −
Classical social democracy and domestic security policy	+ or ++	+ or ++	− or − −	+ or ++
Libertarian model	++(+)	− or − −	− or − −	− or − −
Libertarian model and domestic security policy	++(+)	− or − −	− or − −	+ or ++
Worst possible case	− −	− −	− −	− −

Legend: ++ strongly above average; + above average; − below average; − − strongly below average effectiveness.

contentless classification, making it difficult to recognize policy patterns that lie between the two extremes.

Therefore we combine both ideological preference and best and worst practices in constructing our own typology of five different types of political effectiveness (Table 2.9). The end points are formally defined as the best possible and worst possible cases. The range of types between them comes from the most important ideologies dominating contemporary political discussions: sustainability, classical social democracy, and the libertarian model. These can be regarded as normative models of policy packages, and for each one, patterns are suggested that would exist if the corresponding preferences determined political action and policy outcomes. For each type, a relative measure of effectiveness that extends from strongly above average to strongly below average notes the degree of effectiveness.

The best possible case is characterized by a strongly above-average and the worst possible case by a strongly below-average political effectiveness in all four policy areas. As these limits are conceptualized theoretically, we do not refer to them as 'best practice' or 'worst practice' as would be done in the benchmarking approach. As it is, in a policy pattern that is composed of different, independent dimensions, it is entirely possible that there is no country where strongly above- or strongly below-average effectiveness exists in all four policy areas, hence we need to draw this distinction.

It is possible to derive clear preferences for economic, social, and environmental policies from the sustainability, classical social democracy, and libertarian ideologies that lie between the polar cases. But domestic security, as noted before in the discussion of conflicting and compatibility propositions, is often ignored. In order to take into account its disregard in most ideologies we primarily define ideological policy patterns with respect to economic, social, and environmental goals and distinguish between two subtypes with respect to domestic security. For example, we draw a distinction between 'sustainability' with below-average and 'sustainability and domestic security' with above-average realization of domestic security. Table 2.9 presents a technical description of these types and subtypes of policy patterns by specifying for each policy area whether above- or below-average performance exists. Sustainability, for example, stands for above-average performance in the economy, in social policy, and in the environment. Reading from top to bottom, the number of policy areas with above-average performance decreases, so to some extent we have an ordinal scale from best possible to worst possible case.

Sustainability is the ideologically defined policy pattern with the largest number of above-average markers of effectiveness. The essence of sustainability, following our previous discussion, lies in the equally strong pursuit of economic, social, and environmental goals. Yet such a balanced pattern of effectiveness is only possible if specific goals are not being maximized at the cost of other goals. The prototypical contour of this pattern is therefore not that all three goals are pursued in a 'strongly above average' (++) manner but merely in an 'above average' (+) fashion.

In the case of social democracy, as the discussion of the third way indicates (Giddens 1998, 2000), it is useful to draw a distinction between older, or classical, social democracy and its newer forms. Classical social democracy is characterized by above-average performance in economic and social policy. As Giddens (1998: 11) put it, this ideology 'did not have a hostile attitude towards ecological concerns, but found it difficult to accommodate to them' because the goals of full employment, social security, and equality took precedence. As with sustainability, here too a distinction is made between a classical social democracy with and without domestic security.

The contour of, or consensus about, the 'new' social democracy remains as yet vague; a corresponding policy pattern thus also cannot be determined. However, there are good reasons to regard sustainability as a provisional substitute for a modern social democracy. Speaking for this is the slogan 'Economic Performance, Social Solidarity, Ecological Sustainability: Three Goals—One Path' adopted by the Commission on the Future of the Friedrich Ebert Foundation (1998), a foundation close to the German Social Democratic Party. Giddens (1998) also describes the third way as a new balance between multiple economic goals, equality, environmental protection, and crime prevention.

At the lower end of the ideologically defined types of political effectiveness stands a model that maximizes economic policy performance at the expense of performance in all other policy areas. While this type has thus far been discussed with reference to 'American Exceptionalism', the more general term libertarian model will henceforth be used. Doing so not only makes it applicable to other nations, but its ideological foundations are thereby more appropriately described. It is a broader term than some of the more economy-oriented alternatives, such as economic liberalism or market-oriented capitalism, and it is more neutral than the 'fighting term' neoliberalism (Giddens 1998). Here, too, a subdivision is made whereby the type showing above-average performance in domestic security policy can be regarded as a conservative variant of the libertarian model.

The basic idea behind this typology of political effectiveness is not to incorporate every possible logical combination of policy-specific effectiveness but instead to only include those policy packages that play a central role in contemporary political discussions. It is an open empirical question whether or which of the (five) theoretical policy patterns exist in reality, or—conversely—which empirically existing types are encompassed by this theoretical classification.

Several factors also need to be taken into account with respect to the three ideological types. First, even if actual performance appears to correspond to an ideologically defined policy pattern, one cannot assume that the relevant ideology is the only or decisive factor in creating it. It is quite possible that additional factors such as the degree of socio-economic modernity are important, or even that these other factors are decisive. In other words, these are typological descriptions of ideologically defined policy patterns and not causal models. Second, these ideologies are defined only at the level of policy outcomes in the four policy areas. The respective ideological systems are of course far broader and formulated with reference to values that go well beyond these four policy areas; in particular, they also refer to instruments meant to be used in realizing these goals. Third, sustainability occupies a special place as it articulates a third way between the classical social democratic and the libertarian positions. Such a balanced position was still being called a 'middle way' during the 1980s (Schmidt 1987). With the increasing discussion of sustainability as a new guiding principle in the 1990s, this pattern has gained not only ideological weight und justification but at the same time broader meaning by the inclusion of other preferences and instruments.

General Political Effectiveness

General political effectiveness, the second, quantitative characteristic of the policy package, refers to the overall level of performance in the four policy areas investigated here: domestic security, economic, social, and environmental. The dimension is conceptualized as a composite measure. The construction of such a measure necessitates a variety of theoretical decisions drawn in part from concepts and methods developed in the comparative research on the quality of life. Since its beginnings in the early 1970s, one of the key concerns of this sociological research has been to create a global measure for national welfare—called QOL measure—that is comparable to, but more comprehensive than, GDP.[25]

Such global measures have been employed only rarely in the research of political performance. If and when they are used, the theoretical decisions that enter into their construction are rarely made explicit. Putnam's summary *Index of Institutional Performance* (1993: 65–75), probably the currently best known global measure, illustrates this tendency. The twelve indicators that comprise this index are ordered into three performance dimensions: (*a*) Policy process is measured by cabinet stability, budget promptness, and the breadth of statistical and information services; (*b*) policy pronouncements are measured by reform legislation and legislative innovation; and (*c*) policy implementation is measured by the number of day care centres and family clinics, the industrial policy instruments deployed, spending on agriculture, local health units, and housing and urban development, as well as the degree of bureaucratic responsiveness. The index is based on factor scores, that is, the standardized values for each indicator, weighted by the respective factor loadings, are added up for every single case (Nie et al. 1975: 487–9).

Since this construction does not control (or standardize) for the differing number of indicators per policy performance dimension and per policy area, the result is that the implementation phase is overrepresented relative to earlier phases in the policy process, and welfare state policy is overrepresented relative to other policy areas. Putnam's index therefore primarily measures welfare state outputs. Another problem is that individual indicators are included in the index with different weights (factor loading), but the meaning of these weights remains open. This basic issue of factor scores is particularly serious here because the indicators included are very heterogeneous and quite unequally represent differing theoretical dimensions.

Following a list of criteria that has been suggested for assessing composite measures of performance (Morris 1979: 21–2; Hagerty et al. 2000: 3–7), a good measure should be free of ethnocentric bias and its individual indicators should all measure results or outcomes. An index should also be clear and easy to understand, particularly in its 'social reporting' function. Our normative model and the policy-specific models for evaluating effectiveness were constructed with the first two criteria in mind; the clarity criterion is relevant for constructing the general effectiveness measure. A readily interpretable index is extremely helpful for the descriptive empirical analyses we present,

---

[25] There has been greater interest in comparative welfare research since the 1990s in constructing such global QOL measures (Noll and Zapf 1994; Land 2000). For a summary and discussion of the most current measures used, see Hagerty et al. 2000.

particularly for the description of similarities and differences between countries.

In constructing a composite measure, decisions about the technique of standardization, weighting and aggregation of individual values need to be made (Sangmeister 1994: 424). We discuss the techniques suggested in the literature with reference to their theoretical implications. Based on this discussion we select the techniques for constructing the global measure of general effectiveness.

The fourteen indicators (Figure 2.3), that we derived and justified in the discussion of the policy-specific models for evaluating effectiveness, provide the basis for the composite measure. Each indicator measures one component of the four policy areas. Two components per policy area, taken together, comprise policy-specific effectiveness. In the case of domestic security policy, the components are violent crime and property crime, with the former measured by murder/manslaughter and robbery rates, and the latter by burglary rates. Effectiveness is similarly defined in the other policy areas. General effectiveness is then comprised of the individual measures of effectiveness of the four policy areas taken together. Technically, sub-indices need to be constructed for each policy area before being integrated into a global index; individual pieces of information must be successively aggregated from bottom to top. The decisions as to standardization, weighting, and aggregation apply equally to constructing the sub-indices as they do to the global index.

Standardization. If the measurement units of individual indicators vary, as is the case with the performance indicators, they need to be standardized. Two techniques are available—z-score transformation or an indexing system—if standardization is to take place without losing precision. In case of z-score transformation, divergence from the mean is expressed in standard deviations. Though such transformations are often used in policy research (see Castles and McKinlay 1979: 172), they do not produce measures that are immediately clear.[26] For this reason, and because it is often used in comparative quality of life research, we employ an indexing system (Morris 1979: 41). In this case, the values of each individual indicator are transformed into the same scale, either ranging from 0 to 100 (Morris 1979) or from 0 to 1 (UNDP). Zero thus indicates bad performance, 100 (or 1) good performance.[27] The advantage of indexing over z-score is evident, since the values of all individual indicators are transformed in a single step into a uniform scale.

---

[26] Variables standardized in this manner cannot be simply aggregated, as z-score transformed variables have different starting and end points. They need to be transformed again before they can be aggregated.

[27] Technically, the values of an indicator are determined relative to fixed reference points, in this case fixed minimum and maximum values, though different formulae are used for mathematically transforming the scales.

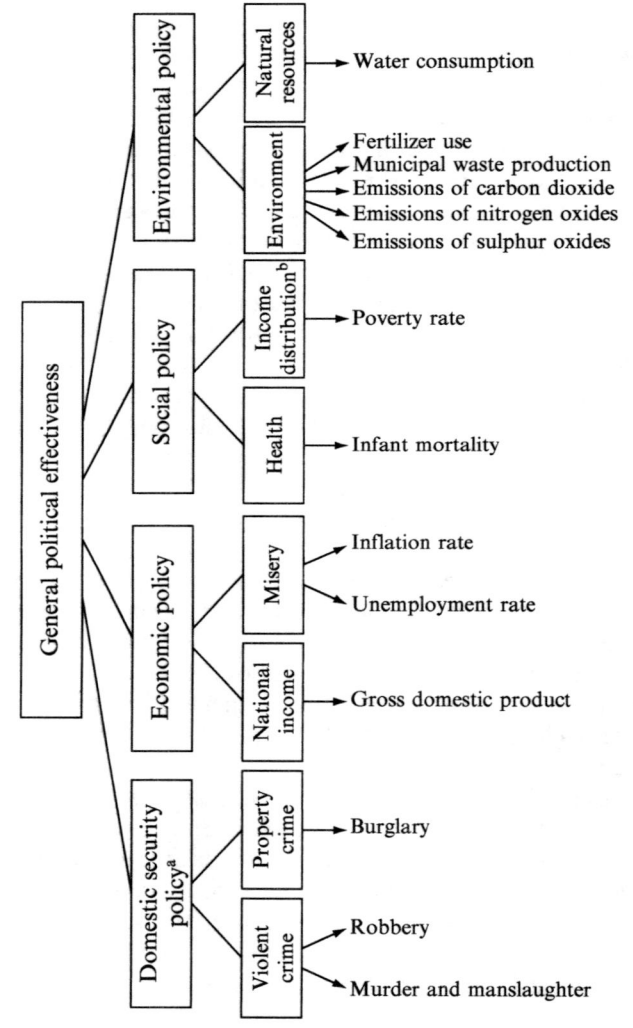

FIGURE 2.3. General political effectiveness

[a]Only protection of life and property. [b]National minimum.

The end points of the scale are readily understood, and the values that lie between can be immediately interpreted as the degree of deviation from maximum and minimum end points. Due to this clarity of individual values, indexing is also used as a form of standardization in the benchmarking of policies (Schütz et al. 1998; Mosley and Mayer 1999).

Indexing defines the values of the scale, but it is still necessary to establish whether the minimum and maximum values are to be defined empirically or theoretically. In the first case, the highest and lowest values are defined by countries; in the second case, the values would be set theoretically, for example, by a normatively defined goal. The *Physical Quality of Life Index* (Morris 1979: 42–6), one of the first composite measures of welfare, covering illiteracy rates, infant mortality figures, and life expectancy, was based on empirical reference points. The *Human Development Index*, by contrast, created in the 1990s by the UNDP and including life expectancy, education, and income, is based on normative reference points. A 100 per cent literacy rate, for example, was defined as the normative goal of education. The degree of literacy a nation reaches is then expressed as a relative deviation from this goal (UNDP 1995: 18).

If an empirically based indexing system is used for longitudinal analysis, another decision is also necessary: Should the best and worst performance be defined on a yearly basis or for the entire time period being investigated? Changes in performance over time can only be measured in the second case, that is, when the best and worst performance over the entire time period studied sets the limits (Morris 1979: 41). A yearly standardization cannot capture relative improvement in the performance of the best nations, as they will always show the highest values.

Weighting. A decision about weighting is necessary when aggregating individual indicators into a composite measure: should they be differently or equally weighted? Different weights can be justified on either empirical or theoretical grounds, with empirical weighting typically determined by factor analysis. While this value-neutral technique may appear attractive, the chief difficulty is the missing information about the meaning of the weights; and statistically determined weights do not necessarily accord with the weights individuals or collective actors ascribe to individual indicators (Carley 1981: 80). Given the lack of precision of performance theories, theoretical arguments to justify unequal weighting can rarely be made. However, theoretical arguments can also be used in favour of equal weighting of indicators. This form of weighting is rarely chosen with reference to a theory but is instead often adopted in the absence of arguments against it.

Aggregation. This is the actual formula used to combine the standardized values of the individual indicators. It is common to sum individual values (see Vogel 1998) or compute an arithmetic mean (see *Human Development Index*). The advantage of the arithmetic mean is that the composite measure has the same scale as the individual indicators and can therefore be interpreted in the same manner. The overall value of the *Human Development Index*, based on a mean of standardized values for health, education, and income, can be taken as the degree of deviation from a normatively set standard of living (UNDP 1995: 18).

Based on these considerations, the following decisions have been taken for determining the concept of general effectiveness. First, the indexing system is used for standardization so as to create readily comprehensible measures for the descriptive analysis. Reference (or end) points are empirically established based on best and worst performance, as the normative model of political effectiveness does not set any particular goals for individual dimensions of effectiveness. So the countries with the worst and best practices fix the end points of the scale, and the value of every other nation is determined relative to these two end points.

Second, both the normative model of, and the policy-specific models for evaluating political effectiveness are based on the premise of an outside and unbiased evaluation of the performance of democracies. No particular weight is given either to individual policy areas or to the components of specific policy areas. For that reason, in constructing both specific and general effectiveness, equal weight was given not just to the two policy-specific components but also to the four policy areas when they were aggregated. This means, for example, that in the domestic security policy area the effectiveness index is constructed of two equally weighted sub-indices: violent crime and property crime. The sub-index violent crime in turn has equally weighted components, murder/manslaughter and robbery, while the sub-index property crime is based solely on burglary. It would not be appropriate to construct this index by weighting the three effectiveness indicators (murder/manslaughter, robbery, and burglary) equally in a sub-index of domestic security policy, as the larger number of indicators of violent crime would then be overrepresented.[28] The indices for all policy areas are constructed the same way, and all four specific effectiveness measures are included with equal weight into the index of general effectiveness.

Third, an arithmetic mean is used to summarize the values of the standardized individual indicators. All sub-indices and the global index, though comprised of different numbers of elements, are thereby expressed in a manner that makes them immediately comparable to one another.

General effectiveness is thus defined by the relative degree to which the four domestic policy area goals have been achieved. No one area is privileged, and below-average performance in one area can be balanced by above-average performance in another. Compared with Putnam's global *Index of*

---

[28] Only by using such a technique is it possible to address the problem of the different number of available indicators for individual components of the policy areas.

Institutional Performance, the index of general political effectiveness both explicitly intends to measure goal-oriented performance, and explicitly does so by measuring the outcomes of political action. That makes it appropriate to call ours a summary measure of performance, which Putnam cannot claim. Technically, the advantage of the global general effectiveness index lies in its equally weighted inclusion of all relevant policy areas and components; no bias exists in favour of numerically over-represented policy components.

Compared with the various QOL measures (Hagerty et al. 2000), general political effectiveness is a *pure* policy measure. Most summary measures in the QOL research tradition only claim to provide information that is relevant to policy formation. It is also a *comprehensive* policy measure specifically constructed so as to encompass effectiveness in the most significant domestic policy areas. The UNDP's *Human Development Index*, in contrast, by measuring effectiveness only in the areas of health, education, and income indicators, limits itself to a few aspects of economic and social policy. This is also why it can differentiate between developing nations but is not sensitive enough to discriminate between highly developed nations in the fashion general political effectiveness can: the latter is both a broader and more differentiated index with respect to the individual policy areas.

Diener (1995) calls summary QOL indices that allow for differentiation between developing nations 'basic', and those measures that can discriminate between highly developed nations 'advanced'. By this perspective, the *Human Development Index* is a 'basic' and our general political effectiveness measure is an 'advanced' index. Put differently, our index can be seen as a further development of the *Human Development Index* that is applicable to highly developed industrial countries. That the level of general effectiveness is not set relative to normative goals, as is true of the *Human Development Index*, but relative to empirical referents, can be seen as one essential feature of an 'advanced QOL index'. In highly developed countries, it is no longer a matter of reaching normative minimum standards but rather of relative effectiveness vis-à-vis the best performer.

SUMMARY

Previous studies and discussions of political performance have utilized an extremely heterogeneous set of performance criteria. We have formulated a concept of *systemic political effectiveness* and have differentiated it from competing concepts. This aspect of performance is concerned with goals all political systems are expected to realize, or put another way, with substantive goals liberal democracies also have to pursue for their own societies.

The theoretical 'Model for Evaluating the Effectiveness of Liberal Democracies' set out in this chapter included both a normative model and an empirical-analytic concept of political effectiveness. The normative model included five criteria for assessing effectiveness in democracies: (*a*) international security, (*b*) domestic security, (*c*) socio-economic security and socio-economic equality, as well as (*d*) environmental protection. All are political goods, which is to say these are goals that guide what political actors do, that reflect the needs or demands of citizens, and that citizens expect from their governments. The empirical-analytic concept, elaborated in terms of models of effectiveness specific to the four domestic policy criteria, intends to establish a systematic relationship to empirically observable phenomena. To do this, goals were differentiated 'vertically' in the sense that general criteria of effectiveness in each policy area were disaggregated into individual components that were in turn assigned indicators. A total of fourteen indicators for measuring political effectiveness in the twenty-one western democracies examined in the period from 1974 to 1995 could be established (see Figure 2.3 and Table 4.1). In addition, two aspects of the 'horizontal' relationship between effectiveness criteria could be specified. Theories and hypotheses regarding the relationship between individual dimensions of performance formed one part, at the centre of which stood propositions of conflict or compatibility between economic and social policies as well as between the economic and environmental policies. Another part was to develop a general typology of political effectiveness that included all the relevant policy areas, and that differentiates between the best and worst possible cases as end points, and three ideologically defined types lying between them: sustainability, classical social democracy, and libertarian. Finally, we developed a concept of general political effectiveness that encompassed the specific policy areas; the corresponding index, unlike the popular *Human Development Index*, may be regarded as a summary QOL index for developed industrial societies.

Thus, four different empirical dimensions of effectiveness have been developed: policy-specific (or specific) effectiveness, general political effectiveness, the relationship between effectiveness in individual policy areas, and a typology of political effectiveness. The last two refer to the structure of political effectiveness. These four dimensions define the object of our investigation and technically constitute the dependent variable(s) of the analysis.

The empirical analysis of the level and development of these four dimensions in western democracies since 1974 is the focus of Chapter 4. Three questions guide our analysis, and they derive from the discussion of theories of globalization, ungovernability, and legitimation crisis with which we began. Has general effectiveness, as well as specific effectiveness, declined since 1974? Have conflicts between goals, particularly between economic and social policy, and between economic and environmental policy, increased? What broad policy patterns have developed in individual nations, and how have they developed?

A widespread current thesis holds that political institutions decisively shape political effectiveness. In Chapter 3 we develop a model for explaining the performance of liberal democracies, and analyse the status and the influence political institutions have on these four dimensions of political effectiveness.

3

A Model for Explaining the
Performance of Liberal Democracies

Do political institutions have an influence on political effectiveness? This is the empirical question that lies at the heart of our study. To address it, we need an explanatory model capable of identifying both the relevant institutional characteristics and the competing, non-institutional factors that may have an impact on political effectiveness. One can only satisfactorily answer the question whether political institutions play a role if other potentially relevant political and non-political determinants can be controlled for in the empirical analysis.

Existing models used to explain political performance in the comparative research on democracy tradition (Powell 1982; Putnam 1993; Lijphart 1999a) inadequately address these issues. They focus primarily on political institutions and neglect other factors such as political actors that are necessary to explain political actions and its consequences (Schmidt 2000a: 347; Armingeon 2002: 89–92). Comparative public policy models, on the other hand, are more comprehensive in this regard (Schmidt 1993), as they take political actors, political institutions, and non-political factors into account, but they ordinarily do not address the interaction between actors and institutions explicitly. Such models in any case are usually trying to explain state activities (or outputs), not political performance. It is true that conceptualizing the interaction between political actors and political institutions is the focus in the new institutionalism, the veto player approach in particular (March and Olsen 1984; Immergut 1992; Tsebelis 2002). But here the problem is that other potential explanatory factors are not taken into account. Some proponents of this approach also narrow the dependent variable and only address policy change. Hence, none of the existing models satisfactorily explain political performance.

A further problem lies in how the term 'political institution' is understood in the existing models, and in particular, how different arrangements of political institutions are conceptualized. The most often used concept is Lijphart's (1984, 1999a) typology of majoritarian and consensus democracies, together with its executives–parties and federal–unitary subdimensions. Though it is comprehensive with respect to the number of structural characteristics included, and though it describes basic variations of informal and constitutional structures, serious theoretical and measurement problems exist regarding both subdimensions.

In addition, the typologies and indices of democratic constitutional structure derived from veto player theory became more important (Huber et al. 1993; Colomer 1996; Schmidt 1996, 2000*a*; Fuchs 2000). Though these typologies are less problematic than Lijphart's in terms of theory and measurement, they are limited to a single aspect of democratic structure, namely the constitutional dimension Lijphart calls federal–unitary (Fuchs 2000: 40; Schmidt 2000*a*: 351). This is a grave disadvantage for our own explanatory purpose, as Lijphart (1999*a*) claims to have found systematic empirical relationships between political performance and the second executives–parties dimension. Some scholars have tried to link and integrate Lijphart's work on majoritarian and consensus democracy with the veto player analysis of democratic constitutional structure (Armingeon 1996; Birchfield and Crepaz 1998; Fuchs 2000; Schmidt 2000*a*). But to date, no unified concept—one with a precise operationalization and measurement of the informal *and* the constitutional dimensions, the two relevant structural aspects of democracies—has yet been suggested.

Given this state of research, the goal of Chapter 3 is to develop an 'integrated model for explaining the performance of democratic institutions' that is derived from the three research traditions noted earlier. This explanatory model should meet three criteria. It should include a precise and well-founded conceptualization and measurement of the relevant democratic structures; it should identify the most significant political and non-political factors, beyond the political institutions themselves, that explain political performance; and it should employ a coherent approach that makes it possible to assess the theoretical significance of individual explanatory factors and how they interact. This last desideratum is meant to ensure that individual factors are not just named and simply added together. Such a procedure, widely used in comparative public policy research and in the comparative research on democracy, can be dubbed 'variables political science', much like the term Esser (1987) coined to describe a certain form of sociological analysis.

First, the explanatory models from the three aforementioned research traditions will be discussed with respect to the object being explained, the explanatory factors, and how they are thought to work. Second, the characteristics relevant for explaining political performance are extracted from these three models, partly reformulated and made more precise, and then integrated into an inclusive model for explaining the performance of democratic institutions. The institutional arrangements relevant for explaining political performance are stated as: (*a*) the constitutionally and formally defined 'governmental system', as well as (*b*) 'the relationship between governing and opposition parties' that is defined by informal rules. Indicators for measuring these two institutions are critically reviewed and some new indices are suggested. The theoretical approach of rational choice institutionalism and its explanatory factors are then discussed. Following this, I suggest hypotheses on the impact of the two institutions of democratic governance on effectiveness. The chapter closes with a summary of the key characteristics of the integrated model.

Though we are primarily interested in explaining effectiveness, this chapter develops a general model for explaining performance. The current state of research does not permit the development of explanatory models for this specific performance dimension. For pragmatic reasons it seems more sensible to start from a general model and to subsequently enhance it as needed with the help of performance-specific explanatory factors.

EXPLANATORY MODELS USED IN COMPARATIVE POLITICAL RESEARCH

Each of the three relevant research traditions—comparative research on democracy, comparative public policy, and the veto player approach—have developed multiple, and differing, explanatory models that can be interpreted as models for explaining political performance. Below we describe only those models that display the following characteristics: a claim to explain political performance, particularly in terms of outcomes, and a focus on the effects of narrowly defined political institutions. As the concept of political institutions will be more precisely detailed later, we begin with a provisional and negative definition that excludes institutions that go 'far beyond governmental structures and even political parties to include things as diverse as the structure of labour-capital relations and the position of a nation within the international economy' (Weaver and Rockman 1993: 8, fn. 16).

Comparative Research on Democracy

Although the explanation of differences in political performance is an original goal of comparative research on democracy, neither an integrated nor a satisfactory explanatory model has emerged yet. The only characteristic common to the three most important models in this tradition developed by Powell (1982), Putnam (1993) and Lijphart (1999*a*) is the central importance all accord to the arrangement of democratic institutions. They differ over which factors are thought to matter in addition, and the selection of factors in turn depends upon the question being pursued in the respective study.

Lijphart's explanatory model is the simplest. Institutional settings take the centre stage, containing ten different structural characteristics (formulated as dichotomous contrasts) that form an informal and a constitutional cluster. For specific empirical analyses he takes into account three factors, the level of economic development, the degree of societal division, and the population size. The arguments for including these factors, that merely function as control variables, are not much elaborated and are based on simple plausibility: economic performance is 'potentially important', controlling for violence is important 'because deep divisions make the maintenance of public order and peace more difficult', and the influence of population 'must be checked . . . if only because our democracies differ widely in this respect' (Lijphart 1999a: 262).

Putnam has developed a much more comprehensive model. Beyond political institutions—that in his study design needs to be held constant—two 'broad possibilities' might exert influence: socio-economic factors like socio-economic modernity and socio-cultural factors like the development of 'civic community', by which he means 'patterns of civic involvement and social solidarity' (1993: 83). Putnam is particularly interested in the influence of long-term cultural factors on political performance.

Powell (1982) has also developed a relatively elaborate model. His focus is on the 'constitutional design', by which he means three constitutionally defined structural characteristics of political institutions, that he tends to analyse separately: the relationship between legislature and executive, the electoral system, and federalism. Both social (population size) and economic (level of development) conditions are regarded as contexts for these institutional factors. Particularly noteworthy is his inclusion of the party system as an additional, fourth factor in the model. If one defines structure to include not just constitutional but also informal elements, then this additional explanatory factor can be interpreted as informal structure.

Figure 3.1 integrates the most significant explanatory factors from these three suggestions—political institutions, socio-economic modernity, and socio-cultural factors—into a common model. Though each study conceptualizes it differently, the object to be explained each time is political performance. The central explanatory factor for both Lijphart (1999a) and

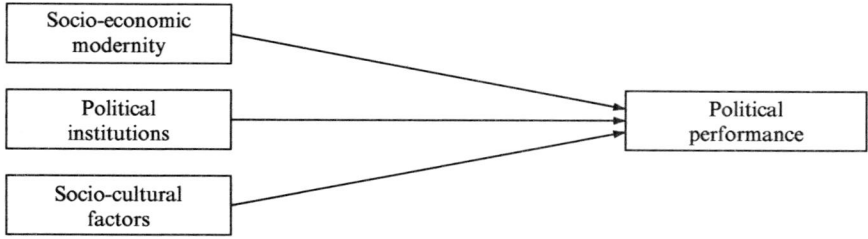

FIGURE 3.1. The explanatory model in comparative research on democracy

Powell (1982) is the arrangement of political institutions, which they define comprehensively to include both constitutional and informal structures. The additional non-political (socio-economic and socio-cultural) factors, that are conceptualized as context for the institutions, are all macroanalytic variables. So the most important characteristic of the key explanatory model developed in this research tradition, is that it is a purely macroanalytic model. Or put another way, political actors, and in particular ruling governments, are given no independent significance for political performance. Given that political performance refers to outcomes or results of political action, this seems questionable (Schmidt 2000a: 347). At least some analyses of political performance conducted in this research tradition include political actors as an explanatory factor (e.g. Birchfield and Crepaz 1998). But they instead made reference to explanatory models used in comparative public policy research, to which we next turn.

Comparative Public Policy

Comparative public policy research employs two very different models. The major model has been suggested in the tradition of analytically separating explaining factors. It is directly linked to the aforementioned explanatory model used in comparative research on democracy. Due to its centrality, it will be called the standard explanatory model of comparative public policy. A complementary, but secondary, model stands in the tradition of integrated nation-based explanations that emphasize the explanatory importance of culture and history. Castles (1993, 1998a), its major proponent, argues that such factors cannot be encompassed using the disaggregating methods of the standard model. Instead it can only be grasped by distinguishing between 'families of nations'.

The standard explanatory model
The first phase in the development of this model was shaped by functionalist approaches that emphasized economic and social factors, such as wealth or the age of the population, and downplayed the importance of political variables (Wilensky 1975). Only later were political factors more taken into account. Initially, the question was what effect political parties, and in particular governing parties had (Castles 1982). With the rise of the new institutionalism in political science, the question 'Do parties matter?' began to be replaced by the question 'Do (political) institutions matter?' (Huber et al. 1993; Schmidt 1997a). Economic and social factors, the role of parties, and the role of institutions were gradually integrated into a more comprehensive explanatory model, so that by now it includes at least two political (governing parties and political institutions) and several other non-political

(socio-economic) explanatory factors. This model has shown itself to be robust in comparative analyses of economic and social policies.

At first glance, this model does not seem that different from the model employed in comparative research on democracy (see Figure 3.1). To be sure, the socio-cultural dimension is not included. But the only other obvious difference is to also take political actors, in this case governing parties, into account. Yet the differences are far more fundamental and far-reaching.

First, in the case of the public policy model each major explanatory factor is part of an independent theory, implying justifications and conceptualizations of the factors as well as the deduction of corresponding hypotheses (Schmidt 1993). Following the socio-economic theories of public policy (e.g. Wilensky 1975), state activity is primarily a reaction to social and economic developments and problems (Schmidt 1993: 373). Following partisan theory (e.g. Hibbs 1977), state activity is primarily shaped by differing policy preferences among ruling parties, themselves reflecting differing preferences of their respective electorates. This theory thereby explicitly establishes a relationship to voters' policy preferences. Following the political-institutional theory (e.g. Huber et al. 1993), state activity is shaped by institutions of opinion formation, decision-making and voting on the one hand, and by the strategic actions of individual and collective actors on the other (Schmidt 1993: 379).[1]

Second, at least some public policy researchers (e.g. Schmidt 1993) have suggested general conceptualizations that place individual explanatory factors into a coherent framework. This integration is possible by interpreting the set of explanatory factors from the perspective of the government. Thus, socio-economic factors, such as the aging of a population, indicate challenges or problems that need to be addressed or resolved by government, or that point to resources, such as wealth, that can be utilized in or for political action. Political parties stand for the choice between various policy alternatives, and institutions provide either constraining or facilitating conditions for the actions of government.

Schmidt, in a work on partisan theory (1996), has formulated this integrated perspective into a 'theory of interaction between governing parties and the constitutional structure'. The ruling government with its ideologically-based policy preferences stands at the centre of his theory. Its preferences, reflecting voters' electoral preferences, are dependant on the party composition of government. The scope of action that is open to government is determined by the constitutional structure that sets the level of institutional constraint. More specifically, institutional constraints define not only how

---

[1] Schmidt has argued that there is a fourth theory that addresses the power resources of organized interests, but because this at least partly overlaps with partisan theory (see Huber et al. 1993) it is not separately considered here.

many but also which constitutional institutions need to agree to executive and legislative decisions. If the constitutional structure places no barriers, a ruling government can assert its interests with relative sovereignty. To the degree to which institutional barriers exist, governments must negotiate with other actors and find compromises. The constitutional structure itself determines whether a 'radical policy change' will be promoted or inhibited (Schmidt 1996: 175). The fewer the barriers are that a government faces, the greater the likelihood of radical policy change or political reform (Huber et al. 1993: 721).

Third, the object being explained is different. The interest in the comparative research on democracy is to explain political performance, that is, the result of political action, while public policy research wants more to explain policy outputs. This is due to the latter focusing on actors, as all they can directly control are their own actions or outputs. However, different research practices have evolved here. In light of the limited ability to control outcomes, a few public policy researchers deliberately only analyse outputs (e.g. Schmidt 1996, 1997b). Most researchers, though they recognize that outputs do not always directly lead to intended results (Castles 1998a: 10), nevertheless fail to use any specific explanatory model to analyse outcomes. This practice is clearest in comparative economic policy research, where outcomes such as unemployment and inflation rates have long been analysed without being aware of their problems (Hibbs 1977; Alvarez et al. 1991). Since outcomes are only controllable to a limited extent, one should assume that the relationship between explanatory factors and outcomes is less stable than that between explanatory factors and outputs (Scharpf 1989: 149). One answer to this potential discrepancy is to bear that in mind when interpreting the empirical results (Castles 1998a: 10). But it is presumably more appropriate to expand the explanatory model to include causal linkages between characteristics of environments, outputs, and outcomes (Scharpf 1989: 149). However, this presumes relatively accurate knowledge of the factors influencing the relationship between outputs and outcomes.

Fourth, international factors have long played a role in explanatory models of comparative public policy in a fashion that they have not in comparative research on democracy. This has long been true in the explanation of economic policy outcomes (Cameron 1978) and the size of government. The interest has generally focused on the openness of the economy, or the degree to which a national economy is integrated into an international market. This dimension normally is measured by foreign trade indicators (Cameron 1978), though more recently also by capital mobility (Garrett 1998). Even when a study is not explicitly interested in the effects an open economy has on national politics (Cameron 1978; Garrett 1998), then this explanatory factor is typically used as a control variable (Alvarez et al. 1991; Huber et al. 1993). The inclusion of an international factor in the explanatory model is justified with the argument that increasing dependence on external economic developments limits the ability of national governments to steer their own policies. This view has become more widespread in the context of the economic globalization discussion (Garrett 1998), though without leading to a theory of its own up to now (Schmidt 1993).

Figure 3.2 summarizes the standard explanatory model in comparative public policy, listing its explanatory factors as socio-economic modernity, political institutions, political (governing) parties, and international factors. The most important characteristic of this model is that not just macroanalytic factors are taken into account but also political actors, in this case governing parties. But many empirical studies do not assign governing parties a prominent role, and just as depicted here, it is simply placed alongside other explanatory factors.

In the more elaborated versions of the standard model (as in Schmidt 1993, 1996), this is not the case. Instead, the entire sphere of action is conceived from the perspective of the government and its ability to carry out its policies. Only with the help of such an approach can we go beyond merely listing potential factors to a level of conceptualizing how factors might interact with one another, and thereby derive working hypotheses. But while Schmidt moves in this direction, his interpretation of the interaction of individual explanatory factors is based on plausibility rather than on a general theoretical approach like that provided by rational choice institutionalism. In his model, as in many other comparative public policy models (e.g. Huber et al. 1993), only constitutional structures are included; informal structures are ignored. Here the veto player approach employed in the new institutionalism can help. Its broad definition of institutions encompasses both constitutional and party-related characteristics, and it also tries to be more precise about the interaction between political actors and political institutions.

Two questions remain open in developing an integrated model for explaining the performance of democratic institutions. One is which factors need to

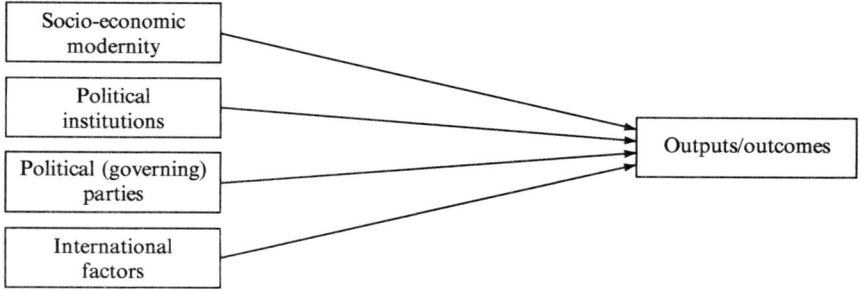

FIGURE 3.2. The standard explanatory model in comparative public policy research

be included in order to turn a model primarily developed to explain outputs into one that can explain outcomes. The other is to discuss the effects of increasing international integration.

The families of nations concept

Castles (1993) has criticized the standard model for neglecting factors such as culture and history that may be just as influential as social, economic, and political determinants. To identify these factors he suggests a complementary 'families of nations' approach. These families are defined 'in terms of shared geographical, linguistic, cultural and/or historical attributes' (Castles 1993: xiii). Commonalities between nations that share such attributes can lead to similar policy patterns arising through different mechanisms. A common culture and a common language may make it easier, for example, to communicate policy ideas between elite and mass and between different nations. Alternatively, similar institutional structures may aid or hinder policy solutions, and previous imperial rule may continue to shape institutional, economic, social, and political developments.

Among the OECD nations, Castles thus finds four families of nations, and the nations and features they share may be seen in Table 3.1. Switzerland and Japan, though modern western democracies, cannot be clearly assigned to any of these families. While Switzerland shares some commonalties with other German-speaking nations, it constitutes a special case in Continental

TABLE 3.1. *Families of nations*

Family of nations	Nations	Common features [sub-groups]
English-speaking	Australia, Canada, Ireland, New Zealand, the USA	Language; political and legal traditions due to historical ties to Great Britain [European colonies in the New World and others]
Scandinavian (nordic)	Denmark, Finland, Norway, Sweden	History; legal traditions; language (except Finland)
Continental Western European	Austria, Belgium, France, Germany, Italy, the Netherlands	History of dynastic connections; culture (particularly religion); policy diffusion due to similarity; charter members of the European Community (except Austria) [German-speaking nations and others]
Southern European	Greece, Portugal, Spain	Ancient culture of the Mediterranean; delayed economic, social, and political modernization
Special cases	Switzerland, Japan	

Source: Castles (1998a: 8–9).

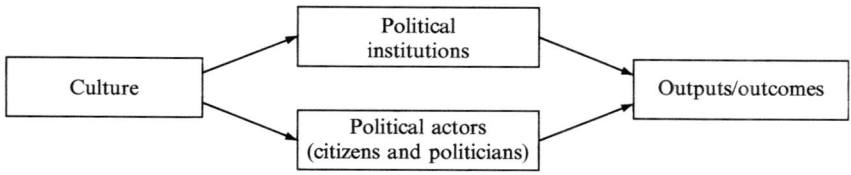

FIGURE 3.3. Families of nations as an explanatory model

Western Europe; Japan is quite unique as it belongs to an entirely different cultural zone or civilization (see Huntington 1996: 45).

The heart of the families of nations concept is that 'history leaves a legacy of ideas, customs and institutions—in sum, a *culture* [author's emphasis]— that influences the present behaviour of those who shape the policies of the state and those who make demands of the state' (Castles 1993: xvi). So such families constitute homogeneous cultural units. The explanatory model underlying this approach is presented graphically in Figure 3.3. Culture determines the development of national institutions and the policy orientations of political actors, whether politicians or citizens. Institutions and policy orientations thereby together influence political decisions (outputs) that lead to particular results (outcomes). As in the standard model, it is outputs that are to be explained, and it is assumed that these are transformed, more or less, into corresponding outcomes. This model bears many similarities to nation-specific models like that of 'American Exceptionalism' (Lipset 1996), with the major difference that the family of nations concept by emphasizing cultural commonalities and differences between nations, thus provides a means to identify cultural explanatory factors.

The two comparative public policy models in fact follow different logics. In the standard model, national configurations are separated into individual components following the tradition in comparative research of disaggregating explanatory factors. In the family of nations concept, national configurations are given 'proper names' (Przeworski and Teune 1970). Due to this difference in logic, it is only possible to investigate these two models in discrete, separated steps. Since we are primarily interested in identifying the impact of political institutions on performance, the theoretical and empirical analyses we present here derive from an explanatory model that separates out individual explanatory factors. It follows the disaggregating tradition much as the standard model does. The family of nations concept, by contrast, is used for describing the level, development, and structure of political effectiveness. It allows for an assessment of the extent to which effectiveness in western democracies is influenced by cultural factors. This heuristic has the added advantage that it is then possible to structure the descriptive analysis of the twenty-one investigated nations in a theoretically meaningful manner.

The Veto Player Approach

Many different models for explaining the impact of political institutions have been suggested by those pursuing the new institutionalism. We limit ourselves here to the veto player approach[2] (Immergut 1992; Tsebelis 1995, 2002), because immediate linkages can be made to the models offered by the other research traditions we have just discussed. This becomes especially evident when some authors working in these other traditions explicitly refer to veto player theory (Huber et al. 1993; Schmidt 1996, 1998a; Birchfield and Crepaz 1998; Lijphart 1999a; Wagschal 1999a; Fuchs 2000; Crepaz 2001). Huber et al. (1993), for example, develop an *Index of Constitutional Structure* in explicit reference to Immergut's theoretical considerations (1992). Both Lijphart (1999a) and Crepaz (2001), following Tsebelis (1995), have reinterpreted the executives–parties and federal–unitary subdimensions into measures of institutional and partisan veto points. Lijphart (1999a: 5) has meanwhile decided that it is more appropriate to refer to these subdimensions as 'joint responsibility/joint power' and 'divided responsibility/divided power', while Birchfield and Crepaz (1998) suggest calling them collective and competitive veto points. The linkage is based on the fact that the arrangement of national political institutions stands at the heart of the veto player approach. They are regarded in the traditional political science terms of the separation of powers (Fuchs 2000).

Immergut (1992) and Tsebelis (1995, 2002) are the best known proponents of the veto player approach. In principle, one can also assign Weaver and Rockman's (1993: 31) decision-making theory to this approach as they place the national decision-making system at the core and analyse 'institutional features . . . [that] tend to diffuse power and add veto points'. However, Weaver and Rockman do so largely in order to compare parliamentary and presidential systems. So we will limit ourselves to the more general approaches Immergut and Tsebelis employ to understand institutions and the interaction between actors and institutions.

Immergut articulated her veto point concept in the context of a comparative study of health policy. She was interested in explaining how and why certain policy choices are made. Her particular question was to what extent different interest groups in individual nations were able to realize their preferences in the crafting of health policy. In her view, the political decision-making structure is shaped by an institutional configuration that combines 'de jure constitutional rules' with 'de facto electoral results' (Immergut 1992: 27). Constitutional rules fix the mode of election and the power granted to representatives. The constitutional rules are seen from the perspective of executive autonomy. They determine to what extent the executive can act

---

[2] The terms 'veto player' and 'veto points' are used synonymously in what follows.

independently of the representatives in other 'arenas' such as the legislature, the courts, and the electorate (Immergut 1992: 26). She distinguishes between unilateral executive decisions, decisions requiring parliamentary support, and decisions (such as referenda) where voters must assent. The de facto rules that result from elections and the party system, define the distribution of votes *within* various institutions. The effective power of the executive, as well as the dynamics of the relationship between executive and legislature, is thus dependent on the party composition of the ruling government and the parliament, and on the existence of a stable parliamentary majority supporting the executive. The de facto rules are non-constitutionally defined rules, though Immergut (1992: 27) points out that many of the rules that follow from election results or that come out of the party system are based on formal electoral laws.

The central actor in this veto player concept is thus the government. Its ability to pass laws is dependent upon whether, or how many, veto (or decision) points the institutional configuration provides, that is, at which points or by whom a governmental proposal must be ratified or can be rejected. The number of veto points is determined partly by constitutional rules, as they establish the political 'arenas' in which decisions must successively be addressed. They are also determined in part by electoral results, as these fix the partisan composition within these arenas. From the point of view of the executive, veto points are 'points of strategic uncertainty where decisions may be overturned' (Immergut 1992: 27). This institutional configuration, with its various veto possibilities, forms the political context in which various actors move, and it offers incentives and places constraints on its strategies and tactics. It also defines the power that interest groups (Immergut's subject) possess, as veto points determine where interests can threaten or intervene.

Tsebelis starts from the assumption that institutions differ in their ability 'to produce policy change' and develops his veto player concept accordingly. The object to be explained is not Immergut's 'policy choices' but rather a particular category of political decisions: the ability to decisively respond to important political problems (Tsebelis 1995: 293–4). Tsebelis (1995: 301) also describes the decision-making structures from the point of view of the veto players, that is, from those collective and individual actors whose consent is necessary before a policy can be changed. The number of veto players determines the degree to which power is dispersed, and the more veto players there are, the less flexibility or ability there is to change policies.

Tsebelis (1995: 302) also differentiates between institutional and partisan veto players. The number of institutional players is set by the constitution, and Tsebelis is particularly interested in two structural characteristics: the regime type (parliamentary versus presidential) and the legislative system (unicameralism versus bicameralism). The number of partisan veto players is set 'endogenously' by the party system and the governing coalition in a nation; Tsebelis is interested in the parties that form the ruling government. Tsebelis gives particular importance to the counting rules for determining the number of veto players in a given political system. He has described the counting procedure to be used as follows: '1. identify and count the institutional veto players; 2. replace institutional veto players by multiple partisan players if there are stable majorities; 3. apply the absorption rule and eliminate redundant veto players' (Tsebelis 2000: 450).

The logic of these rules can be illustrated with respect to Germany (Tsebelis 1999: 593). The German system is characterized by bicameralism (*a*). A stable majority in the lower house usually exists that supports a coalition government comprised of two parties (*b*), thus there are two veto players. If the same majority exists in the upper house as in the lower house (e.g. a CDU/CSU–FDP coalition government in the lower house, and a majority of CDU-governed states in the upper house), then there are still two veto players. If the upper house has a different majority (e.g. there is a majority of SPD-governed states in the upper house), then there are three veto players (*c*). Hence, the counting rules begin with the governing parties and only later are other institutional veto players added. One can interpret this to mean the executive is the central actor.

Tsebelis (1995) also takes the ideological orientation of the veto players into account. This can be seen in the absorption rule, according to which two institutional veto players (such as two chambers) are counted as one if both chambers have similar party majorities. Not only ideological cohesion *within* veto players is regarded as a factor but also ideological congruence *between* them. As a result, Tsebelis proposes three hypotheses: (*a*) policy stability in a political system increases with growing numbers of veto players; (*b*) policy stability decreases as the congruence between veto players grows; and (*c*) policy stability increases as the internal cohesion of the veto players improves (Tsebelis 1995: 313).

Though Immergut and Tsebelis come from different research traditions— Immergut from historical institutionalism (Hall and Taylor 1996) and Tsebelis from formal decision theory—the formulations are parallel. Both concentrate on the decision-making structures and assume that institutions decisively shape these structures. Institutions in turn are defined as rules, they include both constitutionally determined and partisan rules, and these rules authoritatively set the context for executive decisions. At heart, therefore, the veto-player approach is a decision-making model. The most important difference is that while Immergut wishes to explain 'policy choices' or 'policy outputs', Tsebelis limits himself to explaining 'policy change'.

Figure 3.4 illustrates the explanatory model of these two approaches. It indicates that governments interact with institutional contexts and this interaction leads to political decisions (Immergut 1992) or policy changes

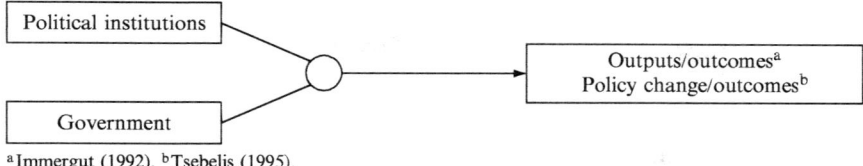

^aImmergut (1992). ^bTsebelis (1995).

FIGURE 3.4. The explanatory model of the veto player approach

(Tsebelis 1995, 2002). A simple mechanism is assumed: With increasing numbers of veto players, governments lose the ability to transform their proposals into law (Immergut) or to respond to important political problems with changes in policy (Tsebelis). Neither approach makes explicit reference to the consequences or results of these political decisions. In the comparative public policy tradition, both approaches quite clearly assume that these decisions will, to a greater or lesser extent, lead to the intended outcomes.

Unlike the earlier two models, the veto player approach is a purely micro-analytic (or action theory) model that places the actors in a decision-making situation at the centre of the analysis. One characteristic trait of this approach is to starkly simplify and focus on the perspective of a *single* political actor, namely the executive, and treat only *one* context as relevant, namely the institutional configuration. The most important aspect of the latter is the number of veto players. The apparent advantage of this simplification is that one can derive a precise hypothesis from it: as the number of veto players increases, the autonomy of the government decreases. One problem in so focusing on the interaction between government and institutional context, however, is that other potential influencing factors noted in the other models, such as socio-economic modernity or international factors, find no place in this decision-making model.

A second characteristic trait is the broad conceptualization of political institutions that includes both constitutionally defined and partisan rules. This theoretical distinction is directly connected to dimensions used in the comparative research on democracy, as in Lijphart's differentiation between federal–unitary and executives–parties dimensions. Given the significance of this distinction, it is incomprehensible why it plays no role in Immergut's and Tsebelis's analyses, and indeed why they fuse the two dimensions together again. The confounding is clearest in Tsebelis's counting rules, in which partisan and institutional veto players are summed together equally into a single measure.

Both approaches are based at least implicitly on the premise that institutional and partisan rules work in the same manner. That means above all that they have the same effect on decisions. Yet this cannot be assumed blindly. A number of studies in the comparative research on democracy tradition have tried to describe how decision-making processes between partisan veto players *within* a constitutionally defined institution differ from decision-making processes *between* different constitutional veto players (Armingeon 1996; Birchfield and Crepaz 1998). A further problem lies in Tsebelis's absorption rule in which, when the same majorities exist in two different institutions, one is eliminated. The questionable assumption is that one can only expect an independent effect on decisions when the majorities differ between two *institutional* veto players. It is more commonly the case, in fact, that different constitutional veto players have independent power bases and sources of legitimation, making veto players not identical even when party majorities are identical. In Germany, for example, the upper house represents the individual German states. Their interests are not a priori congruent with the interests represented in the lower house, when lower and upper house are dominated by the same parties. By Tsebelis's rule, however, if majorities are identical in both houses, then the upper house is not counted as an additional veto player.

In sum, one can say that the veto player approach either negates the important distinction between institutional and partisan rules, or skews it to the benefit of partisan rules. We regard it, first of all, as an empirical question whether institutional and partisan veto players are in fact functionally equivalent with respect to their impact on political decisions, or whether they in fact exert different impacts. For the purposes of our analysis we conclude to separately conceptualize, measure, and empirically investigate both dimensions.

A third trait of the veto player approach is that it places explicit emphasis on searching for and conceptualizing institutional effects. This may be traced back to the fact that the approach is part of the new institutionalism whose goal is to identify institutional effects. Immergut's decision to select 'policy choice' as a dependent variable stands in the comparative public policy research tradition. This is not true of Tsebelis's choice to focus on the narrower question of 'policy change'. In an effort to enhance the value of what is in fact a limitation, he gives the ability of the political system to react effectively to fundamental problems a near-existential significance (Tsebelis 1995: 293–4). The high hopes one has that Tsebelis will provide an analysis of the broad spectrum of effects political institutions have are dashed by his narrow conceptualization.

This narrow conception, however, hides a much more fundamental problem. A basic hypothesis of decision-making theory is that with an increasing number of participating actors the range of interests represented in the decision-making body increases but, at the same time, their decision-making ability declines; the status quo, in short, is preserved (Buchanan and Tullock 1962; Sartori 1987: ch. 8). By this token, Tsebelis has—with much effort—only formally recast one of the basic propositions of decision-making theory: his core hypothesis is that the participation of many veto players leads to 'policy stability'. So while this is a fundamental criticism of Tsebelis's concept of veto players, it also introduces the sceptical note that one should not expect any effects to emanate from political institutions that go beyond this fundamental proposition of decision-making theory.

AN INTEGRATED MODEL FOR EXPLAINING THE PERFORMANCE OF DEMOCRATIC INSTITUTIONS

Our discussion has indicated that though political performance is an original concern of the comparative study of democracy, it has thus far only crafted a rudimentary explanatory model. A more complete model necessitates borrowing elements from allied fields such as comparative public policy, and from the veto player approach used in the new institutionalism. But significant questions remain about the basic theoretical approach, the explanatory factors, how political institutions are conceived, and how political institutions are thought to influence performance.

The more elaborated explanatory models of public policy research describe the connection between individual factors, using aspects borrowed from rational choice institutionalism (Koelble 1995; Ostrom 1995; Hall and Taylor 1996). This *theoretical approach* has not, however, been pursued further by these authors. Comparative public policy has developed the most comprehensive model with respect to the *explanatory factors*, but leaves two questions open. In terms of international factors, it remains to be clarified what consequences increasing economic globalization has on performance. And there should be a discussion whether and which additional factors need to be included in the model to explain outcomes. There is convergence between the comparative study of democracy and the veto player approach with respect to *political institutions*. Both draw a distinction between constitutional and partisan structures, though neither provides a theoretical foundation of the type of rules that underlie these two dimensions. Finally, as for the *impact* of political institutions, at least in Tsebelis's version the veto player approach focuses on explaining 'policy change', which leaves open what other impacts political institutions are expected to have on performance beyond this.

We develop an 'integrated model for explaining the performance of democratic institutions' to try to address these open questions. First, two institutions of democratic governance are posited: the constitutionally defined 'governmental system' and the 'relationship between governing and opposition parties' defined by informal rules. Existing indicators to measure these two institutions are then discussed, wherein Lijphart's executives–parties index that is meant to measure informal democratic structures shows itself to be particularly problematic both for conceptual and measurement reasons. For that reason, we propose alternative indices to measure this informal dimension. Then we turn to the theoretical approach used in rational choice institutionalism, and specify the most important non-institutional explanatory factors for performance. We conclude by formulating hypotheses about the influence these two institutions of democratic governance have on effectiveness. To formulate the integrated model we rely on the explanatory models discussed above.

It is worth restating here what purpose this explanatory model is meant to serve. Our study of the performance of liberal democracies is intended to provide empirical evidence for or against the common assumption that democratic institutions have an impact on performance. The assumption is attractive because if true, it promises simple and expedient solutions to political problems. If political institutions are unambiguously connected to particular levels of performance, then politicians would only have to change institutions to resolve a political problem. This common assumption has two implications for our explanatory model. Those arrangements that build the 'constitutional design' of a democracy stand at the heart of the model, as only they can be 'intentionally shaped' (Fuchs 2000: 34). Only by identifying and holding constant the important non-institutional determinants will it be possible to clarify which impact democratic institutions have on performance. The goal of the model, however, is not to explain as best as possible how political performance comes about.

Institutions of Democratic Governance

The conceptualization of the political institutions relevant to performance proceeds in several steps. In a first step, we define political institutions and describe the key institutional arrangements of liberal democracies with the help of a typology developed by Fuchs (2000). Based on this typology we identify two institutions decisive for political performance: the formal and informal *institutions of democratic governance*. Second, discussion ensues of the most frequently suggestions of types of democracies that are found in the literature—parliamentary and presidential systems, consociational democracy, and majoritarian and consensus democracies—to better specify where our own efforts should be classified. In a third step, we describe the two institutional dimensions more precisely with their central characteristics and discuss their possible impact on political decision-making processes.

A definition and typology of democratic institutions
The interest in the origins and effects of political institution sharply increased in the wake of the new institutionalism, an approach first associated with the work of March and Olsen (1984). A commonly agreed upon definition of 'institution' has yet to emerge, however. Instead, various 'schools of institu-

tional analysis', each working with quite different definitions, have formed (Koelble 1995; Ostrom 1995; Hall and Taylor 1996). One can distinguish these schools by whether they use narrow or broad definitions. That distinction is applied both to what is seen as 'political' and to what is included under the term 'institution'.

Beginning with institutions, the narrow view defines them as 'rules of the game' that steer what actors do. A broader definition, of the kind March and Olsen (1984) or Göhler (1994) have suggested, additionally incorporates organizational structures, or normative, cultural, or symbolic elements that could influence actors (Mayntz and Scharpf 1995: 42; Fuchs 1999: 162–3). Such a broad definition often lacks analytical precision though it is not usable here for a different reason: the thesis that political institutions differ in performance is formulated in terms of the narrow view of institutions. Fuchs (1999: 162) states the core of the narrow view: 'institutions can be defined as lasting rule complexes that steer the actions of individuals in such a manner as to create regular patterns of interaction and by that constitute a social order.' This view is particularly characteristic of rational choice institutionalism.

It is not only institutions themselves that are broadly or narrowly defined; there are also different understandings of *political* institutions. While this aspect is infrequently addressed, it is touched on in Weaver and Rockman's negative definition (1993: 8) that wishes to exclude 'things as diverse as the structure of labour-capital relations and the position of a country within the international economy' from the definition of institutions. Hall (1986: 19) utilizes a broad definition of institution that explicitly includes rules 'that structure the relationships between individuals in various units of the polity and economy'. This broad view of the political dominates in economic policy analyses (Hall 1986; Alvarez et al. 1991; Scharpf 1991) usually encompassing political as well as social and economic institutions. Such a broad definition also makes it possible to include corporatist arrangements and collective economic actors (like labour unions or peak employer associations) into the analysis, as the assumption is that they exert decisive influence over economic policy. If the interest is to provide a broad explanation for economic policy decisions or their consequences (as the above mentioned authors do), then it is certainly advisable to take these institutions of political economy into account.

But such a broad concept of the political is out of the question for us since we are explicitly interested in the performance of the traditional arrangement of political institutions—what Weaver and Rockman call 'governmental structures' or what Hall calls 'polities'. Fuchs (1999, 2000: 31), making reference to systems theory, defines the narrow meaning of the political as 'the making and implementing of generally binding decisions'. By this view, institutions of political economy are not part of political institutions narrowly understood. They do represent institutional arrangements that might be relevant to the analysis of specific policies—accordingly, they can be described as policy-specific institutions.

It follows that we thus work with a doubly 'narrowed' definition of political institutions that can be defined in the following manner: 'Complexes of . . . rules for action that fulfil a strategically significant function in the context of the general function of the political system. This general function rests on making and implementing decisions that are binding for societal community' (Fuchs 1999: 164). The strategic significance element included here derives from Parsonian theory (Parsons 1971). It helps to ascertain those rule complexes constitutive of the political system or needed for its maintenance (thus for democracies, they would include the parliament, the government, and the courts).

Fuchs (2000: 32–3) developed a typology of key institutional arrangements of liberal democracy. It is based on a further differentiation of two essential parts of the definition of political institutions, that is, functions and rules. Following constitutional and democratic theory, the basic functions addressed in the definition can be subdivided between the selection of leaders and the exercise of authority. Following Easton (1990), structures can be differentiated into formal and empirical (or informal) structures. The formal structure is 'the legally binding and constitutionally defined rules that prescribe how the two basic functions are to be translated into procedures' (Fuchs 2000: 33), while the informal structure is guided by rules that arise from interaction between actors and can thus be established empirically. Informal structures differ from actions themselves in that they are defined as relatively lasting constellations of participants that individual actors can or must adjust to when they act.

Combining both dimensions, the 2 × 2 table (Figure 3.5) thus identifies the most important institutional arrangements in liberal democracies. The basic function of *leadership selection* is fulfilled through the formal structure of the 'electoral system' (or right to vote) and through the empirical structure of the party system. The 'party system' in turn is composed of individual

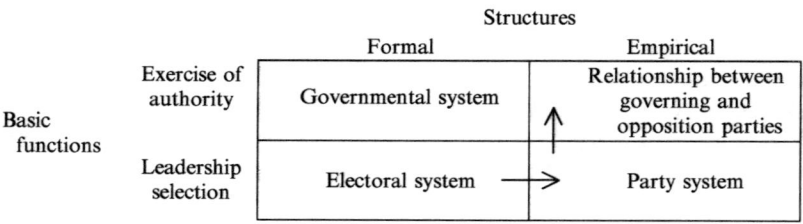

Source: Fuchs (2000: 33).

FIGURE 3.5. Democratic institutional arrangements

parties, the structure of the interactions between them, and their degree of fragmentation. The basic function of the *exercise of authority* is fulfilled through the formal structure of the governmental system and the informal (empirical) structure of the relationship between governing and opposition parties. The 'governmental system' in turn is defined by the institutions that participate in collectively binding decisions and the relations between these institutions. At the centre stand three structural characteristics: (*a*) presidential or parliamentary regime types, (*b*) unicameral or bicameral parliamentary systems, and (*c*) the federal–unitary dimension.[3] Finally, the 'relationship between governing and opposition parties' refers to the rules of interaction which emerge between governing and opposition parties. It is determined by the composition of government (one-party versus coalition government) on the one hand and the parliamentary support for the government on the other.

The main contribution of this typology is to deliver a theoretically justified classification of the key institutional arrangements of liberal democracies. It is significant for a number of reasons. First, the constitutional structure is differentiated into two categories: the electoral system and the governmental system. A number of authors (Huber et al. 1993; Tsebelis 1995) do not *explicitly* separate electoral from governmental institutions and thus do not keep apart two fundamentally different functions, the selection of leaders and the exercise of power. Second, the non-constitutional dimension is theoretically defined as informal rules that emerge from relatively lasting constellation of participants. Because we differentiate basic functions, it is also possible to separate the informal rules arising from the constellation of parties that compete for leadership (party system) from the informal rules that arise from the distribution of parties in keeping leadership roles (relationship between governing and opposition parties). Third, the causal arrows in Figure 3.5 also indicate the relationship between formal and empirical structures. Empirical structures are 'fuzzier, more variable, and harder to predict than constitutional structures' (Fuchs 2000: 33). They are not only decisively influenced by various societal factors but *also* by a constitutionally defined institution, that is, the electoral system. This basic idea was already present in Immergut's veto player approach (1992; see also Lijphart 1999*a*: 303). But here we can provide a causal path: The electoral system, interacting with societal factors and mediated through the electoral results, determines the party system that in turn influences the relationship between governing and opposition parties.

---

[3] For a further differentiation of constitutionally defined institutions into primary and secondary structures see Fuchs (2000: 40). It is discussed in the section 'Formal and informal structures of democratic governance'.

Based on this typology we can specify which institutional arrangements in liberal democracies are decisive for political performance or the realization of specific political goals through what political actors do. Such actions, following Figure 3.5, can be more precisely called the exercise of authority or governing. They take place within the (formal) constitutional structures of the governmental system and within the (informal) empirical structures that determine the relationship between governing and opposition parties. Logically, therefore, an effect on political performance would have to come from these structures involved in the exercise of authority, or in short, from the institutions of democratic governance.

The basic assumption, we noted earlier, that democratic institutions have an impact on performance was primarily based on 'intentionally shaped' constitutional structures (Fuchs 2000: 34). But in the explanatory model, it is necessary to include the empirical (or informal) structures of the relationship between governing and opposition parties in *addition* to the constitutionally defined governmental system. It is widely held that the electoral system (or right to vote) has an effect on political performance. But—at least following Fuchs—that the connection is not direct: an effect of the electoral system on performance can only be mediated through the relationship between governing and opposition parties. To assess the importance of elections for performance, one therefore needs to analyse the direct effect of the relationship between governing and opposition parties on political performance.[4] If such effects are actually found, however, then they can only be treated as indirect proof of the significance of electoral systems, owing to the indirect causal path from the 'electoral system' to the 'relationship between governing and opposition parties'. We think that the formal and informal structures involved in the exercise of authority in democracy, or in short, in democratic governance, are the decisive structural arrangements for performance which we will now describe in greater detail.

Types of democracies
The most important distinctions drawn in the literature have been between parliamentary and presidential democracies, 'consociational' (or concordance) democracies, and majoritarian and consensus democracies (Schmidt 2000a: 309–55). One part of our question is which institutions of democratic governance have already been examined in the literature and where our own efforts to specify and describe formal and empirical institutions would fit. To examine the types of democracies we augment Fuchs's 'structures' and 'basic functions' by a third dimension: the *distribution of power*. This dimension

---

[4] There is another reason to take the relationship between governing and opposition parties into account, and that comes from Lijphart's (1999a) analyses. He finds more significant relationships between performance and the informal executives–parties dimension than between performance and the constitutional federal–unitary dimension.

measures the degree of concentration or dispersion of power. Under the term 'separation of powers' it was already part of the discussion of the constitutional order in the eighteenth and nineteenth centuries (Fuchs 2000: 34).

The contrast between *parliamentarianism* and *presidentialism* is the oldest and simplest typology of democratic systems (Loewenstein 1957; Steffani 1979; Shugart and Carey 1992; Sartori 1994; Fuchs 2000). As is typical of the classic theory of political institutions, it describes the formal rules (Kaiser 1997) governing the relationship between executive and legislature. It is thus a typology purely focused on the governmental system. The concentration of power is reflected in the fusion of executive and legislature characteristic of parliamentary systems; the dispersion of power is reflected in the autonomy of executive and legislature characteristic of presidential systems. This dispersion is also the reason the presidential system in the USA is referred to as a 'system of separation of powers'.

'Consociational democracy' is a term introduced by Lijphart in his examination of the Netherlands as a democracy based on a politics of accommodation (1968). The parallel term 'concordance democracy' was employed at the same time by Lehmbruch (1967) to discuss the 'proportional' democratic practices of Switzerland and Austria. These systems show pronounced power dispersion. The two basic principles are executive power-sharing in the form of grand coalitions as well as group autonomy (Lijphart 1999*b*). They foster the representation and protection of minority interests. For this reason consociational forms of democracy develop particularly in cleavage-ridden, culturally fragmented societies. Even though this type of democracy can be or is in part defined through a constitution (Lehmbruch 1992; Lijphart 1999*a*: 303) its more important characteristic is the prevalence of informal rules that emerge in elite behaviour (Lijphart 1989: 39). If other power-dispersed formal structures like federalism exist in the nation then they merely support such informal rules but are not the core of this type of democracy.

As in the distinction between parliamentary and presidential systems, consociational democracy describes institutions of democratic governance. Here, however, the heart is provided by informal rules that develop between governing and opposition parties. The power-concentrating antithesis to consociational democracy is provided by the Anglo-American competitive or majoritarian democratic systems, whose key features are seen in the majoritarian electoral systems and the resulting two-party system (Lehmbruch 1992; Schmidt 2000*a*: 326). This competing type is often serving as a negative reference point for consociation theorists, though they do not describe or analyse it in detail. It encompasses formal and informal institutions, and in addition to institutions of democratic governance it also incorporates institutions relevant to the selection of leaders.

Lijphart first proposed the distinction between *majoritarian and consensus democracies* as part of an effort to place the consociational type within a larger framework (Lijphart 1997: 249). He began with the assumption that democracies can be built on two different basic principles: 'rule by the majority of the people' or 'rule by as many people as possible'. Starting with these principles and using Great Britain and New Zealand as examples of the former and Switzerland and Belgium as examples of the latter principle, he proposed ten (originally nine in Lijphart 1984) structural characteristics of democracies. Each characteristic is formulated as a continuum with power-concentrating and power-dispersing end points. One structural characteristic, for example, is formulated as 'concentration of legislative power in a unicameral legislature versus division of legislative power between two equally strong but differently constituted houses', while another is 'two-party versus multiparty systems' (Lijphart 1999*a*: 3). Majoritarian democracies are characterized by power concentration while consensus democracies are characterized by power dispersion (Lijphart 1984, 1999*a*: 2). Lijphart derives the power-concentrating characteristics from the same principle. Because they are logically connected he expects them to 'occur together in the real world' (Lijphart 1999*a*: 2); the same applies to the power-dispersing characteristics. He therefore expected all ten variables to be closely related.

The empirical analysis, however, revealed that the distribution of power is not one-dimensional but that 'the variables cluster in two clearly separate dimensions' with five characteristics apiece. Executive power concentration or sharing, the power relationship between executive and legislature, the party system, the electoral system, and the interest group system, define the first *executives–parties dimension*. The second *federal–unitary dimension* is defined by federal versus unitary government, unicameral versus bicameral legislatures, the flexibility or rigidity of the constitution, the absence or presence of judicial review, and central bank autonomy (Lijphart 1999*a*: 3–4).

These designations are based on different logics. While the first dimension encompasses two separate sets of facts (executive and parties) the second focuses on a dichotomized aspect of the degree of centralization (federal–unitary). The main problem of these designations, however, is that both are misleading and imprecise. They do not describe appropriately the respective number of characteristics. In the case of the first dimension, there is the problem that interest groups can be assigned neither to the executive nor to the parties. So including them implies that a quite different dimension slips in 'unnoticed'. The second dimension, in turn, only adequately describes the first characteristic Lijphart lists for it (Schmidt 2000*a*: 350). Lijphart (1999*a*: 4) tries to justify the federal–unitary designation for the other characteristics in this second dimension by arguing that 'strong bicameralism, a rigid constitution, and strong judicial review' are 'secondary' aspects of federalism—though that leaves open the question why a central bank autonomy is then included.

If we overlook the misleading names for these dimensions, then their major problem is their very concreteness, as it hides the fact that these empirically established dimensions should be assigned to quite different theoretical dimensions: executives–parties to informal structures and federal–unitary to formal structures (Fuchs 2000). Majoritarian and consensus democracies are thus types of democracies that include both formal and informal structures. The list of characteristics also shows that while structural elements related to the exercise of authority function (e.g. executive–legislature relationship) predominate, other elements that refer to the category of leadership selection (e.g. electoral system) are included as well.

There is also considerable overlap between consensus and consociational democracies that is particularly evident in the executives–parties dimension. Some of the characteristics of consensus democracy, such as the executive power concentration versus executive power-sharing variable, are also part of consociational democracy. A major difference lies in the fact that consensus democracy incorporates constitutionally defined structures in addition to informal ones (Lijphart 1989: 40). For that reason consociational democracy is regarded 'as an exceptionally "strong" or "extreme" form of consensus democracy' (Lijphart 1997: 249). That consociational democracy provided the model for the more comprehensive, power-dispersing system of consensus democracy is also evident in the latter's name. It has also been repeatedly noted that Lijphart defines his two types at different levels, majoritarian democracy based on the dominant decision rules, and consensus democracy based on the intended results (Czada and Schmidt 1993; Kaiser 1997). Power-dispersing structures do not necessarily lead to positive results, however, and it thus seems more appropriate in these cases to speak not of consensus but of 'negotiation democracy'. Power-dispersive structures necessitate negotiation, but whether they are successful and lead to consensus, or unsuccessful and dissensual, depends on additional factors.

Figure 3.6 summarizes these various types of democracies in terms of the power distribution and structural categories. Since we have discussed them in chronological order, we can also describe the theoretical development of these types as an *expansion* from formal (parliamentary versus presidential

		Power distribution	
		Concentrated	Dispersed
Structure	Formal	Parliamentary democracy	Presidential democracy
	Informal	—	Consociational democracy (Concordance democracy)
	Formal and informal	Majoritarian democracy	Consensus democracy

FIGURE 3.6. Types of democracy by structure and power distribution

democracies) to informal (consociational democracy) to mixed formal and informal (majoritarian and consensus democracies) structures, as well as from exercise of power (seen in both parliamentary or presidential and consociational democracies) to exercise of power combined with leadership selection (seen in majoritarian and consensus democracies) structures. The majoritarian and consensus democracy distinction is the most comprehensive conceptualization to date, as it incorporates a multiplicity of heterogeneous structural characteristics.

The heterogeneity of majoritarian and consensus democracy arise from the fact that Lijphart's original premise was that power distribution in democracies was one-dimensional. All other substantive differentiations, such as between formal or informal structures, or between the exercise of authority and leadership selection, were subordinated and not given independent theoretical significance. The dominance of the power distribution perspective in Lijphart's thinking is most clearly evident in his astonishment that empirical analysis shows 'two clearly separate dimensions'. This limitation leads him to call mixed types, such as the federalist majoritarian democracy (e.g. USA) or the unitary consensus democracies (e.g. Nordic countries), 'logically opposite models of democracy' (Lijphart 1984: 219). A kind of helplessness in addressing this unexpected result can also be seen in the somewhat unfortunate labels he gives the two dimensions. In his major reworking of *Democracies* (1984) that appeared in 1999, Lijphart (1999a: 5) does suggest more precision—'the first dimension could also be labelled the joint-responsibility or joint-power dimension and the second the divided-responsibility or divided-power dimension'—but he does not exploit the potential inherent to these 'more accurate and theoretically more meaningful' designations. He can also provide no satisfactory explanation as to why only the first dimension shows a relationship with the various performance measures, but merely states this as an empirical result (Lijphart 1999a: 301).

Even though all his empirical results, whether factor analyses of the structural characteristics or analyses of the relationship between structure and performance, clearly contradict his theoretical assumption of one-dimensionality of the distribution of power, Lijphart does not draw the corresponding theoretical and empirical conclusion that there are not just two but at least four types of democracies. Thus, he continues to refer to the two types of democracy, majoritarian and consensus, even though he himself has repeatedly provided the empirical proof that not just these pure types exist (Lijphart 1999a: 301 et seq). In his description of consensus democracy, it is also quite evident that what he understands by it, is still primarily consociational democracy based on informal rules. When mentioning consensus democracy, he implicitly or explicitly refers to structural characteristics that define the executives–parties dimension, thereby quietly negating the extension (or limiting the generalizing) of consociational democracy to include constitutionally defined characteristics—which was, after all, the motivation in developing the majoritarian versus consensus democracy framework in the first place.

Unlike Lijphart, we therefore do not start with the concentration or dispersion of power, and then subordinate all structural characteristics underneath it. Instead, we start from the structural categories and draw a distinction between constitutionally defined and informal structures. This is because there are not only constitutionally defined forms of power dispersion but also analogous forms that emerge through the interaction between political actors, and these differing forms of power distribution may well have differing consequences for political decisions. We also regard the analytic distinction between political structures for the exercise of authority and selection of leaders as relevant, and focus on the structures of democratic governance most significant to political performance.

Formal and informal structures of democratic governance
Structures of democratic governance have been discussed thus far in terms of their primary function (exercising power) and the character of rules (formal and informal). Furthermore, the discussion was limited to those rules that define the degree of power distribution. To be able to measure these structures and to predict what impact they will have on performance, a much more detailed conceptualization of these rules is needed. For both, the formal and informal structures, we will first determine how and to what degree they divide power between actors participating in political decision-making. Second, we will discuss the consequences formal and informal rules have on the decision-making process and its results. Here we take up several theoretical hypotheses and considerations that have been put forward by Armingeon (1996) as well as Birchfield and Crepaz (1998).

We start with the more precise *description of the content of the rules*, and in particular, the manner in which these rules distribute power between the veto players involved in collective decision-making. By using the veto player notion we emphasize that not every individual or collective actor is of equal interest analytically. Instead, the decision-making situation is conceptualized from the point of view of those actors whose agreement to adopt a collectively binding decision is necessary. The more veto players involved, the greater the degree of power distribution.

However, the number of veto players alone does not suffice to describe the content of the rules. As we saw in the analysis of the explanatory models from comparative public policy and in the discussion of the veto players approach, hypotheses about the consequences of the degree of power distribution can only be derived if power distribution is addressed from the perspective of *one* relevant political actor, in this case the executive. At stake is formulating the content of the formal and informal rules in such a manner as to reflect the extent to which these rules limit the power of the executive. Or to put more positively, so that the rules reflect the degree of autonomy granted to the executive. The *point of reference* for describing the rules is then the executive autonomy to enforce political decisions. Regarding the (constitutionally defined) governmental system, the issue is the autonomy of the executive as an institution, while in the case of the relationship between governing and opposition parties (based on informal rules), the issue is the autonomy of the government as an actor, which is to say, the autonomy of the governing parties.

So what, from this perspective, is the actual *content* of the rules? Governmental systems fix the rules that define which and how many constitutionally defined institutions need to agree to an executive decision. Fuchs (2000: 40) has suggested to differentiate between primary and secondary structural characteristics that give constitutionally mandated institutions different significance and weight. Primary structural characteristics would apply to those constitutional institutions that need to agree with nearly all executive decisions. This would usually include three characteristics: presidentialism that affords a president's independence, bicameralism that gives the second chamber the power to veto or agree, and federalism that provides independent decision-making authority to sub-national political units (Tsebelis 1995; Fuchs 2000). Secondary structural characteristics differ inasmuch as they encompass only those constitutional institutions that can subsequently, though only under particular conditions or in specifically delimited areas, alter executive decisions or make autonomous decisions, as a constitutional court or an independent central bank might (Fuchs 2000).

The situation is different regarding the relationship between governing and opposition parties. In this case governmental decision-making is restricted for several reasons. For one, a compromise needs to be found between the various actors represented in government, which is that much more difficult the more parties form the government. For another, executive decisions need to find support in parliament, which is again influenced by the number of parties making up the government. A rising number of parties in government increases the need to find compromises, implying in turn that the governing parties are less secure about their support in parliament. Informal rules thus set how many parties need to agree, both within the executive and in the legislature.

Table 3.2 sets out various characteristics of formal and informal structures of democratic governance as well as the assumed consequences for the political decision-making process. Part A (Rules) lists the aspects—character, point of reference, and content of the rules—that distinguish the governmental system and the relationship between governing and opposition parties. Identifying the number of veto players from the point of view of

TABLE 3.2. *Formal and empirical structures of democratic governance*

	Governmental system	Relationship between governing and opposition parties
A. Rules		
Character	Formal rules (anchored in a Constitution or in law)	Informal rules (arising from the interaction between the actors)
Point of reference	Autonomy of the executive as an institution	Autonomy of the government as an actor
Content	(*a*) Which and how many constitutional institutions must agree to an executive decision? (primary rules) (*b*) Which and how many constitutional institutions can, under particular circumstances, subsequently change executive decisions or can make independent decisions in specifically delimited areas? (secondary rules)	How many governing and parliamentary parties must agree to an executive decision?
Type of democracy	Majoritarian or negotiation democracies based on constitutional rules	Majoritarian or negotiation democracies based on informal rules
B. Predicted consequences of power distribution rules		
Decision-making process	Blockage of the executive	Structural need for the government to negotiate and find consensus
Decision-making result	Status quo ('policy stability')	(*a*) proactive and goal-oriented policy ('policy change') (*b*) responsiveness

the executive stands at the centre. Because the basic idea is that with increasing numbers of constitutionally defined or partisan veto players, executive autonomy decreases. This also allows a distinction to be drawn between two *types of democracy*: majoritarian or negotiation democracies based on constitutional rules, and majoritarian or negotiation democracies based on informal rules.

The central premise of this concept of democratic governance is that there are differing forms of power dispersion that are based on different structures, in this case formal and empirical structures. If, unlike Lijphart, one makes an a priori differentiation between different forms of power dispersion, then the logical next question is whether this differentiation would be tied to different *consequences for the political decision-making process* (Armingeon 1996: 284; Birchfield and Crepaz 1998: 181). While research here is in its infancy, some plausible assumptions can be made.

Birchfield and Crepaz (1998: 182–3), for example, draw a distinction between competitive and collective veto points, mirroring the differentiation we have drawn between formal and informal structures.[5] *Competitive veto points* 'occur when different political actors operate through separate institutions with mutual veto powers' (e.g. federalism, strong bicameralism, presidentialism). These actors have independent sources of power and legitimation. Their veto power implies that they can hinder, restrain, or block government and thereby prevent policy change. *Collective veto points* 'emerge from institutions where the different political actors operate in the same body and whose members interact with each other on a face-to-face basis' (e.g. multiparty coalition government, multiparty legislatures). In order to be able to act at all, they must cooperate with one another. A coalition government is a particularly good example, since the need to cooperate results from a necessity to secure its continued viability. The assumption is that compromise and negotiation are characteristic for reaching decisions in these institutions, and that common actions and common responsibility results in greater responsiveness to the demands of citizens. Competitive veto points are seen as 'constraining', in the sense that change does not occur (or the status quo is maintained), and collective veto points are seen as 'enabling', in the sense of proactive, goal-oriented policies (Birchfield and Crepaz 1998: 193).

Armingeon (1996) draws a distinction between two forms of negotiation democracy, one characterized by strong 'secondary governments' and the other consociational democracy. Strong secondary governments designate a situation with many constitutionally defined veto players who strongly limit the autonomy of the central government; this is then a characterization of the governmental system. Consociational democracy is defined in Lehmbruch's (1967) and Lijphart's (1968) terms, as a democracy based on informal practices. Armingeon assumes that his forms describe two structurally different systems of negotiation, with different consequences for policy.

Secondary governments are clearly defined: functionally limited political institutions such as a second legislative house or an independent central bank. They are responsible for different policy areas and must negotiate with the central government because this is fixed in law. However, their politics are primarily 'guided by the goals and interests of their respective institutions in the respective policy area' (Armingeon 1996: 286), so it is likely

---

[5] See Wagschal (1999*a*) for a similar differentiation between competitive and consensual veto players.

that they hinder or block central government policy, and the resulting political decisions are minimal or sub-optimal.

Consociational democracy, by contrast, is a means of regulating relations between socio-cultural groups. All larger groups are represented in decision-making and negotiating and they act together. Here politics is primarily influenced 'by the insight, won over time, that it is of mutual advantage to all to have consensual regulation' (Armingeon 1996: 285). Elites in consociational democracies are confronted with the consequences of their decisions for other policy areas, because they are responsible for the whole range of policies. The result of political decisions is compromise, and the likelihood is great that comprehensive solutions to problems can be found.

So following these studies, different forms of the dispersion of power have wide-ranging and different consequences for the process as well as the result of political decision-making. The cause is seen in the differing character of interaction between veto players that results from the different forms of power dispersion.

Birchfield and Crepaz's reflections on competitive veto points (1998), and Armingeon's on secondary governments (1996) are directly applicable to the governmental system. Both studies focus on the formal structural characteristics assigned to it: presidential systems, bicameralism, federalism, and independent central banks. Both works also predict that in the case of a constitutionally defined dispersion of power, there will be blockage of the executive in the decision-making process and policy stability or maintenance of the status quo as the decision-making result. This reasoning has many parallels to the veto player notions that argue that with increasing numbers of veto players there will be a decreasing ability of the government to enforce its programmes (Immergut 1992) or a decreased ability to react with policy changes to external shocks (Tsebelis 1995, 2002). Still, one of the differences is that Birchfield and Crepaz (1998) and Armingeon (1996) attach these effects exclusively to the constitutionally defined veto players, arguing that these veto players have an independent source of legitimation and have no structural need to be in agreement.

While there is a long, well-established tradition of research on governmental systems (Loewenstein 1957), no such tradition exists for studying the characteristics and functions of informal structures. The analysis of Tsebelis's veto player notion showed that the assumption of independent consequences of informal structures is not universally agreed upon in political science. In fact, it was only with the introduction of the concept of 'consociational democracy' in the late 1960s that informal political structures became part of the comparative research on democracy for the first time. In the 1990s a second research tradition started when empirical analyses found opposite effects of formal and informal structures. Quite varied studies have been able to show that an increase in the number of constitutional veto players is associated with a decrease in social expenditures and in socio-economic equality, while increasing numbers of partisan veto players are associated with increasing social expenditures and an increase in socio-economic equality (Huber et al. 1993; Schmidt 1997*b*, 2000*a*: 347; Birchfield and Crepaz 1998; Crepaz 1998, 2001). While Armingeon (1996) goes back to consociational models to account for informal structures, Birchfield and Crepaz's (1998) work is part of the second research tradition. They suggest that the opposing effects that are found might be explained by a notion of collective veto points that arise through the interaction between parties within institutions. Our question is what consequences power-dispersing structures regarding the relationship between governing and opposition parties have. To discuss this question we will use Birchfield and Crepaz's concept of collective veto points that is at a higher degree of generality.

Birchfield and Crepaz begin with the idea that the decision-making process in a coalition government is characterized by a structural need to negotiate and come to agreement, not only out of the necessity to be able to act, but also because its survival is dependent on parliamentary support. This argument is prevalent in coalition theory that focuses on the interaction between governing parties (Riker 1962). Parties strive to become, and remain, members of a governing coalition, and the primary concern of opposition parties is to become a party in government. Parties already in government are thereby forced to cooperate, both to be able to act and to remain viable decision-makers. They therefore are inclined to make compromises over policies.

The decisive question is what consequences such a structural necessity to negotiate or agree has on the outcomes of political decisions. Birchfield and Crepaz (1998) predict two: on the one hand, proactive and goal-oriented policies that they name reformist policies, that because it is conceived as a counterpart to policy stability can also be called policy change; and on the other hand policies that are responsive to the demands of citizens. Because responsiveness is a democratic criterion of performance and because we are instead concentrating on systemic criteria of effectiveness, we do not consider this aspect in the following analyses.

Part B of Table 3.2 summarizes the predicted consequences of power distribution rules for the decision-making process and the decision-making result. At first glance, it gives an impression that a negotiation democracy based on informal rules is superior to a negotiation democracy based on constitutional rules since it promises reforms or policy change (and responsiveness) rather than deadlock. But it is worth reiterating that our analysis does *not* attempt a comprehensive description of the consequences of these two forms of power dispersion. We are only interested in the consequences for the policies. A more balanced judgment would result from taking other criteria into account. For example, a negotiation democracy based on constitutional rules is generally assumed to ensure that other desirable democratic goals are met, such as preserving liberty or preventing tyranny. In fact, these are the explicit reasons stated in *The Federalist Papers (No. 47)* to justify the separation of powers system in the USA. Conversely, one can assume that a negotiation democracy based on informal rules carries higher decision-making costs because of the greater difficulty in reaching decisions.

It should also be noted that these are only *hypotheses* about the effects different negotiation democracies have on policy; research on the effects of different forms of power dispersion are still in the early stages. Here we would like to state one possible objection to the hypotheses regarding the relationship between governing and opposition parties. A large number of parties in the government and parliament can mean a structural need to negotiate and come to agreement. But it is still open whether and to what extent various collective actors evade—for whatever reason—an 'obligation to agree'. To the extent to which they do so, deadlock sets in with increasing numbers of veto players. This can be seen best in the cases of Italy and the Netherlands: the multiparty coalition governments typical of Italy are of markedly shorter duration than similar governments in the Netherlands. Preventing blockage requires other enhancing conditions, such as mutual trust on the part of elites or elite consensus, which are cultural factors (Lijphart 1968). The overall extremely positive evaluation of negotiation democracies based on informal rules may be due to the fact that even Birchfield and Crepaz's consideration of collective veto points are strongly influenced by the concept of consociational democracy.

The goal here has been to be more precise about what we mean by the governmental system and by the relationship between governing and opposition parties, as well as to examine hypotheses about the consequences these structures have on the decision-making process and its results. Constitutional rules are defined as the number of constitutionally-determined institutions that can limit executive autonomy, and informal rules as the number of parties in government and parliament that must agree to government decisions. These provide the theoretical basis for discussing empirical measures of democratic structures. As for the consequences of power-dispersing structures, deadlock and status quo are predicted for governmental systems, and policy change (and responsiveness) as well as a structural need to be in agreement for the relationship between governing and opposition parties. These general hypotheses about the effects of formal and informal governing structures on policies form the basis for the development of hypotheses about the impact institutions of democratic government have on effectiveness.

Indices for Measuring the Institutions of Democratic Governance

Two different kinds of instruments have been developed in the comparative study of democracy. One is Lijphart's instrument to measure majoritarian and consensus democracies that includes the executives–parties and federal–unitary (sub-) indices. According to the typology of democratic institutional arrangements (Fuchs 2000) applied here, the first index intends to measure informal or partisan structures while the second index aims at formal or constitutional structures. The other is a series of five indicators developed to measure constitutional structures, including the index of constitutional structure (Huber et al. 1993), the index of institutional pluralism (Colomer 1996), the index of institutional constraints of central state government (Schmidt 1996)[6] and the minimal governmental system index with A and B parts (Fuchs 2000).

The construction of all these five additional indices, that constitute alternatives to and variations of Lijphart's federal–unitary index, has been guided by veto player theory. Since, in the meantime, Lijphart himself (1999*a*: 5, fn. 2) sees similarities between his measures and Tsebelis's veto player approach, all seven of these indices can be characterized legitimately as veto player indices (Fuchs 2000).

All of these indices will be examined to establish to what extent they are valid measures of the 'governmental system' or the 'relationship between governing and opposition parties'. We call indices for measuring the governmental system *constitutional veto player indices* and indices for measuring the relationship between governing and opposition parties *partisan veto player indices*. In discussing the validity of the constitutional veto player indices we rely on a theoretical analysis done by Fuchs (2000). Regarding partisan veto player indices the situation is considerably more difficult. Lijphart's executives–parties index suffers major drawbacks, as we will show, so our task is to suggest alternative partisan veto player indices.

All these indices are based on aggregate measurements of various structural characteristics of democracies. First, the type of the structural characteristic reflecting the degree of power distribution is established for each nation. For example, the characteristic 'legislatures' is expressed either as unicameral (power concentration) or bicameral (power dispersion). Applying the veto player logic, the indices then sum up either the power-concentrated characteristics or the power-dispersed characteristics per country.[7] Only in

---

[6] Schmidt's last edition of *Demokratietheorien* includes a 'veto-player index' (2000*a*: 352) based on ten structural characteristics. It is not included here because it covers characteristics that go beyond political institutions (e.g. self-governing structures of welfare states).

[7] Constructing indices in this way is problematic if the numbers of categories vary. So though most characteristics are trichotomized, two of five characteristics (parliamentarism–

the case of the two Lijphart indices were the values of the individual variables first standardized and then averaged.[8] But though all indices measure the degree of power distribution, they differ with respect to the characteristics they rely on. In order to determine the content of these indices we use tabular summaries (see Fuchs 2000) that classify indices by the structural characteristic being measured, in this case classified by the institutional arrangements of democracy: governmental system, electoral system, relationship between governing and opposition parties, and party system (see Figure 3.5 and Fuchs 2000: 40). Table 3.3 lists constitutional veto player indices and Table 3.4 lists the partisan veto player indices.

Constitutional veto player indices
The governmental system encompasses constitutionally defined structural characteristics in which the exercise of authority takes place. Primary structural characteristics describe constitutional institutions that need to agree with nearly all executive decisions (e.g. presidentialism, bicameralism, and federalism), while secondary structural characteristics encompass institutions that can subsequently, though only under particular conditions or in specifically delimited areas, alter executive decisions or make autonomous decisions (e.g. constitutional court, independent central bank). All constitutional veto player indices listed in Table 3.3 measure such structural characteristics. But as one can see they differ sharply regarding three aspects at least.

First, the indices differ with respect to whether or not they include other structural characteristics assigned to institutions outside the governmental system (Fuchs 2000: 41). The index of Huber et al. (1993), for example, measures the electoral system, while the index of Colomer (1996) measures the party system. If one were interested only in a *pure* measure of the governmental system, neither of these indicators would be adequate, quite apart from the other problems these two particular indices have with different number of categories (see fn. 7).

Second, the other indices differ with respect to whether or not they include presidentialism under the primary structural characteristics and third, whether they take secondary characteristics into account (Fuchs 2000: 41). It is surprising to find presidentialism lacking in the Lijphart and Schmidt indices. It calls for some justification since it is regarded as *the* prototype of a power-distributing system (Fuchs 2000: 41). But Schmidt (1996) provides no reasons and Lijphart is of the opinion that the 'parliamentary–presidential

presidentialism, referenda) in Huber et al. (1993), and one of four characteristics (parliamentarism–presidentialism) in Colomer (1996), were included in dichotomized forms.

[8] Lijphart (1999*a*: 247, fn. 1) initially had to standardize because the individual variables 'were originally measured on quite different scales'.

TABLE 3.3. *Content of constitutional veto player indices*

	Huber et al. (1993)	Colomer (1996)	Fuchs A (2000)	Fuchs B (2000)	Schmidt (1996)	Lijphart (1999a)[a]
A. Formal (constitutional) structure						
1. Governmental system						
(a) Primary characteristics						
Presidentialism	X	X		X		
Bicameralism	X	X	X	X	X	X
Federalism	X	X	X	X	X	X
(b) Secondary characteristics						
Constitutional rigidity					X	X
Constitutional court						X
Referenda	X				X	
Independent central bank					X	X
EU Membership					X	
2. Electoral system						
Electoral law	X					
B. Empirical (actor) structure						
1. Relationship between governing and opposition parties						
2. Party system						
Effective number of parliamentary parties		X				

[a] Federal–unitary index.

Source: Fuchs (2000: 40), with author's additions.

distinction does not bear directly on the distribution of power in executive–legislative relationships' (1999*a*: 127). Fuchs sees the only plausible argument for omission in the assumption that the consequences of presidentialism are not contained in the fact that the president is an additional institutional veto player, and therefore provides one version of his index (A) without and another version (B) with presidentialism.

As one can see, both indices of Schmidt and Lijphart include secondary structural characteristics in addition to two primary structural characteristics. Lijphart's index incorporates three and Schmidt's index even four secondary characteristics. Because each characteristic is included with the same weight in the index, the larger number of the secondary characteristics has the effect that they carry a greater weight in the index than the primary characteristics do (Fuchs 2000: 42). Given that there are no theoretical criteria to guide the weighting of primary and secondary characteristics, there are only two alternatives open. One is to employ indices that only measure primary structural characteristics. Fuchs takes this parsimonious path in indices that include only bicameralism and federalism (Index A) or bicameralism, federalism, and presidentialism (Index B). The other is to assume that regardless of whether they are primary or secondary structural characteristics, the 'majority of such veto players *taken together*' constitute a democratic governmental system that 'has the effect of placing considerable restrictions on the decision process *as a whole*' (Fuchs 2000: 42). Under this assumption, Lijphart's federal–unitary as well as Schmidt's institutional constraints of central state government indices could also be considered.

Both alternatives are compatible with the questions we pursue here, so in the empirical analysis we employ four indices: both of Fuchs's minimal governmental indices limited to primary characteristics as well as Lijphart and Schmidt's 'maximal' indices covering primary as well as secondary characteristics.

Lijphart's executives–parties index
Few instruments have been developed to measure the informal structures of democratic governance. The only measure is Lijphart's executive–parties index, but it incorporates not only the relationship between governing and opposition parties but additionally the party system and, moreover, the interest group system in *one* measure (Table 3.4). Before we turn to our specific question, it is worth discussing one conspicuous aspect: the inclusion of interest group systems ranging from pluralist to corporatist.

This characteristic was not included in Lijphart's original index (1984), but was incorporated later with the argument that it was needed 'to try to fill a gap in the theory of consensus democracy' (Lijphart and Crepaz

1991: 235). In his view, this made his measurement instrument richer and more comprehensive (Lijphart and Crepaz 1991: 246). Formally, it means an expansion of the concept of political institutions to include institutions of political economy. Because our question is exclusively about the effect of *political* institutions in a narrow sense, this index is inappropriate.

But the question of the inclusion or exclusion of this particular characteristic has much greater and more fundamental theoretical significance. Unlike the other informal structural characteristics Lijphart includes, such as the composition of the government, dominance of the executive, effective number of parliamentary parties and the disproportionality of elections, interest group pluralism is not a content-neutral characteristic. Corporatist arrangements, characterized by an involvement of interest groups in policy formation, are concentrated in very specific policy areas, namely in economic policy and social policy (Siaroff 1999: 176–7). For that reason, we conceptualized the politico-economic institutions in our theoretical analysis as policy-specific institutions.

But beyond this, the existence of a corporatist structure, representing cooperation between state, union federations and employer associations, also means a strong representation of worker interests (Siaroff 1999: 176). If an index of political structures measures the existence of corporatist arrangements, and given that these arrangements function, one can a priori assume that in analysing performance we will find a relationship with those policies in which workers' interests are expressed, such as full employment and socio-economic equality. Lijphart finds a systematic relationship between the executives–parties dimension and certain performance dimensions, and we do not think it implausible that some of these connections can be traced back to the inclusion of the characteristic of the interest group system. We examined this possibility in the empirical part of our study and found it at least partly confirmed.

Lijphart measures the relationship between governing and opposition parties using two different structural characteristics: 'composition of government' and 'executive dominance'. The number of parties in the government and the relationship of executive to parliament are precisely what specify, in our definition, the relationship between governing and opposition parties. It would thus seem inviting to simply extract these two structural characteristics from Lijphart's executives–parties index and combine them into an index for measuring the relationship between governing and opposition parties. A serious problem stands in the way, however: in measuring both structural characteristics, Lijphart (1999*a*: 116) manipulated the values of some nations, or as he put it, 'several important adjustments are required, especially for presidential systems'.

Lijphart measures the structural characteristic of *government composition*, or degree of power dispersion in the cabinet, by computing the mean value of two variables: one is the percentage of time there have been 'minimal winning cabinets', the other is the percentage of time there have been 'one-party cabinets' in each nation, from 1945 to 1996 (Lijphart 1999a: 100–11). The first variable *minimal winning cabinets* rests on a classification of one-party and coalition governments based on their degree of parliamentary support: (*a*) single party; (*b*) minimal winning coalition; (*c*) surplus coalition; (*d*) single party minority; and (*e*) multiparty minority (Woldendorp et al. 1993, 1998). Lijphart contrasts power-concentrating 'minimal winning and one-party cabinets' (*a*) and (*b*), that contain no parties not needed for a parliamentary majority, with power-dispersing 'oversized' (more parties than necessary for a parliamentary majority) (*c*) and 'minority cabinets' (*d*) and (*e*) (1999a: 103–4).

Lijphart (1999a: 104) then discusses the applicability of the concept of parliamentary support to presidential cabinets: In parliamentary systems, majority support in the legislature is necessary for governments both to stay in office and to pass laws, but because presidents are elected for a fixed term, their survival in office is independent of legislative approval. Regarding one dimension—staying in office—presidents and their cabinets are thus 'minimal winning' by definition. In terms of legislative support for proposed laws, however, the type of government depends 'on the party affiliations of the presidents and of their cabinet members and the sizes of the respective parties in the legislature. This means that whereas cabinets in parliamentary systems can vary between 0 and 100 per cent minimal winning, the variation for presidential cabinets is only between 50 and 100 per cent' (Lijphart 1999a: 105).

Lijphart uses the same logic for discussing the second variable *one-party cabinets*. On the one hand, presidential executives are by definition one-person executives and not collegial, since power is concentrated in the hands of the president. In that respect one can speak also of a one-party cabinet. On the other hand, however, it makes a difference if the presidential cabinet is only composed of members of the president's party or whether members of other parties are included. Lijphart assumes one can weight these two aspects equally, so 'presidential cabinets can vary between 50 and 100 per cent one-party cabinets in contrast with parliamentary cabinets where the range of variation is the full 0 to 100 per cent' (Lijphart 1999a: 106–7). Two of the nations we examine here, the USA and France, are affected by this data manipulation. In both cases the correction of the degree of power concentration along the executives–parties dimension is increased by 50 per cent.[9]

---

[9] Lijphart (1999a: 106–8), in discussing the 'unusual cabinets in Austria, the United States, and Japan', has undertaken further data corrections. But as we are only interested in the systematic problems in applying his concepts, we do not discuss these corrections further.

TABLE 3.4. *Content of partisan veto player indices*[a]

	Executives–parties index (Lijphart 1999a)	Simple partisan veto player index	Veto players in the lower house (Schnapp 2004)	Number of governing parties	Effective number of parliamentary parties
1. Relationship between governing and opposition parties					
Composition of government					
(a) Number of governing parties	X[b]	X	X	X	
(b) Parliamentary support for the government	X[c]	X[d]	X[d]		
Ideological orientation of parties			X		
Executive dominance (government stability)	X				
2. Party system					
Effective number of parliamentary parties	X				X
Electoral disproportionality	X				
3. Other					
Interest group pluralism	X				

[a] The classification of the executives–parties index is based on Fuchs (2000: 40).
[b] Included only as a dichotomy: one-party versus coalition government.
[c] Dichotomized: power-concentrating (one-party majority government, coalition government) versus power-dispersing government (oversized coalition government, one-party and multiparty minority government).
[d] Dichotomized: majority government (one-party majority government, minimal winning and oversized coalition government) versus minority government (one-party and multiparty minority government).

In the case of the second structural characteristic of *executive dominance*, Lijphart employs a less elaborate data replacement procedure. Here the index is also based on the mean of two variables, in this case a broad (measured by changed party composition) and a narrow definition (based on four termination criteria)[10] of mean cabinet duration for the time from 1945 to 1996. However, based on the values Lijphart finds 'a much greater adjustment is necessary' because in certain cases—the USA, France, and Switzerland for example—'cabinet duration gives a completely wrong impression':

> The Swiss average... is obviously completely wrong as a measure of executive dominance because Switzerland is a prime example of executive–legislative balance. Hence, I impressionistically assign it a value of 1.00 year. The same is appropriate for the United States... France must be assigned the highest value for executive dominance—the same as Britain's. (Lijphart 1999*a*: 134)

In the corresponding table Lijphart (1999*a*: 132–3) marks the corrected values with asterisks and merely notes that the values given in the index of executive dominance differ from the calculated mean values. The correction affects eleven of the thirty-six nations studied, and the deviation from the original values can be considerable: the average cabinet duration in the USA is corrected from 4.45 to 1.00 year, of Switzerland from 8.59 to 1.00 year, and that of France from 2.48 to 5.52 years. Thus the US and Swiss systems are corrected towards substantially greater power dispersion while France is corrected towards greater power concentration.

In a recently published article, Lijphart (2002: 110) admits the critical operationalization of the concept of executive dominance. However, he does not suggest a new indicator. Instead he argues that the first variable, measuring cabinet duration between 1945 and 1996 using a broad definition, is sufficient. Yet the logarithm should be calculated, if only to minimize the effects of extremely high values of this variable. Obviously, this is not a satisfactory solution of the problem. Cabinet duration, either narrow or broadly defined, cannot function as an indicator for distribution of power between executive and legislature in presidential systems and in Switzerland.

This detailed description of the measurement problems and their 'creative' solution by Lijphart reveals a basic problem in measuring the relationship between governing and opposition parties. Apparently some of the established concepts for measuring executive composition and the executive–legislature relationship are only able to measure the degree of power distribution in parliamentary but not in presidential systems. Regarding stability of government, there are also problems in the Swiss case as its political system has some presidential features: the executive is only dependent on

---

[10] The four criteria are 'changes in party composition, prime ministership, and coalitional status, as well as new elections' (Lijphart 1999*a*: 132–3).

parliament for its inauguration but during the legislative period it enjoys an independence comparable to that accorded to a president.[11]

Given these problems, Lijphart corrects the data for the presidential systems, and owing to his wide knowledge of the political systems in the individual nations, one can certainly argue that his data corrections are plausible. Yet, the need for such correction is a sure sign that the measurement concepts themselves are inappropriate. This is clearest in the corrections introduced in the executive dominance index. For all their plausibility they are not carried out according to any systematic logic. Lijphart changes the empirical values for cabinet duration 'impressionistically', and in some cases makes enormous corrections (e.g. the Swiss value is reduced from 8.59 to 1.00 year), so that only one conclusion can be drawn from it: cabinet duration cannot be used to empirically establish the distribution of power between executive and legislature in presidential systems. Even if the data replacement procedure used in measures of government composition appears better founded, in the end these are arbitrary decisions as well. Simply as a matter of principle one can challenge the findings that are based on such decisions. The only answer here is to develop operationalizations of the relationship between governing and opposition parties that can be applied to both parliamentary and presidential systems: In the following we suggest three measures with varying degree of complexity: 'the simple partisan veto player index', 'the index veto players in the lower house' developed by Schnapp (2004) and the 'number of governing parties'. Additionally, a fourth and surrogate measure, 'the effective number of parliamentary parties' is suggested.

New partisan veto player indices

The number of parties in the executive and in parliament that must agree to a political decision is the decisive element of the relationship between governing and opposition parties (see Table 3.2). Following the veto player tradition, we focus on the autonomy of government in carrying out political decisions. This has the advantage that it is equally applicable to parliamentary and presidential systems. Lijphart (1999a) additionally takes the dimension of positional independence of legislature and executive into consideration. But that is a *constitutionally* defined form of power separation. It is the core of parliamentarism versus presidentialism and should be measured by constitutional veto player indices.

To carry out political decisions, all governing parties need to agree, and then the majority of the parliamentary parties need to agree as well. Accordingly, the *number of governing parties* must first be determined. More

---

[11] This mixture of parliamentary and presidential elements is the reason that some authors regard this form as a third type: directorial democracy (Lauvaux 1990).

specifically, *each* individual governing party must be counted because, from the veto player perspective, the degree to which power is dispersed rises with increasing numbers of parties. Lijphart's interest, by contrast, is in the existence or absence of one-party governments, and not in the exact number of governing parties. We also assume presidential executives are essentially one-person executives, but unlike Lijphart, we do not investigate whether all cabinet members are also members of the president's party. From the point of view of power dispersion, individual members of a presidential cabinet who do not belong to the president's party are markedly less important than an additional party in a parliamentary coalition government. One can add that one essential element of presidentialism is that a president determines the composition of government, and thus in the end, the course of policies itself (Shugart and Carey 1992).

In terms of the *agreement of the parliamentary parties*, either the governing parties have a parliamentary majority or there is a minority government. This aspect was addressed previously in a classification of the 'type of government' distinguishing one-party and coalition governments on their degree of parliamentary support (Woldendorp et al. 1993, 1998). Since we are interested in a government's ability to carry out its programme, and the degree of power dispersion within the government is already measured by the number of governing parties, unlike Lijphart we assign cases where governments have a surplus coalition to the category of majority government. So we divide parliamentary support of the governing parties into majority governments (minimal winning[12] and oversized or surplus coalition) and minority governments (one-party and multiparty).

The next important question is which counting rule is to be used for parliamentary parties. One can imagine a simple counting rule that states that in the case of a majority government, the number of veto players is defined as the number of governing parties. In the case of a minority government, then one adds *one* additional veto player. This index, that we designate a *single partisan veto player index*, rests on two assumptions. One is that in a majority government, one does not need an independent count of the parliamentary parties, as one can assume the parliamentary parties that have created the government will also agree with the legislative proposals it puts forward. The other assumption is that in a minority government, other veto players become involved. Because the number of additional veto players depends on the actual strength of the opposition parties, and because it varies by individual political decisions, the actual number cannot be determined independent of these specific decisions. The fact that additional veto players exist is only taken into account by adding *one* additional veto player.

---

[12] Subdivided into single party and minimal winning coalition categories (Woldendorp et al. 1993, 1998).

A more complex and differentiated counting rule, at least for minority governments, is provided by Schnapp's *veto players in the lower house index*. To determine the veto players, the ideological positions or preferences as well as the seat distribution of the parliamentary parties are taken into account. This index originated in an effort to explain the manoeuvring room available to the ministerial (or departmental) bureaucracy, as well as out of dissatisfaction with Tsebelis's counting rules in which even in minority governments, it is only the number of governing parties that are counted as veto players. Using formal decision theory, Schnapp (2004) distinguishes between minority governments that need very specific opposition parties to pass laws, and minority governments that can choose between different opposition parties.

In a majority government, only the number of governing parties is counted, but in a minority government, the left–right position of the parties is also taken into account, specifically whether the governing parties are at one of the extremes or in the middle of the left–right spectrum. The party programmes are used to determine the left–right positions.[13] If the parties that comprise a minority government are at the extremes of the left–right spectrum, then they must rely on other parties to pass their laws and are forced to make compromises. If, on the other hand, they are in the centre of the party spectrum, then they are strong because they have alternatives in both directions. If the governing parties adopt extreme positions, as many additional parties are counted as veto players as are needed to reach 50 per cent of the seats. If the governing parties are in a central ideological position, then no parties are counted as additional veto players, since the government can create majorities with help from either direction. An absorption rule is also included for the case of a multiparty minority government where one or more parties exist *between* the governing parties in the left–right dimension that do not belong to the government. In this case as well, no additional veto players are counted.

Both indices just discussed have counting rules applicable to both parliamentary and presidential systems. We will demonstrate this with reference to the simple partisan veto player index, as it has a simpler counting rule. If the president's party has a majority in parliament, then one veto player is counted, but if another party has a majority in parliament (e.g. divided government), then there are two veto players. In a parliamentary system, one veto player is counted in the case of a one-party majority government, and two veto players in a one-party minority government. Since in a presidential system the executive–legislature relationship is also determined by the constitutionally defined independence of both organs, the degree of *total*

---

[13] Schnapp (2004) uses the data from the *Comparative Manifesto Project* (Klingemann et al. 1994; Budge et al. 2001) and Laver and Budge's suggested index to measure party position (1992). Missing data in the party programmes are filled with the help of expert estimations of the party positions (Castles and Mair 1984; Huber and Inglehart 1995).

power concentration is greater in parliamentary than in presidential systems. But it is precisely this constitutionally defined difference that is already encompassed by the constitutional veto player index. The two partisan veto player indices suggested here exclusively refer to the number of different parties that, regardless of the configuration of the constitutional institutions, must agree to a political decision. To stay with our example, there are the same number of parties in both parliamentary and in presidential systems.

The advantage of these two suggested partisan veto player indices lies not only in this parallel application to different systems. It is also that they are constructed following the same veto player logic as Schmidt's (1996) and Fuchs's (2000) constitutional veto player indices. What both indices also have in common is that in addition to the number of governing parties, attention is paid to whether it is a majority or a minority government.

A third partisan veto player index is also conceivable, namely one that ignores the type of government and that focuses only on the *number of governing parties*. This simple index can also be used to measure the degree of power distribution in the relationship between governing and opposition parties, because with increasing numbers of governing parties, the difficulty of making decisions increases, both within government and in achieving a parliamentary majority in support. The empirical analysis will show whether this less theoretically demanding and more parsimonious indicator is sufficient to measure the relationship between governing and opposition parties.

These three indices increase in complexity from 'number of governing parties' to 'simple partisan veto player index' to 'veto players in the lower house', as one can see in Table 3.4: All include the number of governing parties, the second adds parliamentary support, and the third includes the ideological orientation of the parties and the seat distribution in the case of minority governments. For control purposes, the index *effective number of parliamentary parties* is also included. This is a measure of the number of parliamentary parties that takes their relative size (based on the distribution of seats) into account (see Laakso and Taagepera 1979; Taagepera 1997). It is primarily a measure of the distribution of power in the party system and not of the relationship between governing and parliamentary parties. But as there is a close relationship between the party system and this relationship, the effective number of parliamentary parties might serve as a surrogate measure for informal structures of democratic governance. This indicator is also entirely unaffected by the systemic difference between presidential and parliamentary systems because it does not measure executive–legislature relations.

We have, in this last section, suggested some alternative indicators for measuring the relationship between governing and opposition parties, in part because of the difficulties encountered with Lijphart's executives–parties index. All three suggested partisan veto player indices, along with the surrogate measure 'effective number of parliamentary parties' are employed in our empirical analysis on the impact of political institutions on the effectiveness in western democracies.

An Integrated Explanatory Model

After discussing the explanatory models used in comparative political research some theoretical questions are still open. The explanatory models of both comparative public policy and the veto player approach referred to rational choice institutionalism but we need to explore this approach in more detail. Then we turn to two issues that are raised but not further explored in comparative public policy research: how to account for the influence of increasing economic globalization on political performance in our explanatory model, and to what extent outputs need to be included in the model as additional factors for explaining outcomes. We conclude this discussion with describing our integrated model to explain the performance of democratic institutions.

Rational choice institutionalism

The rise of neo-institutionalism in the 1980s (March and Olsen 1984) led to theories of institutionalism that belong to three different schools: historical, sociological, and rational choice (Koelble 1995; Ostrom 1995; Hall and Taylor 1996). Rational choice institutionalism differs from the other two primarily because it uses a narrow, rule-driven definition of institutions, which comes close to the concept of political institutions we apply here, and because it is fairly precise about the relationship between institutions and the behaviour of actors (Hall and Taylor 1996: 966). It brings two research traditions together: a microanalytic rational choice approach that focuses on actors and their behaviour and a macroanalytic institutionalist approach that focuses on structures and their effects. While the microanalytic approach is often criticized for its atomizing point of view, and the macroanalytic approach for its mechanistic explanatory character, the integration has an advantage as it places actors' behaviour within an institutional context. Or seen the other way, it expands the institutionalist perspective by including actors, and thereby giving it a microfoundation (Hall and Taylor 1996: 966; Weingast 1996: 167). Rational choice institutionalism is not a uniform approach (Peters 1999: 46) but rather a variety of heterogeneous approaches of different degrees of specificity whose common goal is the integration of microanalytic and macroanalytic theories. The decision theory variant is the most significant for our study as it focuses on decision rules that determine the process of making and implementing collectively binding decisions.[14]

---

[14] Peters (1999: 46–52), for example, draws a distinction between decision theory, game theory, and 'principal agent' versions of rational choice institutionalism.

Microanalytic rational choice at first means to employ a set of basic behavioural assumptions in which actors have a fixed number of preferences and behave instrumentally (Hall and Taylor 1996: 960). Actors select from the choices available to them those that promise the greatest benefit. Institutions as 'rules of the game' constitute an important part of the actor's context. The relationship between actor's behaviour and institutional contexts is conceptualized through the notion of constraints limiting the sphere of action or choices open to the actors (Windhoff-Héritier 1991: 38).[15] Some authors interpret the fact that institutions structure individual options to mean that rational choice institutionalism utilizes 'bounded rationality' (Simon 1987) rather than a more narrow concept of rationality (Peters 1999: 44). Actors, by this, do not possess complete or perfect information and a perfect capacity to process it. Thus they will settle for a satisfactory alternative (e.g. satisficing) instead of searching for the best one.

The nature of the influence or effect institutions have is the key question here, and various authors have argued that institutions do not determine but merely influence actor behaviour (Koelble 1995: 232; Mayntz and Scharpf 1995: 43; Schmidt 2002: 160). Windhoff-Héritier (1991: 38), following a dual filter model Elster has proposed (1979), argues that every choice is the result of two filters. The first is provided by structural constraints that reduce the universe of possible alternative decisions and determine a small subset of opportunities for the actor. The second is the selection mechanism an actor employs to choose that alternative which promises the greatest benefit from the alternatives still available. Institutions therefore only limit alternatives at the level of the first filter; they do not determine the individual choices actors make. This is extremely consequential, as it means a sharp limitation in the predicted effects institutions have.

Based on these considerations political institutions can be conceptualized as a context restricting the choices of political actors. We further assume rationally behaving actors. Yet, an approach focused on institutions and actors is insufficient for crafting a model to explain the performance of liberal democracies. Performance, at least in the explanatory models used in comparative research, is seen as influenced by additional factors that include socio-economic modernity or international economics. This raises the question whether, or how, such additional factors are to be incorporated in the rational choice institutionalist framework. Elster's two filter theory is helpful here too, since in his conceptualization it is not only institutional constraints that are at work, but also macroanalytic features—economic and technical conditions, value systems—that reduce the sphere of actions

---

[15] Though constraint and restriction are at the centre of the analysis, one should remember that institutions can also act to encourage behaviour. This opposite effect is usually described in terms of reducing uncertainty and minimizing transaction costs (Windhoff-Héritier 1991: 40).

(Windhoff-Héritier 1991: 38). Such additional factors could be thought of as contexts of actors' behaviour that constrain possibilities of action. To the extent that non-institutional factors constitute constraints on actors' choices, it raises the question whether this should continue to be called rational choice institutionalism or rather a more general 'constrained choices' approach (Franz 1986). In our view it remains appropriate to call this approach rational choice institutionalism, since the heart of our analysis is the explanatory power of the institutional setting. Additional potential explanations are seen primarily as competing or controlling factors.

Economic globalization
Comparative research on democracy and on public policies often refer to endogenous factors such as national political actors, national institutions, the national socio-economic level of development, or the national political culture to explain national policies. But the ongoing process of economic globalization that involves an expansion and intensification of transnational interaction (Beisheim and Walter 1997: 157) makes such explanations no longer seem appropriate: to focus on internal explanatory factors at least implicitly assumes autonomy or even isolation of the polity from external influences. There is at least a consensus that the process of economic globalization has intensified since the 1990s, though there are doubts about the empirical significance of this process (Beisheim and Walter 1997; Held et al. 1999; Hirst and Thompson 1999). The general assumption is that globalization processes have the effect of weakening the national ability to steer policy. On the other hand, there is no consensus how increasing international interdependence should be accounted for in social science models. At the moment the discussion is dominated by two contradictory assertions, the one a thesis of convergence, and the other a thesis of divergence. It is no accident that the convergence thesis is stated in theories of crisis and the divergence thesis is based on empirical results from comparative research.

The *convergence thesis* argues that globalization will lead to national policies becoming more similar. Evidence for this is seen in the development of national economies that, due to the high degree of international economic integration, are completely dependent on international business cycles (Garrett 1998; Crepaz 2001). The constraints the global marketplace imposes are also seen as leading to a competition between systems that allows individual nations no autonomy. National institutions and political actors are completely curtailed in their power to make autonomous decisions, and democratic politics are made irrelevant. The more national institutions and political actors lose the ability to craft policy, comparative research is confronted with a fundamental problem: national explanatory factors still carry less explanatory power and the basic premise that the nation-state is the unit of observation or analysis is then put in question. Traditional explanatory models in comparative political research thereby become obsolete (Schmitter 1993: 176; Mair 1996: 324).

The opposite *divergence thesis* argues that globalization has differing effects in individual nations. This argument is based on the findings from comparative research into the effects of open economies, where the degree of openness is determined by the level of foreign trade. Because of the international exchange of goods, open economies are strongly dependent on the development of international markets and prices (Cameron 1978: 1249). So nation-states become subjected to exogenous economic influences outside their control. Older studies find an effect on domestic policy in the sense that open economy nation-states try to reduce market uncertainty by expanding the role of the state and by increasing individual security through expanded social welfare measures (Cameron 1978). This is particularly true in smaller nations whose economies have long been strongly outwardly oriented due to their limited domestic markets (Katzenstein 1985).

Newer studies on the effect of economic globalization confirm this connection between an open economy and national economic and social welfare policies (Garrett 1998; Rodrik 1998; Crepaz 2001). Even when both old and newer research of such open economy effects are challenged—Iversen and Cusack (2000) show that social expenditures vary by degree of endogenous changes of the occupational structure due to de-industrialization rather than the degree of economic openness—they nevertheless support the argument that nation-states are not helpless in the face of economic globalization. Nation-specific protectionism in the face of increasing vulnerability can be taken as an indication that an independent ability to act still exists. This is connected to the theoretical argument that national institutions and actors mediate international developments and that such filtering processes lead to divergent processes of national accommodation (Garrett 1998; Kitschelt et al. 1999; Crepaz 2001; Swank 2002). Here the nation-state as the basic unit of analysis in the explanatory model is not put in question.

The empirical analysis of the effects of economic globalization on national policy is still at the beginning (Garrett 1998; Beisheim et al. 1999; Busch and Plümper 1999; Iversen and Cusack 2000; Crepaz 2001). Given the few, unconfirmed, results thus far, it would be too radical to abandon the traditional explanatory model that rests on the nation-state as the unit of analysis. This is not just because alternative and more complex models are underarticulated (Ebbinghaus 1998). Due to the preliminary state of research it seems more appropriate to turn the effects of economic globalization on political performance into an empirical question. Our approach is to include economic globalization as an independent variable in the model and empirically investigate its effect by controlling for national factors, both political and non-political ones.

The preliminary state of research is also responsible for the fact that the degree of international interdependence can only be empirically established on the basis of foreign trade, measured as a percentage of imports and exports of GNP. We do not use Garrett's measure of capital mobility (1998), as it does not contain sufficient data for the nations and time period we investigate.

The status of outputs

The substantive difference between outputs and outcomes is one of the basic premises of our study. In developing the normative model of political effectiveness of liberal democracies, we argued one could only appropriately analyse effectiveness based on the outcomes of political decisions, unlike what Eckstein (1971) or Putnam (1993) have argued. The question is whether or how outputs must be accounted for in explanatory models as political decisions that occur before outcomes. Comparative public policy researchers do know that outputs do not lead directly to intended results (Castles 1998a: 10) but outputs are nevertheless not treated as an intervening, independent dimension between explanatory factors and outcomes in their models (see Figure 3.2).

In this section we thus discuss the status of outputs in our model. We draw a distinction between an elaborated theoretical model and a model applied in empirical research. While the former is elaborated in this chapter, the empirical model forms the basis of the analysis presented in Chapter 5.

The task of an *elaborated theoretical* model is to identify, describe, and design the individual causal sequences of the process involved in determining the object to be explained, as well as the factors that influence this process. It is out of the question that in such a model outputs are to be treated as political decisions occurring prior to the outcomes. For it is only with the concept of outputs that a connection can be established between the actors themselves and the factors that constrain their choices on the one hand (explanatory factors) and the outcomes or performance (object explained) on the other hand. Outputs function as intervening variables and are causally prior to outcomes, as can be seen in Figure 3.7, the 'theoretical model for explaining the performance of liberal democracies'.

The empirical model, by contrast, is limited to the constructs that are included in the empirical analysis. It contains all constructs whose effects are of interest to the researcher, with the limitation that valid and reliable indicators must exist for these constructs. Interest in including constructs in the empirical model can be motivated either by substantive questions or by the necessity of introducing relevant control variables. We examine whether these two conditions also apply to the case of outputs.

In terms of substantive questions one might be interested in the effect outputs have on outcomes. Questions of this kind might include which instruments produce better results (e.g. whether privately or publicly organized health care systems lead to higher levels of health in the population) or whether more government expenditure is linked to better performance. Such questions are characteristic for the evaluation research that analyses the effectiveness and efficiency of policy programmes (Weiss 1972; Rossi and Freeman 1989). In our study, however, it is not the evaluation of policy programmes that matters but the evaluation of the performance of democracies. Which specific means or instruments democracies use and how successful these means are in reaching articulated goals, is of secondary importance.

Before we address the second question whether outputs must be included in the model as a control variable so that outcomes are not incorrectly ascribed to political institutions and actors, we need to first address the question of measurement of outputs. Typical indicators of outputs refer to the effort or degree of governmental activity as measured by the extent of financial resources utilized, that is, on the basis of governmental expenditure data. The basic problem of such indicators is that individual policies require quite different levels of financial resources (Zimmermann 1973), with the consequence that policy areas steered primarily by regulatory instruments are ignored. Social policy, for example, mainly uses financial means, while domestic security is largely steered by regulatory instruments, and as a result the latter receives very little attention in policy research.

Measures based on fiscal resources also can only be used to a limited degree for making comparisons between individual nations, as different national governments utilize differing instruments in the same policy areas to achieve the same goals. Castles (1998b) has even argued that while continental Europe and Scandinavian welfare states primarily guarantee old age protection through a financially based system of social security, Anglo-American nations may achieve something similar by promoting private home ownership. It is an 'alternative means of accomplishing the horizontal, life cycle redistribution that is one of the primary functions of the welfare state' (Castles 1998b: 5), even when such promotion is not guided by such an explicit socio-political goal. Indicators based on fiscal resources thus can capture only very specific aspects of government activity, and are inadequate for determining the scope of government activity as a whole. In the end, the only alternative to expenditure data is to specify and count laws or regulations, since these are neutral with respect to the instrument employed. Though such data is used in comparative research, it is often limited to very specific policies, such as the number of working hours or working conditions (Tsebelis 1999). Comprehensive data of this sort is simply unavailable for all the policy areas we investigate.[16] So whether or not outputs should be included in the model as a control variable, there is the practical problem that outputs lack valid, reliable indicators as well as adequate data.

So should outputs be included as a control variable in the model? We argue that there is no substantial loss to the empirical model if we do without them. Employing outputs as a control variable would have helped ensure that outcomes were not incorrectly ascribed to political action, and that a connection existed between the political institutions and actors, and political performance. But such a connection is already ensured by the choice of political goals. We established as criteria for evaluating political performance these goals that guide the choices of political actors (see Chapter 2). Therefore, national governments have accepted responsibility for realizing such goals, and if this minimal requirement is fulfilled, it is irrelevant what specific actions a government takes. We have already noted that political action is not merely present when a government takes on a responsibility to fulfill a particular task; it can also simply be taking over the responsibility to guarantee that it will be done (Hoffmann-Riem 1997). Additionally, governments also make conscious decisions not to act or address an issue, particularly when it is assumed that a goal can be reached best in this fashion. This is particularly characteristic of the liberal ideology about the role of the state that prevails in the US. We therefore start from the premise that the selection of political goals already establishes the minimal connection between political factors (actors and institutions) and outcomes, so no additional attention needs be paid to outputs.

In sum, we can say that in the theoretical model, outputs are causally before outcomes. In the empirical model, however, we can do without the outputs because we are not interested in questions about the effectiveness or efficiency of particular policy programmes. Our model does not intend to evaluate the effectiveness of policy programmes, but is rather an explanatory model for the political performance of liberal democracies *irrespective of means*. Outputs also do not need to be introduced as a control variable in the model since we have already established that governments take on the responsibility to realize outcomes in our conceptualization of political performance.

Finally, we want to point at a possible implication of this model. A policy outcome model might have less explanatory power than a policy output model. This is not only due to the fact that it is more difficult to control outcomes than outputs. It is also because national differences in political outcomes are smaller because nations try to realize the same goals by using the most varied and different means (Castles and McKinlay 1997: 105).

---

[16] If there was adequate information about legal activity, one would have another problem. Since given the differing degree of complexity of laws, the question is whether a simple measure of the number of laws or regulations is a valid indicator of the degree of political activity.

Explanatory model

The goal of the integrated model for explaining the performance of liberal democracies is not only to take the most important competing explanations into account, but also to suggest a coherent theoretical approach that captures the status and interaction of the individual explanatory factors. The object of explanation is the outcome or result of political action, also called performance. The models to explain political performance suggested in the comparative study of democracy have shown themselves to be insufficient, so aspects from other research traditions have had to be borrowed to develop a more appropriate model. The relevant explanatory factors could be found in comparative public policy, as it typically studies the origin and effects of policies. With the help of the veto player approach and the general paradigm of rational choice institutionalism that focuses on the interaction between political institutions and political actors, the interaction of explanatory factors can be conceptualized. The main features of the integrated model are described below.

One can draw a distinction between political and non-political explanatory factors. The former includes political actors and political institutions, the latter socio-economic modernity and economic globalization. The political actors stand at the centre of the explanatory model, with the *government* as the most significant political actor. The most important characteristic of a government understood as a rational actor lies in the policy preferences or *ideological orientations* that guide its actions. A democratic government is limited in its ability to act by three factors: first, the institutional arrangements that can be divided into the governmental system (formal structures) and the relationship between governing and opposition parties (informal structures). The governmental system is characterized by constitutionally defined organs that limit executive autonomy, and the relationship between governing and opposition parties is defined by the parties in executive and in legislature that must agree to government decisions. The more constitutional institutions as well as parties in executive and legislature there are, the less room the government has to act. Second, decision alternatives for the government are structured by the degree of socio-economic modernity, which here primarily implies financial resources available to government in carrying out its decisions. Third, economic globalization places constraints on the ability of government to act.

However, in the theoretical model (Figure 3.7) both socio-economic modernity and economic globalization are seen as only having an effect on outcomes, mediated through the government. This is consistent with their conceptualization as constraints. Basically, direct effects on outcomes are not excluded. Wilensky's (1975) theory of socio-economic determinants of policy, for example, suggested such a direct effect as an alternative to political

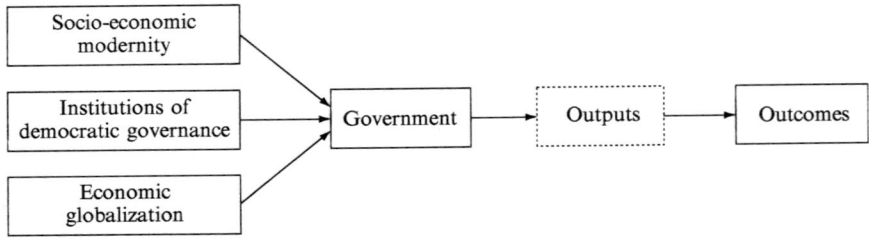

:::: Not considered in the empirical analysis.

FIGURE 3.7. A theoretical model for explaining the
performance of liberal democracies

explanatory factors. Yet, more recent research assumes that the effect of
socio-economic factors can only have an influence when it is mediated
through political factors (Schmidt 1993; Castles 1998a: 301–6). Regarding
economic globalization, the convergence thesis states a direct and the divergence thesis an indirect effect mediated through politics. We find the assumption of divergence theoretically more plausible, and therefore regard
economic globalization as a constraint on government action.

The major difference between this model and that used in comparative
research on democracy (see Figure 3.1) lies in the explicit consideration of
political actors. This is an answer to the critique that it is impossible to
conceive political performance without political actors' behaviour (Schmidt
2000a: 347). Additionally, institutions of democratic governance are divided
into the governmental system and the relationship between governing and
opposition parties. Due to data problems, culture is not included in this
disaggregated explanatory model. However, we try to empirically analyse
the effect of culture on political performance by using the concept of families
of nations (see Table 3.1).

The model suggested here is similar to the standard model of comparative
public policy research, but deviates from it in three respects. One is that
political actors are given a particular role in the explanatory factors. The
actions of the government, as the most important political actor, is influenced or restrained by the other explanatory factors. Another is that an
explicit conceptual distinction is drawn between outputs and outcomes,
even if outputs, as noted, are not addressed in the empirical analysis. Finally,
a broad definition of institution is used that not only includes constitutionally defined institutions (governmental system) but also takes account of the
informal rules that emerge from relatively enduring actor constellations
(relationship between governing and opposition parties).

We noted at the outset that the goal here was to develop a *general* model
for explaining the performance of liberal democracies, and the model should

be applicable to *all* policy areas investigated here. It is in principle quite possible that the explanation for performance in individual policy areas can be improved by taking additional explanatory policy-specific factors into account. The structural arrangement of corporatism might lend additional explanatory power to economic policy performance, or the national welfare state regime might additionally help to explain social policy performance, for example. But because such factors have importance specific to individual policy areas, they are not addressed in this general model.

Some Hypotheses

In this last part of the theoretical analysis we specify the hypotheses to be tested in the empirical analysis. These hypotheses do not refer to performance in general but only to effectiveness as dependent variable and they take only into account institutions of democratic governance as independent variables.

Two types of hypotheses about the influence of political institutions can be found in the literature. The most frequent type ascribes effects to political institutions in terms of the formal characteristic of policies and policy results, either variability or stability of policies (Tsebelis 1995, 2002; Schmidt 1996; Birchfield and Crepaz 1998). The second type assumes political institutions produce differing substantive policy results (Lijphart 1999*a*). The influence of political institutions on a third type, namely the degree of structural balance (or trade-offs) in the policy patterns, is rarely and unsystematically investigated. We thus address these three hypotheses of influence—variability or stability, level, and structural balance—that political institutions might have.

Variability or stability of policies and policy results

We previously discussed three approaches that deal with the influence political institutions have on policy variability or stability: Tsebelis's veto player approach, Birchfield and Crepaz's concept of competitive and collective veto points, and Schmidt's theory of the interaction between governing parties and constitutional structures. All three start from a basic decision-making law, according to which policy stability increases with increasing numbers of actors who participate in decision-making. But this proposition is addressed in quite different ways in the different approaches—and that results in contradictory hypotheses.

Tsebelis (1995, 2002) argues that with increasing numbers of constitutional and partisan veto players, the ability of the polity to react to challenges in its environment by changing its policies decreases. Policy stability and the stability of policy results, increases with increasing numbers of veto players.

In our discussion of Tsebelis, we already noted that constitutional and partisan veto players are treated as functionally equivalent, and that in turn implies this hypothesis applies to both types of negotiation democracies, based on constitutional and informal rules. This general hypothesis is modified in one crucial point by Birchfield and Crepaz (1998), however, as they argue that the two types of negotiation democracies lead to differing results. Policy stability, or maintenance of the status quo, is proposed only for constitutionally defined negotiation democracies—or in their terminology, for democracies with many competitive veto points—while policy change is expected in negotiation democracies based on informal rules, and that have many collective veto points. This is the exact opposite assumption as in Tsebelis.

Schmidt (1996: 175) confines himself to analysing the effects constitutionally defined political institutions. He introduces a further condition that sets it apart from both Tsebelis and from Birchfield and Crepaz. In constitutional majoritarian democracies, policy change only occurs when the governing parties have an unambiguous ideological position with respect to the political decisions on the agenda.

If one then puts the hypotheses about the influence formal and informal political institutions have on the stability or variability of effectiveness together, one finds contradictory if not mutually exclusive assertions:

1. (*a*) Constitutional majoritarian democracies are characterized by a greater variability in political effectiveness than constitutional negotiation democracies (Tsebelis 1995, 2002; Birchfield and Crepaz 1998).
1. (*b*) Constitutional majoritarian democracies are not generally characterized by a greater variability in political effectiveness; variability depends on the policy preferences of the governing parties (Schmidt 1996).
2. (*a*) Informal negotiation democracies are characterized by greater policy stability than informal majoritarian democracies (Tsebelis 1995, 2002).
2. (*b*) Informal negotiation democracies are characterized by greater variability in political effectiveness than informal majoritarian democracies (Birchfield and Crepaz 1998).

The level of political effectiveness
Lijphart (1999*a*) is the most prominent advocate of the thesis that political institutions produce differing substantive policy results. In a first formulation, Lijphart (1994) found that majoritarian and consensus democracies only differed in their degree of representation—in our terminology, in their democratic performance—but showed no differences with respect to effective governing. Lijphart's (1999*a*: 293) later analysis comes to the conclusion not only that the two types of democracies produce different policy results, but even that consensus democracy has 'kinder, gentler qualities'. Since our

discussion of the performance of different democratic types was sparked by Lijphart's assertions, and because in what follows we will not only show certain contradictions between his theoretical interpretation and his empirical findings but that his empirical findings could be interpreted differently, it is helpful to examine his study more closely.

Lijphart (1999*a*: 258) wishes to scrutinize the 'conventional wisdom . . . that there is a trade-off between the quality and the effectiveness of democratic government'. This wisdom holds that consensus democracy may more accurately represent interests, and in particular those of minorities, but that precisely because there is broad participation in decision-making, this form of democracy does not govern effectively. Majoritarian democracy by contrast may only represent the interests of a majority in the population, but because decision-making comes at a lower cost, policymaking is more effective. Lijphart's empirical analyses lead him to conclude that consensus democracies bring more in the way of representation. He finds, for example, that consensus democracies are characterized by a higher parliamentary representation of women than are majoritarian democracies (Lijphart 1999*a*: 280–1).

Lijphart feels he has evidence to contradict the common wisdom that greater representation comes only at the cost of effectiveness. Lijphart (1999*a*: 274) first ascertains that majoritarian democracies are 'not superior to consensus democracies in managing the economy and in maintaining civil peace', which he establishes using indicators for economic growth, inflation, and unemployment for the first, and riots and political deaths for the second (Lijphart 1999*a*: 263–70). Second, he comes to the conclusion that there are even some policy areas in which consensus democracies have a 'significantly better record' than majoritarian democracies do, such as, in fighting inflation on the one hand, and in welfare, environmental, and foreign aid policies on the other (Lijphart 1999*a*: 270, 293–300). He interprets such non-economic policy performance as an expression of the 'kinder, gentler qualities' of consensus democracies that are associated with a strong community orientation and social consciousness, and even calls it 'the more feminine model' of democracy (Lijphart 1999*a*: 293–4).

If we uncritically transfer these results into our conceptual framework, consensus democracies are not only marked by better democratic performance, but Lijphart finds some better results in terms of systemic political effectiveness. Yet, there are at least two cautions here. The first limitation comes from the fact that the differences found between majoritarian and consensus democracies apply only to the executives–parties but not to the federal–unitary dimension (Lijphart 1999*a*: 300–1). There is only a single indicator, the inflation rate, where Lijphart finds an effect of the federal–unitary index. He explains the low inflation rate in power-dispersing systems primarily with the existence of independent central banks: 'the most important reason' why central banks are made independent, he writes, 'is to give them the tools to control inflation' (Lijphart 1999a: 273). Even though Lijphart theoretically predicts the same effects for both of his (sub)-dimensions, he is unsurprised by his findings, and implicitly even corrects his theoretical assumption by stating that 'the conventional wisdom does not concern itself explicitly with the federal–unitary dimension' and focuses on the executives–parties dimension instead (Lijphart 1999a: 272).

The second limitation is of a more methodological nature. Lijphart largely limits his performance analyses to calculating bivariate regression coefficients between his indices for consensus and majoritarian democracies and his performance measures. Though he uses tests of significance for evaluating these coefficients, his criteria are extremely generous: one-tailed tests and 10 per cent levels of significance. But the standard in empirical social research is two-tailed tests when the theories cannot make clear assertions about the direction of the relationship and a maximum 5 per cent significance level.

For that reason we did a re-analysis of Lijphart using more stringent statistical criteria. Taking the *t*-values and number of cases Lijphart presents we identified those bivariate regression coefficients that are significant at the 5 per cent level in a two-tailed test. Under these more severe criteria, it is no longer the case that twenty-five of the twenty-seven regression coefficients indicating the 'kinder, gentler' qualities of consensus democracies remain significant, but only fourteen (see Tables 16.1 and 16.2 in Lijphart 1999a). This reduction by nearly half is considerable, and if one eliminates those that refer to democratic performance (such as the differential satisfaction with democracy of those who support governing or opposition parties), then only seven significant coefficients remain. If one further eliminates those measured with output indicators (such as expenditures for foreign aid as compared to for defence), then only two outcome indicators remain—which measure the degree of socio-economic equality in two different ways.[17]

Employing these harder statistical as well as substantive criteria leaves only a single policy area—social policy—in which consensus democracies are superior to majoritarian democracies along the executives–parties dimension. This finding is interesting inasmuch as it converges with a series of other empirical analyses that have found systematic relationships between social policy indicators and democratic structure (Huber et al. 1993; Schmidt 1997b, 2000a: 347; Birchfield and Crepaz 1998; Crepaz 1998, 2001).[18]

Given this empirical evidence, Lijphart's conclusion in *Patterns of Democracy* that consensus democracies have a better record than majoritarian democracies with respect to performance does seem rather exaggerated. It is

---

[17] Lijphart (1999a: 278) measures the degree of social inequality using the 'rich–poor ratio 1981–93' and the 'decile ratio 1986' from the *LIS* (Atkinson et al. 1995).

[18] It is also true that opposite relationships could be determined for the two types of negotiation democracies, but we will not pursue this issue further here.

more plausible to state a weaker argument, as Lijphart (1994) did in an earlier analysis, that consensus democracies are *no worse* than majoritarian democracies. Given his generous use of significance criteria, and that his earlier work came to a more cautious conclusion, it is hard to avoid the impression that his work is normatively coloured in favour of consensus democracy—and his wording even gives it away: consensus democracy 'should appeal to all democrats' (Lijphart 1999*a*: 293).

Lijphart's original motivation for addressing consociational and consensus democracy was to correct the idealized image of majoritarian democracy that predominated in the American political science literature during the 1950s and 60s (see Almond 1956). In his earlier work, Lijphart was more interested in introducing, developing, and defending consociational or consensus democracies as a second, equivalent type of democracy. In his later work, and particularly in *Patterns of Democracy*, his ambition seems to have increased, to demonstrate that consensus democracies are fundamentally superior to majoritarian democracies. This is clearly evident in what he sees as the practical implications of his findings: 'Because the overall performance record of the consensus democracies is clearly superior to that of the majoritarian democracies, the consensus option is the more attractive option for nations designing their first democratic constitutions or contemplating democratic reform' (Lijphart 1999*a*: 301–2).

Regardless of how sound Lijphart's interpretation of his results is, we are interested particularly in the theoretical question why consensus democracies could produce better performance—if it actually existed. Lijphart himself does not provide any convincing arguments. He situates his work as putting the 'conventional wisdom' in question 'that there is a trade-off between the quality and the effectiveness of democratic government' (Lijphart 1999*a*: 258) and he notes the definitional characteristic that consensus democracies represent a broad array of interests. He then describes the disadvantages of decision-making in majoritarian democracies: fast but not necessarily wise decisions unsupported by a broad consensus (Lijphart 1999*a*: 258–60). Yet, one cannot construct advantages for consensus democracy out of the disadvantages of majoritarian democracies, at least not in such a manner that they would result in 'kinder, gentler' politics or policies.

It is ambitious to want to attribute an ability to produce substantively differing policy results to political institutions, but the theoretical arguments adduced are weak and the empirical result, at least in part, questionable. After critically reviewing his results, we found that that only one policy area remained, social policy, in which a difference still appeared to exist in performance between majoritarian and consensus democracy, and then only on the executives–parties dimension. If one includes the questions we have raised elsewhere about Lijphart's analysis, for example that corporatism is included as a structural characteristic in the executives–parties index or that there are only a few control variables, then the suspicion seems justified that a more scrupulous and sophisticated investigation might find considerably less influence of political institutions on effectiveness, or perhaps no differences at all in the levels of political effectiveness between informal majoritarian and negotiation democracies.

If one takes Lijphart's statements and analyses about the influence formal and informal political institutions have on performance and places them in conjunction with our critical evaluation of his findings, one finds contradictory if not mutually exclusive assertions about the influence of the arrangements of political institutions on the level of political effectiveness:

1. Constitutional negotiation democracies do not differ from constitutional majoritarian democracies in their levels of political effectiveness. The only exception is in the reduction of inflation, where constitutional negotiation democracies perform better (Lijphart 1999*a*).
2. (*a*) Informal negotiation democracies are superior in effectiveness to informal majoritarian democracies particularly in non-economic policy areas, where 'kinder, gentler qualities' come to the fore (Lijphart 1999*a*).
2. (*b*) Informal negotiation democracies are superior to informal majoritarian democracies in only one policy area: social policy.

The structure of political effectiveness (policy patterns)
Because comparative policy research does not have a tradition of simultaneously analysing multiple policy areas, systematic hypotheses as to the effect of political institutions on the structure of political effectiveness, or rather policy patterns, are also lacking. At stake is a formal characteristic, namely the degree of structural balance or trade-offs between different policy areas. Balanced policy patterns exist when the specific goals are not maximized at the cost of other goals. Balance or trade-offs can exist with respect to the relations between individual policy areas as well as with respect to the typology of political effectiveness that simultaneously describes the relationship between all the policy areas investigated here.

The few hypotheses that have been formulated with respect to the typology of political effectiveness have been suggested when explaining individual, nation-specific cases such as the 'American Exceptionalism' or the 'politics of the middle way' in Germany. Yet diametrically opposed effects are asserted as arising from the same kinds of institutional arrangements. Schmidt (1987), for example, regards Germany's *balanced* policy pattern as the result of a constitutionally defined dispersion of power that includes bicameralism and federalism, as well as due to the dominance of coalition governments. Yet King (1973), as well as Amenta and Skocpol (1989), regard the US policy pattern as *imbalanced* due to the constitutionally defined dispersion of power enshrined in the system of 'checks and balances'. This contradiction arises primarily from the fact that the starting point is the respective national policy pattern for which plausible explanations are then sought. We suggest the opposite strategy, and attempt to deduce the impact of the basic principles of constitutional and informal majoritarian and negotiation democracies on the balance of policy pattern.

One can make relatively clear predictions for the majoritarian and negotiation democracies based on informal rules. In informal majoritarian democracies it is primarily the interests of the majority of the citizens that are represented; minority group interests are neglected. The likelihood of an imbalance between different policy areas is thereby enhanced. The opposite is true of negotiation democracies based on informal rules. On the one hand, a broad spectrum of societal interests—especially minorities—is represented in legislature and executive and through a wealth of political parties. On the other hand, parties in government work directly with one another on a daily basis. But of course the ability to act is only possible when they cooperate; the likelihood is thus large that compromise will be sought, and found, in making decisions. Compromise is characterized by concurrent consideration of differing interests. Because the same forum makes many separate political decisions, a balance is also possible over time between interests that consider diverse issues. Accordingly, one can assume finding more balanced policy patterns in informal negotiation democracies than in informal majoritarian democracies.

No such clear hypotheses about balance or imbalance can be formulated for constitutional majoritarian and negotiation democracies. Formal majoritarian democracies have institutional structures that permit interests represented in government to carry out their agendas in a relatively unimpeded fashion. But no predictions can be ventured as to the balance or imbalance in the policy patterns from this, since it is not the constitutional structure that is decisive but rather the party composition of the government. This composition decides whether it is majority interests or a variety of societal interests that are politically represented and that must be taken into account in political decisions.

It is difficult to derive hypotheses about policy pattern balance even for formal negotiation democracies. Goodin's analysis of the 'checks and balances' system in the US (1996), for example, argues that the constitutional separation of powers, in the form of multiple power centres with mutual veto power over one another, means only those policies will be adopted that all the power centres can agree to—so one thus has a system of the smallest common denominator. But what the characteristics of this smallest common denominator are, and whether the policy pattern is balanced or imbalanced, cannot be predicted from this interpretation.

These considerations lead to the following hypotheses about the effect of constitutional and informal political institutions on the policy pattern balance:

1. Constitutional negotiation democracies and constitutional majoritarian democracies do not systematically differ with respect to the balance in policy patterns.
2. Informal negotiation democracies are distinguished from informal majoritarian democracies by more balanced policy patterns.

In sum, it is certainly possible to formulate hypotheses as to the effect of political institutions with respect to the three characteristics of political effectiveness: the level, the development or the stability, and the structure.

What is notable, however, is first that with a single exception (Tsebelis 1995, 2002), different effects are always ascribed to constitutional as opposed to informal political institutions. Second, given the generally shared assumption from decision-making theory that a systematic connection exists between the number of actors who participate in a political decision and the stability of policy, it is surprising just how many contradictory hypotheses have been put forward about the influence of political institutions on policy stability and policy results. Third, the theoretical and empirical basis for the argument that the arrangement of political institutions leads to differing substantive policy results (Lijphart 1999a) is also conspicuously weak. The reason for this weakness might lie in the fact that substantive policy results are to be expected from the formal (and non-substantial) feature of power dispersion. But it is theoretically difficult to imagine varying results coming about solely through formal differences. The hypotheses about the stability or variability in the level of political effectiveness as well as the policy pattern balance are both more restrained and more theoretically consistent than this, since all they predict is that formal features will affect formal characteristics—an aspect we will return to in the discussion of the empirical findings in Chapter 6, the concluding chapter.

SUMMARY

The models to explain political performance employed in the comparative study of democracy have two major problems. They concentrate on political institutions and neglect the political actors who are indispensable—that is, if one wants to explain political action and its consequences. Yet, no consensus exists about the definition of political institutions or which institution will have an effect on political performance. However, there is at least some consistency in definitions in quantitatively oriented empirical analyses. It is established by the indices suggested for measuring the institutional arrangements. These indices include the executives–parties and federal–unitary dimensions Lijphart (1984, 1999a) suggests, and various others (Huber et al.

1993; Colomer 1996; Schmidt 1996; Fuchs 2000) who try to encompass the constitutional structure of democracies. But there are problems here, as some constitutional veto player indices are multidimensional and Lijphart's federal–unitary (sub-) index (1999*a*) has both methodological and conceptual weaknesses.

The theoretical 'Model for Explaining the Performance of Liberal Democracies' that we articulated in this chapter had two parts. The initial part was devoted to developing a concept of institutions of democratic governance, and to suggest indicators with which to measure it. Several stipulations were made in the process. First, the term institution was limited to include only the *rules* that steer the actions of individuals, and to the *political* institutions whose function was to make and implement collectively binding decisions. Second, the governmental system and the relationship between governing and opposition parties were assumed to be the two institutional arrangements of democratic governance from which influences on political performance could be expected. The governmental system was interpreted as formal or constitutionally established rule structures, while the relationship between governing and opposition parties was seen as an informal governing structure that developed out of relatively lasting constellations of participants. Third, based on these categories, four constitutional veto player indices for clearly measuring the governmental system were described: Lijphart's federal–unitary index, Schmidt's institutional constraints of central state government, and Fuchs's minimal governmental system indices A and B. Three partisan veto player indices were suggested to measure the relationship between governing and opposition parties: the simple partisan veto player index, Schnapp's veto players in the lower house, and the number of governing parties. Democracies are often categorized as dichotomies, as in Lijphart's distinction between majoritarian and consensus democracies, but we distinguish between four democratic types: majoritarian or negotiation democracies based on constitutional rules, and majoritarian or negotiation democracies based on informal rules.

An integrated model to explain the performance of liberal democracies was also suggested. It was based on the models developed by comparative public policy research and the veto player approach. Rational choice institutionalism provides the core for our theoretical approach, and according to it, institutions and other macroanalytic factors are seen as constraints on the behaviour of political actors. The executive stands at the heart of our explanatory model, and it is understood in terms of the ideological preferences that guide its actions. Its ability to act, however, is limited both by political institutions—the governmental system as well as the relationship between governing and opposition parties—and by two external factors, the degree of socio-economic modernity, and the level of economic globalization. The outputs of government are causally prior to the outcomes, which themselves in turn constitute policy performance. The empirical model does not include outputs, for reasons we have explained.

Finally, we turn to hypotheses about the effectiveness of institutional arrangements. These have been formulated with respect to three different aspects of effectiveness: level, variability or stability, and policy pattern balance. What they have in common (with one exception) is that they ascribe different effects to constitutional as opposed to informal institutions of democratic governance. Whether these hypotheses are supported by the empirical results will be studied in Chapter 5. In the following chapter, Chapter 4, we first analyse the level, development, and structure of the political effectiveness in western democracies between 1974 and 1995.

Level, Development, and Structure of the Effectiveness of Western Democracies

The empirical analysis has two parts. In this chapter, descriptive questions and hypotheses about the level, development, and structure of political effectiveness in western democracies between 1974 and 1995 are analysed. Chapter 5 is concerned with explanatory questions, where hypotheses about the effects of constitutional and informal institutions of democratic govern- ance regarding these three dimensions of political effectiveness are examined.

The descriptive questions and hypotheses are derived from the general questions we have posed. The first issue is to characterize and compare the investigated nations with respect to the level of their political effectiveness. We are interested not just in the effectiveness specific to the four areas of domestic security, economic, social, and environmental policy, but also in general effectiveness covering all four policy areas. The concept of families of nations (from Castles 1998a) is used as a heuristic to structure these analyses. It is based on the premise that nations with common cultural traditions develop similar political institutions and policy orientations among citizens and politicians, and that these shape political decisions. The result of such similarity is comparable levels of political effectiveness.

The development of political effectiveness is analysed with the help of 'older' (ungovernability and legitimation crisis) and 'newer' (globalization) theories of crisis sketched at the outset of the book. These assert that the 1973 Oil Crisis led to a breakdown in the effectiveness of western democracies. Since then, and increasingly since 1990, the claim is that effectiveness has grown systematically worse due to a diminished capacity on the part of national governments to steer policies. The consequence is an ever-stronger adaptation and thus policy convergence between nations. Hence, what was predicted was not merely deterioration in effectiveness, but also a decrease in variation, both in policy-specific and general effectiveness, between nations. The questions are whether these predicted general trends can be found, or whether they are limited to families of nations, specific nations, or individual policy areas.

The structure of political effectiveness, or the policy patterns, is analysed in order to address three issues. First, we examine the various hypotheses regarding the trade-offs between specific policy areas. In particular, we examine the best known propositions asserting that an effective economic policy is only possible at the cost of an effective social policy and/or an effective environmental policy. The second issue is whether the incompatibility (or tension) between these policy goals has increased from 1974 to 1995, and in particular since 1990, as globalization theory predicted. Third, we investigate what types of political effectiveness have developed in western democracies, whether one can find systematic differences between families of nations, and how stable national policy patterns are over time.

We therefore pursue two different types of questions here: case-oriented questions about nations and families of nations, and variable-oriented questions about the relationship between individual dimensions of effectiveness. First, we discuss the methodological and technical aspects of the empirical analysis, including the data sources and the construction of the performance indices. Then we study the questions regarding the level and development of effectiveness for each selected policy area, and then for general effectiveness. We then turn to questions of policy patterns, trade-offs between policy areas, and more general questions about the structure and types of political effectiveness. We conclude the chapter with a summary of the most important descriptive results for western democracies between 1974 and 1995.

DATA SOURCES AND THE CONSTRUCTION OF THE PERFORMANCE INDICES

In the earlier discussion of the policy-specific models for evaluating effectiveness, fourteen indicators were identified. They provide the basis for investigating the four policy areas: (*a*) domestic security, (*b*) economic, (*c*) social, and (*d*) environmental policy. In what follows, we describe the sources of the data and the selection of the indicators, the strategies used to replace missing data, and the details of constructing the performance indices.

Indicators and data

Table 4.1 lists all fourteen performance indicators, sorted by policy area and component, and giving the data source we have used. The distribution of these indicators by nation and time period, as well as the growth rates between periods are given in Appendix Tables A.1.1 to A.1.14, together with some summary statistics. In order to maximize comparability between indicators, we only use data collected and processed by international organizations or comparative research projects. Ten of the indicators are based on data that come from various statistical series published by the OECD: three economic performance indicators—adjusted GDP, standardized unemployment rate, CPI-based inflation rate (OECD 1986*b*, 1987, 1995*c*; 1999*a*); one

TABLE 4.1. *Indicators and data*

Policy areas	Indicators	Source
Domestic security policy[a]		
(*a*) Violent crime	Murder and manslaughter (per 100,000 residents)	WHO, *World Health Statistics Annual*
	Robbery (per 100,000 residents)	Interpol, *International Crime Statistics*
(*b*) Property crime	Burglary (per 100,000 residents)	
Economic policy		
(*a*) National income	Gross domestic product (adjusted for price and purchasing power, in US dollars per capita)	OECD, *National Accounts*
(*b*) Misery	Standardized unemployment rate	OECD, *Main Economic Indicators*
	Inflation rate (consumer price index)	
Social policy		
(*a*) Health	Infant mortality (per 1,000 live births)	OECD, *Health Data*
(*b*) Income distribution (national minimum)	Poverty rate (below 50 % of the median of equivalent income)	LIS
Environmental policy		
(*a*) Environment	Emissions of sulphur oxides (kg per capita) nitrogen oxides (kg per capita) carbon dioxide (kg per capita)	OECD, *Environmental Data Compendium*
	Municipal waste production (kg per capita)	
	Fertilizer use (tons per square kilometer)	
(*b*) Natural resources	Water consumption (cubic meters per capita)	
Standardization information	Population size (in thousands) Area (in square kilometers)	UN, *Demographic Yearbook*

[a] Protection of life and property only.

health policy indicator—infant mortality (OECD 1998*c*); and six environmental indicators—sulphur oxides, nitrogen oxides, and carbon dioxide emissions, municipal waste production, fertilizer use, and water consumption (OECD 1993, 1995*b*, 1997). The quality of the economic and health policy data can be regarded as good, both according to expert opinion and by how often these data are employed in comparative research. More scepticism is warranted for the quality of the environmental indicators, as both definition and measurement procedures of individual indicators not only vary between nations but even vary over time in some nations (see Binder 1996). Nevertheless, there is consensus in comparative environmental policy research that these environmental data are the best currently available (Crepaz 1995: 407; Jänicke et al. 1996a: 42).

Domestic security policy data comes from two different sources. Murder and manslaughter data come from the WHO's *World Health Statistics*, regarded as the best comparative source for such data (Kalish 1988: 2; Huang and Wellford 1989: 36) while robbery and burglary data are taken from the *International Crime Statistics* published by Interpol. Poverty data are based on the *LIS* using microanalytic household data. Experts regard it as the best available comparative data on income inequality, an evaluation evidently shared by the OECD as it relies on this data in its publications on income distribution (1995a, 1998d). Poverty is defined in relative terms, as an income level below 50 per cent of the average income, with the median of the equivalent income as measure of average income (for details of this poverty definition, now used as an informal standard, see OECD (1998d), the LIS home page, Smeeding 1997, and Smeeding et al. 1990: 58).

All measures, with the exception of two indicators, are standardized with respect to population size or the size of specific population groups, in order that they can be directly interpreted as the per person effects of political action.[1] The exceptions are the inflation rate that measures the yearly growth of the consumer price index, and fertilizer use that employs an areal measure. The UN's *Demographic Yearbook 1969* supplies the standardization information.

A second selection criterion, in addition to data comparability, is completeness: as far as possible, the data series should include all western democracies and the period from 1974 to 1995. Of the twenty-three OECD nations with longer democratic traditions, Iceland and Luxembourg could not be included because too much statistical information was lacking.[2] But data was missing even for the other twenty-one nations: Australia, Austria, Belgium, Canada, Denmark, Finland, France, Germany (up to 1991 West Germany), Great Britain, Greece, Ireland, Italy, Japan, the Netherlands, New Zealand, Norway, Portugal, Sweden, Switzerland, Spain, and the USA. Seven of these nations lacked data for specific indicators: Australia

---

[1] Standardization based on economic performance, as it is used in part in comparative environmental policy research (see OECD 1994), is ignored here because it measures a relationship between policy areas.

[2] As it is, these two nations are often omitted in comparative public policy research and in the comparative research on democracy simply due to their small size (less than half a million residents; see Castles 1998a: 6). Because such nations are 'extremely vulnerable to international influences', their inclusion would have a 'disturbing impact' on the analysis, Lijphart argues (1999a: 263).

(sulphur oxides emissions), Great Britain (municipal waste), Greece (poverty), Italy (burglary), Japan (poverty), New Zealand (poverty, sulphur and nitrogen oxides emissions), and Portugal (poverty). Individual periods of measurement in some nations are also lacking for the domestic security, poverty, and environmental performance indicators. Missing data is one of the basic problems in the comparative analysis of macro data (Gurr 1972), and it is typically addressed with data replacement procedures.

Data replacement and data estimation procedures
The two most frequent data replacement procedures in macroanalytic policy research are interpolation and substitution using the variable mean. Interpolation is used to estimate missing values that lie between two time points (Gurr 1977: 47; Schmidt 1997*b*: 168). Substitution using the variable mean is applied if data is missing for entire cases or nations, as occurs particularly in environmental or poverty indicators. Here missing values are replaced by the average for all other nations for which data exist on the respective indicator (Jahn 1998: 127; UNDP 1998: 28). In both cases, the unknown values are simply replaced by estimated values based on the information available for that variable.[3] We use such data replacement procedures as well, though in part go beyond the typical practices. The following four examples illustrate the various methodological strategies that have been used to substitute for missing values:

- *Missing values between two time points*: Carbon dioxide emission data is missing for the time from 1981 until 1984 for Great Britain (see Table A.1.11), so interpolation was used to estimate it. That is, the values between the available data points in 1980 and 1985 are estimated by means of a linear regression.
- *Missing values at the beginning or end of a time series*: The Interpol data series on robbery only begins in 1977 (see Table A.1.2), and the Canadian data series on sulphur oxides ends in 1994 (see Table A.1.9). In these cases, extrapolations are made on the basis of the longer-term trends in the respective nation.[4] These long-term trends are established with the use of

---

[3] Other data replacement procedures use additional information for estimation. Thus, for estimating environmental performance indicators, one could utilize information about energy or automobile use, or levels of economic development. Newer procedures and programmes to impute missing values use such methods (King et al. 2001; Schafer 2000). These more demanding procedures could not be used here because additional estimation information is missing for most performance variables.

[4] An extrapolation based on short-term trends, that might, for example, include the first or last five years, was not considered because in the case of rather volatile indicators, this would have resulted in extremely distorted trends. Only in the case of Greece was a short-term trend used to estimate values for robbery and burglary indicators at the beginning of the time series because negative values would have resulted from using the long-term trend.

regression analysis, with missing data at the beginning or end of a data series estimated on the basis of the regression coefficient. Thus, an estimation strategy is used that also assumes a linear trend.

- *Missing data for a specific indicator in a nation*: This is the case for the seven nations and five variables listed earlier. Unlike common practice, these values are *not* replaced with the mean value of all other nations in the sample where data exist for this indicator. Instead, the mean value is calculated only for those nations that belong to the same family. The assumption is that due to the many similarities between family of nations this is a better estimate.
- *Only one time point for an indicator is available for a nation*: This is particularly true of data on poverty rates (see Table A.1.8), municipal waste production (see Table A.1.12), and water consumption (see Table A.1.14). In such cases the missing values are based on an extrapolation of longer-term trends in the respective family of nations, which means this method combines the two strategies just described. The assumption is that estimation based on the respective family of nations is superior to one based on all investigated nations.

If one of these types of missing values was found in one of the fourteen indicators, then the same data replacement procedure was employed.

There was only one performance indicator, the standardized unemployment rate, for which a different procedure was used. Here data was missing for certain periods in some nations; the data series for Denmark only begins in 1988, for example (see Table A.1.5). In such cases, the *un*standardized unemployment rate, also published by the OECD, was used instead. While this procedure is not uncommon (Schmidt 1992a: 29; Castles 1998a: 228; Armingeon et al. 1999), it is not always documented. It rests on the assumption that unstandardized data more accurately reflect the actual developments in the respective nations than would estimated data.

The use of these five data replacement procedures is unavoidable if one wants to empirically study the question of effectiveness in western democracies at all. Even when replacement procedures can claim some plausibility, the basic problem remains that these data do not capture actual developments but only estimate them. The only practical, and at the same time, acceptable answer for this problem lies in disclosing and documenting the replacement procedures (see the footnotes to Tables A.1.1–A.1.14 providing the original values for all performance indicators). The most missing values are found in the poverty indicator (see Table A.1.8), but as noted previously, this indicator is the only one which measures the distribution of political goods rather than just their volume. However, for control purposes, the most important analyses are conducted a second time without this particular indicator.

There is an important consequence when one uses such estimation procedures. Because they are based on linear regression, development over time is 'smoothed' in the respective cases. This needs to be taken into account particularly when analysing and interpreting longer-term developments. For performance indicators whose change depends on longer-term factors such as wealth (as in some environmental indicators), this kind of estimation poses no problems. If, however, the indicator is subject to situationally specific fluctuations (as is true for some criminal offences in a few nations), the deviations from the actual developments are likely to be greater.

The construction of performance indices
We are less interested in analysing the fourteen performance indicators than in analysing the broader concepts of policy-specific and general political effectiveness. This requires composite measures. In our discussion of general political effectiveness we examined the principles that govern such composites and came to three decisions. First, the individual indicators and all three indices used—the indices of the policy-specific components, the indices of policy-specific effectiveness, and the global index of general effectiveness—were standardized on a 0 to 100 scale. The end points were set as the best (100) and worst (0) performance over the entire time investigated; a value between these end points immediately indicates a nation's deviation from the best and worst practice, such that 50 means the nation lies exactly in the middle. Second, in constructing these three summary indices, individual parts are equally weighted. Third, the aggregation of the standardized individual indicator values, as well as of the sub-indices, is done with the help of an arithmetic mean. The precise nature, and implications, of the standardization technique deserves discussion.

We already noted that standardization based on best and worst practice is used both in QOL research (Morris 1979), and in studies where benchmarking is used to evaluate policies (Schütz et al. 1998; Mosley and Mayer 1999), as this produces clearer measures than can be achieved with a z-score transformation. It is also superior to a simple ranking of nations (as in Schmidt 1998b: 192), because it is possible to more precisely determine the distance between individual nations. We use the formulae employed in policy benchmarking for standardizing the values. They vary depending upon whether the best practice is specified by a minimum value (e.g. robbery) or a maximum value (e.g. GDP) (Mosley and Mayer 1999: 48):[5]

---

[5] To increase clarity in interpreting these values, we employ 0 and 100 as end points of the scale, unlike Mosley und Mayer (1999: 48) who use 0 and 1.

1. For indicators in which the *minimum* values represent the best practice, then

$$i = 100 - (((\min -x)/\min)^* F)$$

where $F = \min/(\min - \max)^* 100$; $x =$ original value, $i =$ standardized value; if $x = \min$, then $i = 100 - 0 = 100$; if $x = \max$, then $i = 100 - 100 = 0$.

2. For indicators in which the *maximum* values represent the best practice, then:

$$i = 100 - (((\max -x)/\max)^* F)$$

where $F = \max/(\max - \min)^* 100$; $x =$ original value, $i =$ standardized value; if $x = \max$, then $i = 100 - 0 = 100$; if $x = \min$, then $i = 100 - 100 = 0$.

The individual indicators are first standardized using these formulae. For all subsequent levels of aggregation—policy-specific components, policy-specific effectiveness, and general effectiveness—the values are standardized anew such that the respective performance indices will go into the next aggregation with the same weighting. All individual indicators and all three indices are thus measured with a uniform scale from 0 to 100; low values thus always indicate poor effectiveness, and high values always indicate good effectiveness.

There is no question that this indicator is more readily understood than the z-score—commonly used in macroanalytic studies—that measures deviations from the mean in units of standard deviation (Castles and McKinlay 1979; Ricken 1995; Lijphart 1999a). However, there are some questions about the implication of such standardization. Mosley and Engelmann (2000: 20), for example, have drawn attention to the fact that extreme outliers also lead to extremely skewed distributions. So when a nation has extremely high values for criminal offences, as is the case for murder and manslaughter in the USA (see Table A.1.1), the values of all other nations are all shifted upwards. These skewed variables thereby are also given greater weight in composite measures. According to Mosley and Engelmann (2000: 20) one can only reduce this problem with 'more rigorous standardization of the underlying data' as through a z-score transformation. Still, this solution would come at the cost of transparency.

While this objection has some merit, it is less problematic in terms of content. In fact, if there are positive or negative outliers then it is justified to represent the exceptional nature of these nations in the composite measures. More serious is the question whether skewed distributions create statistical problems for subsequent methods of analysis that assume normally distributed variables. This particular objection is mitigated by the fact that we employ regression analysis based on ordinary least squares estimates, which is robust against violations of normality assumption (Pennings et al. 1999: 194).[6]

---

[6] In addition, the most important statistical analyses here were conducted not only with the described performance indices, but also with z-score transformed indices. No systematic deviations could be found between the variables transformed by one method or the other.

LEVEL AND DEVELOPMENT OF POLICY-SPECIFIC AND GENERAL EFFECTIVENESS

A number of questions need to be answered in the following empirical analysis. First, which nations have the best and worst policy effectiveness? Are there systematic differences between the families of nations with respect to effectiveness, either general or policy-specific? Second, has effectiveness in western democracies generally worsened between 1974 and 1995? Or does it vary instead by policy area and nation, or families of nations? Third, did western democracies converge with respect to their effectiveness in this period? Or has this development varied as well by policy area?

The empirical analysis proceeds in three steps. The first is to examine the level and development of effectiveness in the four policy areas of (*a*) domestic security, (*b*) economic policy, (*c*) social policy, and (*d*) environmental policy. Each analysis begins with a short description of the original indicators (the details are documented in the appendix), then the indices of the policy-specific components are described, and at the end the index of policy-specific effectiveness is analysed. In this manner, the most important information about the individual performance indicators is provided in a comprehensible way. At the same time the content and homogeneity of the composite measures are described. The second step analyses the general effectiveness encompassing all the policy areas examined. The third step directly compares the level and development of policy-specific and general effectiveness between time periods (before and after 1990) and among families of nations.

The empirical analyses are uniformly structured. First, the data contained in the tables as to level and development of effectiveness are grouped into the five *families of nations* that Castles proposes (1998*a*), and listed in the order presented in Table 3.1—first English-speaking, then Scandinavian, Continental Western European, Southern European, and the special cases of Switzerland and Japan at the end. These families are optically separated in the tables, and mean values are calculated for each family. With the exception of the special cases the countries within a family are listed alphabetically. The values for Switzerland are presented before those of Japan because the nation has more in common culturally with the other four families than does Japan.

Second, Greece, Portugal, and Spain are not only a cultural family but also have in common that they are all young democracies. Democracy was introduced in Greece by a plebiscite in 1974, a democratic constitution came into force in Portugal in 1976, and the first democratic elections took place in Spain in 1977. Since we investigate the development of effectiveness in democratic systems since 1974, Portuguese effectiveness is only measured as of 1976, and Spanish only after 1977 (Schmidt 2000*a*: 381).

Third, for reasons having to do with content and presentation, some analyses of the development of effectiveness were based on time periods. Since we assume that economic cycles have an influence on effectiveness, these time periods are defined accordingly, and four periods were distinguished: 1974 to 1979, 1980 to 1984, 1985 to 1989, and 1990 to 1995. With one exception, these time periods mirror the way economic cycles are described in comparative policy research (Castles and Dowrick 1990: 180; Hicks and Kenworthy 1998: 1644). The exception is the division of the time from 1980 to 1989 into two periods, undertaken in order that the lengths of the periods remained fairly close.

In all, three aspects of effectiveness were investigated: the level, the development of this level, and the development of differences between the nations. Different statistical measures were used in the analysis of these three dimensions, as follows:

- *Level of effectiveness*:
  A nation's level of effectiveness is studied on the basis of a mean value per time period for a specific performance index. Means are also calculated for each nation and for all families of nations.
- *Development of the level of effectiveness*:
  1. Change in the level of effectiveness is determined by calculating the difference between levels in the first time period (1974–9) and the last time period (1990–5). This measure shows by how many points a nation has risen or fallen with respect to the 0 to 100 performance scale over the entire 1974–95 period. Thus the absolute change in a nation's position, or in the position of a family of nations, is measured on the performance scale.[7]
  2. In addition, the mean absolute *annual* change over the entire time period is determined with the help of the unstandardized regression coefficient b. This coefficient provides information not only about the annual trend but also about its linearity and its statistical significance.
  3. The structure of the development is established with the help of a correlation coefficient that calculates the relationship between the level of effectiveness in the first time period (1974–9) and the change of the level of effectiveness between the first and last periods (see point 1 above). A negative sign indicates that the development can be characterized as one of 'catching-up' on the part of lagging nations (Castles 1998a: 16). A positive sign indicates by contrast, that the difference between the best and worst performing nations has grown larger over the entire period (this coefficient is presented as a correlation in the lower right-hand corner; in Table 4.1 it is −0.02).

---

[7] In addition, in the tables presenting the distribution of the original indicators (see appendix), relative growth is used as an indicator of change.

- *Development of national differences*:
  1. The question of national convergence is measured by the coefficient of variation 'V' (see the row 'V' in the following tables). The advantage of this coefficient over other measures of variance such as the standard deviation is that it is a relative, or standardized, measure of variance rather than an absolute measure. This means that it can be used to directly compare different variables. The coefficient of variation may be obtained by dividing the standard deviation by the arithmetic mean. In other words, the standard deviation is expressed in units of the mean (Wagschal 1999*b*: 115).
  2. To be able to make statements about the stability of the ranking between nations over time (or about 'cross-national variation'; see Castles 1998*a*: 16), the level of effectiveness of the nations at the first time period (1974–9) is correlated with all following time periods.

In addition, the variability or stability of effectiveness per nation over time is measured with a coefficient of variation. This coefficient is also included in the following tables (in the column 'V') but will only be systematically investigated in conjunction with the later causal analysis.

The descriptive analyses are uniformly structured in the same manner for each of the four policy areas and for general effectiveness: first the level, then the development of the level, and finally the development of differences between nations are studied. We are interested in a description of the effectiveness of western democracies, and the hypothesis that these democracies are converging on a low level of effectiveness is investigated. This general hypothesis is specified for each of the policy areas.

Domestic Security Policy

Social disintegration has become increasingly central in arguments during the 1990s about the pernicious influence of economic globalization. The presumption is that globalized markets lead to a dismantling of national welfare states and thus to unfettered capitalism; the consequences can be seen in manifold societal phenomena (Habermas 1998: 68–9; Münch 1998: 9–10), including increased poverty and social inequality, insecurities, anomie, and social exclusions. If one uses a narrower definition of social integration, then it is the illegal acts of members of a society that are the centre of attention. Crime rates can then be interpreted as proximate 'expressions of failing social integration' (Friedrichs 1997; Fuchs 1999: 153).

The level and development of the two basic forms of criminal offences, violent crimes and property crimes, are measured here, the former by murder and manslaughter as well as robbery rates, the latter by burglary rates. These three serious criminal offences were selected because it is more possible to ensure comparability between nations with these indicators than with other crime indicators (Gurr 1977, 1979; Lynch 1995; Kalish 1988). All of these crimes also belong to the core of domestic security.

These three crimes are quite differently distributed. In all nations, increasing frequency is associated with decreasing severity of the crimes, though there is considerable variation between the nations with respect to individual offences. Overall, the frequency increases from the offences of murder and manslaughter (a mean of 1.8 deaths per 100,000 population) through robbery (a mean of 58 offences per 100,000 residents) to burglary (a mean of 1,161 offences per 100,000 residents) (see Appendix Tables A.1.1–A1.3).

The greatest differences between nations are found with respect to *murder and manslaughter*. The USA has the highest level, with 9.4 dead per 100,000 residents, far ahead of Finland (3.0) and Canada (2.2). At the lowest level, with less than 1 dead per 100,000 residents, one finds Ireland, Greece, and Japan. Two facts are noteworthy here, namely the negative outlier position of the USA, and the great similarity in values between all the other nations. The public discussion of the exceptionally high murder rate in the USA often attributes it to specific cultural norms, but international comparative analyses have been able to show that the widespread possession and availability of guns in the USA is an important contributory factor. The likelihood that violent altercations take a deadly turn increases with the diffusion of guns in the population (Gurr 1989: 18; Lynch 1995: 37). Murder and manslaughter crimes in western democracies have risen slightly from an average of 1.7 (1974–9) to 1.9 (1990–5). But this is not a general trend since in seven of the twenty-one nations investigated the situation has actually improved.

For the violent crime of *robbery*, the USA also holds the negative record with 225 cases per 100,000 residents; Spain is in second place with 154 and Canada, with 101 crimes, is in third. Japan (1.7) and Greece (5.3) have the lowest rates. Unlike with murder and manslaughter, however, there has been a distinct increase in the crime of robbery. Between 1974–9 and 1990–5 the number of robberies has nearly doubled, from a mean of 39 across all nations to a mean of 78, a trend that can be observed in every case except Japan.

The performance index *violent crimes* (Table 4.2) aggregates the data on murder and manslaughter as well as robbery into the aforementioned standardized measure that ranks nations by their degree of effectiveness from 0 (worst practice) to 100 (best practice). The USA (13.7) stands, at conspicuous distance, at the bottom of the ranking. The best performance with respect to violent crimes is provided by Japan (98.2), Greece (97.4), Norway (93.6), Switzerland (92.4), Portugal (90.5), and Denmark (90.2). The special cases of

TABLE 4.2. *Violent crimes (performance index[a]) 1974–95*

	Level (mean per period)					Trend		
	1974–9	1980–4	1985–9	1990–5	1974–95	V	Difference	b
Australia	86.4	81.7	81.5	78.8	82.1	0.04	−7.5	−0.44**
Canada	71.9	72.3	75.5	72.9	73.1	0.03	1.0	0.13
Great Britain	90.2	90.0	86.0	83.5	87.4	0.04	−6.8	−0.45**
Ireland	92.1	89.1	90.6	87.8	89.9	0.03	−4.3	−0.23**
New Zealand	94.4	94.3	85.5	83.3	89.3	0.06	−11.1	−0.76**
USA	16.7	13.9	18.0	6.9	13.7	0.48	−9.8	−0.38
	75.3	73.5	72.9	68.9	72.6	0.05	−6.4	
Denmark	95.7	91.4	89.7	84.2	90.2	0.05	−11.5	−0.66**
Finland	80.2	81.2	81.3	78.0	80.1	0.03	−2.1	−0.10
Norway	95.9	93.2	92.8	92.3	93.6	0.02	−3.7	−0.22**
Sweden	89.9	89.2	86.9	83.9	87.4	0.03	−6.0	−0.36**
	90.4	88.8	87.7	84.6	87.8	0.03	−5.8	
Austria	90.4	89.5	90.8	86.5	89.2	0.02	−3.9	−0.19**
Belgium	93.1	87.3	81.8	81.0	85.9	0.07	−12.1	−0.70**
France	87.4	81.5	79.7	75.0	80.9	0.06	−12.4	−0.73**
Germany	90.5	88.4	88.5	84.3	87.9	0.03	−6.2	−0.35**
Italy	91.1	88.4	85.5	80.8	86.4	0.05	−10.4	−0.62**
The Netherlands	93.0	90.8	84.7	77.2	86.3	0.08	−15.8	−1.00**
	90.9	87.6	85.2	80.8	86.1	0.05	−10.1	
Greece	99.4	98.6	97.4	94.2	97.4	0.02	−5.2	−0.31**
Portugal	92.1	92.3	90.7	87.7	90.5	0.05	−4.5	−0.42**
Spain	92.4	82.0	58.1	56.9	69.4	0.25	−35.6	−2.52**
	94.7	91.0	82.1	79.6	85.8	0.09	−15.1	
Switzerland	94.4	92.5	92.8	89.9	92.4	0.02	−4.5	−0.24**
Japan	96.6	97.8	98.8	99.6	98.2	0.01	3.0	0.19**
	95.5	95.2	95.8	94.8	95.3	0.02	−0.7	
All countries	87.33	85.01	82.70	79.28	83.40	0.05	−8.1	−0.47**
V	0.20	0.20	0.21	0.24	0.21			
Correlation with 1974–9		0.99	0.90	0.91			−0.02	

** $p < 0.01$; * $p < 0.05$ (two-tailed).
[a] Values range from 0 to 100 (0 = worst practice … 100 = best practice) from 1974–95. Values are the mean of the standardized variables for murder and manslaughter (see Table A.1.1) and robbery (see Table A.1.2) with subsequent standardization of the mean.
Legend: V = coefficient of variation; difference = difference between 1974–9 and 1990–5; b = unstandardized regression coefficient (OLS-estimate).

Switzerland and Japan show themselves to be particularly effective with respect to violent crimes, in the sense of minimizing violence.

The general trend is that of an increase in violent crimes. Only in Japan and Canada did performance improve by a small amount (by 3 points in

Japan, 1 point in Canada) on the 0 to 100 performance scale. The greatest continuous increase in violent crimes, by far, was seen in Spain, whose position worsened by an average of 2.52 points per year (b) on the performance scale from 92 (1974–9) to 57 (1990–5). At first glance, this development would appear to be one of the effects accompanying the transition from dictatorship to democracy and to increasing affluence. But the increase in violent crimes in the other newer democracies Greece (b = −0.31) and Portugal (b = −0.42) is sufficiently varied that one cannot assume that the increase in violence is a general characteristic of such system transformations.

It is noteworthy that the USA does *not* have the worst performance among property crimes as measured by *burglaries* (see Table A.1.3). With 1,345 burglaries per 100,000 residents, it takes only a middling position: New Zealand (2,211), the Netherlands (2,183) and Denmark (2,072) have the highest values. The lowest values are found in Portugal (88), Norway (109) and Greece (147). Other studies (Lynch 1995: 15) have also noted that the negative outlier role of the USA is limited to violent crimes, and interpret it as a refutation of the 'conventional wisdom' that the nation is the 'most crime-ridden'. For all nations taken together, the mean number of burglaries has risen by 1.5 times, from 909 (1974–9) to 1,366 (1990–5), though one cannot speak of a general trend. In some nations, notably Canada, the USA, Norway, Sweden, Switzerland, and Japan, the situation has actually improved.

The mean annual change reflected in the standardized performance index of *property crimes*[8] (Table 4.3) shows the greatest loss of effectiveness between 1974 and 1995, and thus the greatest increase, in the Netherlands. This nation's position on the performance scale reduces per year by 3.61 points on the scale (b) on average. The level of effectiveness sinks dramatically between the first (75) and last (17) time period investigated; we will discuss this special case in more detail later.

The empirical results based on the *domestic security policy* performance index (Table 4.4) do not contribute much new information beyond the results already discussed for the partial aspects of violent crime and property crime. At this general level, the USA has the worst level of performance (12.4) by a wide margin, followed by the Netherlands (50.1), Finland (50.8), and New Zealand (51.8). The best performance is found in Greece (95.5), Japan (94.5), Norway (93.4), and Portugal (91.6). At this policy-specific level, one can therefore see two families of nations with opposite patterns. In terms of above-average performance, we have the two special cases of Switzerland and Japan. In terms of below-average performance, we find the English-speaking nations, excepting Ireland.

---

[8] The name of the theoretical concept (in this case, property crimes) is used for the standardized performance index (standardized scale from 0 to 100) rather than the indicator name (in this case, burglary), even though, as here, the performance index is based on only a *single* indicator.

TABLE 4.3. *Property crimes (performance index^a) 1974–95*

	Level (mean per period)					Trend		
	1974–9	1980–4	1985–9	1990–5	1974–95	V	Difference	b
Australia	73.2	63.8	53.1	48.0	59.7	0.19	−25.2	−1.60**
Canada	62.9	62.7	65.0	63.2	63.4	0.03	0.3	0.09
Great Britain	69.1	63.0	55.0	45.3	58.0	0.17	−23.8	−1.43**
Ireland	81.0	77.9	78.2	77.4	78.7	0.04	−3.6	−0.21*
New Zealand	59.8	49.0	35.3	33.2	44.5	0.28	−26.6	−1.61**
USA	62.5	63.5	67.2	71.6	66.3	0.07	9.2	0.62**
	68.1	63.3	59.0	56.5	61.8	0.12	−11.6	
Denmark	57.8	50.0	40.0	43.2	48.0	0.16	−14.6	−0.90**
Finland	52.9	52.5	52.1	52.2	52.5	0.01	−0.7	−0.05*
Norway	97.0	97.2	97.2	97.6	97.3	0.00	0.6	0.04**
Sweden	56.1	58.0	57.7	56.4	57.0	0.04	0.3	0.05
	66.0	64.4	61.8	62.4	63.7	0.04	−3.6	
Austria	82.7	79.1	78.7	70.7	77.7	0.06	−12.1	−0.68**
Belgium	89.4	84.1	84.8	76.9	83.8	0.08	−12.5	−0.74**
France	88.7	83.4	82.1	80.4	83.7	0.04	−8.3	−0.48**
Germany	70.4	64.6	53.1	52.3	60.2	0.14	−18.1	−1.19**
Italy	81.2	73.5	66.2	59.5	70.1	0.13	−21.7	−1.34**
The Netherlands	74.8	56.0	32.5	17.3	45.2	0.55	−57.5	−3.61**
	81.2	73.5	66.2	59.5	70.1	0.14	−21.7	
Greece	100.0	98.6	94.9	91.9	96.3	0.04	−8.1	−0.51**
Portugal	98.1	97.8	98.2	97.3	97.8	0.01	−0.8	−0.07
Spain	96.0	84.7	69.3	76.2	79.7	0.13	−19.8	−1.17**
	98.0	93.7	87.5	88.5	91.3	0.06	−9.6	
Switzerland	74.1	74.3	74.7	74.4	74.4	0.01	0.4	0.05
Japan	93.2	93.7	94.4	95.2	94.1	0.01	2.0	0.12**
	83.7	84.0	84.6	84.8	84.3	0.01	1.2	
All countries	77.19	72.74	68.09	65.73	70.88	0.09	−11.5	−0.65**
V	0.20	0.22	0.29	0.33	0.24			
Correlation with 1974–79		0.95	0.80	0.73			0.05	

** $p < 0.01$; * $p < 0.05$ (two-tailed).
^a Values range from 0 to 100 (0 = worst practice . . . 100 = best practice) from 1974–95. Values are the standardized variables for burglary (see Table A.1.3).

Legend: V = coefficient of variation; difference = difference between 1974–9 and 1990–5; b = unstandardized regression coefficient (OLS-estimate).

The overall averages show effectiveness in this policy area has worsened over the entire time period. It is largest, by a considerable margin, for the Netherlands (b = −3.37) and Spain (b = −2.69); we have already noted that the former nation was a negative outlier in property crime, and the latter

TABLE 4.4. *Domestic security policy (performance index^a) 1974–95*

	Level (mean per period)					Trend		
	1974–9	1980–4	1985–9	1990–5	1974–95	V	Difference	b
Australia	70.6	60.3	52.4	46.7	57.6	0.18	−23.9	−1.49**
Canada	52.4	52.7	56.7	53.4	53.7	0.06	1.0	0.16
Great Britain	70.4	65.8	57.1	48.1	60.2	0.16	−22.4	−1.38**
Ireland	80.5	76.0	77.3	74.7	77.2	0.04	−5.8	−0.32**
New Zealand	66.7	58.7	42.3	39.1	51.8	0.24	−27.5	−1.73**
USA	11.9	10.5	16.2	11.4	12.4	0.45	−0.5	0.17
	58.7	54.0	50.3	45.6	52.2	0.14	−13.2	
Denmark	66.2	57.4	48.8	47.1	55.0	0.15	−19.1	−1.14**
Finland	51.2	51.7	51.5	49.2	50.8	0.03	−2.1	−0.11*
Norway	95.0	93.1	92.8	92.8	93.4	0.01	−2.2	−0.13**
Sweden	60.7	61.5	59.7	56.5	59.5	0.04	−4.2	−0.23**
	68.3	65.9	63.2	61.4	64.7	0.05	−6.9	
Austria	80.5	77.2	77.8	68.8	75.9	0.06	−11.6	−0.64**
Belgium	87.3	79.2	75.7	69.4	78.0	0.10	−17.9	−1.05**
France	82.7	74.5	72.2	67.5	74.3	0.09	−15.1	−0.89**
Germany	71.6	65.8	57.5	53.8	62.2	0.13	−17.8	−1.12**
Italy	79.9	72.3	64.8	56.5	68.4	0.14	−23.4	−1.43**
The Netherlands	76.6	61.2	39.7	23.0	50.1	0.46	−53.5	−3.37**
	79.8	71.7	64.6	56.5	68.1	0.14	−23.2	
Greece	99.7	98.1	94.5	90.0	95.5	0.04	−9.7	−0.60**
Portugal	93.0	92.9	92.0	89.1	91.6	0.04	−3.8	−0.35*
Spain	91.7	75.8	47.1	51.2	63.0	0.31	−40.5	−2.69**
	94.8	88.9	77.9	76.8	83.3	0.11	−18.0	
Switzerland	77.1	75.9	76.4	74.1	75.8	0.02	−3.0	−0.14**
Japan	92.7	93.9	95.1	96.4	94.5	0.02	3.6	0.23**
	84.92	84.91	85.76	85.23	85.19	0.02	0.3	
All countries	74.20	69.25	64.17	59.94	66.71	0.11	−14.3	−0.82**
V	0.26	0.28	0.32	0.37	0.29			
Correlation with 1974–9		0.97	0.79	0.77			−0.19	

** $p < 0.01$; * $p < 0.05$ (two-tailed).
^{a} Values range from 0 to 100 (0 = worst practice . . . 100 = best practice) from 1974–95. Values are the mean of the standardized variables for violent crimes (see Table 4.2) and property crimes (see Table 4.3) with subsequent standardization of the mean.
Legend: V = coefficient of variation, difference = difference between 1974–9 and 1990–5; b = unstandardized regression coefficient (OLS-estimate).

nation for violent crimes. Only three nations deviate from this general negative trend: in Japan, the situation has minimally improved, while in both Canada and the USA no linear trend appears to exist, since criminality increased until 1985–9 and then began decreasing.

The number of criminal offences has continually increased from 1974 to 1995 in all the nations examined here, with the exception of Japan, Canada, and the USA. There appears to be no specific pattern, however, as it is neither the case that nations are (negatively) 'catching up', nor does it seem to be the case of a further worsening on the part of the (worst) performers—as the correlation coefficient ($r = -0.19$) between the level of the first time period and the difference between first and last time periods indicates. Effectiveness has diminished, but against what one might expect, the nations have not converged at a lower level.

In fact, the tendency has been for the nations to become even more dissimilar. The coefficient of variation increases from 0.20 (1974–9) to 0.24 (1990–5) for violent crimes and even from 0.20 to 0.33 for property crimes; for domestic security policy, it is an overall increase from 0.26 to 0.37. This increasing divergence can be traced back to the fact that criminality has dramatically increased in certain nations, particularly Spain and the Netherlands, indicating that domestic security is not just influenced by general factors but also by nation-specific factors, which in turn is relevant for the variance between nations.

It is also noteworthy that the national ranking only changes marginally for violent crimes (the correlations over time are all over 0.90) but that there is much greater variation for property (the correlations decrease continuously over time from 0.95 to 0.73). This can be interpreted as meaning that violent crimes, particularly murder and manslaughter, are a relatively stable national characteristic, while property crimes are to a far greater degree influenced by nation-specific factors.

If one excludes Japan, Canada, and the USA for the moment, then it would seem at first glance that the social disintegration processes predicted by the crisis theory are confirmed by the data. But to place this negative development in perspective, one should remember that crime rates, and particularly property crimes, were rising continuously from 1945 through 1974 in both the USA and Europe (Gurr 1977). Switzerland and Japan were already positive and special in this earlier period; Swiss property crime rates were relatively stable and Japanese rates even went down. Thus, if the negative development we note did not first begin with the economic recession in 1973, then other and longer-term factors must be responsible for a process that has lasted since 1945.

Criminology has suggested two different clusters of factors—motivations and opportunities—which can explain the level and development of crime rates (Cohen and Felson 1979; Lynch 1995). Among the motivating factors, one can count the relative size of delinquency-prone groups, the proportion of young men in the population, and how widespread unemployment and poverty are (Gurr 1989: 15). The opportunities include such diverse aspects as the increase in private property, the availability of weapons, and how well organized crime prevention is. In this framework, the general increase in property crimes in western democracies is interpreted as an increase in opportunities that come about because more private property is acquired as wealth continues to rise (Gurr 1977: 73). This standard explanation also fits with the data we present here, inasmuch as property crime frequency— specifically burglary and robbery, where robbery is both a property and a violent crime—has increased significantly between 1974 and 1995, while the pure violent crimes of murder and manslaughter have barely increased.

Economic Policy

Our study begins after the end of the 'golden age of the post-war era' in western industrial societies that lasted from 1950 until 1973 (Maddison 1991: 1). The end of this era of unprecedented increase in wealth was most clearly marked by the changes in economic performance: a significant slowing of economic growth, increasing unemployment, and rising inflation rates (Maddison 1991, 1995). The collapse of the Bretton Woods system of fixed exchange rates that had provided a stable economic environment during the 'golden age', the 'Oil Shock' of a twelve-fold increase in the price of crude oil, and the subsequent price increases in other products that the Oil Shock unleashed, were all seen as contributory factors for this sharp change in performance (Maddison 1991: 132).

In the meantime, there is growing agreement that this also ushered in the era of increasing interdependence of national economies, accelerating the process of economic globalization. If the 'golden age' was marked by a growing convergence between western industrial societies, then the period since 1974 has been a new phase of economic divergence. Nations experienced the economic recession differently, and responded in different ways and at different speeds to it. The economic performance of western democracies since 1973 has often been documented and analysed (Maddison 1991, 1995; Scharpf 1991; Cusack 1995; Castles 1998a). In the following, we briefly summarize the key aspects of the level and development of economic performance for all three components: national income, full employment, and price stability, whereby the last two are combined into a component that, like its corresponding index, is designated as misery.

The national income is measured, in US dollars, by *GDP* per capita adjusted for price and purchasing power. This measure differs from others commonly utilized, inasmuch as it can be used for longitudinal as well as for cross-national comparison because it employs purchasing power parity exchange rates.[9] The mean for all nations is an income of $11,676 per capita

---

[9] The first to develop such a GDP-measure suited to cross-national comparison were Summers and Heston (1991); they published it in the context of the *Penn World Table* dataset. The

(see Table A.1.4). The USA shows the highest value, at $16,440, but it no longer occupies the dominant position it did during the 1950s and 1960s (Maddison 1995: 22). Switzerland, at $15,670 mean per capita income, already takes second place, followed by Canada at $13,597. Norway is close behind, at $13,132, its wealth primarily due to oil production and export. The poorest nations are in southern Europe—Greece ($7,098), Portugal ($7,240), and Spain ($9,159)—though Ireland ($8,179) also provides them company.

GDP has increased by a factor of three in all western democracies, from a mean of $5,887 (1974–9) to $17,676 (1990–5). The annual mean increase, as given in Table 4.5, is again the highest for the USA (b = 4.04), soon followed by Japan (b = 3.79), Switzerland (b = 3.78) and Norway (b = 3.74); Greece (b = 1.86) has the lowest value. The level of wealth in the richer nations has markedly increased in comparison with the poorer ones, as can be seen in the correlation between the first period and the subsequent growth (r = 0.74).[10] Correspondingly, there has been little change in the ranking between the nations over the entire time period (the correlation has diminished from 0.98 to 0.89). The finding that national divergence has significantly decreased, from 0.42 (1974–9) to 0.23 (1990–5), is particularly arresting since it indicates that the development of national income is clearly deviating from the predicted general trend: Nations are not converging on a low but rather on a higher level of effectiveness.

The standardized *unemployment rate* that measures the number of unemployed in relation to the working population is on average 6.8 per cent (see Table A.1.5). Switzerland (1.1 per cent) has the lowest rate, followed by Japan (2.3 per cent), Austria (3.0 per cent), Norway (3.3 per cent), and Sweden (3.4 per cent). Two of the poorest nations, Spain (16.8 per cent) and Ireland (12.3 per cent), have the highest unemployment rates. On average, in all nations, the unemployment rate has nearly doubled (from 4.4 to 8.4 per cent), with only the USA and Portugal providing the exceptions to this negative trend.

The *inflation rate*, measured on the basis of the consumer price index,[11] showed a mean of 7.8 per cent for the period under investigation (see Table A.1.6). Germany's inflation rate (3.5 per cent) was the lowest—its tight fiscal policy is often explained with reference to the experience of hyper-inflation

OECD has since then made such a measure available in the context of their *National Accounts*, and covering the time since 1970.

[10] However, there is a catching-up in terms of *relative* rates of growth; that is, the growth rates in the poorer nations are distinctly higher than in the richer nations.

[11] The consumer price index measures price increases that comprise about 60 per cent of the economic activities contained in GDP. The alternative measure, the GDP deflator, is more comprehensive (OECD 2000). However, because government policy is primarily oriented toward the CPI, this measure was selected (Schmidt 1982: 207).

TABLE 4.5. *National income (performance index^a) 1974–95*

	Level (mean per period)					Trend		
	1974–9	1980–4	1985–9	1990–5	1974–95	V	Difference	b
Australia	14.6	30.6	45.8	62.0	38.2	0.51	47.4	2.97**
Canada	18.5	37.1	55.5	70.8	45.4	0.47	52.3	3.29**
Great Britain	12.9	27.4	43.9	58.9	35.8	0.53	46.1	2.90**
Ireland	3.8	14.5	24.2	48.0	22.9	0.80	44.2	2.72**
New Zealand	13.0	27.5	39.0	50.4	32.4	0.47	37.4	2.34**
USA	25.1	46.5	67.5	89.7	57.2	0.46	64.6	4.04**
	14.6	30.6	46.0	63.3	38.7	0.52	48.7	
Denmark	15.7	33.1	50.6	70.6	42.6	0.53	54.9	3.44**
Finland	11.1	28.2	44.3	56.0	34.8	0.53	44.9	2.81**
Norway	13.9	33.7	51.9	74.2	43.5	0.56	60.3	3.74**
Sweden	16.2	33.3	49.2	61.3	39.9	0.46	45.0	2.81**
	14.3	32.1	49.0	65.5	40.2	0.52	51.3	
Austria	13.6	31.1	45.5	67.3	39.4	0.55	53.7	3.31**
Belgium	14.4	31.5	45.4	68.7	40.1	0.54	54.2	3.34**
France	16.4	34.1	48.5	67.1	41.5	0.49	50.7	3.12**
Germany	12.8	29.1	43.9	65.6	38.0	0.56	52.7	3.26**
Italy	12.2	29.2	44.4	63.6	37.4	0.55	51.4	3.17**
The Netherlands	14.9	29.7	43.3	62.9	37.8	0.51	48.1	2.98**
	14.1	30.8	45.2	65.9	39.1	0.53	51.8	
Greece	4.0	13.8	21.5	34.0	18.4	0.66	30.0	1.86**
Portugal	2.9	10.6	19.2	36.5	19.0	0.71	33.6	2.25**
Spain	9.0	16.9	27.5	43.8	27.0	0.51	34.8	2.42**
	5.3	13.8	22.7	38.1	21.4	0.61	32.8	
Japan	11.8	29.4	46.9	73.3	40.6	0.61	61.5	3.79**
Switzerland	23.6	44.9	62.3	85.1	54.0	0.46	61.5	3.78**
	17.7	37.1	54.6	79.2	47.3	0.52	61.5	
All countries	13.36	29.15	43.83	62.37	37.43	0.53	49.0	3.04**
V	0.42	0.31	0.28	0.23	0.26			
Correlation with 1974–79		0.98	0.96	0.89			0.74	

** $p < 0.01$; * $p < 0.05$ (two-tailed).
^{a} Values range from 0 to 100 (0 = worst practice ... 100 = best practice) from 1974–95. Values are the standardized variables for gross domestic product (see Table A.1.4).

Legend: V = coefficient of variation; difference = difference between 1974–9 and 1990–5; b = unstandardized regression coefficient (OLS-estimate).

during the Weimar Republic in the 1920s as well as the currency reform in 1948 (Schmidt 1989: 68)—along with Switzerland (3.5 per cent) and Japan (4.3 per cent). Greece (17.4 per cent), Portugal (16.3 per cent), and Spain (10.3 per cent), along with Italy (11.1 per cent), showed the highest inflation rates. Unlike the unemployment rate, the inflation rate in western democracies has markedly reduced since the 1973 economic recession, falling by nearly two-thirds from 11.7 to 4.1 per cent overall. This positive trend can be seen in all nations. Even though the unemployment and inflation rates have moved in opposite directions since 1974, they have one great similarity—the correlation of the national ranking between the time periods is nearly identical, falling from 0.85 to 0.55 for the unemployment rate, and 0.86 to 0.55 for the inflation rate (see Tables A.1.5 and A.1.6). Compared with all other investigated indicators, these are the two dimensions of effectiveness with the largest variability in ranking between nations over the entire period.

The misery performance index aggregates unemployment and inflation rates, with the name—but not its construction—taken from its origins in the 'misery index' that sums together the national unemployment and inflation rates. The performance index is constructed in the same manner as all the other indices, that is, first the unemployment and inflation rates are standardized in a 0 to 100 scale and then an arithmetic mean is calculated. Families of nations only partly evident at the level of the individual performance indicators can thereby be discerned at the level of this composite measure (Table 4.6).

The best practice is found among the special cases of Switzerland and Japan, while the worst is among the southern European family together with Ireland. However, there is *no* continuous development at this more general level that combines unemployment and inflation rates. Given that these two rates developed in opposite directions over the entire time period, this is hardly astonishing. On average across all nations, the economic situation worsened between 1974–9 and 1980–4, but became better in the following time period (1985–9) and remained stable subsequently. No uniform trend is evident at the level of the individual nations either. The only noteworthy nation was Portugal, with an above-average positive annual trend (b = 3.22), but in all other nations, the development was not nearly as linear. Unlike national income, one can see a catching-up process in the misery dimension: economic performance between 1974 and 1995 has improved particularly in those nations that directly experienced this slump (r = −0.52).

As a final step, the standardized performance indices of national income and misery are integrated into a general measure of *economic policy*, as seen in Table 4.7. Switzerland has, by a considerable margin, the best performance value (79.5), followed at a comparably high level by Japan (68.7), the USA (67.6), and Austria (66.9). Spain (26.6), Greece (32.5), Portugal (32.7), and Ireland (34.2) have the worst values. Here, too, the special cases show the best and the southern European family shows the worst performance. By including national income, economic performance increases by an average, across all nations, of 40 to 70 points on the scale. The nation with the highest average annual increase is Portugal (b = 3.04), closely followed by the USA

TABLE 4.6. *Misery (performance index^a) 1974–95*

	Level (mean per period)					Trend		
	1974–9	1980–4	1985–9	1990–5	1974–95	V	Difference	b
Australia	57.3	56.7	59.6	64.2	59.6	0.09	6.8	0.46**
Canada	57.4	49.8	63.7	63.2	58.7	0.12	5.8	0.55*
Great Britain	49.5	47.6	57.9	62.5	54.5	0.17	13.0	1.02**
Ireland	42.3	28.9	40.5	49.4	40.8	0.24	7.1	0.67*
New Zealand	68.1	60.1	60.0	67.8	64.4	0.11	−0.2	0.09
USA	60.5	57.8	74.1	73.7	66.6	0.13	13.2	1.06**
	55.9	50.2	59.3	63.5	57.4	0.14	7.6	
Denmark	57.6	48.8	72.0	70.2	62.3	0.17	12.6	1.03**
Finland	58.5	63.3	75.3	56.9	63.0	0.16	−1.5	0.03
Norway	76.7	70.7	77.8	78.6	76.1	0.07	1.9	0.28
Sweden	73.9	69.2	82.5	69.6	73.6	0.09	−4.4	−0.03
	66.7	63.0	76.9	68.8	68.7	0.12	2.1	
Austria	82.8	79.8	86.8	83.5	83.2	0.04	0.7	0.18
Belgium	62.3	51.2	66.4	69.8	62.8	0.13	7.5	0.63*
France	62.9	50.8	61.7	61.7	59.5	0.09	−1.1	0.09
Germany	81.8	74.1	79.5	74.0	77.4	0.07	−7.8	−0.39*
Italy	41.7	39.0	57.1	57.4	48.9	0.21	15.7	1.15**
The Netherlands	69.9	63.7	75.7	75.8	71.4	0.09	5.9	0.53*
	66.9	59.8	71.2	70.4	67.2	0.10	3.5	
Greece	58.4	32.6	37.4	38.6	42.3	0.32	−19.8	−0.82
Portugal	18.8	23.7	50.5	65.5	42.0	0.53	46.7	3.22**
Spain	33.3	19.1	20.2	23.5	23.0	0.40	−9.8	−0.40
	36.8	25.1	36.0	42.5	35.8	0.42	5.7	
Switzerland	92.7	91.1	96.1	85.7	91.2	0.06	−7.0	−0.23
Japan	73.1	86.2	92.1	91.2	85.3	0.13	18.2	1.27**
	82.9	88.6	94.1	88.5	88.3	0.10	5.6	
All countries	60.93	55.43	66.04	65.85	62.22	0.14	4.9	0.39**
V	0.29	0.35	0.28	0.24	0.27			
Correlation with 1974–9		0.91	0.80	0.67			−0.52	

** $p < 0.01$; * $p < 0.05$ (two-tailed).
^{a} Values range from 0 to 100 (0 = worst practice … 100 = best practice) from 1974–95. Values are the mean of the standardized variables for standardized unemployment rate (see Table A.1.5) and inflation rate (see Table A.1.6) with subsequent standardization of the mean.

Legend: V = coefficient of variation; difference = difference between 1974–9 and 1990–5; b = unstandardized regression coefficient (OLS-estimate).

(2.83), and Japan (2.81). Greece (b = 0.57) has by far the lowest average annual increase.

The various predictions of loss of effectiveness in western democracies were strongly influenced by the post-1973 economic dynamics, and were

TABLE 4.7. *Economic policy (performance index^a) 1974–95*

	Level (mean per period)					Trend		
	1974–9	1980–4	1985–9	1990–5	1974–95	V	Difference	b
Australia	38.7	47.3	57.3	68.9	53.1	0.24	30.1	1.90**
Canada	41.0	47.1	65.0	73.2	56.6	0.25	32.3	2.14**
Great Britain	33.5	40.4	55.3	66.2	49.0	0.30	32.8	2.17**
Ireland	24.4	22.9	34.7	52.9	34.2	0.40	28.5	1.88**
New Zealand	43.8	47.4	53.8	64.4	52.5	0.18	20.6	1.35**
USA	46.3	56.8	77.4	89.5	67.6	0.28	43.2	2.83**
	38.0	43.7	57.3	69.2	52.2	0.27	31.2	
Denmark	39.6	44.3	66.9	77.0	57.1	0.30	37.5	2.48**
Finland	37.5	49.6	65.2	61.5	53.1	0.23	24.1	1.58**
Norway	49.1	56.7	70.9	83.6	65.2	0.23	34.5	2.23**
Sweden	48.9	55.7	71.9	71.5	61.8	0.18	22.6	1.54**
	43.8	51.6	68.7	73.4	59.3	0.23	29.6	
Austria	52.3	60.4	72.3	82.5	66.9	0.19	30.2	1.94**
Belgium	41.4	44.7	60.8	75.7	55.9	0.27	34.2	2.20**
France	42.8	45.9	60.0	70.3	54.9	0.22	27.5	1.78**
Germany	51.4	56.1	67.3	76.3	62.9	0.17	24.9	1.59**
Italy	28.7	36.7	55.1	66.0	46.7	0.34	37.3	2.40**
The Netherlands	45.9	50.7	64.9	75.9	59.5	0.22	30.0	1.95**
	43.8	49.1	63.4	74.5	57.8	0.23	30.7	
Greece	33.5	24.6	31.5	39.1	32.5	0.25	5.6	0.57**
Portugal	10.9	17.9	37.5	55.5	32.7	0.59	44.6	3.04**
Spain	22.3	18.8	25.3	36.2	26.6	0.32	13.9	1.12**
	22.2	20.4	31.4	43.6	30.6	0.39	21.4	
Switzerland	63.4	74.3	86.8	93.7	79.5	0.16	30.3	1.97**
Japan	45.9	63.0	76.0	90.2	68.7	0.27	44.2	2.81**
	54.7	68.7	81.4	91.9	74.1	0.21	37.2	
All countries	40.06	45.78	59.81	70.00	54.14	0.25	29.9	1.9**
V	0.29	0.32	0.27	0.22	0.25			
Correlation with 1974–9		0.94	0.85	0.78			0.01	

** $p < 0.01$; * $p < 0.05$ (two-tailed).
^{a} Values range from 0 to 100 (0 = worst practice ... 100 = best practice) from 1974–95. Values are the mean of the standardized variables for national income (see Table 4.5) and misery (see Table 4.6) with subsequent standardization of the mean.

Legend: V = coefficient of variation; difference = difference between 1974–9 and 1990–5; b = unstandardized regression coefficient (OLS-estimate).

often formulated amidst that crisis. But our analysis of the central economic dimensions of performance corrects an all too simplistic view of this development: the 'golden age', with its above-average economic growth, may have come to an end, but wealth has continued to rise in western democracies since

1974, if at a less steep rate. The dramatic rise in inflation that was part of the new era after the Oil Crisis seems to have been alleviated in most nations by the mid-1980s; only in Greece does one still find an above-average inflation rate in the 1990s. The only dimension that develops negatively is the unemployment rate; with the exception of the USA and Portugal, it has continuously worsened since 1974. Unemployment is thus the characteristic negative aspect of the new age.

Social Policy

1973 was a turning point in western democracies not just for economic policy but also for social policy. Economic recession had negative effects on welfare state programmes and expenditures since it led to a reduction of government resources for such purposes. In the earlier 'golden age', welfare states continued to expand, but after 1973, this trend slowed. At various times and to various degrees, western democracies responded to tighter financial resources with cuts in benefits and the dismantling of welfare state programmes. Though there is disagreement about how to characterize the degree of policy change—whether only incremental adjustment, as some (Pierson 1996; Garrett 1998; Stephens et al. 1999) argue, or a more radical change (Clayton and Pontusson 1998)—there is at least agreement that a new phase of restructuring and dismantling the welfare state began after the mid-1970s. Many feel that this process has only intensified since the 1990s with increasing economic globalization (Beisheim and Walter 1997; Habermas 1998; Münch 1998; Zürn 1998).

There is a widespread argument that holds that the openness of economies and the accompanying capital mobility exerts pressure to lower sociopolitical standards, as in this fashion one can increase national economic competitiveness (Beisheim and Walter 1997). This process of 'social dumping', it is further argued, leads to race to the bottom as all try to underbid each other. The result is that western democracies then end up converging on a lower welfare state level (Alber and Standing 2000). All such theories and hypotheses as to the restructuring or dismantling of the welfare state at least implicitly assume that such changes or reforms go hand-in-hand with corresponding losses of effectiveness. Yet since the majority of the relevant empirical studies focus on analysing welfare state outputs, the question remains open to what extent benefit cuts and programme dismantling actually leads to the assumed effectiveness losses. Our analyses of welfare state performance since 1974 can provide the first answer.

Available data unfortunately limit our consideration to only two components of social policy: health and income distribution (national minimum). Health is measured by infant mortality per 1,000 live births, or in other words, the proportion of infants who die within a year of their birth

(OECD 1998*c*). The national minimum is measured by the poverty rate, defined by the proportion of persons who live in a household whose income lies under the poverty level (Smeeding et al. 1990). The poverty level is set as under 50 per cent of the average income, itself defined by the median of equivalent income. The poverty level defined this way has become an informal standard in international comparative research, and this relative measure, based on a concept of the 'economic distance of the individual income earner to the average citizen' is based on the following definitions and methodological choices (Smeeding et al. 1990; Kohl 1992; Förster 1994):

- Income is defined as the income still available to a household *after* subtraction of taxes and transfer of benefits. A household is thus only poor if it remains under the poverty level even after benefits have been accounted for.
- The individual economic well-being (equal to the equivalent available income) is determined based on the available household income, weighted with the help of an equivalence scale that takes differing size of households, or number of persons in a household, as well as their composition (parents, children) into account.[12]
- The income of the average citizen is determined based on the median equivalent income, since the arithmetic mean is readily skewed upward by the presence of a few extremely high incomes. In an income distribution skewed to the left, the arithmetic mean is normally higher than the median. Using a median as the basis leads to a more cautious estimation of the poverty level (Kohl 1992: 279).

At this juncture, it should again be reminded that this measure of income distribution is only one that reflects a *minimum standard of living* for the members of the society. A more radical interpretation involving flattening income differences cannot be used as a criterion for evaluating the performance of western democracies because 'the Model for Evaluating Effectiveness in Liberal Democracies' is limited to those criteria about which there is a consensus.

The concept of families of nations is also used here as a heuristic for describing differences between nations. In the context of the welfare state, these families have a meaning that goes beyond their cultural similarities, as they also group different welfare states together. That is, the families more or less reflect the different types of welfare state regimes as they have been proposed in comparative welfare state research (Castles 1998*a*: 319). There, differences have been drawn between liberal welfare states of the

---

[12] The *LIS* uses the following formula: $W = D/S^e$, where W = economic well-being or 'adjusted' income (equivalent available income), D = disposable household income, S = household size, and e is a coefficient of elasticity that accounts for economies of scale and equals 0.5.

Anglo-Saxon type, Scandinavian social democratic welfare states, and the conservative welfare states of Continental European nations (Esping-Andersen 1990). Newer studies add an additional type of 'Latin Rim' or southern European welfare states (Leibfried 1992; Bonoli 1997) that includes not only the family we have noted but also Italy. These types vary primarily in their degree of decommodification (the independence of market participation to uphold a socially acceptable standard of living), stratification (the levelling of inequalities), and the welfare mix (the role of the state relative to other producers of welfare such as the market or the household). Given the convergence between the 'families of nations' typology of Castles (1998a) and the 'worlds of welfare capitalism' of Esping-Andersen (1990), in what follows we can analyse at least indirectly the effectiveness of different welfare state regimes (see Schmidt 1998b; Goodin et al. 1999; Kohl 1999).

The key characteristic of the health indicator *infant mortality* is not just that it distinguished between highly developed and underdeveloped nations, but also that it can distinguish within the group of highly developed industrial societies examined here. The mean infant mortality across all investigated counties is at 10 infants per 1,000 live births (see Table A1.7). There are some nations, notably Japan (6.4), Sweden (6.6), and Finland (6.7) where infant mortality is distinctly below the mean, and others, notably Portugal (17.4) and Greece (14.4), where it is distinctly above. Scandinavian nations (mean 7.3) are all above average in effectiveness, or in other words are marked by a low infant mortality. Still, one cannot conclude from this that social democratic welfare state regimes show particularly good performance, since the special cases of Switzerland and Japan show themselves to be no less effective (mean 7.1).

On average, in all nations over the entire time period, mean infant mortality has been halved, dropping from 14.3 to 6.7, and the trend is universal. As one can see in Table 4.8, the unstandardized regression coefficient for the health performance index shows the least improvement in mean annual rates for Scandinavia, and the most improvement for the southern European nations. This development has the character of a catching-up process, as one can see from the correlation between the level of effectiveness in 1974–9 and the ensuing improvements in effectiveness ($r = -0.99$). In Scandinavia, as well as in Switzerland and Japan, all of which had already achieved a low infant mortality in the 1970s, the improvement was much less large. A 'ceiling effect' ensued in these nations once they reached an infant mortality rate of 4–6 per 1,000 live births. Conversely, growth was above average in those nations that still had high infant mortality rates in the 1970s. Portugal was the most extreme case ($b = 4.44$), but even comparatively wealthy nations such as Germany ($b = 2.32$), Italy ($b = 2.49$), and Austria ($b = 2.44$) saw above-average improvement. Overall, the level of effectiveness clearly

TABLE 4.8. *Health (performance index^a) 1974–95*

	Level (mean per period)					Trend		
	1974–9	1980–4	1985–9	1990–5	1974–95	V	Difference	b
Australia	68.1	79.7	83.6	90.9	80.5	0.12	22.8	1.41**
Canada	69.3	82.5	88.1	91.7	82.7	0.11	22.4	1.39**
Great Britain	64.1	76.9	82.7	90.7	78.5	0.14	26.6	1.64**
Ireland	60.5	78.2	85.6	90.3	78.4	0.16	29.8	1.84**
New Zealand	65.0	72.4	77.5	87.8	75.7	0.12	22.8	1.38**
USA	63.2	74.1	79.0	84.7	75.1	0.12	21.5	1.33**
	65.0	77.3	82.7	89.4	78.5	0.13	24.3	
Denmark	81.0	86.5	86.4	92.2	86.5	0.06	11.3	0.68**
Finland	82.8	91.2	92.9	96.8	90.8	0.07	14.0	0.86**
Norway	80.4	86.5	85.7	94.6	86.8	0.07	14.2	0.83**
Sweden	85.4	90.5	93.0	96.2	91.2	0.05	10.8	0.69**
	82.4	88.6	89.5	95.0	88.9	0.06	12.6	
Austria	52.0	70.7	81.2	90.4	73.3	0.22	38.4	2.44**
Belgium	63.7	76.1	81.8	86.8	77.0	0.13	23.1	1.45**
France	72.2	81.9	86.8	91.7	83.0	0.10	19.4	1.24**
Germany	55.8	76.2	85.9	92.7	77.4	0.20	37.0	2.32**
Italy	48.7	69.1	80.6	88.5	71.4	0.23	39.8	2.49**
The Netherlands	79.4	85.0	88.5	92.4	86.3	0.06	13.0	0.82**
	62.0	76.5	84.1	90.4	78.1	0.16	28.5	
Greece	40.6	60.4	73.7	84.3	64.5	0.28	43.7	2.73**
Portugal	12.6	44.4	64.0	82.4	54.3	0.49	69.8	4.44**
Spain	61.9	75.0	84.5	90.8	80.4	0.13	28.9	1.83**
	38.4	59.9	74.1	85.8	66.4	0.28	47.5	
Switzerland	79.1	87.0	90.1	93.7	87.4	0.07	14.6	0.92**
Japan	82.3	90.9	96.5	98.7	91.9	0.08	16.4	1.04**
	80.7	88.9	93.3	96.2	89.7	0.08	15.5	
All countries	65.14	77.86	84.20	90.88	79.68	0.13	25.7	1.54**
V	0.26	0.14	0.08	0.05	0.11			
Correlation with 1974–79		0.98	0.89	0.81			−0.99	

** $p < 0.01$; * $p < 0.05$ (two-tailed).
^{a} Values range from 0 to 100 (0 = worst practice ... 100 = best practice) from 1974–95. Values are the standardized variables for infant mortality (see Table A.1.7).
Legend: V = coefficient of variation; difference = difference between 1974–9 and 1990–5; b = unstandardized regression coefficient (OLS-estimate).

improved between 1974 and 1995, and the ranking of the nations remained relatively stable. As in the case of the national income, the nations converged at a higher level of effectiveness: the coefficient of variation, significantly, sank from 0.26 (1974–9) to 0.05 (1990–5). This means that by the 1990s, no significant differences in infant mortality existed among western democracies.

The *poverty rate* indicator is unusual, since unlike all other performance indicators, it measures distribution rather than volume. On the other hand, the data gaps here are relatively extensive, leading to frequent recourse to data replacement procedures. We thus limit ourselves in interpreting by focusing on those findings that are relatively robust. Based on the 'cautious' measure employed here (Kohl 1992: 279), a mean of 9.2 per cent of the population in western democracies lived in poverty in the investigated time period (see Table A.1.8). As was already true for violent crime, the USA at 16.9 per cent provides the negative outlier, followed by Australia and Canada at about 12 per cent. At the other end, Belgium (4.7 per cent), the Netherlands (5.4 per cent), and Finland (5.5 per cent) have relatively low poverty rates.

One can also discern a fairly clear structural difference between the families of nations: all English-speaking nations have above-average and all Scandinavian have below-average poverty rates. This is an indication of the differing ideologies and political practices of the two types of welfare state regimes represented in these two families of nations; they take opposite positions with respect to flattening inequalities (see Kohl 1999). The mean poverty rate in all nations increased slightly from 9.05 to 9.61, though this did not reflect a general trend. In Canada, Denmark, and Spain, the poverty rate did not increase but instead decreased, and the only nations that showed a relatively continuous increase were Great Britain and the Netherlands. The mean annual change that one can see in the standardized performance index of *income distribution* (national minimum) was at −2.05 (b) points for Great Britain and −1.13 (b) for the Netherlands (Table 4.9). In addition, this negative development, to the extent that it is based on more secure data, only began in the 1980s.

The data on infant mortality and the poverty rate are aggregated into a *social policy* index, the results of which can be seen in Table 4.10. At this more general level, the families of nations become still more distinct. Above-average performance can be seen in the Scandinavian nations as well as in the special cases of Switzerland and Japan. Below-average performance is evident in the English-speaking as well as the southern European nations. Continental Western European nations are quite heterogeneous, and if, as is done in the typology of welfare state regimes (Leibfried 1992; Bonoli 1997), one takes Italy out of this group, then one finds above-average performance for all the remaining nations. Given the suggested typology of welfare state regimes, the question is why it is not only the Scandinavian social democratic welfare states that show above-average performance but also Switzerland and Japan. Overall, socio-political performance has improved in western democracies between 1974 and 1995, and all southern European nations

TABLE 4.9. *Income distribution: national minimum (performance index[a]) 1974–95*

	Level (mean per period)					Trend		
	1974–9	1980–4	1985–9	1990–5	1974–95	V	Difference	b
Australia	42.5	43.9	41.4	30.1	39.2	0.17	−12.4	−0.78**
Canada	30.4	39.9	45.8	49.3	41.2	0.20	18.9	1.19**
Great Britain	62.2	62.2	53.1	27.9	50.8	0.31	−34.3	−2.05**
Ireland	53.6	50.8	48.2	45.4	49.5	0.07	−8.2	−0.51**
New Zealand	40.6	41.0	37.9	30.8	37.4	0.12	−9.7	−0.59**
USA	14.0	8.2	0.9	1.4	6.3	0.93	−12.7	−0.81**
	40.6	41.0	37.9	30.8	37.4	0.19	−9.7	
Denmark	54.8	61.4	62.0	73.9	63.1	0.13	19.2	1.11**
Finland	88.0	88.4	88.7	88.6	88.4	0.01	0.6	0.05*
Norway	87.3	85.7	78.1	80.3	83.0	0.05	−7.0	−0.51**
Sweden	84.4	86.5	76.4	79.5	81.7	0.05	−4.9	−0.41**
	78.6	80.5	76.3	80.6	79.1	0.06	2.0	
Austria	85.7	82.6	79.9	76.8	81.2	0.04	−8.9	−0.56**
Belgium	96.0	94.5	95.0	91.4	94.2	0.02	−4.6	−0.26**
France	72.5	74.6	68.3	67.7	70.7	0.05	−4.8	−0.37**
Germany	81.3	86.5	85.6	80.3	83.2	0.05	−1.0	−0.08
Italy	58.8	51.4	52.4	42.6	51.2	0.17	−16.1	−1.01**
The Netherlands	95.4	92.9	93.4	76.4	89.2	0.11	−19.1	−1.13**
	81.6	80.4	79.1	72.5	78.3	0.07	−9.1	
Greece	42.7	43.3	50.9	57.0	48.6	0.13	14.4	0.95**
Portugal	43.5	43.3	50.9	57.0	49.4	0.13	13.5	1.01**
Spain	44.0	43.3	50.9	57.0	49.7	0.12	13.1	1.06**
	43.4	43.3	50.9	57.0	49.2	0.13	13.6	
Switzerland	72.2	71.2	67.3	61.8	68.0	0.07	−10.4	−0.65**
Japan	72.2	71.2	67.3	61.8	68.0	0.07	−10.4	−0.65**
	72.2	71.2	67.3	61.8	68.0	0.07	−10.4	
All countries	62.96	62.99	61.62	58.92	61.63	0.09	−4.0	−0.31
V	0.37	0.37	0.36	0.39	0.36			
Correlation with 1974–79		0.99	0.95	0.83			−0.29	

** *p* < 0.01; * *p* < 0.05 (two-tailed).

[a] Values range from 0 to 100 (0 = worst practice … 100 = best practice) from 1974–95. Values are the standardized variables for poverty rate (see Table A.1.8).

Legend: V = coefficient of variation; difference = difference between 1974–79 and 1990–95; b = unstandardized regression coefficient (OLS-estimate).

display an above-average increase in effectiveness. There are only two nations that show a clearly negative trend, and they are Great Britain (b = −0.27) and the Netherlands (b = −0.20), the two nations that had the sharpest declines in performance regarding poverty.

TABLE 4.10. *Social policy (performance index[a]) 1974–95*

	Level (mean per period)					Trend		
	1974–9	1980–4	1985–9	1990–5	1974–95	V	Difference	b
Australia	46.1	54.9	55.8	53.1	52.2	0.08	7.0	0.43**
Canada	38.7	54.1	61.7	66.6	55.0	0.21	27.8	1.74**
Great Britain	56.6	65.2	63.0	51.5	58.6	0.11	−5.2	−0.27
Ireland	48.5	58.4	61.7	63.0	57.7	0.11	14.5	0.89**
New Zealand	42.7	48.0	49.3	51.5	47.8	0.08	8.8	0.53**
USA	23.6	27.1	25.4	29.5	26.4	0.11	6.0	0.35**
	42.7	51.3	52.8	52.5	49.6	0.12	9.8	
Denmark	63.0	71.2	71.5	83.5	72.4	0.12	20.5	1.20**
Finland	86.6	92.5	93.9	96.5	92.3	0.05	9.9	0.62**
Norway	84.5	87.6	81.9	89.4	86.0	0.04	4.8	0.22
Sweden	86.0	90.8	85.7	89.9	88.1	0.03	4.0	0.19
	80.0	85.5	83.3	89.8	84.7	0.06	9.8	
Austria	64.3	74.9	80.0	84.2	75.7	0.12	19.9	1.27**
Belgium	79.2	86.5	90.7	91.7	86.9	0.06	12.5	0.80**
France	69.1	77.0	76.1	78.9	75.1	0.06	9.9	0.59**
Germany	63.9	81.2	87.1	88.1	79.7	0.14	24.2	1.51**
Italy	44.0	52.7	61.2	59.9	54.2	0.15	15.9	1.00**
The Netherlands	89.3	91.4	94.1	85.3	89.8	0.05	−4.1	−0.20
	68.3	77.3	81.5	81.3	76.9	0.09	13.1	
Greece	27.6	41.4	55.5	66.8	47.8	0.34	39.1	2.48**
Portugal	9.4	30.6	49.0	65.5	41.4	0.53	56.1	3.68**
Spain	42.9	51.2	62.7	71.2	59.2	0.19	28.3	1.95**
	26.6	41.1	55.7	67.8	49.5	0.33	41.2	
Switzerland	73.5	78.1	77.6	76.4	76.3	0.03	2.8	0.18
Japan	75.6	80.8	81.9	79.7	79.3	0.03	4.1	0.26**
	74.6	79.4	79.7	78.0	77.8	0.03	3.4	
All countries	57.86	66.46	69.80	72.48	66.76	0.11	14.6	0.83**
V	0.39	0.30	0.25	0.23	0.27			
Correlation with 1974–79		0.98	0.90	0.76			−0.66	

** $p < 0.01$; * $p < 0.05$ (two-tailed).
[a] Values range from 0 to 100 (0 = worst practice ... 100 = best practice) from 1974–95. Values are the mean of the standardized variables for health (see Table 4.8) and income distribution: national minimum (see Table 4.9) with subsequent standardization of the mean.

Legend: V = coefficient of variation; difference = difference between 1974–9 and 1990–5; b = unstandardized regression coefficient (OLS-estimate).

It was generally thought that the restructuring and dismantling of the welfare state after 1974 would lead to declines in effectiveness. But at least in the case of infant mortality, this predicted negative trend did not occur between 1974 and 1995. The data instead show the opposite development, indicating that certain health precautions are part of the core elements of the welfare state, and are not negatively affected by budget cuts and programme retrenchment. Even in nations in the need of catching up, such as Germany, such programmes were expanded.

By contrast, the predicted negative development in the poverty rate does seem to have been confirmed since the 1980s. However, this trend is not a particularly strong one, and some nations are exempt from it. It is in any case much more difficult to come to a judgment to what extent this moderately negative trend is based on welfare state restructuring or dismantling efforts. On the one hand, many studies have argued that extensive welfare state benefits or programmes have a positive effect on the national poverty rate (Kenworthy 1995; Smeeding 1997; OECD 1998*d*). On the other hand, both national and comparative studies of the development of inequality have indicated that increasing income inequality arising from deindustrialization in western democracies since 1980 is the cause of increasing inequality (Gottschalk and Smeeding 1997; Gottschalk et al. 1997; Gustafsson and Johansson 1999). There is only one study thus far that has directly compared both influencing factors, changes in taxation and welfare state benefits as well as labour market change, and it was able to demonstrate that it is primarily labour market changes that are responsible for increasing inequality, though taxes and benefits also play a part (Gottschalk and Smeeding 1997). One can conclude that, at least in the case of the USA, welfare state benefits are not comprehensive or generous enough to compensate for poverty brought about through economic changes. It is an open question for research whether or to what extent this is also true in other western democracies.

A possible contradiction should also be addressed here, inasmuch as our finding of a moderately negative development in the poverty rate needs to be placed in conjunction with increasing social inequality in western democracies since the 1980s. Many national and comparative studies show *income inequality* has risen perceptibly in the vast majority of western democracies after 1980, most significantly so in Great Britain and the USA. The Gini coefficient, by which one measures income inequality, rose by 33 per cent in Great Britain and 13 per cent in the USA between 1979 and 1995 (Gottschalk and Smeeding 2000: Appendix Table A.2), and only in Ireland, Finland, and Italy was no increase in income inequality found (Gottschalk, et al. 1997; Gottschalk and Smeeding 2000; OECD 1998*d*). Comparative studies have been able to show that increasing income inequality does not go hand-in-hand with growing poverty (Smeeding 1997: 31; OECD 1998*d*: 9). Instead, while poverty and inequality are both subdimensions of income inequality and are intercorrelated, the poverty rate only encompasses the bottom part of the income distribution; inequality measures like the Gini coefficient describe the entire income distribution. This is also the reason why both dimensions can, at least to some extent, develop independently of one another.

Environmental Policy

Unlike the previous three policy areas, environmental policy is a comparatively new area that only came onto the political agenda of western democracies at the end of the 1960s and only became institutionalized in course of the 1970s (Jörgens 1996). The ability to take action over environmental policy matters has steadily increased since then, helped by ministries for the environment, national environmental bureaus and reports, and growing knowledge and technical know-how (Jänicke and Weidner 1997). Increasingly, too, environmental measures and programmes have been passed with the goal of slowing if not halting the continuing destruction of the environment, and to improve environmental quality as well as the quality and quantity of natural resources.

Environmental policy is also different from domestic security, economic, or welfare state policy in its degree of internationalization. Much environmental degradation, whether in the form of air pollution, water pollution, or climate change, occurs in ways that do not respect national borders, making halting or mitigating it a matter of international cooperation (Hucke 1992: 444). For this reason, it is a policy area characterized by a large degree of international activity and multilateral agreements (for a list of multilateral conventions on the environment, see OECD 1997: 261–3). Given how internationalized environmental policy has become, Jänicke and Weidner (1997: 15) even argue that globalization plays 'a positive role in supporting and stimulating national environmental protection'. In this, however, they go against the more widespread opinion that increasing economic globalization sets a process of deregulating environmental standards in motion that will lead to a convergence of western industrial nations at a lower level of environmental performance (Beisheim and Walter 1997; Münch 1998).

Given the intensification of environmental policy activities in western industrialized societies since the 1970s, one might assume that environmental effectiveness has also risen in these nations. This is too simple and linear an assumption, however, that does not do justice to the complexity of environmental conditions in these developed nations. That complexity is best expressed in the research on the ecological Kuznets curve (Shafik 1994; Ricken 1995; Jänicke et al. 1996a) that sees the relationship between economic development and burdens on the environment as an upside-down U-shaped curve. In the initial phase of economic development, wealth increases at the cost of the environment, because industrial production and modern lifestyles go hand-in-hand with higher emissions of pollutants and greater use of resources. But in the second phase, both goals can be achieved at the same time. This is in part because sufficient technical (modern environmental technologies), economic (monetary), and cultural (sensitivity to environmental issues) resources are available to reduce the damage to the environment. But it is also in part due to the beneficial side effects generated for the environment from the shift from an industrial to a service sector economy.

Comparative environmental policy research argues that the ability to resolve an environmental problem determines whether a performance indicator is trending negative (first phase) or positive (second phase) (Shafik and Bandyopadhyay 1992; Arrow et al. 1995; Jänicke et al. 1996*a*). So reducing sulphur oxides emissions is an easy problem to solve due to the use of filtering technology that is compatible with economic growth, while it is not easy to resolve the problems of municipal waste production because these call for direct intervention into the structures of their production (Jänicke et al. 1996*a*).

Two consequences follow from these considerations of the relationship between wealth and environmental protection. First, one cannot expect to find any general upward or downward trends for the individual indicators in this policy area, since the trend depends upon whether the performance indicator measures an environmental policy problem that is easy or hard to resolve. Second, one will see a negative 'catching-up' process in at least some performance indicators, in which economic stragglers such as the southern European nations and Ireland will also reach higher levels of damage to the environment and resource exploitation as their per capita income rises and becomes more like that of the wealthier nations. To the extent to which this negative catching-up process exists, one can also assume that convergence in effectiveness in environmental policy will also start being evident between western democracies.

Two different dimensions of effectiveness are investigated here: protecting environmental quality, and protecting the quality and quantity of natural resources. Five indicators are available to measure the first—sulphur oxides, nitrogen oxides, carbon dioxide emissions, municipal waste production, fertilizer use, and one—water consumption—is available to measure the second dimension. Of course, these six indicators measure only a slice of the damage done to the environment or the resources consumed. But at the moment statistical data sufficient to our purposes is not available. All of these indicators also measure environmental policy outcomes or impacts, since in light of our conceptualization, we do not consider any output or response indicators (OECD 1994), such as the number of sewage treatment plants built or nature reserves set aside, or how extensive recycling measures are (Jänicke et al. 1996*a*; Jahn 1998; Scruggs 1999).

All emissions of pollutants into the air are measured in kilograms per capita. Sulphur oxides are primarily a by-product of burning at stationary sources (power plants, industrial heating, and private households) and in various industrial production processes (OECD 1997: 18). Nitrogen oxides are also a by-product of burning, less from stationary sources than from mobile sources such as motor vehicles (OECD 1997: 18). The carbon dioxide indicator only measures emissions from burning fossil fuels (oil and natural gas) for primary energy use, thus in transportation, in energy conversion, and in industry (OECD 1997: 45). Sulphur and nitrogen oxides are harmful particularly because of their acid-creating properties; carbon dioxide is a greenhouse gas that plays a particular role in warming the earth's atmosphere.

Over the entire time period investigated, *sulphur oxides emissions* were 53 kilograms per capita on average across all nations (see Table A.1.9). Canada (154 kg) had by far the highest emissions, followed by the USA (92 kg), with Great Britain at third place (73 kg).[13] Japan (11 kg) and Switzerland (12 kg) had the lowest emissions. The continuous downward evolution here is quite impressive, however, since between 1974–9 and 1990–5 the average emission of this pollutant has been cut in half, from 72.7 to 36.6 kilograms per capita, across all nations. In this one can see the success of the first large-scale environmental measures to clean the air, introduced and implemented in most western democracies in the early 1970s (Knoepfel and Weidner 1985). With the exception of Portugal, sulphur oxides emissions have fallen in every nation. As we shall see, this is the only environmental policy indicator that can show such an unusually positive development since 1974. It is also the only environmental quality indicator where the evolution does *not* have the character of a negative catching-up process on the part of latecomers ($r = -0.04$), and is the only environmental indicator where differences between nations are increasing rather than decreasing (the coefficient of variation rises from 0.66 to 0.73).

As for *nitrogen oxides emissions,* an average of 45 kilograms per capita were produced in the nations studied (see Table A.1.10), with Australia (130 kg) by far the largest producer, followed by the USA (88 kg) and Canada (77 kg). Japan (13 kg) and Portugal (17 kg) had the lowest values. Apart from some smaller fluctuations, the average for all nations remains stable, though nation-specific patterns are thereby hidden. Nations with low initial nitrogen oxides emissions, such as Ireland, Italy, and the southern European family saw above-average increases, while in some nations with initial high emissions, such as Germany, Austria, or the USA, they decreased. There are at least some indications in this of a (negative) catching-up process on the part of the economic stragglers ($r = -0.34$), which is leading to increasing convergence between western democracies (the coefficient of variation has decreased from 0.64 (1974–9) to 0.57 (1990–5)).

---

[13] New Zealand sulphur oxides emissions are 92 kilograms on average, but because this value is based on an estimate, it is not considered here.

There are considerable parallels between the nitrogen oxides and *carbon dioxide emissions* indicators (see Table A.1.11). On average across all nations, 9.5 kilograms per capita of carbon dioxide emissions were produced, with the USA (20 kg) producing the most, followed by Canada (16.5 kg) and Australia (15 kg). The southern European family of Portugal (3.4 kg), Spain (5.3 kg) and Greece (5.8 kg) produced the least. The mean for all nations shows neither a positive or negative trend. But though the data indicate stability, there also seems to be a negative catching-up process among the stragglers of Ireland, New Zealand, Greece, and Portugal. The correlation value ($r = -0.60$) is considerably higher than was the case for nitrogen oxides ($r = -0.34$). One consequence of catching-up is also that western democracies have become somewhat more similar; the coefficient of variation for carbon dioxide emissions has declined from 0.46 (1974–9) to 0.39 (1990–5).

But if the picture of air pollutants thus far has either been one of improvement (sulphur oxides) or at least overall stability (nitrogen oxides, carbon dioxide) in environmental performance, this is certainly not the case for *municipal waste production*: the situation here has continuously worsened (see Table A.1.12). On average per capita across all nations and for the entire time period, 426 kilograms of waste were produced. The largest producers are Australia (694 kg) and the USA (638 kg); the smallest producers are in southern Europe—Portugal (261 kg), Greece (290 kg), and Spain (297 kg)— as well as Ireland (288 kg). There is a clear covariance between waste production and level of affluence. Other than in Germany, waste production has increased across the board, from 384 to 478 kilograms per capita. This is also a catching-up process on the part of economic stragglers ($r = -0.58$), that has led to greater similarities between western democracies (the coefficient of variation has reduced from 0.34 to 0.27).

The last indicator for the environmental quality dimension addresses *fertilizer use*, where it is particularly the nitrogen and phosphate contained in the fertilizers that degrade water quality (OECD 1997: 238). In the nations investigated, an average of 5.6 tons of fertilizer per square kilometre was used (see Table A.1.13).[14] The Netherlands (15 tons), Denmark (14 tons) and Belgium (13 tons) all show above-average use, and these are small nations with comparatively little arable land and intensive agricultural exploitation. Australia (0.2 tons), Canada (0.2 tons), Norway (0.7 tons), and Sweden (0.9 tons) show relatively little fertilizer use, possibly due to their not having much arable land. Over time there has been little change in fertilizer use, though by the third and fourth time periods, a small reduction from 5.9 to 5.2 tons can be seen. This reduction in the last time periods exists in all but five nations—the English-speaking ones, except Great Britain. As with the

---

[14] It would be more appropriate to standardize with respect to agricultural land, but the corresponding data to do so are regarded by the OECD (1997: 100) as insufficient.

nitrogen oxides emissions, one can see a moderate catching-up process among the stragglers Ireland, Greece, and Spain ($r = -0.33$), and as a consequence, convergence increases between the western democracies (the coefficient of variation decreases from 0.90 to 0.82).

All five indicators are aggregated in an *environmental quality index* (Table 4.11). Each performance indicator, after being standardized on a 0 to 100 scale, is included with the same weight into this composite measure.[15] As was true in the other policy areas, one can see structural similarities between families of nations that are not nearly as clear in the individual indicators. The southern European family of Portugal (92), Spain (76.8), and Greece (76.5) has by far the best environmental performance—though one should not conclude from it that a comparative low level of wealth has a positive influence on the environment. After all, the special cases of Switzerland (75.5) and Japan (73.6), among the wealthiest nations, also have above-average environmental performance. At the other end of the scale, the three worst environmental polluters by far are Australia (5.1), the USA (6.4), and Canada (13.8). Given the differing trends in the individual indicators, it is not surprising that this composite measure, on average, shows considerable stability across all nations. Opposite developments in individual nations balance each other out. Generally speaking, environmental performance improves in those nations that were among the worst polluters in the mid-1960s, and worsens in those nations that began with relatively good values. The largest continual improvement can be seen in Canada (b = 1.2) and Germany (b = 0.93), while the largest deterioration is in Ireland (b = −1.66) and Portugal (b = −1.03). The correlation coefficient that captures the (negative) catching-up process on the part of the economically under-developed nations stands at −0.60, and the coefficient of variation that describes the divergence between nations decreases from 0.56 to 0.45.

Only one indicator, measuring *water consumption*, is available for the second environmental policy dimension, the quality and quantity of natural resources (see Table A.1.14). Western democracies used 712 cubic meters of water per capita on average. The greatest users by far were the USA (2,052) and Canada (1,571), followed by Spain (1,032), a comparatively poor nation. Great Britain (211) and Denmark (224) had the lowest usage. The pattern of individual nations and families of nations is quite distinct from that seen in the indicators for the first dimension of environmental quality; the separation of the components is thus not only analytically but also empirically justified. The performance index of the *quality and quantity of natural resources* (Table 4.12) calculates means for the families of nations, and indicates that it is not the southern European but rather the Scandinavian family

---

[15] The three air pollutants are not aggregated into a separate index (see Ricken 1995) because they arise from different sources and have different consequences.

TABLE 4.11. *Quality of environment (performance index[a]) 1974–95*

	Level (mean per period)					Trend		
	1974–9	1980–4	1985–9	1990–5	1974–95	V	Difference	b
Australia	1.0	5.5	6.9	7.3	5.1	0.62	6.3	0.39**
Canada	2.3	13.8	16.8	22.7	13.8	0.60	20.3	1.20**
Great Britain	34.8	32.2	27.8	30.2	31.4	0.10	−4.6	−0.32**
Ireland	73.4	66.4	55.7	47.5	60.7	0.18	−26.0	−1.66**
New Zealand	44.4	45.6	43.4	37.1	42.4	0.13	−7.4	−0.49**
USA	4.5	7.6	7.4	6.5	6.4	0.37	2.0	0.11
	26.8	28.5	26.3	25.2	26.6	0.21	−1.5	
Denmark	22.8	24.2	20.7	27.0	23.8	0.16	4.2	0.20
Finland	56.2	58.3	55.9	59.8	57.6	0.07	3.6	0.17
Norway	69.4	69.3	63.6	61.0	65.8	0.06	−8.4	−0.57**
Sweden	65.4	70.4	71.1	72.9	69.9	0.05	7.5	0.45**
	53.5	55.6	52.8	55.2	54.3	0.07	1.7	
Austria	64.7	62.4	66.1	70.9	66.2	0.05	6.2	0.41**
Belgium	32.6	35.7	42.8	43.9	38.7	0.14	11.4	0.75**
France	45.7	47.8	53.1	56.8	50.9	0.10	11.2	0.70**
Germany	42.4	44.6	50.0	57.6	48.8	0.14	15.3	0.93**
Italy	73.4	71.7	69.6	61.7	69.0	0.08	−11.7	−0.73**
The Netherlands	27.4	28.9	31.7	32.9	30.2	0.10	5.5	0.33**
	47.7	48.5	52.2	54.0	50.6	0.10	6.3	
Greece	82.1	79.2	73.0	71.6	76.5	0.06	−10.5	−0.70**
Portugal	97.8	95.9	93.7	82.6	91.8	0.07	−15.2	−1.03**
Spain	80.9	79.3	78.3	71.3	76.8	0.05	−9.5	−0.65**
	87.0	84.8	81.7	75.2	81.7	0.06	−11.7	
Switzerland	78.7	73.9	72.4	76.2	75.5	0.04	−2.5	−0.15
Japan	72.5	75.2	75.0	72.4	73.6	0.02	−0.1	−0.01
	75.6	74.6	73.7	74.3	74.6	0.03	−1.3	
All countries	51.07	51.80	51.18	50.95	51.18	0.09	−0.1	−0.08
V	0.56	0.50	0.48	0.45	0.49			
Correlation with 1974–79		0.99	0.97	0.93			−0.60	

** $p < 0.01$; * $p > 0.05$ (two-tailed).

[a] Values range from 0 to 100 (0 = worst practice ... 100 = best practice) from 1974–95. Values are the mean of the standardized variables for emissions of sulphur oxides, nitrogen oxides, carbon dioxide, municipal waste production, and fertilizer use (see Tables A.1.9–A.1.13) with subsequent standardization of the mean.

Legend: V = coefficient of variation; difference = difference between 1974–9 and 1990–5; b = unstandardized regression coefficient (OLS-estimate).

that has above-average performance, that is, it shows the lowest water consumption rates. On average across all nations, water consumption first rises (until 1980–4) and then falls continuously to a level (by 1990–5) below

Effectiveness of Western Democracies

TABLE 4.12. *Quality and quantity of natural resources (performance index^a) 1974–95*

	Level (mean per period)					Trend		
	1974–9	1980–4	1985–9	1990–5	1974–95	V	Difference	b
Australia	67.8	68.9	64.8	67.3	67.2	0.03	−0.5	−0.09
Canada	43.9	31.5	29.3	27.4	33.2	0.22	−16.5	−1.01**
Great Britain	96.7	96.9	97.8	98.8	97.6	0.01	2.1	0.14**
Ireland	92.8	92.6	92.5	92.2	92.5	0.00	−0.5	−0.03**
New Zealand	90.8	85.5	79.8	80.4	84.3	0.06	−10.4	−0.67**
USA	2.5	6.1	16.4	17.1	10.5	0.67	14.7	0.97**
	65.7	63.6	63.4	63.9	64.2	0.06	−1.8	
Denmark	96.5	96.5	96.6	98.1	97.0	0.01	1.7	0.10*
Finland	71.6	70.1	75.5	85.1	75.8	0.09	13.5	0.84**
Norway	80.3	83.0	83.1	84.0	82.6	0.02	3.7	0.22**
Sweden	83.8	86.8	90.8	92.0	88.3	0.04	8.2	0.53**
	83.1	84.1	86.5	89.8	85.9	0.04	6.8	
Austria	92.3	94.0	93.7	93.8	93.4	0.01	1.5	0.08
Belgium	64.2	64.9	65.0	64.8	64.7	0.01	0.7	0.04
France	81.2	77.1	76.7	75.1	77.6	0.03	−6.1	−0.37**
Germany	79.6	75.4	73.8	72.3	75.3	0.04	−7.3	−0.46**
Italy	64.2	62.0	63.3	62.0	62.9	0.02	−2.1	−0.12**
The Netherlands	65.6	77.0	78.5	82.1	75.6	0.09	16.5	0.99**
	74.5	75.1	75.2	75.0	74.9	0.04	0.5	
Greece	79.1	79.9	80.4	82.0	80.4	0.02	2.9	0.18**
Portugal	69.9	68.0	68.8	74.2	70.4	0.04	4.3	0.33**
Spain	58.2	54.6	55.6	65.0	58.7	0.09	6.9	0.62**
	69.1	67.5	68.3	73.8	69.8	0.05	4.7	
Switzerland	95.5	88.2	88.4	89.5	90.6	0.04	−6.0	−0.36**
Japan	71.0	72.3	73.0	73.2	72.4	0.01	2.2	0.14**
	83.3	80.2	80.7	81.4	81.5	0.03	−1.9	
All countries	73.69	72.91	73.52	75.09	73.86	0.04	1.4	−0.06
V	0.29	0.30	0.28	0.28	0.28			
Correlation with 1974–79		0.98	0.95	0.93			−0.29	

** $p < 0.01$; * $p < 0.05$ (two-tailed).
^{a} Values range from 0 to 100 (0 = worst practice ... 100 = best practice) from 1974–95. Values are the standardized variables for water consumption (see Table A.1.14).

Legend: V = coefficient of variation; difference = difference between 1974–9 and 1990–5; b = unstandardized regression coefficient (OLS-estimate).

the initial (1970–4) rates. No identifiable pattern of catching-up or of convergence is evident. Particularly noteworthy is the above-average increase (deterioration) in Canada ($b = -1.01$) and above-average decrease (improvement) in the Netherlands ($b = 0.99$) and the USA ($b = 0.97$).

Finally, the two performance indicators of environmental quality and the quality and quantity of natural resources are aggregated into an *environmental policy index* (Table 4.13).[16] Switzerland (91.6), Portugal (89.4), Austria (88), and Sweden (87) have the best performance at this general level, while the worst effectiveness, by far, can be seen in the USA (8), Canada (25), and Australia (39), respectively. Two families of nations show themselves to be relatively homogenous at this level: the southern European nations as well as the special cases of Switzerland and Japan have the best environmental performance. The English-speaking nations fall into two opposite groups, one comprised of the USA, Canada, and Australia, showing a performance that is the worst compared to all other nations, and the other comprised of Great Britain, Ireland, and New Zealand, showing above-average performance. The level of environmental performance is stable, when seen in the average of all nations, though there are two opposite processes at work that balance each other out in the aggregate: a worsening among the economic stragglers and a bettering among the economic pioneers. As a consequence of this catching-up process ($r = -0.54$), the nations have become somewhat more similar, and the coefficient of variation has reduced from 0.35 (1974–9) to 0.30 (1990–5). It is worth noting in this context that the national ranking in this summary index (as in all the other environmental performance indicators), remains comparatively stable over time; the correlations over time are always larger than 0.90. The opposite developments—improvements in environmental performance on the part of pioneers (such as the USA and Germany), and deterioration in environmental performance on the part of the economic stragglers (such as the southern European nations and Ireland)—have no effect on the ranking of the individual nations relative to one another.

We can conclude that the development of environmental performance follows no simple pattern, and this corresponds with our original expectations. There is only one performance indicator (sulphur oxides emissions) where effectiveness has continually and significantly improved since 1974, though in some others (fertilizer use, water consumption) there have been small increases in effectiveness in the 1980s and 1990s. In the other indicators, the pattern is either one of stability (nitrogen oxides and carbon dioxide emissions) or effectiveness has continually deteriorated (municipal waste). If one places the development of these individual environmental dimensions into a summary environmental policy index, then one can observe that environmental performance has stagnated across all investigated nations between 1974 and 1995. At this general level, therefore, one cannot confirm

---

[16] Following the logic of constructing composite measures, the two components (environmental quality and quality and quantity of natural resources) go into this index with equal weights, and not the indicators, whose numbers are quite different in the two components.

T ABLE 4.13. *Environmental policy (performance index[a]) 1974–95*

	Level (mean per period)					Trend		
	1974–9	1980–4	1985–9	1990–5	1974–95	V	Difference	b
Australia	37.0	40.1	38.6	40.2	38.9	0.04	3.3	0.17**
Canada	24.3	23.8	24.2	26.5	24.7	0.08	2.2	0.11
Great Britain	72.2	70.8	68.9	70.8	70.8	0.02	−1.4	−0.10*
Ireland	91.7	87.7	81.6	76.8	84.4	0.07	−14.9	−0.95**
New Zealand	74.3	72.0	67.6	64.3	69.5	0.07	−10.0	−0.65**
USA	2.2	6.0	11.7	11.6	7.8	0.60	9.4	0.61**
	50.3	50.1	48.7	48.4	49.4	0.07	−1.9	
Denmark	65.3	66.1	64.2	68.6	66.2	0.04	3.3	0.17
Finland	70.2	70.5	72.2	79.8	73.3	0.07	9.6	0.57**
Norway	82.4	83.9	80.7	79.8	81.7	0.02	−2.6	−0.20**
Sweden	82.2	86.6	89.3	91.0	87.2	0.04	8.8	0.55**
	75.0	76.8	76.6	79.8	77.1	0.04	4.8	
Austria	86.5	86.2	88.1	90.8	88.0	0.02	4.3	0.28**
Belgium	52.7	54.8	58.9	59.4	56.4	0.06	6.8	0.45**
France	69.6	68.5	71.2	72.4	70.5	0.03	2.8	0.19*
Germany	66.9	65.7	67.9	71.3	68.1	0.04	4.5	0.27**
Italy	75.6	73.5	73.0	67.8	72.4	0.05	−7.8	−0.47**
The Netherlands	50.6	57.8	60.2	62.9	57.8	0.09	12.3	0.75**
	67.0	67.7	69.9	70.8	68.9	0.05	3.8	
Greece	88.9	87.7	84.5	84.7	86.5	0.03	−4.3	−0.29**
Portugal	92.6	90.4	89.6	86.4	89.4	0.03	−6.1	−0.39**
Spain	76.4	73.6	73.5	74.9	74.4	0.02	−1.5	−0.02
	86.0	83.9	82.5	82.0	83.5	0.02	−4.0	
Switzerland	96.2	89.4	88.6	91.4	91.6	0.04	−4.8	−0.28**
Japan	79.0	81.2	81.5	80.1	80.4	0.01	1.2	0.07
	87.6	85.3	85.0	85.8	86.0	0.03	−1.8	
All countries	68.42	68.39	68.38	69.14	68.57	0.04	0.7	−0.08
V	0.35	0.32	0.31	0.30	0.32			
Correlation with 1974–9		0.99	0.98	0.96			−0.54	

** $p < 0.01$; * $p < 0.05$ (two-tailed).

[a] Values range from 0 to 100 (0 = worst practice . . . 100 = best practice) from 1974–95. Values are the mean of the standardized variables for quality of environment (see Table 4.11) and quality and quantity of natural resources (see Table 4.12) with subsequent standardization of the mean.

Legend: V = coefficient of variation; difference = difference between 1974–9 and 1990–5; b = unstandardized regression coefficient (OLS-estimate).

the diagnoses of crisis that argue for systematic loss of effectiveness, nor can one confirm the hypotheses that increasing environmental policy activism since the 1970s has led to an increase in environmental performance. The cause for the overall stagnation is that moderate environmental policy improvements in some nations are balanced out by policy deterioration among other (economically lagging) nations. We often see the predicted negative catching-up process in this policy area, and it is a process with the expected consequence that environmental performance converges in western democracies.

General Political Effectiveness

Having analysed the individual policy areas, we now turn to the spectrum of policies, or policy package, as a whole. To do so, we aggregate the four policy-specific performance indices of (*a*) domestic security, (*b*) economic policy, (*c*) social policy, and (*d*) environmental policy into a single measure of general political effectiveness. This summary index measures policy effectiveness both comprehensively, inasmuch as a broad spectrum of policy areas is included, and in a differentiated manner, as the performance indices include two components per policy area. According to the crisis diagnoses with which we began—ungovernability, legitimation crises, and the negative effects of globalization—we should be able to discern a continuous worsening in western democracies at this aggregated level of general effectiveness.

In the ensuing analyses, we use two versions of this global index. The first, general effectiveness, encompasses all eight policy-specific components. The second, general effectiveness without wealth, only includes the misery dimension that incorporates the unemployment and inflation rates in the economic policy area (see Figure 2.3).[17] There is a particular reason for employing this second index. Given that western democracies have seen a continuing, significant increase in GDP since 1973, it is unlikely that the general effectiveness index, which includes this dimension, would show a negative trend over time. The hypotheses about the deterioration of effectiveness in western democracies must therefore be examined based on a summary performance index that does not include wealth. Another general argument for using this additional index lies in the ambivalent nature of wealth itself. Wealth can, as we have argued in the normative model of political effectiveness in liberal democracies, be seen as a performance dimension. But it also reflects the degree of socio-economic modernity of a nation, and from this perspective primarily indicates the extent of financial resources available for achieving other policy goals, particularly in social policy and the environment. Wealth then is also a determinant of other dimensions of effectiveness, and this

---

[17] Because there are a relatively large number of estimated values in the poverty data, a third index of general effectiveness without poverty was also constructed for control purposes. The results found on the basis of this indicator did not systematically differ from those found for the two indices of general effectiveness and general effectiveness without wealth.

second conceptualization is given its due through the additional summary index where national income is excluded as a dimension.

Performance index: general effectiveness
The general effectiveness index, the most comprehensive evaluation criterion that integrates all the analytically separated performance dimensions, shows (Table 4.14) that the highest values are reached in Norway (90.3), Switzerland (89.2), and Japan (89.1); the three differ little on the 0 to 100 performance scale. The spread is larger in the nations with the worst values. The clearly lowest general effectiveness is found in the USA (15.3), followed at considerable distance by Canada (42.2) and then Australia (46.3). The gap between the USA and Canada strikingly shows what was already evident in some of the individual indicators, namely the negative outlier role played by the USA.

That the three nations with the best practice, namely Norway, Switzerland, and Japan, belong to the group of the five wealthiest nations could be taken as an indication that affluence plays a decisive role in high general effectiveness—except that this cannot be the only decisive factor, since the USA and Canada are the other two richest nations and they are at the bottom of the performance scale. The USA is even the nation with the highest per capita income of the western democracies. The dominating economic performance of the USA is, at least statistically speaking, not sufficient to compensate for its very poor performance in domestic security, poverty, and environmental policies, nor for the fact that it has the worst general effectiveness by far. This imbalanced libertarian effectiveness pattern will be discussed in more detail later.

This extraordinarily poor result for the USA may raise doubts about the data and indicators utilized here, or about the standardization procedures. As to the reliability of the data and indicators, one can look at a similarly conceptualized comparative study: Bok's *The State of the Nation* (1996). Bok was interested in comparing the USA to six other industrial democracies—Canada, France, Germany, Great Britain, Japan, and Sweden—with respect to wealth, quality of life, equal opportunity, individual security, and values (such as liberty, responsibility, and solidarity). His time frame stretched from 1960 to 1990, and he measured the level and development of a total of sixty-six indicators, most of which measured outcomes, and some of which were derived from sources other than the ones used in our study. Bok (1996: 367) came to the conclusion that in two-thirds of the indicators, the USA was below the mean of the nations, and in more than half the indicators, the USA had the worst or near-worst values. Thus, in this comparative study as well, the USA had the worst performance by far.

TABLE 4.14. *General effectiveness (performance index[a]) 1974–95*

	Level (mean per period)					Trend		
	1974–9	1980–4	1985–9	1990–5	1974–95	V	Difference	b
Australia	43.0	46.6	47.1	48.8	46.3	0.07	5.8	0.36**
Canada	30.3	37.7	48.4	52.6	42.2	0.23	22.3	1.46**
Great Britain	57.2	60.6	61.3	58.6	59.3	0.05	1.4	0.15
Ireland	61.6	61.6	65.2	69.5	64.6	0.06	7.9	0.53**
New Zealand	55.4	54.9	50.2	52.5	53.3	0.06	−2.8	−0.18*
USA	4.6	10.4	21.2	25.2	15.3	0.63	20.5	1.40**
	42.0	45.3	48.9	51.2	46.8	0.12	9.2	
Denmark	57.7	59.4	63.8	72.6	63.6	0.11	14.9	0.96**
Finland	61.7	68.4	74.9	76.4	70.2	0.09	14.7	0.94**
Norway	84.9	88.5	90.3	97.1	90.3	0.06	12.2	0.75**
Sweden	73.1	79.1	83.3	84.2	79.8	0.06	11.0	0.72**
	69.4	73.9	78.1	82.6	76.0	0.08	13.2	
Austria	75.2	80.5	87.5	90.3	83.3	0.08	15.1	1.01**
Belgium	67.1	68.7	76.1	79.7	73.0	0.08	12.6	0.85**
France	68.3	69.0	73.8	77.2	72.1	0.06	8.9	0.59**
Germany	64.7	70.0	73.9	77.3	71.4	0.08	12.7	0.79**
Italy	55.6	58.1	64.8	63.4	60.4	0.07	7.8	0.53**
The Netherlands	67.7	67.3	66.5	62.3	65.9	0.06	−5.4	−0.31**
	66.4	68.9	73.8	75.0	71.0	0.07	8.6	
Greece	63.2	64.0	69.0	74.1	67.7	0.08	10.9	0.77**
Portugal	47.7	56.9	69.7	79.8	65.1	0.20	32.1	2.11**
Spain	57.5	52.5	48.7	57.5	53.9	0.09	0.1	0.12
	56.1	57.8	62.5	70.5	62.2	0.12	14.3	
Switzerland	84.6	87.3	91.4	93.6	89.2	0.05	8.9	0.61**
Japan	78.6	87.7	93.2	97.4	89.1	0.09	18.8	1.19**
	81.6	87.5	92.3	95.5	89.2	0.07	13.9	
All countries	60.00	63.30	67.64	70.96	65.53	0.09	11.0	0.7**
V	0.30	0.29	0.26	0.25	0.27			
Correlation with 1974–9		0.98	0.92	0.89			−0.27	

** $p < 0.01$; * $p < 0.05$ (two-tailed).

[a] Values range from 0 to 100 (0 = worst practice ... 100 = best practice) from 1974–95. Values are the mean of the standardized variables for domestic security policy (see Table 4.4), economic policy (see Table 4.7), social policy (see Table 4.10), and environmental policy (see Table 4.13) with subsequent standardization of the mean.

Legend: V = coefficient of variation; difference = difference between 1974–9 and 1990–5; b = unstandardized regression coefficient (OLS-estimate).

A second objection can be raised about the standardization of performance indicators that, as it is borrowed from the practices used in policy benchmarking, lends negative and positive outliers a greater weight in composite measures (Mosley and Engelmann 2000: 20). To address this objection, a general effectiveness index based on z-score transformed values was also constructed. A comparison of the distribution shown in these differently standardized indices reveals that the nations with best and worst practices were identical. The differences between the indices were exclusively confined to the ranking of nations in the middle (data not shown). We can therefore conclude that the poor results for the USA are neither an artefact of the data and indicators, nor an artefact of the standardization procedures used here.

General effectiveness has, when viewed as an average of all nations between 1974 and 1995, continually improved, increasing by nearly 11 points from first to last period (Table 4.14). This positive evolution was well above average in three nations: the economic straggler Portugal (b = 2.11), as well as Canada (b = 1.46) and the USA (b = 1.40). The last two are also the nations with the worst effectiveness values across the entire time period. The positive development in these three nations is quite marked: from 1974–9 to 1990–5, Portugal improved from 48 to 80, Canada from 30 to 53, and the USA from 5 to 25 on the performance scale. Evidently, these three nations have an above-average capacity for reform, and we will address them in greater detail in the discussion of the second general performance index without wealth.

At this juncture we wish to confine ourselves to an analysis of the two nations that actually demonstrate the negative trend predicted by the theories of crisis: the Netherlands (b = −0.31) and New Zealand (b = −0.18). Overall, the reduction in effectiveness is minimal, with the Netherlands slipping from 68 to 62, and New Zealand from 55 to 53 on the performance scale over the entire time period. Yet, given the fact that such slippage is occurring in these nations despite the positive trend of wealth in the general effectiveness index, the question is how such a particular development could come about. One possibility is that this negative development might be traced back to fundamental reforms in economic and social policy that were introduced in both nations in the early 1980s.

New Zealand saw a 'great capitalist restoration' begin in 1984, a process of deregulation and liberalizing the economy that meant a radical rejection of the comprehensive welfare state and Keynesian policies that had previously been in effect (McClintock 1998; Kamp 2000). This reform continued through 1990, and was not only radical but also very rapidly implemented. It included the privatization of state enterprises, drastic curtailments of subsidies and welfare expenditures, partial privatization of health and education systems, and reducing import duties and foreign investment restrictions. As an impressive consequence of this liberalization, inflation was stopped in its tracks, dropping from 11.3 to 2.8 per cent between 1985–9 and 1990–5 (see Table A.1.6). But this positive development evidently occurred at the cost of developments in other policy areas. Thus, in the same time period, unemployment increased from 5.0 to 8.7 per cent (see Table A.1.5), and environmental performance worsened, at a rate greater than average, from 68 to 64 points (see Table 4.13). This radical reform was also associated with great social costs, since both violent and property crimes increased dramatically between 1980–4 and 1985–9 (see Tables A.1.1–A.1.3): the murder rate increased 1.5 times (from 1.3 to 2.0), robberies nearly tripled (from 10.8 to 39.4) and the number of burglaries went up by a quarter (from 2,031 to 2,579).

The Wassenaar agreement between unions and employers in 1982 in the Netherlands also ushered in fundamental economic reforms, the heart of which was the reduction of unemployment and an increase in employment through wage restraints. Cutting state expenditures and privatizing some public services, as part of this reform process (in particular by curtailing welfare payments and tightening eligibility restrictions for claiming them), reduced the budget deficit. The employment rate increased, from 1983 to 1993, from 52 to 63 per cent (OECD 1999*a*) while the unemployment rate dropped from 9.7 to 6.6 per cent (OECD 1999*a*; 1999*b*: 137),[18] leading this 'polder model' of employment growth to be praised as a 'miracle' (Visser and Hemerijck 1997). Though this successful employment policy has since been criticized because it was primarily poorly paid, part-time jobs that were created for women who were pressing into the labour market (Becker 1998; Schmid 1998), it has also been realized that one of the drawbacks of such economic liberalization is an increase in poverty (SCP 1998). The poverty rate increased from 3.9 to 8.1 per cent between 1983 and 1994 (LIS 2000, see also Table A.1.8), due largely, it is thought, to reducing welfare benefits (SCP 1998).

This negative development of general effectiveness in the Netherlands is not only due to the increase in poverty, but is also due to a comparatively dramatic increase in criminality. We already noted, in our earlier analysis, that the Netherlands had by far the greatest annual deterioration of performance in domestic security policy. But unlike in New Zealand, this negative evolution did not just begin with the economic and social policy reforms but was instead part of a much longer-term trend that began already in the mid-1950s (SCP 1998). Given this longer-term trend, it is not likely that increased criminality is causally connected with these reforms, but is likely due to other factors. The Dutch *Social and Cultural Planning Bureau* has

---

[18] Older publications, also utilizing OECD data, even report a reduction in the Dutch unemployment rate from 11.9 to 6.3 per cent (Becker 1998: 13; Schmid 1998: 98). The discrepancy arises because the *Labor Force Statistics* published by the OECD after 1996 retrospectively include data for all EU member nations (Greece excepted) that are based on Eurostat values since 1982 (OECD 1999*b*: 133).

not been able to pinpoint specific causes for the increase in its national social report, but cites excessive alcohol and drug consumption, the increased availability of weapons, and diminishing social control as possibilities (SCP 1998).

Accordingly, it is possible to argue with some assurance that in New Zealand the negative trend in general effectiveness finds its causes in the radical economic and social policy reforms begun in 1984, since reform efforts and the negative trend of the performance indicators fall together. In the Netherlands, by contrast, one can only assert a temporal connection between economic and social reforms and the increase in poverty. As we previously indicated with respect to the comparative studies of poverty in western democracies (Gottschalk and Smeeding 1997; Gottschalk et al. 1997), this development was not confined to the Netherlands. De-industrialization has had the effect in all western democracies of replacing well-paid industrial jobs for the poorly qualified or unqualified with poorly paid service sector jobs. Social benefits have also been reduced in many western democracies, and the eligibility criteria for obtaining such benefits have been restricted. From this perspective, the Dutch developments are part of more general changes in economic and social policy such as de-industrialization or the reorganization or dismantling of the welfare state. The 'polder model' thus only reinforces the existing trends.

Performance index: general effectiveness without wealth
The role wealth plays in the level and development of general effectiveness can be seen by comparing the global index of general effectiveness with the global index of general effectiveness without wealth. Table 4.15 provides data for the latter index. In addition, Table 4.16 directly compares both indices with respect to level and development of the nations. It ranks the nations and assigns them to a scale differentiating between best, above average, average, below average and, worst practice. The statistical indicator for development is the difference between the level of effectiveness in the first (1974–9) and the last time period (1990–5) investigated.

In terms of the *level* of effectiveness, what is striking is that the same groups of nations are found in the 'best practices' as well as 'worst practices' groups in both indices, respectively (see Table 4.16). At the top, the only difference is a small change in the rank order, such that in general effectiveness without wealth, Japan (95.3) has the best performance (compared to 89.1 in the general effectiveness index), followed by Norway (94.4 vs. 90.3) and Switzerland (93.6 vs. 89.2). At the bottom, and here without changes in ranking, one finds the USA (13.8 vs. 15.3), Canada (42.2 vs. 42.2) and, Australia (48.0 vs. 46.3) with the worst practices. In the other categories, there are also minimal differences between the indices, with individual

TABLE 4.15. *General effectiveness without wealth (performance index^a) 1974–95*

	Level (mean per period)					Trend		
	1974–9	1980–4	1985–9	1990–5	1974–95	V	Difference	b
Australia	49.0	49.4	47.3	46.6	48.0	0.06	−2.4	−0.16
Canada	35.3	38.0	47.3	48.5	42.2	0.15	13.2	0.92**
Great Britain	62.6	62.8	61.9	56.9	61.0	0.06	−5.7	−0.26*
Ireland	67.7	63.4	67.0	68.1	66.7	0.05	0.4	0.10
New Zealand	63.7	59.0	51.9	53.2	57.1	0.09	−10.4	−0.63**
USA	8.4	9.6	18.9	18.5	13.8	0.47	10.1	0.79**
	47.8	47.0	49.1	48.6	48.1	0.10	0.9	
Denmark	63.8	60.7	65.4	70.1	65.2	0.06	6.2	0.45**
Finland	69.0	73.1	78.5	74.7	73.6	0.06	5.7	0.40**
Norway	95.0	93.7	93.0	95.6	94.4	0.02	0.7	0.06
Sweden	82.0	84.0	87.2	83.6	84.1	0.03	1.5	0.17
	77.5	77.9	81.0	81.0	79.3	0.04	3.5	
Austria	86.1	87.5	92.9	90.9	89.3	0.04	4.8	0.39**
Belgium	74.4	70.9	78.1	77.6	75.3	0.05	3.2	0.30*
France	75.3	70.5	74.3	74.1	73.7	0.03	−1.3	−0.01
Germany	75.4	76.3	78.1	76.5	76.5	0.04	1.1	0.09
Italy	59.9	58.5	65.2	60.0	60.8	0.06	0.2	0.09
The Netherlands	76.2	71.7	70.2	62.0	69.9	0.09	−14.2	−0.82**
	74.5	72.6	76.5	73.5	74.3	0.05	−1.0	
Greece	71.9	66.6	70.9	73.9	71.0	0.07	1.9	0.28
Portugal	50.0	58.6	74.2	83.4	68.2	0.20	33.4	2.22**
Spain	61.0	52.1	46.3	52.5	52.1	0.11	−8.5	−0.42
	61.0	59.1	63.8	69.9	63.8	0.13	9.0	
Switzerland	95.3	93.5	95.0	91.0	93.6	0.03	−4.3	−0.17*
Japan	88.4	96.2	99.3	98.1	95.3	0.06	9.7	0.66**
	91.8	94.8	97.1	94.6	94.5	0.04	2.7	
All countries	67.16	66.49	69.67	69.32	68.19	0.07	2.2	0.17
V	0.30	0.30	0.28	0.28	0.28			
Correlation with 1974–9		0.98	0.91	0.88			−0.33	

** $p < 0.01$; * $p < 0.05$ (two-tailed).
^{a} Values range from 0 to 100 (0 = worst practice … 100 = best practice) from 1974–95. Values are the mean of the standardized variables for domestic security policy (see Table 4.4), misery (see Table 4.6), social policy (see Table 4.10), and environmental policy (see Table 4.13) with subsequent standardization of the mean.

Legend: V = coefficient of variation; difference = difference between 1974–9 and 1990–5; b = unstandardized regression coefficient (OLS-estimate).

nations moving up or down in the rank ordering by no more than two positions. In only a few cases do nations move from the category 'below average' to 'average' (Ireland), or from 'above average' to 'average' (the

TABLE 4.16. *Ranking of nations according to general effectiveness with and without wealth*[a]

Practice	General effectiveness		General effectiveness without wealth	
	Level	Trend	Level	Trend
Best	1. Norway (90.3) 2. Switzerland (89.2) 3. Japan (89.1)	1. Portugal (32.1) 2. Canada (22.3) 3. USA (20.5)	1. Japan (95.3) 2. Norway (94.4) 3. Switzerland (93.6)	1. Portugal (33.4) 2. Canada (13.2) 3. USA (10.1)
Above average	4. Austria (83.3) 5. Sweden (79.8) 6. Belgium (73) 7. France (72.1) 8. Germany (71.4) 9. Finland (70.2) 10. Greece (67.7)	4. Japan (18.8) 5. Austria (15.1) 6. Denmark (14.9) 7. Finland (14.7) 8. Germany (12.7) 9. Belgium (12.6) 10. Norway (12.2)	4. Austria (89.3) 5. Sweden (84.1) 6. Germany (76.5) 7. Belgium (75.3) 8. France (73.7) 9. Finland (73.6) 10. Greece (71) 11. The Netherlands (69.9)	4. Japan (9.7) 5. Denmark (6.2) 6. Finland (5.7) 7. Austria (4.8) 8. Belgium (3.2)
Average	11. The Netherlands (65.9) 12. Portugal (65.1) 13. Ireland (64.6)	11. Sweden (11) 12. Greece (10.9)	12. Portugal (68.2)	9. Greece (1.9) 10. Sweden (1.5)
Below average	14. Denmark (63.6) 15. Italy (60.4) 16. Great Britain (59.3) 17. Spain (53.9) 18. New Zealand (53.3)	13. France (8.9) 14. Switzerland (8.9) 15. Ireland (7.9) 16. Italy (7.8) 17. Australia (5.8) 18. Great Britain (1.4)	13. Ireland (66.7) 14. Denmark (65.2) 15. Great Britain (61) 16. Italy (60.8) 17. New Zealand (57.1) 18. Spain (52.1)	11. Germany (1.1) 12. Norway (0.7) 13. Ireland (0.4) 14. Italy (0.2) 15. France (−1.3) 16. Australian (−2.4) 17. Switzerland (−4.3) 18. Great Britain (−5.7)
Worst	19. Australia (46.3) 20. Canada (42.2) 21. USA (15.3)	19. Spain (0.1) 20. New Zealand (−2.8) 21. The Netherlands (−5.4)	19. Australia (48) 20. Canada (42.2) 21. USA (13.8)	19. Spain (−8.5) 20. New Zealand (−10.4) 21. The Netherlands (−14.2)
	All countries (65.5)	All countries (11)	All countries (68.2)	All countries (2.2)

[a] Level = mean for the time period 1974–95; trend = difference between the means of the time periods 1974–9 and 1990–5.

Source: General effectiveness (see Table 4.14) and general effectiveness without wealth (see Table 4.15).

Netherlands) when one compares the general effectiveness without wealth index with the general effectiveness index. Therefore, at least in terms of effectiveness level, including wealth has no real effect on the ranking of the nations.

The situation is somewhat different in the *development* of effectiveness. For one, the average for all nations over the entire time period shows an increase of only 2 points on the performance scale in the general effectiveness without wealth index, even though it stands at 11 points in the general effectiveness index. Leaving wealth out also has the consequence that now seven (rather than two) nations show a negative trend, whereby this trend is significant in the Netherlands (b = -0.82) and New Zealand (b = -0.63) at the 1 per cent level, and in Great Britain (b = -0.26) and Switzerland (b = -0.17) at the 5 per cent level. In the case of the last two, this slight negative trend can be ascribed particularly to domestic security and environmental policies. In this index of general effectiveness without wealth, Portugal (b = 2.22), Canada (b = 0.92), and the USA (b = 0.79) show an above-average positive trend as was the case in the first global index that indicated that these nations were among those with the greatest improvement. In terms of the performance scale, Portugal improved from 50 to 83, Canada from 35 to 49, and the USA from 8 to 19 between 1970–4 and 1990–5. Thus, in these three nations, above-average improvement in effectiveness is not solely due to above-average increases in wealth. These three nations do share a commonalty, for as we indicated in Table 4.15, these nations had (along with Australia), the worst initial values in the first 1974–9 time period. This speaks for a kind of 'floor effect'; given that the effectiveness values are at the bottom end, the likelihood of further worsening shrinks and that of improvement grows. This kind of effect is not enough to explain the positive trend in these nations, however, since in the case of Australia there is actually stagnation or even a small decline from 49 (1974–84) to 47 (1985–95). In Portugal, Canada, and the USA, it is thus likely that explanations for the positive improvement in effectiveness lie in political reforms.

In the Portuguese case, one can note two reforms that could have caused the above-average evolution, particularly in the health and the misery dimensions. Social reforms were already begun in the time after the military coup of April 1974, and before the formal introduction of democracy in April 1976. Various interim governments introduced minimum wage guarantees and began to expand the health, education, and welfare systems (Bernecker 1990; Maravall 1993). Between 1976 and 1979, Portugal still had the highest infant mortality rate (29.7 per 1,000 live births) of all western democracies, but with the introduction of the reforms, this rate declined precipitously, and was only one-third as high (9.2) by 1990–5 (see Table A.1.7). Though this was still the highest infant mortality rate among the western democracies, no other nation had seen such a large increase in performance on this indicator as Portugal.

Economic reforms were begun during the same transitional era as the social reforms. They initially included socialist programmes, as banks, insurance companies, and infrastructure enterprises were nationalized, and large landowners dispossessed (Bernecker 1990; Maravall 1993). The consequences included rising inflation rates and growing unemployment; in the time period from 1976–9, Portugal had the highest inflation rate (25.1 per cent) by far of all western democracies (see Table A.1.6), and an unemployment rate (7.4 per cent) only exceeded by Ireland (7.6; see Table A.1.5). A change of economic course had already begun in 1976 under the first socialist government, and by the early 1980s, many of these reforms were rescinded. Insurance companies and industries were re-privatized, subsidies were reduced, and labour laws (including those to do with dismissing workers) were liberalized (Bernecker 1990; Maravall 1993). The motivation was partly to bring the budget into balance and to improve economic competitiveness, but it was also to better position the nation to make it eligible for EU membership.

The consequence of introducing this second set of more economically liberal reforms is reflected in the sharp reduction both in the inflation rate, which fell from 22.7 (1980–4) by two-thirds to 8.3 (1990–5), and in the unemployment rate, which sank from 7.7 to 5.5 over the same time span. The turning away from socialist ideals, which can be seen among other things in the deletion of all socialist language in the 1988 revision of the Constitution (Bernecker 1990: 27), meant Portugal experienced a near exemplary economic upturn. In the 1990s, the nation is among those (along with Ireland) with the largest increase in GDP.

Canada and the USA, unlike Portugal, are established democracies and wealthy industrialized nations. This may be one reason why the increase in effectiveness lags slightly behind Portugal's. Still, the increase in both nations is above average, and that is particularly noteworthy given the extremely low levels of effectiveness they demonstrate. Canada is unusual in comparative perspective as it is the only case in which the poverty rate clearly sank, from 13.6 (1974–9) to 10.9 (1990–5) (see Burniaux et al. 1998b: 9 and Table A.1.8). Canadian studies of income inequality have been able to show that by the mid-1980s, at the latest, while inequality of market income increased, it was possible to compensate for this negative development by increasing income transfer payments and by increasing the progressiveness of the tax system (Osberg et al. 1997; Burniaux 1998b: 10). Canada has thus been able to prove its ability to carry out social policy reforms.

The third positive example of a reform that the USA provides is specifically evident in unemployment and environmental policy. While unemployment initially increased (from 6.8 in 1974–9 to 8.3 by 1980–4), it fell back again to 6.4 in 1990–5; (see Table A.1.5). Portugal and the USA are the only nations where the unemployment rate is lower in 1990–5 than it was in 1970–4. The low unemployment rate in the USA, and its associated job creation was praised as an 'employment miracle', and served in part as a positive model for labour market policy reforms in European democracies, particularly in Germany, where unemployment was increasing at the time.

The favourable development in the USA was ascribed to the greater flexibility in its labour market, as it was able to react to changes in the world economy that include increasingly global economic competition, technological change brought about through de-industrialization, and a vanishing demand for unqualified or underqualified workers, by increasing the wage spread and reducing labour costs (Barrell et al. 1996; Addison 1997). This evolution was helped by falling unionization rates and stagnation of the minimum wage (Addison 1997). But the above-average performance in the labour market is associated with greater costs, since increasing the wage spread may be one cause of increasing inequality and poverty in the USA, at least if one regards the last value (17.6) in 1990–5 as significantly greater than the first (15.9) in 1970–4 (see Table A.1.8).

Environmental policy is the other policy area in which the USA was able to increase its performance, at least until the 1990s, in an above-average manner, and showed its particular ability to reform. Overall, in the performance scale (see Table 4.13) it was able to raise its value from 2 to 12, though this positive development stagnated after 1990. After 1970, the USA was accounted the environmental pioneer that had passed and implemented the farthest-reaching national laws and regulations to protect the environment (Andrews 1997). This political direction halted by the mid-1990s, and the support for regulatory measures and governmental expenditures for environmental issues have had to face greater opposition.

We can conclude that even if we take as a basis a global index of general effectiveness that does not include wealth, we cannot find empirical support for the hypothesis that there is a continual worsening in the effectiveness of western democracies, as theories of crisis would have it. Nations showing a negative trend are a minority (the Netherlands, New Zealand, Great Britain, Switzerland), and the dominant trend is nations showing improvement (Portugal, Canada, USA, Japan, Denmark, Finland, Austria, Belgium) or a steady-state condition (Australia, Ireland, Norway, Sweden, Germany, France, Italy, Greece, Spain). A closer analysis of nations like New Zealand or the Netherlands that seem to confirm the diagnosis of crisis indicates that their negative developments either need to be seen in the context of national reforms in economic and social policy or that there are nation-specific developments (as in rising crime in the Netherlands). These few confirming nations are evidently special cases rather than typical examples for the theoretically predicted negative trend.

A picture of stability dominates at the level of general effectiveness without wealth, and this is not just based on the fact that the mean level of effectiveness has only increased by 2 points between the first and last time periods investigated. It is also that there are only marginal changes in the ranking of the nations over time (the correlation over time decreases from 0.98 to 0.88) but also because there is minimal change in the coefficient of variation (sinking from 0.30 to 0.28).[19] The national level of general effectiveness is thus evidently a relatively stable characteristic of western democracies. This suggests in turn that to explain national levels of effectiveness, relatively stable factors such as cultural patterns or institutional arrangements may play a much more decisive role.

The data presented here indicate that a loss of general effectiveness in western democracies predicted in theories of crisis cannot be confirmed. On the other hand, there is also no empirical evidence for an opposite, positive development in the manner partly suggested in modernization theories. Eight nations show an increase in effectiveness after 1974, but only in Portugal is this very pronounced. A closer look at the three significantly positive examples of Portugal, Canada, and the USA indicated that the increased effectiveness there seemed more related to nation-specific constellations and conditions rather than general conditions influencing all western democracies. Based on the data analysed here, there was general progress and a corresponding convergence between nations after the economic recession began in 1973. But this was confined to only a few economic and social policy components, particularly national income and health, both dimensions usually accounted as part of socio-economic modernity.[20] Unlike such a narrow concept of modernization, our concept of political effectiveness encompasses a broader spectrum of the most important policy areas, including not only progress but also the costs or drawbacks of socio-economic modernity, such as social disintegration tendencies (reflected in declines in domestic security), environmental degradation and the exploitation of natural resources, as well as—though here with caveats—rises in poverty rates. Applying this more comprehensive conceptualization of welfare, one can hardly call the developments in western democracies since 1973 progressive.

[19] Only in the index of general effectiveness, that also includes wealth, does the coefficient of variation slip from 0.30 to 0.25 (see Table 4.14).

[20] Beyond this, such a positive development would certainly be noticeable in education, if corresponding comparable data existed about educational attainment rates.

Time Periods and Families of Nations Compared

Earlier we discussed, in some detail, the individual policy areas as well as general effectiveness, and this leaves several questions open. The first is with reference to the development of political effectiveness. In the analyses conducted so far, we could not confirm a continual decrease in effectiveness after 1973 either in specific policy areas or in general effectiveness. However, this does not exclude the possibility that the negative effects of economic globalization have only manifested themselves since 1990 and thus the predicted decline in effectiveness would only set in after that date (Beisheim and Walter 1997; Garrett 1998). This possibility, which is a modified hypothesis about the development of political effectiveness, would have to be answered empirically.

The second is a question about the families of nations that were introduced as a heuristic to structure the analysis of the level and development of policy-specific and general effectiveness. Based on the presented frequency distributions, a variety of similarities and differences between particular families of nations seem to stand out with respect to the level of effectiveness.[21] These could be interpreted to mean that culture has an influence on the level of political effectiveness. However, beyond these individual observations, the more general question whether families of nations systematically differ with respect to their effectiveness is unsettled. We address these various questions below.

The development of effectiveness before and after 1990

The various crisis theories predict losses of effectiveness in western democracies after 1973. The predicted negative trend can be seen for some performance indicators such as the unemployment and poverty rates, and in the production of municipal waste. But this trend does not exist at the level of the policy areas themselves. The negative trend in domestic security policy is a longer-term process, the trend in both economic and social policy is positive, and in environmental policy there is no movement at all in either direction. It also cannot be seen at the level of general effectiveness (for a summary, see Table 4.17, column 1974–95). The general hypothesis that there is a continuous decline in political effectiveness since 1973 simply does not have empirical evidence to support it.

At least some globalization theories suggest that the negative effects will be manifested particularly after 1990 (Beisheim and Walter 1997; Garrett 1998),

---

[21] There is only one case where a connection appears to exist between a family of nations and the *development* of the level of effectiveness, and that is in the southern European family where, between 1974 and 1995, the socio-political performance improved the most (see Table 4.10).

TABLE 4.17. *Development of effectiveness before and after 1990[a] (regression analysis)*

	1974–95	1974–89	1980–9	1990–5
Domestic security policy	−0.82**	−0.83**	−1.02*	0.18
(a) Violent crimes	−0.47**	−0.41*	−0.48	0.09
Murder and manslaughter[b]	0.00	0.00	0.00	−0.02
Robbery[b]	2.34**	2.11**	2.66*	0.10
(b) Property crimes (burglary)	−0.65**	−0.72**	−0.93*	0.16
Economic policy	1.9**	1.80**	2.72**	1.73*
(a) National income	3.04**	2.87**	2.97**	3.23**
(b) Misery	0.39**	0.38	1.93**	−0.15
Unemployment rate[b]	0.25**	0.30**	0.11	0.55*
Inflation rate[b]	−0.51**	−0.58**	−0.96**	−0.71**
Social policy	0.83**	1.04**	0.71	0.56
(a) Health	1.54**	1.76**	1.30**	1.30**
(b) Income distribution (poverty rate)	−0.31	−0.22	−0.25	−0.47
Environmental policy	−0.08	0.05	0.05	0.19
(a) Environmental quality	−0.08	0.17	−0.04	0.15
Sulphur oxides emissions[b]	−2.41**	−2.88**	−3.19**	−2.26
Nitrogen oxides emissions[b]	−0.05	0.07	0.16	−0.85
Carbon dioxide emissions[b]	−0.01	−0.05	0.00	0.04
Municipal waste[b]	5.71**	4.60**	7.16*	6.11
Fertilizer use[b]	−0.02	0.03	−0.01	−0.02
(b) Quality and quantity of natural resources				
Resources (water consumption)	−0.06	−0.00	0.13	0.19
General effectiveness	0.7**	0.73**	0.87*	0.94
General effectiveness without wealth	0.17	0.23	0.60	0.28

** $p < 0.01$; * $p < 0.05$ (two-tailed).
[a] Unstandardized regression coefficients (OLS-estimate); $N=457$.
[b] Refers to original indicators; performance indices ranging from 0 to 100 are unmarked. In the case of the original indicators, positive signs indicate improved effectiveness, and in the case of performance indices, negative signs indicate worsened effectiveness.

assuming that the collapse of state socialism in central and eastern Europe would reinforce the process of economic globalization. This modification would mean the predicted general decline in political effectiveness would only be noticeable after 1990. We have examined this possibility for all levels of performance: the individual indicators, the index of policy-specific components, the indices of policy-specific effectiveness, and the two indices of general effectiveness, both with and without wealth. The empirical analysis is undertaken by comparing the mean annual change for the time before and after 1990. The statistical measure used is the unstandardized regression coefficient. The mean annual change before 1990 is calculated both for the time between 1974 and 1989 as well as for the time from 1980 to 1989, since this second, shorter time period does not include the negative consequences resulting from the economic recession after 1973. If there is a negative turn in the development of effectiveness after 1990, then it should be seen particularly as a contrast to the trend in this shorter, 1980–9 period.

The data presented in Table 4.17 indicate that even this modified hypothesis of a negative development of effectiveness for the time period after 1990 is not confirmed. There are changes in two policy areas after 1990. In the case of domestic security policy, the negative trend comes to an unexpected halt. Only in the misery dimension does one find any evidence for the predicted negative trend, since the mean annual increase in the unemployment rate rises from 0.11 (1980–9) to 0.55 (after 1990) (in the original indicators, positive signs denote a worsening of effectiveness). There are also a few, if weak, indications that the negative development in the poverty rate has increased since 1990, but neither coefficient for the time from 1980 to 1989 (−0.25) nor for the time from 1990 to 1995 (−0.47) is statistically significant.

So one can conclude that at least until 1995, the end of the time period investigated here, there is no empirical evidence that effectiveness in western democracies has generally worsened as a consequence of economic globalization. One sees the predicted worsening of effectiveness only in the case of the unemployment, whereas the possibility of a similar trend cannot be excluded in the case of the poverty rate.

Families of nations

The families of nations concept is based on the premise that the nations that constitute a family are relatively homogenous cultural units. It also assumes that culture influences the form national institutions take, as well as the policy orientations of citizens and politicians, and that these lead to political decisions and their corresponding results. The descriptive analyses of levels of effectiveness have indicated numerous commonalties as well as differences between certain families of nations, but there is a question whether these are systematic differences or not.[22]

To answer this question, at first the distributions of the performance indices were analysed to determine whether individual families of nations differ, based on higher or lower levels of performance. A dummy variable was constructed for each family, and this variable was correlated with the policy-specific as well as with the general performance indices. This correlation coefficient has an advantage over the level of effectiveness measure presented earlier. It provides information about the relative extent of the family of nations' level of effectiveness as well as how strong the relationship is between the families of nations and the level of effectiveness (Castles 1998a: 316).

The correlation coefficients presented in Table 4.18 show a very clear pattern. On one side stand the English-speaking nations with consistently

---

[22] On differences between the families of nations regarding public policy making or outputs see Castles 1993, 1998a as well as Obinger and Wagschal 2001.

TABLE 4.18. *Families of nations and level of effectiveness (correlations)*[a]

	Families of nations				
Effectiveness	English-speaking	Nordic	Continental Western European	Southern European	Switzerland, Japan
Domestic security policy	−0.44**	−0.05	0.05	0.33**	0.29**
Economic policy	−0.08	0.13**	0.12*	−0.49**	0.34**
Misery	−0.18**	0.16**	0.16**	−0.56**	0.46**
Social policy	−0.56**	0.44**	0.32**	−0.35**	0.18**
Environmental policy	−0.57**	0.20**	0.01	0.28**	0.27**
General effectiveness	−0.65**	0.28**	0.19**	−0.07	0.42**
General effectiveness without wealth	−0.66**	0.28**	0.19**	−0.08	0.44**

** $p < 0.01$; * $p < 0.05$ (two-tailed).
[a] Correlations (Pearson's r) between dummies for the respective family of nations and performance indices ($N = 457$).

negative coefficients. In other words, compared with the other nations they have lower values both in policy-specific and in general effectiveness. This negative difference is only marginal in the case of economic policy and on the misery dimension. At the other end stand the special cases of Switzerland and Japan, showing consistently positive deviations, though in the case of social policy, this positive deviation is the lowest compared with the other effectiveness dimensions. The correlations are also consistently positive for the Continental Western European and for the Scandinavian nations (with one, slightly negative, exception in latter case in domestic security effectiveness). But only in social policy do both families of nations show notably higher values than those found for other nations.

In the southern European family there are, by contrast, both positive and negative correlations: positive correlations in domestic security and environmental policies, and negative correlations for economic and social policy. In other words, the economic and social policy stragglers are simultaneously better in domestic security and environmental policies and worse in economic and social policy. This indicates the existence of a quite specific, imbalanced type of political effectiveness to which we wish to turn next.

It is evident that families of nations differ with respect to effectiveness. The decisive question, however, is just how good the families of nations concept is in explaining political effectiveness and which families of nations statistically differ from one another. To analyse these questions empirically, an analysis of variance was conducted, followed by a comparison of the means of the families of nations. The results of the analysis presented in Table 4.19 shows that there are statistically significant differences between the families of nations not only with respect to policy-specific effectiveness but also with

TABLE 4.19. *Families of nations and level of effectiveness (analysis of variance)[a]*

| | Families of nations | | | | | | | |
Effectiveness	English-speaking	Nordic	Continental Western European	Southern European	Switzerland, Japan	All nations	F	eta
Domestic security policy	52.2	64.7	68.1	**84.1**	**85.2**	66.6	50.5**	0.56
Economic policy	52.2	59.3	57.8	30.7	74.1	54.4	58.9**	0.59
Misery	57.4	68.7	67.2	36.2	88.3	62.6	124.6**	0.72
Social policy	49.6	84.7	**76.9**	49.3	**77.8**	66.9	160.1**	0.77
Environmental policy	49.4	77.1	68.9	83.7	86.0	68.4	72.4**	0.63
General effectiveness	46.8	76.0	71.0	62.5	89.2	65.6	140.7**	0.75
General effectiveness without wealth	48.1	79.3	74.3	64.2	94.5	68.3	150.2**	0.76
N	132	88	132	61	44	457		

** $p < 0.01$ (two-tailed).
[a] Numbers in italics or bold indicate families of nations *not* differing significantly ($p < 0.05$) from one another (Scheffe-test).

respect to both forms of general effectiveness. Membership in a particular family of nations quite clearly plays a central role in questions of effectiveness. But as the *F*-values and eta (coefficient of association) indicate, the importance of the family varies according to the particular policy area under discussion.

Thus, the explanatory power of the families of nations is higher for social policy and the economic misery dimension than it is for domestic security, economic policy (which also includes national income), and environmental policy. One should not overinterpret the differences between the various policy areas, but it seems that cultural differences that determine preferences of politicians and citizens, as well as policies and institutions, are greatest in economic and social policy. Such differences can be seen particularly well in the differing welfare state regimes that have developed in various western democracies (Esping-Andersen 1990).

Commonalities and differences between the individual families of nations can be more closely identified on the basis of a comparison of the means. For each family of nations, we first look at the number of policy areas that have means that differ, in a statistically significantly sense, from the means of the other families. Here the English-speaking family has the most differences, as it shows statistically significant deviations from the other families in three out of five policy areas, with the worst values for domestic security and environmental policies, and an average value for the misery dimension.

The Scandinavian and Continental Western European family, by contrast, differ systematically only by a single dimension from the other families. The special features are that the Scandinavians show an above-average social policy performance, while the Continental Western European nations have an above-average environmental performance. Both families have the most commonalties with other families of nations, and in this, the commonalties between these two nations dominate. In fact, the differences are so small that one can argue that there are large cultural commonalties between the Scandinavian and the Continental Western European families.

The other families fall in between these two poles. The special cases of Switzerland and Japan as well as the southern European nations differ in a statistically significant fashion from all other families of nations on the economic policy and economic misery dimensions, whereby Switzerland and Japan show the highest, and southern Europe the lowest performance values.

An even clearer pattern of difference can be seen at the level of general effectiveness. The differences between the Scandinavian and the West European continental families completely vanish by this level, and with the exception of these two families, the means of all the families vary from another in a statistically significant fashion. The special cases of Switzerland and Japan have by far the best general effectiveness, followed by the Scandinavian and Continental Western European nations. The southern European nations are in third place, while the English-speaking nations show by far the worst performance.

Of course one cannot exclude the possibility that the influence of the families of nations on political effectiveness is overestimated inasmuch as missing data in the time series are replaced by the mean values of the respective family of nations. This problem is greatest for the poverty index, where the missing values for New Zealand, Greece, Portugal, and Japan were replaced in this manner (see Table A.1.8). To answer this objection, a second analysis of variance was carried out using only the seventeen nations for which original values for poverty exist. Based on this re-analysis, differences between families of nations remain statistically significant as before, and the influence on social policy was only minimally reduced from an eta value of 0.77 (all nations) to 0.71 (seventeen nations). Thus, the results presented here on the effect of families of nations are not an artefact of the estimation procedure used to replace missing values.

The premise that performance varies systematically by families of nations is confirmed by these analyses. Since this categorization primarily reflects common cultural foundations, one can conclude from this that cultural differences have an influence on the level of effectiveness. This general result must be qualified in two respects, however.

First, the families of nations do not have completely distinct performance patterns; instead, in every policy area there are overlaps between individual families. The English-speaking nations distinguish themselves by having the least overlaps, and that means that they also can claim the greatest degree of uniqueness. The special cases of Switzerland and Japan, as well as the southern European family, are also relatively distinct. It is among the Scandinavian and Continental Western European nations that one finds so many commonalties that only individual policy areas make each group unique. In the case of the Scandinavian family, it is an above-average social policy performance, reflecting the superiority of the social democratic welfare state regime compared to other regimes (Esping-Andersen 1990; Schmidt 1998b; Goodin et al. 1999; Kohl 1999). The continental Western European nations are not either above or below average; their distinctiveness appears in an average level of environmental performance.

The second qualification is with reference to the composition of the families of nations. English-speaking and Continental Western European families are more heterogeneous internally, while the Scandinavian and southern European families are more homogenous. Ireland is an exception within its family, as it has better performance than the other English-speaking nations in domestic security and environmental policy, but worse performance in economic policy. Italy stands out among the Continental Western European nations as well, given its below-average economic and welfare state performance.

With these two qualifications, the family of nations concept has shown itself to be a productive concept for explaining the differing levels of political effectiveness. Based on the results of the analyses presented here, we can assume that culture is an important determinant of political effectiveness.

STRUCTURE OF EFFECTIVENESS (POLICY PATTERNS)

Having analysed the level and development of policy-specific and general effectiveness, we now turn to the descriptive questions about the structure of political effectiveness or policy patterns. The bivariate analysis of the relations between individual effectiveness dimensions is a first aspect. Here the key issues are the well-known propositions arguing that there is conflict between economic and social policy as well as between the economic and environmental policy. Further issues refer to the hypotheses formulated in the context of crisis theories that argue that the incompatibility or tension between these various dimensions of effectiveness have increased after the Oil Crisis in 1973, but particularly since 1990. The second aspect deals with the entire spectrum of policy-specific effectiveness. Using the suggested typology of political effectiveness, we investigate which types of political effectiveness have emerged in western democracies, whether there are systematic differences between the families of nations, and how stable these policy patterns are over time.

Trade-offs between Individual Policy Areas?

Democracies and national governments are expected to achieve a multiplicity of heterogeneous political goals. Every political decision in pursuit of one particular goal, however, is associated with costs. Hence, it cannot be excluded that there are trade-offs between individual goals, that is, that one goal can only be realized at the cost of another goal, and vice versa. The economy stands at the centre of the most well-known theories of conflict. It is suggested that it conflicts with social policy on the one side, and with environmental policy on the other.

However, these theories of conflict are not based on assertions that have a solid empirical foundation, but rather they are theoretical hypotheses based in part on normative assertions. The theory that economic policy and social policy are in conflict is derived from economic liberalism, while asserted conflicts between economic and environmental goals come primarily from the left-liberal ecological theory tradition. In both cases, contradictory hypotheses are put forward, either asserting that the policies are complementary or that one dimension is independent of the other. In part, these alternative hypotheses, particular those emphasizing complementarity, are also based on normative convictions and are elements of general ideological belief systems. We therefore now turn to an empirical examination of which of these competing hypotheses about the relationship might find confirmation.

The different hypotheses describe relations that refer to different levels of the policy areas. Thus, connections are predicted between policy areas in general (e.g. economic and environmental policy), between individual components of differing policy areas (e.g. national income and income distribution), or between policy areas and individual components of policy areas (e.g. environmental policy and national income). It is for that reason that the relationships between the indices measuring individual policy areas and individual components of the policy areas are analysed. The relationships are measured by means of correlation coefficients.

For control purposes, two other correlation coefficients were utilized. One of these does not include the USA, since it is an outlier in many of the dimensions of effectiveness. The fundamental problem of outliers is that the probability that the relationships between two variables are in fact created by the outlier increases. The other, second coefficient is a partial correlation that measures the relationship between two performance indices by holding wealth (the indicator is GDP) constant. As noted previously, GDP or national income is not just a dimension of economic policy, but also expresses the extent of fiscal resources available for achieving policy goals. By holding this factor constant, we can control for the fact that a relationship between two performance variables is created through the existence of this third variable. This partial correlation coefficient also controls for the different composition of the sample of nations, as it includes not only well-established democracies but also newer as well as comparatively poorer southern European nations. In interpreting the correlation coefficients, it should be kept in mind that all the dimensions of effectiveness are measured with performance indices standardized on a 0 to 100 scale, thus low values indicate worse and high values indicate better performance.

Because our primary interest here is descriptive, we have not included other explanatory factors such as the size of state expenditures or the openness of the national economy, as control variables. We are interested in which relationships or configurations exist in western democracies between the individual dimensions of effectiveness, but we are not interested under which specific conditions these relationships are established. The interest in these configurations is also why the relationships between the individual effectiveness dimensions are not analysed and interpreted as causal relationship. It is true that the correlation matrices include information on the relationship between domestic security and the variables per capita income, poverty, and unemployment, all of which are regarded as determinants of criminality (Cohen and Felson 1979; Blau and Blau 1982; Messner 1989; Norström 1988). We are not interested in analysing such explanatory models but instead want to identify the character of the relationship between the various effectiveness dimensions—in particular to what extent these relations are conflict-laden, complementary, or independent.

The empirical analyses are organized as follows: first, the hypotheses about the conflict between economic and social policy, and then the conflict between the economic and environmental policy, are investigated. Domestic security, for which there is no independent conflict proposition, is analysed in connection with these two propositions. For both propositions, the relationships are first investigated over the entire time period from 1974 to 1995, and then are analysed separately for the time before and after 1990 in order to find empirical evidence whether the incompatibility between effectiveness dimensions increased during this time. Much, and quite varied, information is presented in the correlation matrices, though we limit ourselves primarily to analysing and interpreting the relations regarded as most relevant in the theoretical part of our study. The results of the analysis of the relationships between the individual effectiveness dimensions are summarized and discussed later.

The conflict between economic and social policy
There are two propositions about the conflict between economic and social policies, one comprehensive and the other limited. Following the comprehensive proposition, a conflict exists between all economic policy components and the welfare state goal of income equality (Lindert and Williamson 1985; Kenworthy 1995). The limited proposition only asserts that a conflict exists between national income and income equality (Okun 1975). What these two economic liberal propositions also have in common is that conflict is seen only with one component of the welfare state, namely income distribution (poverty rate). Other welfare state components such as health and education are interpreted as investments in human capital and are thus seen as having a complementary relationship to economic goals.

Turning to the limited proposition first in our empirical examination, we find a complementary, strongly positive (correlation coefficient of 0.70) connection between national income and health, as predicted (Table 4.20). But the proposed conflictual, negative relationship between national income and poverty cannot be found. This relation is, however, also not complementary, as the social democratic hypothesis would have it, but instead the two dimensions are independent of one another ($r = -0.08$). Our analysis thus confirms neither the economic liberal nor the social democratic hypotheses about the relationship between national income and poverty. Instead, we empirically confirm independence, and while this is not part of a political ideology, it has been suggested as a possibility in a few empirical studies (Korpi 1985; Castles and Dowrick 1990).

TABLE 4.20. *Correlations between economic, social, and domestic security policy*[a]

	Social policy			Health			Poverty		
	All countries	Excluding USA	Controlling for wealth	All countries	Excluding USA	Controlling for wealth	All countries	Excluding USA	Controlling for wealth
Economic policy	0.44**	0.54**	—	0.67**	0.69**	—	0.13**	0.28**	—
National income	0.29**	0.39**		0.71**	0.74**		−0.08	0.06	
Misery	0.46**	0.54**	0.39**	0.39**	0.40**	0.16**	0.34**	0.45**	0.41**
Price stability	0.50**	0.57**	0.43**	0.69**	0.70**	0.40**	0.21**	0.31**	0.36**
Full employment	0.11*	0.15*	0.15**	−0.16**	−0.17**	−0.10*	0.24**	0.29**	0.23**

	Domestic security policy			Violent crimes			Property crimes		
	All countries	Excluding USA	Controlling for wealth	All countries	Excluding USA	Controlling for wealth	All countries	Excluding USA	Controlling for wealth
Economic policy	−0.28**	−0.20**	—	−0.17**	−0.08	—	−0.26**	−0.28**	—
National income	−0.39**	−0.34**	—	−0.32**	−0.28**	—	−0.29**	−0.31**	—
Misery	−0.05	0.04	0.14**	0.08	0.19**	0.24**	−0.14**	−0.14**	−0.02
Price stability	−0.33**	−0.30**	−0.09	−0.19**	−0.18**	0.05	−0.32**	−0.33**	−0.18**
Full employment	0.27**	0.34**	0.24**	0.29**	0.43**	0.26**	0.14**	0.14**	0.10*
Social policy	0.16**	−0.09	0.31**	0.37**	−0.03	0.52**	−0.12*	−0.13**	−0.04
Health	−0.28**	−0.36**	0.00	−0.08	−0.25**	0.23**	−0.35**	−0.36**	−0.21**
Poverty	0.38**	0.09*	0.38**	0.54**	0.10*	0.54**	0.07	0.05	0.05

** $p < 0.01$; * $p < 0.05$ (two-tailed).

[a] Correlations (Pearson's r) between performance indices; excluding USA = calculations without the USA using newly constructed performance indices; controlled by wealth = partial correlation coefficients controlling for wealth (indicator: GDP); $N = 457$ (all countries), $N = 435$ (excluding the USA).

As our theoretical discussion indicated, the relationship between national income and income equality is not just of interest from the perspective of the competing political ideologies. It is also the economic Kuznets curve that describes the relationship between economic development and income equality as an upside-down U-shaped curve. Following the expanded Kuznets curve, suggested since the 1970s as an explanation for increasing poverty and inequality in the USA and Great Britain (Atkinson 1996: 33; Barro 1999: 9), de-industrialization has the effect of changing the relationship between level of wealth and income equality from a positive and complementary into a negative and conflictual relationship. Seen from the vantage point of this theory, our empirical finding of independence could be the first signs that western democracies find themselves at the cusp of the shift from a positive to a negative relationship.

The comprehensive proposition of conflict, unlike the limited proposition, includes not just per capita income but also the other dimensions of economic performance, namely price stability and full employment. It asserts that they all stand in conflict with poverty. But as one can see from the coefficients given in Table 4.20, this hypothesis is not supported by the data. Price stability is positively correlated with poverty, and so is full employment—and that means low inflation rates and low unemployment on the one side, and low poverty on the other side, are not mutually exclusive but instead more often complementary. Thus, with respect to these two economic dimensions of performance, the social democratic hypothesis of a complementary relationship is more strongly supported. Though given that the coefficients range from 0.23 to 0.45, one can speak instead of an empirical confirmation for a moderate social democratic hypothesis.

As a first, partial result, we can assert that the proposition that there is conflict between economic and social policy—or, as Okun asserts, 'our biggest socioeconomic trade-off' (1975: 2)—finds no empirical confirmation in the period between 1974 and 1995. Depending upon the indicator used for economic policy, poverty is either independent (in the case of national income) or moderately complementary (in the case of price stability or full employment) with economic performance. Of course, we should note the limitation that poverty only reflects one aspect of income distribution, namely the national minimum, and thus refers only to the bottom part of the income distribution. It is possible that the economic liberal proposition of conflict between economic and social policy would find empirical confirmation if one did not restrict the analysis to this national minimum but instead investigated the relationship between economic policy and income equality as a whole. Income equality is not addressed here, however, as it does not fulfil the criteria of our 'normative model of political effectiveness'.

Domestic security occupies a particular place in this context. It is frequently argued that the one-sided pursuit of economic growth without providing guarantees for minimum subsistence has negative consequences for domestic security. Accordingly, we can suggest three hypotheses and assess them with the help of the empirical results found in Table 4.20. The first argues that one should expect to find a conflictual relationship between national income and domestic security. The second argues for a complementary relationship between full employment and domestic security. This hypothesis takes into account comprehensive welfare state models, of the kind Esping-Anderson (1990) proposes. According to these models full employment is one of the basic goals of the welfare state, as is reducing income inequality and providing financial security. The third hypothesis argues one should expect complementarity between the poverty rate and domestic security.

The first hypothesis is confirmed by the empirical results: increasing national income is associated with increasing violent and property crimes. It is worth emphasizing that this relationship also exists even when one omits the outlier of the USA from the analysis, as it has both the highest per capita income as well as the highest criminality rate. To judge by the size of the coefficient, however, which varies from -0.28 to -0.39, the degree of conflict in this relationship should be regarded as only moderate. The second hypothesis is also confirmed, though even more weakly: Increasing criminal offences go along with increasing unemployment. But the third hypothesis, according to which low poverty is associated with low criminality, cannot be confirmed by the data. True, the correlation coefficient is positive for the whole sample of countries, but this connection is apparently entirely an artefact of including the outlier of the USA. If one excludes it, as it has both the highest poverty rate and the highest criminality rate, then one can no longer find any connection between poverty and criminality rates. This result contradicts a widespread belief that low poverty rates guarantee low rates of criminality, a belief likely engendered through observations of the 'exceptional' case of the USA where high poverty co-varies with high criminality. Following the analysis pursued here, this is a nation-specific pattern and not a general rule that one could find in other nations.

Table 4.21 examines whether the incompatibility or tension between the different goals has increased since 1990, along the lines suggested by globalization theories, by comparing the period before and after 1990. The coefficients suggest three changes, of which only the first could be interpreted as a confirmation of this increase. This first change involves a weakening of the complementary, positive relationship between poverty and price stability as well as between poverty and full employment since 1990. After 1990, the relationship moves from complementarity to independence from poverty for both price stability and full employment, though in the latter case this is not upheld when one excludes the USA from the calculations. The second change involves the relationship between national income and poverty.

Effectiveness of Western Democracies

TABLE 4.21. *Correlations between economic, social, and domestic security policy before and after 1990*[a]

	Poverty					
	All countries		Excluding USA		Controlling for wealth	
	1974–89	1990–5	1974–89	1990–5	1974–89	1990–5
Economic policy	0.25**	0.07	0.42**	0.29**	—	—
National income	−0.03	−0.04	0.15**	0.25**	—	—
Misery	0.41**	0.16	0.52**	0.27**	0.47**	0.24**
Price stability	0.31**	0.08	0.44**	0.12	0.42**	0.13
Full employment	0.27**	0.14	0.29**	0.24**	0.27**	0.16
	Domestic security policy					
Economic policy	−0.26**	−0.09	−0.18**	0.12	—	—
National income	−0.42**	−0.22*	−0.35**	0.01	—	—
Misery	−0.05	0.05	0.01	0.20*	0.15**	0.25**
Price stability	−0.30**	−0.25**	−0.24**	−0.22*	−0.04	−0.16
Full employment	0.25**	0.20*	0.28**	0.35**	0.24**	0.31**
Social policy	0.14*	0.37**	−0.11*	0.10	0.30**	0.39**
Health	−0.27**	0.07	−0.34**	−0.05	0.00	0.20*
Poverty	0.37**	0.39**	0.06	0.11	0.39**	0.38**

** $p < 0.01$; * $p < 0.05$ (two-tailed).
[a] Correlations (Pearson's r) between performance indices; all countries: $N = 331$ (1974–89), $N = 126$ (1990–5); excluding the USA: $N = 315$ (1974–89), $N = 120$ (1990–5).

In all nations, this relationship is characterized by independence, though if one excludes the USA from the analysis, then the complementarity between these two dimensions increases substantially after 1990. The third change is also an example of increasing complementarity, since after 1990, the conflictual relation between national income and domestic security decreases.

We conclude from this that though there is some empirical evidence for the assumption that economic and social policy are increasingly incompatible, there is simultaneously other empirical evidence for the opposite development, namely increasing compatibility between policies.

The conflict between economic and environmental policy
Limited and comprehensive propositions have also been formulated for the conflict between the economic and environmental goals. According to the limited proposition, national income and environmental performance are in conflict; according to the comprehensive proposition, there is also a conflict between full employment and environmental performance. Common to both propositions is that no differentiation is made between the environmental policy components of 'environmental quality' and 'quality and quantity of

natural resources'. Instead, a generally conflictual relationship between economic performance and environmental performance is predicted.

In the comparative environmental policy research, largely devoted to empirical investigations of the ecological Kuznets curve, a distinction is drawn instead between environmental problems that are relatively easier and relatively more difficult to solve (Shafik and Bandyopadhyay 1992; Arrow et al. 1995; Jänicke et al. 1996a). Difficulties are defined not only in terms of how readily a problem can be solved technologically but also how politically difficult it is to implement the solution. According to this literature, there is a complementary relationship with an 'easily resolved' problem such as sulphur oxide emissions; emissions go down as economic performance goes up. A 'harder to resolve' problem such as municipal waste production means there is conflict; waste production goes up as economic performance goes up. Unlike our previous analysis, we therefore analyse three different aspects of environmental policy: environmental policy in general, sulphur oxides emissions, and municipal waste production, with these emissions serving as indicators of relatively more easily resolved problems, and waste production as an indicator of relatively more difficult to resolve environmental problems.

We start with an empirical analysis of national income, as it stands at the heart of the limited proposition of conflict. To judge by the coefficients given in Table 4.22, the predicted complementary relationship between national income, in the case of the easily resolved environmental problem (sulphur oxides emissions), as well as the predicted conflictual relationship in the case of the harder to resolve environmental problem (municipal waste production), in fact exist, though both correlation coefficients are only moderate. The fact that increasing national income is associated with decreasing sulphur oxides emissions can be seen as refutation of the radical ecology hypothesis and as confirmation of the technocratic hypothesis. It also indicates that the economy and the environment are not logically incompatible but rather that both of their goals can, in principle, be 'made' compatible by employing particular policies or instruments.

Given this positive example of the compatibility between wealth and reduced environmental damage, it does *not* seem appropriate to interpret the conflictual relationship between national income and waste production that also exists as confirmation of a radical ecology hypothesis. It is much more the case that one can merely diagnose a conflictual relationship that, by using specific instruments and economic resources, can under certain circumstances be transformed into a complementary, positive relationship.

If, in a final step, one aggregates all the environmental performance dimensions into an index of environmental policy effectiveness, and analyses its relationship to national income, then complementary and conflictual relations along the individual environmental dimensions balance each other

TABLE 4.22. *Correlations between economic, environmental, and domestic security policy*[a]

	Environmental policy			Sulphur oxides emissions			Municipal waste		
	All countries	Excluding USA	Controlling for wealth	All countries	Excluding USA	Controlling for wealth	All countries	Excluding USA	Controlling for wealth
Economic policy	-0.11*	-0.01	—	0.34**	0.38**	—	-0.45**	-0.42**	—
National income	-0.19**	-0.09	—	0.29**	0.35**	—	-0.47**	-0.42**	—
Misery	0.03	0.10*	0.12*	0.27**	0.28**	0.17**	-0.27**	-0.27**	-0.10*
Price stability	-0.17**	-0.15**	-0.06	0.25**	0.27**	0.07	-0.38**	-0.38**	-0.10*
Full employment	0.21**	0.27**	0.19**	0.11*	0.11*	0.16**	0.02	0.02	-0.05
Social policy	0.35**	0.11*	0.43**	0.45**	0.41**	0.40**	0.16**	0.05	0.36**
Health	-0.04	-0.10*	0.14**	0.22**	0.20**	0.02	-0.31**	-0.35**	0.03
Poverty	0.47**	0.20**	0.47**	0.44**	0.40**	0.49**	0.41**	0.27**	0.43**
Domestic security policy	0.66**	0.50**	0.64**	0.40**	0.42**	0.58**	0.55**	0.43**	0.45**
Violent crimes	0.72**	0.52**	0.71**	0.34**	0.43**	0.48**	0.44**	0.29**	0.34**
Property crimes	0.32**	0.31**	0.28**	0.28**	0.28**	0.40**	0.42**	0.44**	0.34**

** $p < 0.01$; * $p < 0.05$ (two-tailed).

[a] Correlations (Pearson's r) between performance indices; excluding USA = calculations without the USA using newly constructed performance indices; controlling for wealth = partial correlation coefficients controlling for wealth (indicator: GDP); $N = 457$ (all countries), $N = 435$ (excluding the USA).

out. What remains is independence between national income and environmental performance. If one includes all the nations, this relationship is actually slightly negative or conflictual, but after excluding the USA, the coefficient sinks down to zero. At the general level that includes all environmental indicators, one cannot confirm the propositions of conflict.

The theoretical discussion of the conflict proposition regarding the economy and the environment argued that this connection was also relevant from the perspective of the ecological Kuznets curve, as it describes the relationship between per capita income and the burdens placed on the environment as an upside-down U-shaped curve (Jänicke et al. 1996*b*; Stern et al. 1996). The studies have thus far been able to show the existence of an ecological Kuznets curve using samples of nations that had differing levels of economic development and differing political systems (democratic, non-democratic). Our analysis confirms its existence even among the relatively homogenous group of wealthy democracies. What is noteworthy is that in this homogenous group of nations, the majority of whom were environmental policy pioneers, the positive side of the curve described as 'getting rich–getting clean' (Jänicke et al. 1996*a*), is only confirmed for certain environmental policy indicators (such as sulphur oxides emissions) but not for all. For the first time, the existence of the ecological Kuznets curve was analysed for all environmental performance dimensions taken as a whole, but at this general level there is, as yet, no empirical evidence for such a positive trend.

Following the comprehensive proposition of conflict between economic and environmental policy, there should also be a conflictual relationship between full employment and environmental performance. The argument here is that too high environmental policy standards for businesses result in insufficient jobs being created or made available. By this token, full employment would be associated with poorer environmental performance and vice versa. The correlations presented in Table 4.22 indicate that while the relationship between full employment and sulphur oxides emissions is positive, there is no correlation with waste production, and in addition, the relationship is slightly positive for environmental performance taken as a whole. That means, again against commonly held beliefs, an improvement in environmental performance does not go hand-in-hand with an increase in unemployment. In the case of easier to resolve environmental problems, there is even a complementarity between both effectiveness dimensions.

Table 4.22 also contains the correlations between environmental policy and other policy areas, in particular social and domestic security policies. In the absence of corresponding propositions of conflict, we can assume that there is at least an implicit complementary relationship in these cases. In fact, the empirical results do show a complementary relationship between environmental policy and poverty rates, though the correlation is not particularly strong. Complementary and much more significant relationships exist between environmental and domestic security policies. These three non-economic policy areas of welfare state, environment, and domestic security, represent a relatively homogenous bundle of policies that, at least in Lijphart's (1999a: 275, 293) view represent 'kinder, gentler qualities' of polities. Thus, nations with good environmental performance also tend to have good welfare state and good domestic security performance. By the same token, nations comparatively worse in one of these three areas tend to also show poor performance in the other two policy areas.

How did these relationships evolve after 1990? The correlation coefficients in Table 4.23 indicate that that there is only one clear change: that is, an increase in the complementary relationship between poverty rates and environmental policy. Hence, one can observe increased complementarity and not, as predicted, increasing incompatibility between policies.

If one reviews the analyses of environmental policy presented in this section, then what is characteristic of this policy area is an absence of a clear pattern. This may have to do with the relative novelty of this policy area, and be based on the fact that one can observe quite different developments in the different environmental indicators. It is a heterogeneous policy area comprised of aspects of environmental damage that have either been markedly reduced, or whose further expansion has been slowed or halted, or where the environmental damage has actually worsened. Yet, if one takes all these differing environmental dimensions together, then there is no empirical evidence of a conflictual relationship to the economy. In the case of national income, there is independence, and in the case of full employment even a complementary relationship.

Less conflict and more independence or even complementarity between policy goals?
At the centre of the political and economic discussions about the relationship between policy goals are propositions of conflict that assert that there are trade-offs between economic and social policies as well as between economic and environmental policies. The prominence of these arguments, doubtless due in part to the greater attention usually accorded to 'conflict' rather than 'harmony', nevertheless stands in contradiction to the results of the empirical analyses presented here. These show, first, that there is evidence of less conflictual relations between economic and social policy as well as between the economic and environmental policy, than there is of independence or even complementary relationships. A second significant result of the analysis is that the three economic dimensions of performance do not behave in the same fashion, such that national income shows quite different characteristics than full employment and price stability.

TABLE 4.23. *Correlations between economic, environmental, and domestic security policy before and after 1990*[a]

| | Environmental policy | | | | | |
| | All countries | | Excluding USA | | Controlling for wealth | |
	1974–89	1990–5	1974–89	1990–5	1974–89	1990–5
Economic policy	−0.12*	−0.19*	−0.02	−0.00	—	—
National income	−0.26**	−0.35**	−0.15**	−0.13	—	—
Misery	0.03	0.00	0.09	0.11	0.16**	0.30**
Price stability	−0.19**	−0.21*	−0.16**	−0.22*	−0.03	−0.01
Full employment	0.26**	0.12	0.30**	0.24**	0.25**	0.29**
Social policy	0.28**	0.58**	0.05	0.32**	0.39**	0.64**
Health	−0.09	0.24**	−0.16**	0.08	0.11	0.48**
Poverty	0.44**	0.58**	0.16**	0.32**	0.45**	0.60**
Domestic security policy	0.70**	0.62**	0.54**	0.46**	0.67**	0.60**
Violent crimes	0.75**	0.71**	0.58**	0.45**	0.73**	0.67**
Property crimes	0.36**	0.26**	0.32**	0.32**	0.30**	0.25**

** $p < 0.01$; * $p < 0.05$ (two-tailed).
[a] Correlations (Pearson's r) between performance indices; all countries: $N = 331$ (1974–89), $N = 126$ (1990–5); excluding the USA: $N = 315$ (1974–89), $N = 120$ (1990–5).

For national income, the predicted conflictual relations with poverty and environmental policy could not be found; instead, the empirical analysis largely shows independence. The conflictual relationship with domestic security moved towards independence after 1990 as well. An explanation for the discrepancy between the prominence of the propositions of conflict and these empirical findings could, as previously indicated, lie in the fact that the beliefs in the incompatibility of these dimensions were influenced by the example of the USA. This is a nation that explicitly sets itself apart ideologically from Western Europe and quite consciously pays the price in high poverty, high criminality, and high levels of environmental pollution in order to one-sidedly pursue the goal of increasing wealth. Such a pursuit of a libertarian model contains the idea that above-average wealth is at least partly incompatible with the three other non-economic goals. However, the comparative analysis of relationships, based on a broad sample of nations, was able to demonstrate that wealth does not necessarily carry with it worse performance in these other policy areas. Switzerland, Japan, Norway, and Austria are exemplary in showing that high levels of wealth can occur together with good domestic security, economic, and social policy. In the co-variation of high national income, high poverty rates, high crime rates and a higher level of environmental pollution, one thus has the nation-specific pattern called 'American Exceptionalism' and not a general regularity.

In the case of full employment, and partly also for price stability, we also could not find the predicted conflictual relationships with poverty, domestic security and environmental policy. Unlike in the case of national income, one mostly finds complementary or positive relationships. However, one should note the limitation that the relationships are not particularly strong and the fact that since 1990, the complementary relationship between price stability and full employment with poverty has also weakened. The relatively homogeneous package that includes the non-economic policy areas of domestic security, social, and environmental policy that we found in the empirical results at least partly includes the economic performance dimensions of full employment and price stability.

Overall, the relations between the policy areas are relatively stable over time. In only one single case, namely the relationship between full employment and price stability with poverty was it possible to see the predicted incompatibility between the performance dimensions increase in the time after 1990. There are thus a few, if empirically weak, indicators for the end of 'relative balancing' in politics that has been predicted in globalization theories (Münch 1998: 17; Zürn 1998: 13), but at the same time there are also indicators of the opposite development, namely that policies are becoming increasingly compatible.

Empirical Types of Political Effectiveness

Having discussed the relations between the individual dimensions of effectiveness, we will next analyse the whole policy packages. Unlike the exclusively quantitative method we used to examine policy packages in the case of general effectiveness, here we primarily describe policy packages in qualitative terms. We described five different patterns in our theoretical typology of political effectiveness: the worst and best possible cases, and the three ideologically defined categories provided by the libertarian model, classical social democracy, and sustainability. Three questions are of interest here. First, is empirical reality completely encompassed by this theoretical typology of political effectiveness, or are there other policy patterns? Second, which nations demonstrate which types of political effectiveness—and are there systematic differences between the families of nations? Third, how stable are these types of political effectiveness over time?

The types of political effectiveness were constructed on the basis of the four performance indices specific to the domestic security, economic, social, and environmental policy areas (Table 4.24). Using the mean value of every index, each nation is coded according to whether it shows a strongly above-average (++), above-average (+), below-average (−), or strongly below-average (− −) effectiveness in that particular policy area. 'Strongly' is defined 25 per cent above or below the mean. In the very few

TABLE 4.24. *Types of political effectiveness 1974–95*[a]

	Domestic security policy		Economic policy		Social policy		Environmental policy		Types of political effectiveness
Australia	57.6	(−)	53.1	(−)	52.2	(−)	38.9	(−−)	Worst possible case 1
Canada	53.7	(−)	56.6	(+)	55.0	(−)	24.7	(−−)	Libertarian model
Great Britain	60.2	(−)	49.0	(−)	58.6	(−)	70.8	(+)	Economic & socio-political straggler
Ireland	77.2	(+)	34.2	(−−)	57.7	(−)	84.4	(+)	Economic & socio-political straggler⁺
New Zealand	51.8	(−)	52.5	(−)	47.8	(−−)	69.5	(+)	Economic & socio-political straggler
USA	12.4	(−−)	67.6	(++)	26.4	(−−)	7.8	(−)	Libertarian model
Denmark	55.0	(−)	57.1	(+)	72.4	(+)	66.2	(−)	Classical social democracy
Finland	50.8	(−)	53.1	(−)	92.3	(++)	73.3	(+)	Economic straggler
Norway	93.4	(++)	65.2	(+)	86.0	(++)	81.7	(+)	Best possible case 1(a)
Sweden	59.5	(−)	61.8	(+)	88.1	(++)	87.2	(++)	Sustainability
Austria	75.9	(+)	66.9	(+)	75.7	(++)	88.0	(++)	Best possible case 1(b)
Belgium	78.0	(+)	55.9	(+)	86.9	(++)	56.4	(−)	Classical social democracy⁺
France	74.3	(+)	54.9	(0)	75.1	(+)	70.5	(+)	Sustainability⁺
Germany	62.2	(−)	62.9	(+)	79.7	(+)	68.1	(+)	Classical social democracy
Italy	68.4	(+)	46.7	(−)	54.2	(−)	72.4	(+)	Economic & socio-political straggler⁺
The Netherlands	50.1	(−)	59.5	(+)	89.8	(++)	57.8	(−)	Classical social democracy
Greece	95.5	(++)	32.5	(−−)	47.8	(−−)	86.5	(++)	Economic & socio-political straggler⁺
Portugal	91.6	(++)	32.7	(−−)	41.4	(−−)	89.4	(++)	Economic & socio-political straggler⁺
Spain	63.0	(−)	26.6	(−−)	59.2	(−)	74.4	(+)	Economic & socio-political straggler
Switzerland	75.8	(+)	79.5	(++)	76.3	(+)	91.6	(++)	Best possible case 1(c)
Japan	94.5	(++)	68.7	(++)	79.3	(+)	80.4	(+)	Best possible case 1(d)
Average	66.7		54.1		66.8		68.6		

[a] Policy-specific performance indices ranging from 0 to 100: domestic security policy (see Table 4.4), economic policy (see Table 4.7), social policy (see Table 4.10) and environmental policy (see Table 4.13).

Legend: (++) = strongly above average, (+) = above average, (0) = average, (−) = below average, (−−) = strongly below average ('strongly' is defined as 25 % above or below the mean).

cases where the national value equals the mean value for all nations, it is coded as average (0).

Because domestic security policy plays a marginal role in the three political ideologies, the ideological types of political effectiveness are defined primarily by the differing importance given to the other three domestic policy areas. *Sustainability* means that an above-average performance exists in economic policy, social policy, and environmental policy; *classical social democracy* has an above-average or strongly above-average performance only in economic policy and social policy; while the *libertarian model* has an above-average performance only in economic policy. To give domestic security policy its due, two versions are differentiated: one with below-average or strongly below-average effectiveness, and one with above-average or strongly above-average effectiveness in domestic security policy. Thus, 'sustainability' stands for above-average performance in economic, social, and environmental policy as well as below-average or strongly below-average performance in domestic security; 'sustainability$^+$' by contrast stands for above-average performance in economic, social, and environmental policy as well as above-average or strongly above-average performance in domestic security.

Theoretically, the best possible and the worst possible cases are defined as strongly above- or strongly below-average performance in all four policy areas. However, these two possible cases do not exist in reality—a first important empirical finding—so the *worst possible case* is defined as when there is at least below-average effectiveness in all four policy areas. Conversely, the *best possible case* exists when there is strongly above-average effectiveness in at least one policy area, and above-average effectiveness in the other three policy areas. The major difference between 'the best possible case' as the 'sustainability$^+$' case lies in the fact that in the former, at least one policy area shows a strongly above-average effectiveness. It is vital for sustainability that the different policy goals are equally strongly pursued, so one could regard the best possible case as sustainability at a still higher level.

As the last column of Table 4.24 indicates, all five theoretical types of political effectiveness can be found among the twenty-one nations investigated. On the other hand, the typology is insufficient to completely describe empirical reality, as there are two other patterns. The first pattern, the most frequent single type and found in seven cases, is characterized by a below-average or strongly below-average performance in economic as well as social policy, but an above-average or strongly above-average performance in environmental policy. This type might be called the mirror image of classical social democracy, and is found in Great Britain, Ireland, and New Zealand, as well as in Italy, Greece, Portugal, and Spain. This pattern is apparently characteristic not only of the comparatively poorer straggler nations, but also for those nations whose economic and social policy performance is backward compared to other western democracies. This policy pattern is thus not ideologically driven but rather a specific type of poor performance that we will burden with the term *economic and socio-political straggler*. As with the other ideologically defined types, two versions are distinguished depending upon the domestic security policy.

The second pattern, only found in Finland, is another type of poor performance, characterized by below-average or strongly below-average effectiveness in economic policy, coupled with above-average or strongly above-average effectiveness in social and environmental policy. This type belongs to the category of *economic straggler*.

How are the other nations distributed among the theoretical types of political effectiveness? Among the best possible cases, one finds Norway, Switzerland, Japan, and Austria, the same nations listed in the first four ranks under general effectiveness. This convergence between the two concepts indicates that the overall superior general effectiveness in these nations does not come about through the balancing of a below-average effectiveness in one policy area by a strongly above-average effectiveness in another policy area. Rather, it indicates that nations with the best general effectiveness simultaneously have above-average performance in all policy areas. The sustainability policy pattern, shown in an above-average economic, social, and environmental policy effectiveness, exists in Sweden and in France, and the classical social democratic pattern is characteristic of Denmark, Belgium, Germany, and the Netherlands.

The policy pattern in the USA reflects the libertarian model, with its strongly above-average economic effectiveness coupled with strongly below-average effectiveness in all other policy areas. This assignment could have been expected theoretically, but this empirical result is nevertheless not self-evident. To this point, analyses of US policy patterns have been undertaken with reference to only a few other nations, or have used other indicators than our own. In particular, they have been limited to qualitative interpretations of national difference (Bok 1996; Lipset 1996). Here, for the first time, based on a systematic, comparative, quantitative analysis involving twenty-one nations and numerous outcome indicators, it is possible to unequivocally empirically identify the libertarian policy pattern of the USA.

This policy pattern exists not only there but also in Canada. Canada's above-average performance is also limited to economic policy. The difference between the two nations is evident only at a more subtle level: economic effectiveness in Canada is 'only' above-average and not strongly above-average. Additionally, domestic security and social policy effectiveness is also 'only' below-average and not strongly below-average. This finding supports other assessments that have argued for the many similarities between these two North American nations but at the same time emphasized their significant differences in values and institutions at secondary levels (Lipset 1990).

Only one nation falls into the category of worst possible case, and that is Australia. In the global index of general effectiveness, Australia, together with the USA and Canada, was among the nations with the lowest levels of effectiveness (see Table A.1.16), though Australia ranked ahead of both the USA and Canada in terms of general effectiveness.

Three aspects are noteworthy in this distribution of political effectiveness types. First, there are only three nations with very imbalanced patterns, which is to say, cases in which both strongly above- and below-average effectiveness exists in different policy areas. In addition to the USA, with its extremely imbalanced libertarian pattern, one also finds Greece and Portugal that have been categorized as economic and socio-political stragglers. These latter two both have a strongly above-average effectiveness in domestic security and environmental policy coupled with a strongly below-average effectiveness in economic policy (and in Portugal also a strongly below-average social policy effectiveness). The vast majority of western democracies do not show large differences between the levels of effectiveness in the selected policy areas. This supports what was found earlier, namely that there is comparatively little conflict between the different policy goals.

Second, the two most frequent types are the economic and socio-political stragglers (seven nations) and sustainability (six nations—i.e. if one includes not only these examples but also the four 'best possible cases' interpreted as sustainability at a higher level). Given how new sustainability is as a guiding concept for societal development, this rather good result was unexpected.

Third, there was also no systematic relationship between domestic security and the three ideologically defined types of political effectiveness and the two straggler types. All that does exist is the positive relationship to environmental policy, as found earlier.

One can also find systematic differences between the families of nations in these different types of political effectiveness. The special cases of Switzerland and Japan both are 'best possible cases' while the southern European family all belongs to the 'economic and socio-political stragglers'. It is also typical of the English-speaking nations that one only finds policy patterns that could be called 'negative': the 'worst possible case', the 'economic and socio-political straggler', and the 'libertarian model'. As was already the case for policy-specific and general effectiveness, no systematic differences can be found between the Scandinavian and the Continental Western European nations. Against the background of the many differing typologies that have emphasized the uniqueness or superiority of aspects of Nordic welfare capitalism compared with that found in Continental Western European nations (Schmidt 1987, 2000b; Esping-Andersen 1990), this is a rather surprising result. One can summarize this by stating that what is specific to the Nordic nations is not their general, above-average performance but rather their comparative superiority, relative to the Continental Western European family, reflected in but limited to, an above-average social policy performance.

This brings us to the question about the development of these types of political effectiveness over time. Given the relatively large stability we were able to show earlier of both policy-specific and general effectiveness, we do not anticipate large shifts in the typology of political effectiveness. However, as this concept incorporates the configuration between all four dimensions of effectiveness in a relatively detailed fashion, it is possible that individual interesting shifts exist that are not revealed by the preceding analyses. In order to analyse these possible shifts in the policy patterns, the analysis was redone to compare the early (1974–9) to the late (1990–5) time period, as one can see in Tables 4.25 and 4.26.

Five nations showed changes in their type of political effectiveness in this comparison: New Zealand, the Netherlands (whose systematic decline was already mentioned in the analysis of general effectiveness), Germany, Italy, and Spain.

- New Zealand declined from 'socio-political straggler' to 'worst possible case' in the time period under investigation, due to losses in performance in domestic security, economic, and environmental policies.
- The policy patterns in the Netherlands changed from 'classical social democracy^{+}' to 'classical social democracy' because domestic security performance worsened from above average (+) to a strongly below average effectiveness (− −).
- Italy, though it could still count as an 'economic and socio-political straggler' in the first period, fell to the 'worst possible case' category by the 1990s, due to a worsening in domestic security policy and in environmental policy.
- Germany is the only nation that showed improvement. Owing to an increase in environmental performance, it moved from 'classical social democracy' into the 'sustainability' category.
- Spain changed from 'economic and socio-political straggler^{+}' to 'economic and political straggler' due to losses in domestic security policy.

In four out of five of these changes, there were declines, and in each one worsening of domestic security performance played a role. This is also the only policy area where the mean for all nations worsened over time (see Table 4.4). There are no cases in which the imbalance between the types of political effectiveness increased, and Germany was the only nation where there was an improvement in the policy pattern. In its change from 'classical social democracy' to 'sustainability' categories one can also see reflected what environmental policy research argued, namely that Germany developed into a

TABLE 4.25. *Types of political effectiveness 1974–9*[a]

	Domestic security policy		Economic policy		Social policy		Environmental policy		Types of political effectiveness
Australia	70.6	(–)	38.7	(–)	46.1	(–)	37.0	(– –)	Worst possible case 1
Canada	52.4	(– –)	41.0	(+)	38.7	(– –)	24.3	(– –)	Libertarian model
Great Britain	70.4	(–)	33.5	(–)	56.6	(–)	72.2	(+)	Economic & socio-political straggler[+]
Ireland	80.5	(+)	24.4	(– –)	48.5	(–)	91.7	(++)	Economic & socio-political straggler[+]
New Zealand	66.7	(–)	43.8	(+)	42.7	(– –)	74.3	(+)	Socio-political straggler
USA	11.9	(– –)	46.3	(+)	23.6	(– –)	2.2	(– –)	Libertarian model
Denmark	66.2	(–)	39.6	(0)	63.0	(+)	65.3	(–)	Classical social democracy
Finland	51.2	(– –)	37.5	(–)	86.6	(++)	70.2	(+)	Economic straggler
Norway	95.0	(++)	49.1	(+)	84.5	(++)	82.4	(+)	Best possible case 1(a)
Sweden	60.7	(–)	48.9	(+)	86.0	(++)	82.2	(+)	Sustainability
Austria	80.5	(+)	52.3	(++)	64.3	(+)	86.5	(++)	Best possible case 1(b)
Belgium	87.3	(+)	41.4	(+)	79.2	(++)	52.7	(–)	Classical social democracy[+]
France	82.7	(+)	42.8	(+)	69.1	(+)	69.6	(+)	Sustainability[+]
Germany	71.6	(–)	51.4	(++)	63.9	(+)	66.9	(–)	Classical social democracy
Italy	79.9	(+)	28.7	(– –)	44.0	(–)	75.6	(+)	Economic & socio-political straggler
The Netherlands	76.6	(+)	45.9	(+)	89.3	(++)	50.6	(– –)	Classical social democracy[+]
Greece	99.7	(++)	33.5	(–)	27.6	(– –)	88.9	(++)	Economic & socio-political straggler[+]
Portugal	93.0	(++)	10.9	(– –)	9.4	(– –)	92.6	(++)	Economic & socio-political straggler[+]
Spain	91.7	(+)	22.3	(– –)	42.9	(– –)	76.4	(+)	Economic & socio-political straggler[+]
Switzerland	77.1	(+)	63.4	(++)	73.5	(++)	96.2	(++)	Best possible case 1(c)
Japan	92.7	(++)	45.9	(+)	75.6	(++)	79.0	(+)	Best possible case 1(d)
Average	74.2		40.1		57.9		68.4		

[a] Policy-specific performance indices ranging from 0 to 100: domestic security policy (see Table 4.4), economic policy (see Table 4.7), social policy (see Table 4.10) and environmental policy (see Table 4.13).

Legend: (++) = strongly above average, (+) = above average, (0) = average, (–) = below average, (– –) = strongly below average ('strongly' is defined as 25 % above or below the mean).

TABLE 4.26. *Types of political effectiveness 1990–5*[a]

	Domestic security policy	Economic policy	Social policy	Environmental policy	Types of political effectiveness
Australia	46.7 (−)	68.9 (−)	53.1 (− −)	40.2 (− −)	Worst possible case 1(a)
Canada	53.4 (−)	73.2 (+)	66.6 (−)	26.5 (− −)	Libertarian model
Great Britain	48.1 (−)	66.2 (−)	51.5 (− −)	70.8 (+)	Economic & socio-political straggler
Ireland	74.7 (++)	52.9 (−)	63.0 (−)	76.8 (+)	Economic & socio-political straggler[+]
New Zealand	39.1 (− −)	64.4 (−)	51.5 (− −)	64.3 (−)	Worst possible case 1(b)
USA	11.4 (− −)	89.5 (++)	29.5 (− −)	11.6 (− −)	Libertarian model
Denmark	47.1 (−)	77.0 (+)	83.5 (+)	68.6 (0)	Classical social democracy
Finland	49.2 (−)	61.5 (−)	96.5 (++)	79.8 (+)	Economic straggler
Norway	92.8 (++)	83.6 (+)	89.4 (+)	79.8 (+)	Best possible case 2(a)
Sweden	56.5 (−)	71.5 (+)	89.9 (+)	91.0 (++)	Sustainability
Austria	68.8 (+)	82.5 (+)	84.2 (+)	90.8 (++)	Best possible case 2b
Belgium	69.4 (+)	75.7 (+)	91.7 (++)	59.4 (−)	Classical social democracy[+]
France	67.5 (+)	70.3 (0)	78.9 (+)	72.4 (+)	Sustainability[+]
Germany	53.8 (−)	76.3 (+)	88.1 (+)	71.3 (+)	Sustainability
Italy	56.5 (−)	66.0 (−)	59.9 (−)	67.8 (+)	Worst possible case 1(c)
The Netherlands	23.0 (−)	75.9 (+)	85.3 (+)	62.9 (−)	Classical social democracy
Greece	90.0 (++)	39.1 (− −)	66.8 (−)	84.7 (+)	Economic & socio-political straggler[+]
Portugal	89.1 (++)	55.5 (−)	65.5 (−)	86.4 (+)	Economic & socio-political straggler[+]
Spain	51.2 (−)	36.2 (− −)	71.2 (−)	74.9 (+)	Economic & socio-political straggler
Switzerland	74.1 (+)	93.7 (++)	76.4 (+)	91.4 (++)	Best possible case 1(a)
Japan	96.4 (++)	90.2 (++)	79.7 (+)	80.1 (+)	Best possible case 1(b)
Average	59.9	70.0	72.5	69.1	

[a] Policy-specific performance indices ranging from 0 to 100: domestic security policy (see Table 4.13), economic policy (see Table 4.4), social policy (see Table 4.7), economic policy (see Table 4.10) and environmental policy (see Table 4.13).

Legend: (++) = strongly above average, (+) = above average, (0) = average, (−) = below average, (− −) = strongly below average ('strongly' is defined as 25 % above or below the mean).

pioneer in environmental policy in the 1980s, replacing the USA (Jänicke and Weidner 1997: 19).

This change in Germany's political effectiveness type is related to work Schmidt has done on the nation's policy patterns (1987, 2000*b*). Schmidt argued that it was characteristic of the German political economy (referring to various characteristics in economic and social policy) to have found a 'middle way' characterized by a balance between competing policy goals and means. Using our comparative and longitudinal data, we can show that this policy pattern existed in Germany at the end of the 1970s, since the nation had an above-average effectiveness in both economic and social policy. The expansion of this politics of the middle way can be seen in the 1990s as it includes above-average effectiveness in the rather new area of environmental policy. The politics of the middle way evidently is a basic, characteristic principle of German policy-making that, at least since the 1990s, is no longer confined to political economy.

SUMMARY

The analysis of descriptive questions and hypotheses about the level, development and structure of political effectiveness in western democracies between 1974 and 1995 was the focus of this first empirical chapter.

Our focus on the level of policy-specific and general effectiveness was first to identify those nations with the (relatively) best and worst levels. Table 4.27 summarizes the results, listing the three nations with both the best and worst practices over the entire time period from 1974 to 1995, and even at this simple level one can see a pattern. The USA is present in all five effectiveness dimensions, and with the exception of economic policy, always among those with the worst practices. One can say nearly the opposite of the southern European nations of Greece, Portugal, and Spain. These three constitute the group with the worst practice in economic policy. Portugal and Greece are also in the category 'worst practice' in social policy, though at the same time Greece has the 'best practice' in domestic security policy, while Portugal has nearly the 'best practice' in environmental policy.

A systematic analysis of all the nations indicates that the families of nations (English-speaking, Scandinavian, Continental Western European, Southern European, as well as the special cases of Switzerland and Japan) differ in policy-specific as well as general performance. Since this 'families of nations' concept is primarily a proxy for cultural differences, one can draw the conclusion that cultural differences that influence politicians, citizens, policies, and political institutions, play a central role in questions of performance. However, the differences between the Scandinavian and the Continental Western European families of nations are comparatively marginal.

In terms of the development of political effectiveness, it has been an article of faith in various crisis theories that western democracies have been converging at a lower level of performance since the economic recession that set in after 1973. This general hypothesis could not be confirmed by our empirical analysis. First, the development varies by policy area. There has been a reduction in effectiveness only in domestic security, yet this is a longer-term trend that began already after 1945 and not just since 1973. Economic policy, by contrast has as a whole seen an increase in performance, even with the negative trends seen in employment statistics. This increase is primarily due to a continuous increase in per capita income. In the case of social policy, one also sees a positive trend, due here to continuous reductions in infant mortality rates. Finally, in the case of environmental policy, one finds stability, at least when viewed in terms of the means for all nation. Hidden behind this, however, one can find two developments that move in opposite directions: increasing performance in pioneering environmental policy nations like the USA and Germany, but decreasing effectiveness in economic stragglers like the southern European nations and Ireland.

Second, the different developments in the four policy areas of domestic security, economic, social, and environmental policy largely balance each other out. There has been a slight rise between 1974 and 1995 in general effectiveness, but this is due primarily to increasing wealth.

Third, there was little empirical evidence even for a modified hypothesis that asserted a decline in effectiveness particularly in the period after 1990; evidence for this existed only in the case of unemployment and, with limits, for poverty rates.

Fourth, western democracies converge with respect to certain dimensions of performance (national income, infant mortality, environmental policy) but that occurs at the same time as divergence with respect to other dimensions (domestic security).

Thus, the general hypothesis that an overall loss of effectiveness was to be expected in western democracies could not be empirically confirmed. The negative development predicted could only be found in individual policy areas (domestic security), individual performance indicators (unemployment, municipal waste production), or in individual nations. Table 4.28 provides an overview of the three nations with the worst and best development with respect to policy-specific and general effectiveness. The Netherlands and New Zealand are the two nations most frequently found in the category 'worst practice' in specific policy areas (the Netherlands in domestic security policy and social policy, New Zealand in domestic security policy and environmental policy). These are also the only two nations whose situation has generally worsened overall, as one can see in the general effectiveness column. By contrast, the developments in Portugal, the USA, and Canada most clearly contradict the thesis that there has been a general

TABLE 4.27. *Level of policy-specific and general effectiveness 1974–95*

	Domestic security policy	Economic policy	Social policy	Environmental policy	General effectiveness
Best practice	1. Greece 2. Japan 3. Norway	1. Switzerland 2. Japan 3. USA	1. Finland 2. The Netherlands 3. Sweden	1. Switzerland 2. Portugal 3. Austria	1. Norway 2. Switzerland 3. Japan
Worst practice	1. USA 2. The Netherlands 3. Finland	1. Spain 2. Greece 3. Portugal	1. USA 2. Portugal 3. Greece/New Zealand	1. USA 2. Canada 3. Australia	1. USA 2. Canada 3. Australia

TABLE 4.28. *Development of policy-specific and general effectiveness 1974–95[a]*

	Domestic security policy	Economic policy	Social policy	Environmental policy	General effectiveness
Best practice	1. Japan 2. USA 3. Canada	1. Portugal 2. Japan 3. USA	1. Portugal 2. Greece 3. Spain	1. The Netherlands 2. Finland 3. USA	1. Portugal 2. Canada 3. USA
Worst practice	1. *The Netherlands* 2. *Spain* 3. *New Zealand*	1. Greece 2. Spain 3. New Zealand	1. *Great Britain* 2. *The Netherlands* 3. Switzerland	1. *Ireland* 2. *New Zealand* 3. *Italy*	1. *The Netherlands* 2. *New Zealand* 3. Spain

[a] Countries in italics show a negative trend (indicator: difference between levels of effectiveness between 1974–9 and 1990–5).

loss in effectiveness. One should particularly note the USA, as it can be found among the three nations showing the best practice in improving performance in domestic security, economic, and environmental policies (but not in social policy). This overall positive development both here and in Canada corrects the negative image created by the generally low performance levels in both nations and indicates their above-average ability to reform and change, or catch up to other western democracies.

Hypotheses about the structure of political effectiveness or about policy patterns are primarily biased towards conflict, whether they assert trade-offs between individual goals (between economic policy and social policy, or between economic policy and environmental policy), or predict that there will be increasing incompatibility or tension between policy goals as a consequence of economic globalization. The prominence of propositions of conflict may be due to the fact that unlike harmony or compatibility, conflict draws greater attention. It may also be nourished by the example provided by the USA where a very unbalanced policy pattern exists, characterized by above-average prominence given to economic policy and relative neglect or lack of support for the other non-economic policy areas (social policy, environmental policy, and domestic security).

Such hypotheses of conflict between policy goals also cannot be empirically confirmed. First, the dominant pattern in the time period under investigation is, in fact, the complementarity or the independence of goals, in particular for the relationship between economic policy and social policy as well as between the economy and the environment. The incompatibility between economic policy and social or environmental policy characteristic for the USA simply cannot be generalized for other nations. There are nations such as Switzerland, Japan, and Norway, that are able to realize all three policy goals simultaneously, and that at a high level. Second, the thesis of increasing incompatibility or increased conflict between goals after 1990 also finds no empirical confirmation. There is only one relationship that finds support along the lines of this thesis, and that is between full employment and poverty, which prior to 1990 was complementary but since then one finds only independence. Thus, our empirical analysis of the relationship between individual dimensions of performance leads us to conclude that the likelihood that policy goals will be in conflict is exaggerated not only in academic but also in political discussions.

We also developed a new typology of political effectiveness to characterize policy patterns, and used it to describe the configurations of policy-specific effectiveness found in western democracies. In so doing, we were able to find eight different policy patterns: three ideologically defined models (sustainability, classical social democracy, libertarian), two poles (the best possible and worst possible cases), and three types of negative effectiveness: economic stragglers, socio-political stragglers, and economic and socio-political stragglers. Only three nations have extremely imbalanced policy patterns: the USA (libertarian model), Greece, and Portugal (both are economic and socio-political stragglers).

Here, too, clear differences between the families of nations exist. The special case nations of Switzerland and Japan are the 'best possible' cases, the southern European nations are the 'economic and socio-political stragglers' and the English-speaking nations display the three 'negative' effectiveness patterns of the 'libertarian model' (USA, Canada), the 'worst possible case' (Australia) and the 'economic and socio-political stragglers' (Great Britain, Ireland). No systematic differences can be found between the Scandinavian and the Continental Western European families of nations. Overall, the western democratic type of political effectiveness shows itself to be relatively stable. There were changes in type in only five nations between 1974–9 and 1990–5, and only in the case of Germany was there an improvement in performance. In Germany's change from the 'classical social democracy' type (1974–9) to the 'sustainability' type (1990–5) one can see documented that the typical German political style of taking the 'middle way' now also includes environmental policy.

5

The Influence of Political Institutions on the Effectiveness of Western Democracies

Having provided a descriptive empirical analysis in Chapter 4, we now turn to explanatory analysis. We are interested in the influence political institutions have on the effectiveness of western democracies. At the centre stands the examination of the hypotheses formulated in Chapter 3, namely whether institutions do matter with respect to the level, stability, and structure of political effectiveness.

In examining the level, we are primarily interested in whether negotiation democracies are actually superior to majoritarian democracies, that is, whether their policy outcomes are in fact 'kinder and gentler', as Lijphart (1999a) claims to have empirically proven. By examining stability, we are addressing one of the central premises of decision-making theory regarding the mutability of policies and policy outcomes. Following this argument, taken up and reformulated in the context of the veto player approach (Tsebelis 1995, 2002), negotiation democracies cannot address challenges in their environment by policy change due to the larger number of veto players. Unlike majoritarian democracies, therefore, their policy outcomes are thus more stable. In this context, it is particularly interesting whether this thesis of policy stability applies to both types of negotiation democracy, the one based on constitutional rules and the other based on informal rules. At least some proponents of consensus democracy (Birchfield and Crepaz 1998) assert that negotiation democracies based on informal rules are also capable of policy change. As to the third dimension, the structure of political effectiveness, we examine the hypothesis that more balanced policy patterns exist in informal negotiation democracies than in informal majoritarian democracies due to the greater representation of societal interests and the structural need to form compromises.

The analysis proceeds in three steps. The first step is an investigation of the dimensionality of the constitutional and partisan veto player indices for measuring the institutions of democratic governance. One part of this involves addressing methodological questions previously raised when these indices were first introduced. The second step is a re-analysis of Lijphart's *Patterns of Democracy* (1999a) that is designed to answer two questions.

What is the implication of the broad conceptualization of informal structures in the executives–parties index for the classifying of western democracies as majoritarian and negotiation democracies? And to what extent are the empirically asserted relationships between the executives–parties index and the various performance dimensions, particularly in economic and social policy, the result of including corporatism as a structural characteristic that is specific to these two policy areas and not interest-neutral? The third step is the heart of the explanatory analysis. Here we investigate the influence of constitutional and informal institutions of governance on the level and stability of policy-specific and general effectiveness, as well as the balance between policy patterns. The chapter ends with a summary of the most important findings about the effects of constitutional and informal institutions as well as the quality of the various veto player indices.

THE DIMENSIONALITY OF THE VETO PLAYER INDICES

In the theoretical part of the analysis, the formal and empirical institutions of democratic governance were identified as the two structural elements where one might expect to find an effect on performance (Fuchs 2000; and Figure 3.5). The former is the constitutionally established 'governmental system' defined by the institutions that participate in collectively binding decisions as well as the relationship between them; the latter is the 'relationship between governing and opposition parties' defined by the informal rules of interactions that develop between these parties.

The pure constitutional veto player indices for measuring the governmental systems can, following Fuchs (2000), be distinguished by whether they are based only on primary and minimal structural characteristics such as bicameralism, federalism, and presidentialism—as Fuchs himself does in his minimal governmental system indices A and B—or whether they go beyond this to include secondary structural characteristics such as the jurisdiction of constitutional courts or the existence of an independent central bank. Examples of this second type of maximal index are Schmidt's index of institutional constraints of central state government (1996) and Lijphart's federal–unitary index (1999a).[1]

Lijphart's executives–parties index has become established as a measure of informal democratic structures. However, this index is too imprecise, because while it does measure the relationship between governing and opposition parties we are interested in, it also measures the degree of power dispersion in the party system as well as the system of interest groups. It also uses concepts

---

[1] The constitutional structure index of Huber *et al.* (1993) and the institutional pluralism index of Colomer (1996) that also intend to measure the governmental system are not addressed here. They are not pure measures of the governmental system and are also methodologically problematic (see Chapter 3).

to measure the relationship between governing and opposition parties that are only applicable to parliamentary systems. We suggest using three partisan veto player indices—the *simple partisan veto player index*, Schnapp's (2004) *veto players in the lower house*, and the *number of governing parties*—as a means to take into account and answer these problems with Lijphart's executives–parties index.

The first two indices follow the veto player research tradition and are based on the number of parties needed in government and parliament for making political decisions. The simple partisan veto player index sums the number of governing parties together, and in the case of a minority government, adds an additional veto player. The veto players in the lower house index (Schnapp 2004) also takes the number of governing parties into account and whether it is a majority or minority government. In the case of a minority government, depending upon the ideological position of the governing party or parties and the percentage of seats held by the opposition parties, formal decision-making theory is applied to determine how many additional parties, or rather veto players, are needed to make political decisions. The third index limits itself only to the number of governing parties and makes no further distinctions about type of government. For control purposes, a fourth *effective number of parliamentary parties* index is suggested to measure the distribution of power in the party system. Given the close relationship between the party system and the relationship between governing and opposition parties (see Figure 3.5), this last index may be a surrogate measure of the relationship between governing and opposition parties.

To construct these indices, we relied on data collected, prepared, corrected, and updated by the 'Institutions and Social Change' unit of the Social Science Research Center Berlin (WZB). Data on the number of governing parties and type of government are drawn from the information presented in *Party Government in 20 Democracies* (Woldendorp et al. 1993, 1998), while information on parliamentary parties, electoral results, and distribution of seats come from the *International Almanac of Electoral History* (Mackie and Rose 1991). Both data collections were supplemented and updated based on *Keesings's Contemporary Archives and Record of World Events*. Schnapp (2004) calculated the ideological positions of the parties based on the data collected as part of the *Comparative Manifestos Project* (Klingemann et al. 1994; Budge et al. 2001), and where there were gaps in the data, relied on expert judgment (Castles and Mair 1984; Huber and Inglehart 1995).

In constructing these indices, two decisions had to be made: how to address caretaker governments that are only temporarily in office and cannot 'undertake any kind of serious policy-making' (Woldendorp et al. 1993: 9), and which method should be used in annualizing the data collected for elections and legislative periods. In the simple partisan veto player and the number of governing parties indices, caretaker governments were ignored, and those governments with the longest terms in office per year were selected as the units for annualization. For the veto players in the lower house index, caretaker governments were treated like multiparty coalition governments with little decision-making ability (Schnapp 2004), with the data weighted per day. The effective number of parliamentary parties index was also annualized on a per day basis. All these veto player indices were coded in such a fashion that high values measure power dispersion and low values measure power concentration.

An exploratory factor analysis was undertaken to check the validity of these indices for measuring formal and empirical institutions of democratic governance. Included in this analysis are not only the four constitutional veto player indices and the three partisan veto player indices we have suggested but also the proxy index effective number of parliamentary parties and Lijphart's executives–parties index. The data basis is provided by the twenty-one nations investigated in our study and the time from 1974 to 1995. A mean value for the entire time period was calculated for the individual indices.[2]

The factor analysis presented in Table 5.1 comes to a clear conclusion. The four constitutional veto player indices—the federal-unitary index (Lijphart 1999a), the index of institutional constraints of central state government (Schmidt 1996)[3] as well as the minimal governmental system indices A and B (Fuchs 2000)—constitute one factor. The five partisan veto player indices—the executives–parties index (Lijphart 1999a), the simple partisan veto-player index, the veto players in the lower house index (Schnapp 2004) as well as the indices number of governing parties and the effective number of parliamentary parties—constitute a second factor. In no cases are there significant loadings on the other (respective) factor. We can therefore conclude that the three partisan veto player indices we have suggested, together with the effective number of parliamentary parties and the executives–parties index measure the same dimension of informal structures.

A closer examination of the factor structure permits five important qualifications to be added. The first four refer to the first factor, defined by the relationship between governing and opposition parties.

---

[2] Data on the executives–parties and the federal–unitary index, as well as for all individual indicators of these indices, are available for the time periods 1945–96 and 1971–96 (Lijphart 1999a: 312–14). The data for the second period were used, as they are almost identical with the time period under investigation in our study.

[3] All analyses are based on the data as presented in Schmidt (1996). Updated data (as of the end of 1999) as given in the latest edition of *Demokratietheorien* (Schmidt 2000a: 352) were not used, as our investigated period ends in 1995.

TABLE 5.1. *Factor analysis of veto player indices 1974–95[a]*

	Relationship between governing and opposition parties	Governmental system
Executives–parties index (Lijphart 1999*a*)	0.886[b]	−0.018
Simple partisan veto player index	0.983	0.036
Veto players in the lower house (Schnapp 2004)	0.978	0.075
Number of governing parties	0.961	0.105
Effective number of parliamentary parties	0.960	−0.060
Federal–unitary index (Lijphart 1999*a*)	−0.059	0.942
Institutional constraints of central state government (Schmidt 1996)	0.125	0.937
Minimal governmental system index A (Fuchs 2000)	0.023	0.976
Minimal governmental system index B (Fuchs 2000)	−0.063	0.953

[a] Principal components analysis: varimax rotation; explained variance = 91.4 %; $N=21$.
[b] Factor loadings for executives–parties index without the structural characteristic of interest group system: 0.907.

1. Lijphart's executives–parties index shows the—comparatively—smallest factor loading. This might be regarded as empirical evidence for the assertion that this index is not a pure partisan veto player index. Confirmation for this interpretation also comes from an additional factor analysis that was conducted using the executives–parties index but *omitting* the structural characteristic of the interest group system, which yielded a factor loading somewhat higher (0.907) than when the interest group system characteristic was included (0.886; see Table 5.1).

2. The proxy effective number of parliamentary parties index also resulted in an identical factor loading (0.960) as the number of governing parties index (0.961), from which one can conclude that the assumed close relationship between power distribution in parliament and in the executive exists.

3. There is also a difference, though a marginal one, between those indices based on the number of parties in government or parliament, and those indices that also include the type of government. Factor loadings on the number of governing parties (0.961) and the effective number of parliamentary parties (0.960) are slightly lower than those for the simple partisan veto player (0.983) and veto players in the lower house (0.978) indices. One conclusion from this is that the parsimonious number of governing parties index can certainly be used as a measure for the relationship between governing and opposition parties. Beyond this, the effective number of parliamentary parties, though it primarily measures power

distribution in the party system, can apparently also function under certain circumstances as a surrogate measure for the relationship between governing and opposition parties.

4. The small difference in the factor loading between the simple partisan veto player index (0.983) and the veto players in the lower house index (0.978) is also noteworthy, since the additional differentiation of types of minority governments that form part of the latter index (Schnapp 2004), apparently do not contribute to a substantial improvement of the factor loading.

A fifth and final observation is related to the second factor of the governmental system. The factor loadings of the two minimal governmental system indices A and B (Fuchs 2000) indicate that very parsimonious indices based only on primary structural characteristics of the governmental system can measure the latent construct (governmental system) just as well as the more complex federal–unitary (Lijphart 1999*a*) and institutional constraints of central state government (Schmidt 1996) indices that also include secondary structural characteristics.

In summary, we want to reiterate the most significant findings of the factor analysis. First, the theoretically asserted difference between the constitutional and partisan veto player indices is impressively empirically confirmed. The indices seem to be valid measures of the two dimensions of democratic governance—the governmental system and the relationship between governing and opposition parties. Second, the three indices that we have suggested for the relationship between governing and opposition parties are clearly indicators of this dimension. This is, following our expectation, somewhat less true for Lijphart's executives–parties index (1999*a*). Third, the validity of the simpler indices is at least equivalent to that of the more complex ones.

However, a factor analysis only establishes the degree of covariance between indicators. Even within this very clear factor structure, one cannot exclude the possibility that individual indices have different explanatory power due to characteristics specific to the indicators themselves. In the language of measurement theory, the construct validity of the indicators can certainly still vary.

A RE-ANALYSIS OF LIJPHART'S 'PATTERNS OF DEMOCRACY'

Lijphart's executives–parties index (1999*a*) is a broad measure of informal structures. It contains not only indicators measuring the distribution of power in the relationship between governing and opposition parties, but also indicators measuring the party system and the system of interest groups (see Table 3.4). The troubling implication of including corporatism has been addressed repeatedly, for in doing so, Lijphart has expanded the definition of political institutions by including not only a policy-specific but at the same time an institution that is not neutral with respect to interests. Based on all ten structural characteristics Lijphart (1999a: 246) employs, his factor analysis can show that this variable has a high factor loading on the executives–parties dimension. That is, political systems characterized by power dispersion in the relationship between governing and opposition parties, as well as in the party system, disproportionately also lead to corporatist systems of interest groups. But because corporatism is an institution of political economy, it is not theoretically plausible to classify the *political* structure of a nation based on this index. Given its policy-specificity and how interest-guided it is, one can also assume that—unlike other informal institutions—corporatism primarily has positive effects on economic and social policy performance. One can therefore not exclude the possibility that Lijphart's empirically derived result that consensus democracies display 'kinder and gentler' policies may be primarily based upon the inclusion of the corporatism variable in the index.

The second difference between the executives–parties index and the pure partisan veto player indices favoured here—the addition of the *party system*—may likely have an effect on the classification of nations as well as on the results of the performance analysis. The party system describes the parties and the structure of relationships between them. The key characteristic with respect to the criterion of power distribution is fragmentation, counting the number of parties and taking their relative size into account (Sartori 1976; Niedermayer 1996). Following Laakso and Taagepera (1979), Lijphart (1999a) measures this characteristic primarily through the effective number of parliamentary parties. But the variable electoral disproportionality, which measures the degree of deviation between votes cast and the proportion of seats parties obtain (Gallagher 1991), can also be assigned to this concept.[4] Power dispersion at the level of party system means a representation of societal interests in parliament as broad and comprehensive as possible. This implies that minority interests are also represented in parliament, and the probability that such interests are taken into account in the legislative bargaining process increases.

The consequence of this broader conceptualization of the informal structures in the executives–parties index, are examined in terms of its implication for the assignment of western democracies as majoritarian or negotiation

---

[4] Electoral disproportionality is not a direct measure for dispersion in the party system (due to its empirical basis it also cannot be assigned to the constitutionally defined electoral system). Assigning it to the party system, however, is justified with the argument that increasing electoral disproportionality is an indicator of power concentration in the party system (Lijphart 1999a: 165–9).

democracies, and for the performance of majoritarian and negotiation democracies.

Classifying democracies

To investigate the first question, namely what effect a broad concept of informal structure has on the classification of nations, we contrast two classifications of the twenty-one western democracies, one based on Lijphart's executives–parties index (1999a: 255) and the other using the simple partisan veto player index. The latter is chosen because it is a pure measure of the relationship between governing and opposition parties that shows the highest factor loading of all institutional indices on the first factor. To differentiate informal majoritarian from informal negotiation democracies, the zero point of z-score transformed (standardized) variables was selected, the same criterion Lijphart (1999a: 248) also used to classify nations as majoritarian or consensus democracies.

As one can see in the tabular summary (Table 5.2), the broad definition of institutions used in the executives–parties index evidently has the result that the proportions of informal majoritarian and informal negotiation democracies are exactly reversed in the comparison between indices: Lijphart finds thirteen informal negotiation democracies and eight informal majoritarian democracies, while the simple partisan veto player index finds eight informal negotiation democracies and thirteen informal majoritarian democracies. There are six nations (Austria, Germany, Ireland, Japan, Norway, Portugal) that Lijphart classified as informal negotiation democracies, classified here as informal majoritarian democracies based on the more restrictive index, and one nation (France) that moves in the opposite direction, from an informal majoritarian to an informal negotiation democracy. While we will not discuss these differences in detail here, it is worth noting that at least on the basis of a more narrow definition of informal structures based only on institutions that exercise rule, it is not the informal negotiation democracies that predominate but the informal majoritarian democracies.

The broader definition of institutions in the executives–parties index also has consequences for the classification of nations based on the constitutional *and* the informal structural dimensions. Lijphart used the federal–unitary index for measuring the constitutional structures. We rely instead on Fuchs's (2000) minimal governmental system index B, that unlike Lijphart's index only includes primary structural characteristics and the classic separation of powers characteristic of presidentialism. As the results presented in Table 5.2 indicate, there are only marginal differences in the classification of the nations as constitutional majoritarian and constitutional negotiation democracies that result from using either a minimal or maximal constitutional veto player index. Under both indices, both types are approximately equally

TABLE 5.2. *A typology of western democracies by veto player indices*

Type of democracy[b]	Veto player indices[a]	
	Executives–parties index	Simple partisan veto player index
Informal majoritarian democracy	Australia, Canada, *France*, Great Britain, Greece, New Zealand, Spain, USA	*Austria*, Australia, Canada, *Germany*, Great Britain, Greece, *Ireland, Japan,* New Zealand, *Norway, Portugal,* Spain, USA
Informal negotiation democracy	*Austria*, Belgium, Denmark, Finland, *Germany, Ireland,* Italy, *Japan,* the Netherlands, *Norway, Portugal*, Sweden, Switzerland	Belgium, Denmark, Finland, *France*, Italy, the Netherlands, Sweden, Switzerland
	Federal–unitary index	Minimal governmental index B
Constitutional majoritarian democracy	Denmark, Finland, *France*, Great Britain, Greece, Ireland, *Italy*, New Zealand, Norway, Portugal, Sweden	Denmark, Finland, Great Britain, Greece, Ireland, New Zealand, *the Netherlands*, Norway, Portugal, Sweden
Constitutional negotiation democracy	Australia, Austria, Belgium, Canada, Germany, Japan, *the Netherlands*, Spain, Switzerland, USA	Australia, Austria, Belgium, Canada, *France*, Germany, *Italy*, Japan, Spain, Switzerland, USA
	Federal–unitary and executives–parties indices	Minimal governmental system B and simple partisan veto player indices
Pure majoritarian democracy	*France*, Great Britain, Greece, New Zealand	Great Britain, Greece, *Ireland*, New Zealand, *Norway, Portugal*
Constitutional majoritarian and informal negotiation democracy	Denmark, Finland, *Ireland, Italy, Norway, Portugal,* Sweden	Denmark, Finland, *the Netherlands*, Sweden
Constitutional negotiation and informal majoritarian democracy	Australia, Canada, Spain, USA	Australia, *Austria*, Canada, *Germany, Japan*, Spain, USA
Pure negation democracy	*Austria*, Belgium, *Germany, Japan, the Netherlands*, Switzerland	Belgium, *France, Italy*, Switzerland

[a] Federal–unitary and executives–parties indices for the period 1971–96 (Lijphart 1999*a*: 255); minimal governmental system index B (Fuchs 2000) and simple partisan veto player index for the period 1974–95.

[b] Majoritarian and negotiation democracies are differentiated by the zero points of z-score transformed (standardized) variables. Countries classified differently by the various veto player indices are in italics.

represented, with differences in only three nations: according to the federal–unitary index, France and Italy are constitutional majoritarian democracies and the Netherlands is a constitutional negotiation democracy, while the minimal governmental system index B results in the opposite classification.[5]

If one combines the executives–parties index with the federal–unitary index and contrasts that with the combination of the simple partisan veto player index and Fuchs's minimal governmental system index B, one sees what consequences a broader conceptualization of informal structures have for a typology of nations that includes both constitutional and empirical structures. The resulting typology of democracies, comparable to Lijphart's (1999*a*: 248) two-dimensional conceptual map of democracy, includes four types: 'Pure majoritarian democracies' are marked by a governmental system and a relationship between governing and opposition parties in which power is concentrated; 'pure negotiation democracies' are the opposite, marked by a dispersion of power in both respects. The two mixed types of 'constitutional majoritarian and informal negotiation democracies' as well as 'constitutional negotiation and informal majoritarian democracies' are marked by a combination of power-dispersing and power-concentrating structures.

Lijphart's broader institutional understanding results in the mixed type 'constitutional majoritarian and informal negotiation democracy' as the largest category (with seven nations), closely followed by the 'pure negotiation democracy' (with six), while our narrower understanding results in the complementary mixed type of 'constitutional negotiation and informal majoritarian democracy' as the most frequent (with seven nations), followed by 'pure majoritarian democracy' (with six). The narrower definition has the greatest consequence in the case of France, for while it it is classified as a pure majoritarian democracy under Lijphart's broader definition, it is classified as a pure negotiation democracy under the narrower. The different classification of France is a familiar pattern, given the hybrid character of its semi-presidential system (Sartori 1994).

Performance of democracies
Bivariate regressions are used to answer the second question as to the effect of the broader understanding of institutions on the performance of informal majoritarian and negotiation democracies. The dependent variables here are the effectiveness dimensions that were constructed and analysed in Chapter 4. The mean of these variables over the entire time period were employed. The independent variables were the executives–parties index as well as various sub-indices of this global index. The sub-indices were constructed on the

---

[5] One should bear in mind that the typology is dichotomous. France, for example, shows only a weak constitutional negotiation democracy. The values of the minimal governmental system index B are only barely above zero.

basis of the distribution of the individual indicators of the executives–parties index, following the figures presented in Appendix A of *Patterns of Democracy* (Lijphart 1999*a*: 312–14). Like the executives–parties index, these sub-indices are themselves based on the mean value of z-score transformed (standardized) individual indicators (1999*a*: 247).

Before discussing the results of this re-analysis, we need to explain its comparability with the performance results reported by Lijphart (1999*a*). We use Lijphart's data to measure the institutional arrangements, and like Lijphart, our analysis rests on a cross-sectional design using performance measures whose mean is calculated over time periods. But our analysis diverges from Lijphart's study in four significant ways.

First, though Lijphart's *Patterns of Democracy* is a study of the democratic structure in thirty-six nations, the performance analyses only rarely encompass all these nations, and it is far more often the case that his analyses are based on about twenty OECD nations. Some of his analyses include less than twenty—in one case only eleven nations (see Chs. 15 and 16)—the reason for which is the quite varied availability of data for individual performance dimensions. Since one of our selection criteria for the performance indicators was a complete data series, the following analyses are always based on the same twenty-one nations. The results of our performance analysis, across all indicators, are thus directly comparable to one another, which is not the case in Lijphart.

Second, the comparability of the results is also enhanced by the fact that our performance indicators always cover the same time period under investigation (1974 to 1995), while Lijphart's longitudinal data for individual performance dimensions vary sharply. In some cases, this data is only for individual years.

Third, our performance analysis is limited to the dimension of political effectiveness, and it is measured with pure outcome indicators. Lijphart, by contrast, includes effects of political institutions on various dimensions, uses both output and outcome measures, relies on citizen attitudes and behaviours, and investigates the characteristics of democratic institutions themselves.

Finally, to evaluate the strength of the bivariate regression coefficients we use two-tailed tests of statistical significance with at most a 5 per cent significance level—both more a stringent standard than Lijphart uses and the standard levels employed in empirical social research.

The starting point of the analysis is the bivariate regression of the individual effectiveness dimensions on Lijphart's original executives–parties index. As the results displayed in Table 5.3 indicate, the regression coefficients are all positive, with the sole exception of property crimes. Seven of the nineteen effectiveness dimensions show statistically significant relationships (noted in Table 5.3). Compared with informal majoritarian democracies, informal

TABLE 5.3. *Lijphart's executives–parties index with sub-indices and the levels of political effectiveness 1974–95 (bivariate regression analysis)*[a]

	Executives–parties index		...without interest groups		Relationship between governing and opposition parties		Party system		Interest groups	
	b (t-value)	beta	b (t-value)	beta	b (t-value)	beta	b (t-value)	beta	b (t-value)	beta
Domestic security	3.39 (0.796)	0.18	3.89 (0.744)	0.17	1.36 (0.271)	0.06	5.73 (1.17)	0.26	3.04 (0.686)	0.16
(a) Violent crimes	4.67 (1.259)	0.28	4.77 (1.036)	0.23	0.94 (0.209)	0.05	7.76 (1.868)	0.39	5.44 (1.434)	0.31
(b) Property crimes	−0.003 (−0.008)	−0.02	0.56 (0.118)	0.03	0.93 (0.207)	0.05	0.08 (0.017)	0.00	1.29 (0.324)	0.07
Economic policy	5.02 (1.807)	0.38	4.01 (1.125)	0.25	3.52 (1.034)	0.23	3.76 (1.103)	0.25	8.71** (3.655)	0.64**
(a) National income	2.17 (1.033)	0.23	1.81 (0.693)	0.16	2.34 (0.951)	0.21	0.95 (0.375)	0.09	3.57 (1.719)	0.37
(b) Misery	6.87 (2.06)	0.43	5.41 (1.244)	0.27	4.00 (0.954)	0.21	5.83 (1.419)	0.31	12.12** (4.625)	0.73**
Unemployment	4.99 (1.659)	0.36	4.13 (1.082)	0.24	3.69 (1.014)	0.23	3.81 (1.042)	0.23	8.46** (3.136)	0.58**
Inflation	3.56 (1.538)	0.33	2.60 (0.882)	0.20	1.29 (0.454)	0.10	3.44 (1.246)	0.28	6.61** (3.244)	0.60**
Social policy	11.29** (3.601)	0.64**	10.79* (2.498)	0.50*	6.12 (1.356)	0.30	13.51** (3.746)	0.65**	15.05** (6.284)	0.82**
(a) Health	3.13 (1.656)	0.36	2.63 (1.096)	0.24	2.00 (0.871)	0.20	2.78 (1.218)	0.27	5.03* (2.877)	0.55**
(b) Poverty	13.63** (3.588)	0.64**	13.38* (2.584)	0.51*	7.08 (1.291)	0.28	17.28** (4.145)	0.69**	17.32** (5.463)	0.78**
Environmental policy	7.20 (1.59)	0.34	7.97 (1.421)	0.31	4.59 (0.834)	0.19	9.91 (1.923)	0.40	7.15 (1.52)	0.33
(a) Environment	7.68 (1.45)	0.32	9.91 (1.541)	0.33	7.95 (1.278)	0.28	10.07 (1.65)	0.35	4.51 (0.795)	0.18
Sulphur oxides emissions	7.28* (2.798)	0.54*	8.17* (2.486)	0.50*	6.12 (1.85)	0.39	8.72** (2.901)	0.55**	7.02* (2.546)	0.50*
Municipal waste	9.60* (2.212)	0.45*	13.23* (2.585)	0.51*	10.36 (2.021)	0.42	13.68* (2.884)	0.55**	3.52 (0.71)	0.16
(b) Resources	5.13 (1.144)	0.25	4.26 (0.763)	0.17	0.21 (0.04)	0.01	7.58 (1.475)	0.32	8.21 (1.864)	0.39
General effectiveness	9.51* (2.931)	0.56**	9.42* (2.208)	0.45*	5.51 (1.263)	0.28	11.64** (3.134)	0.58**	12.00** (4.057)	0.68**
...without wealth	10.35* (2.890)	0.55**	10.10* (2.14)	0.44*	5.79 (1.202)	0.27	12.60** (3.063)	0.58**	13.45** (4.209)	0.70**
...without economy	9.13* (2.331)	0.47*	9.45 (1.896)	0.40	5.04 (1.00)	0.22	12.17* (2.776)	0.54*	10.53* (2.70)	0.53*

** $p < 0.01$; * $p < 0.05$ (two-tailed).

[a] Unstandardized (b) and standardized (beta) regression coefficients (OLS-estimate); beta equals Pearson's r; $N = 21$. Significant coefficients are in italics.

negotiation democracies reveal, on average, better performance levels, particularly in social policy, poverty rate, sulphur oxides emissions, and municipal waste.[6]

In addition, informal negotiation democracies show better overall performance. General effectiveness includes all the performance indicators investigated here, and the general effectiveness without wealth index has been previously discussed. Here we have added a third global measure of effectiveness that includes all non-economic performance indicators. This general effectiveness without economy includes domestic security, social, and environmental policy, the three policy areas for which Lijphart (1999a: 293) uses the adjectives 'kinder' and 'gentler' since they are associated with the attributes of 'a strong community orientation and social consciousness'.

The differences between informal majoritarian and informal negotiation democracies are clearest in the case of social policy and the poverty rate. The standardized regression coefficient beta, which is identical with the correlation coefficient Pearson's r in the case of bivariate regressions, is at 0.64 in both cases, and is significant at the 1 per cent level. This result accords with the critical review we conducted of Lijphart's own performance analyses at the end of Chapter 3. Using more severe criteria in that analysis, we found that statistically significant differences between majoritarian and consensus democracies only exist in the case of social policy.

We can therefore summarize that based on our effectiveness indicators, informal consensus or negotiation democracies show better policy outcomes, or are 'kinder and gentler'. We can do so using a better data basis and more stringent criteria than Lijphart. One should again point to the limitation that informal majoritarian and informal negotiation democracies were defined on the basis of the theoretically and methodologically problematic executives–parties index.

The critical question that remains to be investigated is to what extent these relationships are due to taking into account (policy-specific and not interest-neutral) corporatist arrangements into account. A first indication for the assumed importance of corporatism can be seen in the 'interest group' sub-index (Table 5.3), derived from Siaroff's corporatism index (1999). Eleven of the nineteen relationships are statistically significant. This means that the effectiveness of corporatist interest group systems are better, at a level greater than chance, than pluralist interest systems. The interest group sub-index therefore works better than the executives–parties index, with standardized

---

[6] Given the considerable heterogeneity among the various environmental indicators, we chose also to run regressions on the individual indicators of sulphur oxides and municipal waste, in addition to the two analytic dimensions of environmental quality and the quality and quantity of natural resources. In the cases of sulphur oxides emissions, the burden on the environment has, as a mean of all twenty-one nations under investigation, continuously reduced, while municipal waste has continued to increase.

regression coefficients higher (except in the case of municipal waste production). As one might expect from the interest-driven nature of corporatism
and its policy specificity, significantly higher performance can be seen particularly in the two economic misery dimensions and in social policy, and not
only in the poverty rate but also in the indicator for health. Consequently, the
relationships with the global effectiveness measures (general effectiveness,
general effectiveness without wealth, and general effectiveness without economy) are all significant.

An 'executives–parties index without interest groups' sub-index was also
constructed to directly test the thesis that the performance effects that were
found are due to the inclusion of corporatism in the executives–parties index.
Unlike the executives–parties index, this sub-index does not include the
structural characteristic of corporatism but instead is based only on four
other structural characteristics: the effective number of parliamentary parties, the percentage of minimal winning one-party cabinets, executive dominance and the disproportionality index. As one can see from the results
presented in Table 5.3, there are also only positive relationships with respect
to the effectiveness dimensions. As expected, the standardized regression
coefficients are lower for this sub-index than for the executives–parties
index, again with the exception of municipal waste production. However,
though this sub-index omits corporatism, there continue to be statistically
significant positive effects in the case of social policy, poverty rate, sulphur
oxides emissions, and municipal waste production, as well as for general
effectiveness and general effectiveness without wealth. Our assumption that
differences in performance between informal majoritarian and informal
negotiation democracies is attributable to the inclusion of corporatism, and
that this is particularly true in the case of the economic and social policies can
be confirmed, though with reservations. A significant portion of the covariance between the executives–parties index and individual performance indicators can be attributed to this structural characteristic.

We also argued that including the party system into Lijphart's executives–
parties index was theoretically problematic, and therefore investigated to
what extent effects of this index might be due to this characteristic. First
we constructed a 'party system' sub-index based on the effective number of
parliamentary parties and electoral disproportionality. Here again, all the
regression coefficients were positive (Table 5.3), and the relationship with
social policy, the poverty rate, sulphur oxides emissions, municipal waste
production, and all three general effectiveness measures were statistically
significant.

If, beyond the characteristic of corporatism, we also remove the two
characteristics of the party system from the executives–parties index, then
we are left with the two—albeit problematic—indicators that encompass the
'relationship between governing and opposition parties', namely government

composition (measured by the proportion of 'minimal winning one-party cabinets') and executive dominance. As one can see in Table 5.3, all the relationships with the dimensions of effectiveness we have investigated remain positive, but none of them are statistically significant. This 'remainder' index, based on problematic indicators, does not reveal any significant differences in performance between informal majoritarian and informal negotiation democracies.

Finally, we examined whether the positive relationship between the executives–parties index and the various sub-indices with the effectiveness dimensions remains if one controls for national levels of wealth. Lijphart utilizes this at least partly as a control variable. While we do not present this analysis in detail here, it showed not only that the positive relationships remained even after controlling for this factor,[7] but also that all the statistically *significant* relationships between the executives–parties index and the various sub-indices with the individual performance dimensions also continued to be significant.

In sum, we have found that informal negotiation democracies, as determined on the basis of Lijphart's executives–parties index, tend to show better performance than informal majoritarian democracies. However, significant differences exist only in the cases of social policy, poverty rate, some environmental aspects, and in general effectiveness. These positive relationships persist even after controlling for national levels of wealth. These positive relationships are not solely due to the inclusion of corporatism, as we had originally surmised, but also because the party system is included in the executives–parties index. A pure measure of the relationship between governing and opposition parties, based on two dubious Lijphart indicators (government composition and executive dominance), no longer shows statistically significant relationships with effectiveness. Given the weak explanatory power of these two indicators, the question is whether this is a substantiated finding or merely a result of the poor quality of the indicators themselves. We address this in the next section with the help of various partisan veto player indices suggested here.

Our analysis argues that it is primarily Lijphart's broad understanding of institutions, based on the inclusion of corporatism and party system characteristics in his executives–parties index, that is responsible for one of his central findings, namely that informal negotiation (or rather consensus) democracies are superior to informal majoritarian democracies along many performance dimensions, and that they are 'kinder and gentler' in their policies.

---

[7] There are only two exceptions: the positive relationship between the inflation rate and the executives–parties index with sub-indices turned negative after controlling for national levels of wealth. It is noteworthy that the only negative relationship, between property crime and the executives–parties index, turned positive.

DO CONSTITUTIONAL AND INFORMAL
INSTITUTIONS MATTER?

In the theoretical part of our analysis we discussed the somewhat contradict-ory hypotheses suggested as to the influence the political institutions have on the level and stability of political effectiveness as well as the balance of policy patterns. These hypotheses, predicting quite differing effects of con-stitutional and informal institutions of democratic governance, are examined empirically.

Formal and informal political institutions are measured using different constitutional and partisan veto player indices. The governmental system is measured with the two maximal (Lijphart's federal–unitary and Schmidt's institutional constraints of central state government) and the two minimal (Fuchs's minimal governmental system A and B) constitutional veto player indices. The four partisan veto player indices previously suggested (including the surrogate index) are used to measure the relationship between governing and opposition parties. These differ primarily in whether they only include parties (number of governing parties and effective number of parliamentary parties) or additionally take into account the type of government (simple partisan veto player index and Schnapp's veto players in the lower house) into account. The use of differing indicators provides information on the validity of the individual indices, but also minimizes the problem that the relationships found are an artefact of a particular measurement. The follow-ing discussion proceeds by examining the influence of constitutional and informal institutional arrangements first on the level and then on the stability of policy-specific and general effectiveness, and then turns to the structure of political effectiveness, or rather the policy patterns.

Levels of Policy-specific and General Effectiveness

In a first step, the relationship between institutions of democratic governance and level of political effectiveness is studied using bivariate regressions. In order to adequately determine the effect of institutional arrangements, how-ever, it is necessary to control for the most important theoretically presumed explanatory factors—national level of wealth, ideological orientation of the government, and openness of the economy—that were identified in the integrated model for explaining the performance of democratic institutions. But with a maximum of five explanatory factors and twenty-one nations under investigation, we are confronted with the typical problem of compara-tive, macroanalytic research: 'too many explanatory variables and too few cases' (Lijphart 1971; Collier 1993). A simultaneous consideration of all control variables in a multivariate regression model is not possible for statistical reasons, because there are insufficient degrees of freedom. Many comparative macroanalytic analyses address the problem by 'stacking' cross-sectional data gathered at different points in time and using a pooled time-series cross-sectional analysis. When introduced, this method was hailed as a 'panacea' (Mair 1996; Shalev 1998). In the meantime critical reflection has led both to methodological suggestions and to reflections on how to better specify the conditions necessary for using this method (Beck and Katz 1995; Kittel 1999). In a second step, the applicability of pooled analysis for our study is discussed, and reasons are given why a traditional cross-sectional design is used to analyse the influence of political institutions on the level of political effectiveness. In a third step, we present the results of the multivariate analysis that we conducted based on this design.

Bivariate analyses
We first carried out bivariate analyses on the relationship between 'the governmental system' and effectiveness and then between 'the relationship between governing and opposition parties' and effectiveness. In the case of the *governmental system* we were guided by Lijphart's hypothesis that constitutional negotiation democracies do not differ from constitutional majoritarian democracies—with the exception of fighting inflation, where the former type show better results.

Table 5.4 presents the bivariate regressions between all the effectiveness dimensions and the four constitutional veto player indices noted earlier (Lijphart's federal–unitary, Schmidt's institutional constraints of central state government, and Fuchs's minimal governmental system A and B). As was true for the preceding re-analysis of *Patterns of Democracy*, this is a cross-sectional design, utilizing the mean value of effectiveness from 1974 to 1995 per nation.

It is noteworthy that positive relationships exist that indicate superior performance of constitutional negotiation democracies not just in the case of the inflation rate but also for another economic policy indicator, namely national income. At the same time, the relationship to all other effectiveness dimensions – domestic security, social (health partly excepted), and environmental policies, as well as with general effectiveness—have negative signs. If one only examines the statistically significant coefficients, then constitutional negotiation democracies are superior to constitutional majoritarian democracies inasmuch as they show lower inflation rates and a higher national income, but inferior with regard to having more violent crimes, worse environmental policies, and an above-average consumption of natural resources. Relative to Lijphart, therefore, the difference between the two forms is not limited to fighting inflation. In some respects constitutional negotiation democracies actually show worse results than constitutional majoritarian democracies, and this is of considerable theoretical importance. If at least

TABLE 5.4. *Constitutional veto player indices and the levels of political effectiveness 1974–95 (bivariate regression analysis)*[a]

	Federal–unitary index (Lijphart 1999a)		Institutional constraints of central state government (Schmidt 1996)		Minimal governmental system index A (Fuchs 2000)		Minimal governmental system index B (Fuchs 2000)	
	b (t-value)	beta	b (t-value)	beta	b (t-value)	beta	b (t-value)	beta
Domestic security policy	−5.42 (−1.554)	−0.34	−2.52 (−0.886)	−0.20	−4.02 (−1.385)	−0.30	−3.83 (−1.645)	−0.35
(a) Violent crimes	−6.76* (−2.319)	−0.47*	−4.46 (−1.882)	−0.40	−4.98 (−2.02)	−0.42	−5.19* (−2.768)	−0.54*
(b) Property crimes	−0.65 (−0.199)	−0.05	1.02 (0.398)	0.09	−0.52 (−0.193)	−0.04	−0.05 (−0.024)	−0.01
Economic policy	4.81 (2.073)	0.43	3.56 (1.938)	0.41	3.70 (1.91)	0.40	3.34* (2.153)	0.44*
(a) National income	4.38* (2.826)	0.54*	3.50** (2.912)	0.56**	3.47* (2.683)	0.52*	3.19** (3.173)	0.59**
(b) Misery	4.29 (1.429)	0.31	2.92 (1.226)	0.27	3.19 (1.281)	0.28	2.83 (1.397)	0.31
Unemployment	0.49 (0.178)	0.04	0.51 (0.239)	0.06	0.28 (0.123)	0.03	0.81 (0.441)	0.10
Inflation	4.84* (2.721)	0.53*	3.11* (2.105)	0.44*	3.69* (2.454)	0.49*	2.71* (2.13)	0.44*
Social policy	−1.58 (−0.458)	−0.11	−2.24 (−0.84)	−0.19	−2.22 (−0.789)	−0.18	−2.31 (−1.013)	−0.23
(a) Health	0.46 (0.267)	0.06	−2.22 (−0.161)	−0.04	0.26 (0.184)	0.04	0.11 (0.09)	0.02
(b) Poverty	−2.81 (−0.677)	−0.15	−3.11 (−0.969)	−0.22	−3.56 (−1.058)	−0.24	−3.53 (−1.302)	−0.29
Environmental policy	−9.81* (−2.847)	−0.55*	−5.79 (−1.977)	−0.41	−6.76* (−2.247)	−0.46*	−5.27* (−2.114)	−0.44*
(a) Environment	−7.98 (−1.815)	−0.38	−4.27 (−1.188)	−0.26	−5.68 (−1.535)	−0.33	−3.71 (−1.20)	−0.27
Sulphur oxides emissions	−2.12 (−0.817)	−0.18	−0.41 (−0.198)	−0.05	−1.03 (−0.476)	−0.11	−0.55 (−0.308)	−0.07
Municipal waste	−5.36 (−1.35)	−0.30	−0.21 (−0.649)	−0.15	−4.28 (−1.306)	−0.29	−3.19 (−1.182)	−0.26
(b) Resources	−9.47* (−2.862)	−0.55*	−6.04* (−2.18)	−0.45*	−6.36* (−2.183)	−0.45*	−5.67* (−2.436)	−0.49*
General effectiveness	−4.24 (−1.327)	−0.29	−2.47 (−0.969)	−0.22	−3.29 (−1.244)	−0.27	−2.85 (−1.326)	−0.29
General effectiveness without wealth	−4.51 (−1.28)	−0.28	−2.75 (−0.981)	−0.22	−3.53 (−1.213)	−0.27	−3.09 (−1.305)	−0.29
General effectiveness without economy	−7.01 (−2.041)	−0.42	−4.41 (−1.578)	−0.34	−5.43 (−1.895)	−0.40	−4.76 (−2.062)	−0.43

** $p < 0.01$; * $p < 0.05$ (two-tailed).

[a] Unstandardized (b) and standardized (beta) regression coefficients (OLS-estimate); beta equals Pearson's r; $N = 21$. Significant coefficients are in italics.

some of these negative coefficients remain even after controlling for other factors, and for outliers, then there would be empirical evidence for the 'conventional wisdom' that majoritarian democracies are more effective than negotiation democracies—a wisdom that Lijphart claims to have disproved in his analyses.

In terms of the validity of the various constitutional veto player indices, we expected that the two minimal (primary characteristics) and the two maximal (primary and secondary) indices would behave, respectively, in a similar fashion. This expectation was only borne in the case of the minimal indices A and B. In only one dimension, namely for violent crimes, was the beta value significantly higher for Index B (-0.54) than for Index A (-0.42). This is almost certainly due to the fact that presidentialism is included in Index B, but not in Index A, and because the presidential system of the USA has by far the highest rate of violent crime.

There were, by contrast, much clearer differences between the two maximal indices: Schmidt's institutional constraints of central state government index showed lower values for the coefficients than Lijphart's federal–unitary index in nearly all of the effectiveness indicators. The difference can also be clearly seen in the fact that while only three of the relationships are statistically significant in the case of the former index, five are significant in the latter. While both indices include the same primary structural characteristics (bicameralism, federalism), they differ both in the *number* of secondary characteristics they include (Lijphart with three and Schmidt with four), but also in the *nature* of these secondary aspects (see Table 3.3). Both take constitutional rigidity and the existence of an independent central bank into account, but Lijphart also includes constitutional court jurisdiction (which Schmidt omits) in his index, while Schmidt includes referenda and EU membership (which Lijphart omits). Lijphart in fact explicitly omitted referenda after his first analyses in *Democracies* (1984) revealed that this dimension could not be clearly assigned either to the federal–unitary or to the executives–parties dimension. That Schmidt's index has twice as many secondary as primary characteristics, and the fact that these secondary characteristics are only selectively relevant for certain decisions or decisions in particular policy areas, gives this index a very specific character that comes out not just in the comparison with the federal–unitary index. It is also seen in the fact that Schmidt's index is the only one of the four whose coefficient actually has the opposite sign in two cases (property crimes and health) than is the case in any of the other constitutional veto player indices.

As to the *relationship between governing and opposition parties* and the effectiveness dimensions, Lijphart expects to find consistently higher levels of effectiveness in informal negotiation democracies in the non-economic policy areas, where the 'kinder and gentler qualities' come to the fore. A different hypothesis, based on a critical evaluation of Lijphart's research results, asserts instead that informal negotiation democracies are superior to informal majoritarian democracies in only one policy area, namely in social policy. Table 5.5 presents the bivariate regressions between all the effectiveness dimensions and the four partisan veto player indices (number of governing parties, simple partisan veto player index, veto players in the lower house, and the effective number of parliamentary parties). With a single exception, namely in the case of property crimes, informal negotiation democracies consistently show better performance than informal majoritarian democracies. It is also noteworthy that the only statistically significant relationships exist with the poverty rate and with social policy as a whole; and this pattern is valid for all four indices used. Thus, the empirical findings do not support Lijphart's hypothesis of generally better performance on the part of informal negotiation democracies but rather only the alternate hypothesis that they are superior only in the area of social policy.

All four indices show a similar pattern relative to the level of political effectiveness, but a number of important differences remain, particularly in the case of the poverty rate. The value of the standardized regression coefficient is highest for the effective number of parliamentary parties index (0.62) and lowest for the number of veto players in the lower house (0.48). The coefficients for the other indices lie in between (0.55 for the number of governing parties and 0.53 for the simple partisan veto player index).

As in the previous discussion, these results are illuminating for assessing the validity of the respective indices, in particular Lijphart's executives–parties index. We had constructed a sub-index 'relationship between governing and opposition parties' as part of the re-analysis of Lijphart's study which excluded all those characteristics of the executives–parties index that for theoretical reasons could not be regarded as a measure of this construct. This left only two indicators (government composition, executive dominance) that were of dubious methodological quality. Though statistically significant relationships with poverty can be found for all four suggested partisan veto player indices (see Table 5.5), in the case of this Lijphart sub-index (see Table 5.3), no statistically significant relationship could be found. One can draw the conclusion from this that the absence of such a relationship is due to the poor quality of the Lijphart indicators.

The four partisan veto player indices were originally constructed to measure the autonomy of the government as an actor in carrying out political decisions, and it is noteworthy that they show considerable differences particularly with respect to the poverty rate. The indices start from the premise that governmental autonomy would diminish proportionately as the number of parties in government and parliament that needed to approve a political decision increased. But political parties are not only veto players in the political decision-making process, they are also and primarily the representatives of quite specific societal interests and groups. This makes them

TABLE 5.5. *Partisan veto player indices and the levels of political effectiveness 1974–95 (bivariate regression analysis)*[a]

	Number of governing parties		Simple partisan veto player index		Veto players in the lower house (Schnapp 2004)		Effective number of parliamentary parties	
	b (t-value)	beta	b (t-value)	beta	b (t-value)	beta	b (t-value)	beta
Domestic security policy	1.34 (0.326)	0.08	0.46 (0.111)	0.03	0.63 (0.159)	0.04	2.02 (0.627)	0.14
(a) Violent crimes	3.22 (0.895)	0.20	1.84 (0.504)	0.12	1.89 (0.539)	0.12	3.07 (1.087)	0.24
(b) Property crimes	-1.39 (-0.381)	-0.09	-1.21 (-0.333)	-0.08	-1.03 (-0.29)	-0.07	-0.30 (-0.104)	-0.02
Economic policy	3.22 (1.167)	0.26	3.23 (1.170)	0.26	3.18 (1.195)	0.26	2.38 (1.082)	0.24
(a) National income	2.03 (1.017)	0.23	2.51 (1.271)	0.28	2.36 (1.236)	0.27	1.64 (1.034)	0.23
(b) Misery	3.77 (1.109)	0.25	3.31 (0.967)	0.22	3.37 (1.022)	0.23	2.65 (0.974)	0.22
Unemployment	1.77 (0.584)	0.13	1.43 (0.47)	0.11	1.85 (0.633)	0.14	0.95 (0.394)	0.09
Inflation	2.92 (1.307)	0.29	2.69 (1.196)	0.27	2.34 (1.072)	0.24	2.34 (1.323)	0.29
Social policy	*8.72* (2.639)*	*0.52**	*8.75* (2.648)*	*0.52**	*7.23* (2.165)*	*0.45**	*8.16 (3.37)*	*0.61***
(a) Health	1.66 (0.878)	0.20	2.17 (1.165)	0.26	1.22 (0.666)	0.15	2.07 (1.429)	0.31
(b) Poverty	*11.29** (2.903)*	*0.55***	*10.82* (2.731)*	*0.53**	*9.50* (2.409)*	*0.48**	*10.04** (3.466)*	*0.62***
Environmental policy	3.47 (0.77)	0.17	3.33 (0.737)	0.17	1.98 (0.452)	0.10	2.98 (0.835)	0.19
(a) Environment	3.37 (0.644)	0.15	3.51 (0.669)	0.15	2.24 (0.440)	0.10	2.16 (0.517)	0.12
Sulphur oxides emissions	4.07 (1.465)	0.32	4.16 (1.498)	0.33	3.45 (1.269)	0.28	3.39 (1.545)	0.33
Municipal waste	7.77 (1.822)	0.39	7.92 (1.862)	0.39	6.75 (1.614)	0.35	5.51 (1.603)	0.35
(b) Resources	2.80 (0.643)	0.15	2.42 (0.553)	0.13	1.29 (0.305)	0.07	3.14 (0.92)	0.21
General effectiveness	5.92 (1.713)	0.37	5.57 (1.60)	0.34	4.60 (1.344)	0.30	5.49 (2.065)	0.43
General effectiveness without wealth	6.23 (1.629)	0.35	5.70 (1.475)	0.32	4.76 (1.257)	0.28	5.69 (1.922)	0.40
General effectiveness without economy	5.64 (1.406)	0.31	5.23 (1.292)	0.28	4.11 (1.037)	0.23	5.49 (1.773)	0.38

** p < 0.01; * p < 0.05 (two-tailed).

[a] Unstandardized (b) and standardized (beta) regression coefficients (OLS-estimate); beta equals Pearson's r; N = 21. Significant coefficients are in italics.

different from constitutionally defined institutions that are only veto players. Thus, though increasing numbers of political parties in parliament and government makes it harder to make political decisions, it also increases the extent to which societal interests are represented in these institutions. One can therefore assume that the probability increases that minority interests will be that much more addressed in the legislative bargaining process.

It thus follows that the various partisan veto player indices will not only measure the construct 'governmental autonomy in decision-making' but will also measure the construct 'representation of societal interests'. The degree to which this second construct will be measured will likely vary among the indices. We assume that it will be lowest in the index number of veto players in the lower house, as it measures the number of governing parties and, depending upon the type of minority government, varying numbers of additional veto players. We assume it will be highest in the effective number of parliamentary parties, conceived as a surrogate instrument, as it measures not only the distribution of power in the relationship between governing and opposition parties but also in the party system itself. This index, which determines the number of parliamentary parties based on weighted seat distribution (Laakso and Taagepera 1979; Taagepera 1997), measures the breadth or entire spectrum of the societal interests represented in parliament. Such theoretical assertions are mirrored in the empirical results of our regression analysis inasmuch as the relationship between the poverty rate and the number of veto players in the lower house index shows the lowest, and the effective number of parliamentary parties index shows the highest value.

Finally, we wish to emphasize that unlike constitutional veto players, political parties are not only veto players but also the representatives of societal interests and groups. Partisan veto player indices thus measure two theoretical constructs with different impact, and this is of central importance for the theory about the effects of political institutions, which will be discussed in Chapter 6.

Multivariate analyses: design and methods

The bivariate regressions have shown that constitutional majoritarian and constitutional negotiation democracies as well as informal majoritarian and informal negotiation democracies differ systematically from one another in several effectiveness dimensions. The next question is whether these empirically established differences would continue to hold even after controlling for the most important rival explanatory factors.

We already identified three such factors in the theoretical part of our study: the national level of wealth, the ideological orientation of the government, and the openness of the economy. In the majority of his analyses,

Lijphart (1999*a*) already controlled for the national level of wealth, but he did not pay attention to the government as a central political actor—without which political action and performance would not even be possible (Schmidt 2000*a*: 347). He also did not account for economic globalization as a factor, one that has been much discussed of late as an important determinant of performance. Beyond these general factors there are, in principle, policy-specific factors that determine the level of effectiveness. In the case of economic and social policy, for example, the institutional arrangement of corporatism that we have addressed repeatedly could play a role, as the percentage of foreigners in a nation might in domestic security policy, and in environmental policy the same might be true of the use of automobiles. However, our goal is not to explain policy-specific or general effectiveness as well as possible, but rather to pursue the question whether institutional arrangements have an influence on effectiveness. To answer this question, it is adequate to control for the most important competing potential explanations.

As noted above, when comparative macroanalytic research is confronted with the problem of many explanatory factors and few cases, one answer has been to pool cross-sectional data covering different time periods and to conduct a time-series cross-sectional analysis. This method is particularly often encountered in comparative research on economic and social policy (see Alvarez et al. 1991; Huber et al. 1993; Schmidt 1997*b*; Birchfield and Crepaz 1998; Iversen and Cusack 2000). The advantage is that of a simple and elegant increase in the number of observations (n = nations × time periods), thereby permitting the empirical analysis of complex explanatory models.

The difficulty, however, is that pooled data are not simply 'more data' in the sense of an increase in the amount of data (Shalev 1998), because a change of design also results in a change in what is being explained. In the case of simple cross-sections, differences in the levels between the nations are explained, while in the case of pooled cross-sections, additional variations over time (or developments) are explained (Hicks 1994; Kittel 1999). Both cross-sectional and time-series dimensions go into the regression coefficients, but this coefficient gives no information about the relative importance of both dimensions. Its interpretation remains open because it is not clear whether it is the *differences* between nations or the nation-specific *development* over time that is responsible for the effects seen (Kittel 1999: 231; Shalev 1998). This situation has notable consequences, because one cannot assume that differences between nations as well as temporal developments are caused by the same factors (Shalev 1998). Additional analyses are needed to separate cross-sectional from longitudinal effects, and they in turn are based on a small number of cases (Kittel 1999). In the end, the decision whether to use time-series cross-sectional analysis or not is dependent on the questions under investigation.

In our discussion of various theories and hypotheses on the impact of political institutions, we have identified two types of effects. The first is limited to the level of effectiveness, and Lijphart, the most prominent proponent of this hypothesis, merely asserts that consensus or negotiation democracies produce better policy outcomes than majoritarian democracies. He does not assume that they also directly influence the development of the level of effectiveness. The systematic reason for limiting the consideration to differences in levels lies in the fact that among the political institutions, particularly the constitutionally defined institutions, one is dealing with relatively stable factors and that therefore a co-variation between temporal developments of institutional factors and temporal development of performance would either be small or be entirely excluded.

The second type of effects focuses on the development, but no predictions are made about the direction (either positive or negative) of the level of effectiveness, but only about its variability or stability over time. The empirical examination of this premise of political decision-making theory, reformulated primarily in Tsebelis's veto player approach (1995, 2002), also does not call for a typical time-series design but rather a cross-sectional design with a measure for the variability or stability of the level of effectiveness for each nation as a dependent variable.

If, despite the fact that the hypothesis is focused on the level of effectiveness, one nevertheless employed a time-series cross-sectional analysis, then the explained object would decisively change. In the case of relatively stable dependent variables, as is the case for the effectiveness dimensions examined here, there is a problem of the autocorrelation of the residuals. In this case, to calculate an unbiased and consistent standard error, the regression equation has to include a correction for this autocorrelation. The most frequently used method to correct this error is to introduce a 'lagged dependent variable' into the explanatory model (Beck and Katz 1996).

But there are disadvantages here as well. First, only a small amount of the variance of the dependent variable remains unexplained. This reduces the chance that other, exogenous variables will have an effect. Second, only short-term changes in the dependent variable remain, because the influence of longer-term factors has already been included in the endogenous lagged dependent variable (Pennings et al. 1999: 211). In such a situation where only a 'partial adjustment of the dependent variable to changes in the independent variables' is explained (Kittel 1999: 230–1), it is relatively unlikely that comparatively stable explanatory factors such as political institutions can even reveal explanatory power. If under such conditions institutional arrangements show no significant effects then this does not mean that these arrangements have no influence on political effectiveness. It only means that they cannot explain these specific, short-term changes or adaptation processes in effectiveness. When running a time-series cross-sectional analysis with our effectiveness data, the lagged dependent variable was the most powerful independent variable while institutional variables (measured by constitutional and partisan veto player indices) revealed no significant effects on effectiveness dimensions (not shown here). Given this methodological situation, the theories and hypotheses we have put forward as to the influence the political institutions have on the level of political effectiveness, such influence can only be appropriately analysed with the use of a traditional cross-sectional design. As it is, in a regression model with twenty-one investigated nations, it is only possible to include a maximum of three explanatory factors, given the degrees of freedom.

We use the 'backwards' procedure (Pennings et al. 1999: 215) contained in the SPSS package to identify the statistically significant explanatory variables. First all independent variables are included in the regression equation, and then those variables not significant at the 5 per cent level are sequentially excluded, starting with the variable with the lowest level of significance. In addition, for two selected effectiveness variables (dependent variable), a pairwise comparison is undertaken to match the effect of the institutional variables with the effect of competing explanatory factors.

In using such cross-sectional designs, three problems can arise that lead to biased, inefficient, or unrobust estimates: outliers, multicollinearity, and heteroscedasticity (Berry and Feldman 1985; Pennings et al. 1999: 193). The 'split files' SPSS procedure was used to find outliers, and multicollinearity was checked with the help of the SPSS statistical measure of 'level of tolerance'. The residual scatterplots for the independent variable were inspected for heteroscedasticity. Neither multicollinearity nor heteroscedasticity could be found in the data we used, but outliers could be identified in various regression equations. They will be discussed in the presentation of the empirical findings.

The means for the dependent variables (effectiveness dimensions) as well as for the independent variables (national level of wealth, ideological orientation of the government, openness of the economy, constitutional and partisan veto players) were calculated for the entire investigated time period (1974–95).

- The national level of wealth, introduced and justified on the one hand as a performance dimension, but at the same time also a determinant of performance, is measured by GDP per capita in US dollars (adjusted for price and purchasing power). The standardized performance index using a scale from 0 to 100 is used in the empirical analysis (see Table 4.5).
- The ideological orientation of the government is measured using Schmidt's (1992*b*) party composition of government measure, updated for the years after 1990 by Armingeon et al. (1999). It measures government party composition by length (in days) and strength (per cent cabinet seats) and

differentiates parties by ideological family. The measure differentiates between five types of governments: (*a*) hegemony of right-wing and centre parties; (*b*) dominance of right-wing and centre parties; (*c*) balance between left and right parties; (*d*) dominance of social democratic and other left parties; and (*e*) hegemony of social democratic and other left parties.
- The openness of the economy is measured by foreign trade, that is, that proportion of GNP that is composed of imports and exports. This index is based on OECD *National Accounts* data (OECD 1999*a*).

Each of these explanatory factors stands for a particular theory in comparative public policy (Schmidt 1993). National levels of wealth are at the centre of the theory of socio-economic determinants of public policy (Wilensky 1975), the ideological orientation of the government is central to the partisan theory (Hibbs 1977) and the openness of the economy stands for the new and still imprecise theory of globalization.

Each effectiveness dimension (dependent) is investigated, using multivariate regression analysis, to establish whether the political–institutional theory we have proposed stands up to these competing theory traditions. For measuring the governmental system and the relationship between governing and opposition parties, each of the four veto player indices introduced previously were utilized—though the analysis is made considerably easier by the fact that systematic differences did not exist between all of them. Therefore, only the results of the multivariate regressions for the *minimal governmental system index B* and the *simple partisan veto player index* are presented, and only those regression coefficients either statistically significant at the 1 per cent or 5 per cent level, or that are very close to the 5 per cent significance level, are included in the tables.

Multivariate analyses: the results
Based on the bivariate regression analyses previously presented, we found statistically significant effects for the *governmental system* in five areas: violent crimes, national income, inflation rate, quality of the environment, and the use of natural resources. The multivariate regression results presented in Table 5.6 show the following: First, the violent crime effect can be attributed to the outlier of the USA. In the case of the inflation rate, the statistically significant effect vanishes after controlling for national level of wealth and for the openness of the economy. This result is noteworthy, since this is the only effect that Lijphart attributes to the arrangement of constitutional institutions. Our results indicate that it is a spurious correlation after controlling for competing factors. Second, even after controlling for competing factors, the statistically significant effect of the governmental system on national income and the use of natural resources remain. Third, an additional effect of the governmental system on health appears after con-

trolling for level of wealth, at just slightly above the 5 per cent significance level. This is clearly due to a so-called suppressor effect (Kühnel and Krebs 2001) that appears particularly in cases when the correlations between two independent and one dependent variable do not have the same signs. Here the two independent variables—national income and governmental system—positively correlate with one another, while national income correlates positively but the governmental system correlates negatively with health.

Thus, after controlling for the most important competing explanatory factors, we still find two significant effects and one nearly-significant effect of constitutional veto players. As in the case of the bivariate regressions, these effects go in opposite directions. Positive effects that indicate better performance of constitutional negotiation democracies only exist in the case of one economic performance variable (national income). The relationships to socio-political (health) and environmental effectiveness (natural resource use) are negative and indicate a lower performance on the part of constitutional negotiation democracies. This pattern contradicts Lijphart's hypotheses about the difference between constitutional negotiation and constitutional majoritarian democracies in two ways. One was the assumption that, as a rule, there were no differences in performance between the two types of democracy. The other was the assumption that the few differences he asserted favoured constitutional negotiation democracies. Even if these assumptions appear unsubstantiated, it does not clearly imply that the opposite 'conventional wisdom' is confirmed, namely that constitutional majoritarian democracies are superior in their performance. Rather, the inconsistent pattern that includes both positive and negative effects instead leads to the surmise that other factors decide what effect constitutional settings have on performance. This thought will be taken up in Chapter 6, in the discussion of the theoretical implications of our empirical findings.

In the bivariate regressions with the indices for *the relationship between governing and opposition parties* (see Table 5.5), it was only possible to find one statistically significant relationship, namely with the poverty rate and with general social policy. As one can see from the multivariate regressions presented in Table 5.6, only the first of these effects remained after controlling for other determinants. However, three other statistically significant (or nearly-significant) effects were added in the multivariate model. After controlling for the level of wealth, the simple partisan veto player index showed an effect on municipal waste production as well as on general effectiveness without economy. Controlling for ideological orientation also revealed an effect on general effectiveness. In four of five cases, the unstandardized regression coefficient for the partisan veto player index increased after controlling for additional explanatory variables. Here suppressor effects, as was already the case for constitutional veto players, also exist, due to the partially

TABLE 5.6. *Determinants of the levels of political effectiveness 1974–95 (multivariate regression analysis)*[a]

Independent variables	Domestic security polices	Violent crimes	Property crimes	National income	Misery	Unemployment
Minimal governmental system index B (Fuchs)	—	−5.19* (−2.768)	—	3.19** (3.173)	—	—
Simple partisan veto player index	—	—	—	—	—	—
Ideological orientation of the government (Schmidt)	—	—	—	—	—	—
Gross domestic product	−0.94* (−2.316)	—	—	—	—	—
Openness of the economy		—	—		1.18** (4.165)	0.59 (1.896)
Constant	101.89** (6.503)	61.88** (7.328)	—	50.65** (11.194)	18.04 (1.648)	49.58** (4.102)
Adjusted R^2	0.18	0.25	—	0.31	0.45	0.12
Outlier	—	USA	—		—	—

	Inflation	Social policy	Health	Poverty	Environmental policy	Environment
Minimal governmental system index B (Fuchs)	—	—	−2.32 (−2.073)	—	—	—
Simple partisan veto player index	—	9.08** (2.926)	—	8.12 (2.102)	—	—

	Sulphur oxides emissions	Municipal waste	Resources	General effectiveness	General effectiveness without wealth	General effectiveness without economy
Ideological orientation of the government (Schmidt)	—	6.88 (1.890)	—	8.36 (2.064)	—	—
Gross domestic product	0.93** (6.063)	—	0.76** (3.682)	—	−1.09* (−2.452)	−1.24* (−2.381)
Openness of the economy	12.53* (2.244)	—	—	28.23 (1.788)	—	—
Constant	32.69** (4.554)	29.60* (2.46)	41.69** (3.722)	6.10 (0.429)	109.45*** (6.364)	97.44* (4.86)
Adjusted R^2	0.65	0.32	0.37	0.43	0.20	0.19

	Sulphur oxides emissions	Municipal waste	Resources	General effectiveness	General effectiveness without wealth	General effectiveness without economy
Minimal governmental system index B (Fuchs)	—	—	−5.67* (−2.436)	—	—	—
Simple partisan veto player index	—	11.96** (3.968)	—	5.91 (1.788)	—	7.57 (1.961)
Ideological orientation of the government (Schmidt)	—	—	—	6.93 (1.788)	—	—
Gross domestic product	—	−1.61** (−4.795)	—	—	—	−0.93* (−2.163)
Openness of the economy	—	—	—	—	—	—
Constant	—	84.90** (6.583)	50.37** (4.809)	35.39* (2.76)	—	90.65** (5.491)
Adjusted R^2	—	0.59	0.20	0.17	—	0.19

** $p < 0.01$; * $p < 0.05$ (two-tailed).

[a] Unstandardized regression coefficients (OLS-estimate) and t-values in parentheses; $N = 21$.

opposite relationship (seen in the signs) between two independent and one dependent variable (Kühnel and Krebs 2001).

However, unlike what was found in the case of the constitutional veto players, the statistically significant coefficients that measure the effect of partisan veto players on the level of performance have only positive signs. This indicates that informal negotiation democracies generally produce better policy performance than informal majoritarian democracies, particularly in social policy and poverty rates, in municipal waste production, as well as in the case of general effectiveness and general effectiveness without economy. Still, in these last two cases they explain less than 20 per cent of the variance in the dependent variable, a very small amount. The two explanatory models, for poverty rates and municipal waste production, reach distinctly higher values, with explained variances of 0.43 and 0.59, respectively.

So what is the meaning of these results for the hypothesis on the influence of informal institutions on effectiveness? According to Lijphart's broad hypothesis informal negotiation democracies, almost as a rule, show significantly better performance in non-economic policy areas. This hypothesis is not confirmed by these data. But the 'Lijphart-critical' thesis that differences between informal majoritarian and informal negotiation democracies were limited to social policy was also not wholly confirmed because there are significant differences in one of the environmental performance dimensions. There are therefore empirical indications for a 'kinder and gentler' policy of the informal negotiation democracies, but these are considerably more limited in both scope and strength than Lijphart (1999a) has asserted.

To throw more light upon how informal institutional settings influence the level of political effectiveness, we have conducted more detailed analyses of the most satisfactory models, namely the models that explain the poverty rate and municipal waste production. We conducted both pairwise comparisons of the explanatory variables, and examined how stable the effect of the institutions was over time.

The multivariate analysis of the poverty rate indicated that three determinants have weak significant effects: the simple partisan veto player index, the ideological orientation of the government, and the openness of the economy. That all three of these just miss the 5 per cent significance level indicates that the poverty level is also influenced by other factors. To establish a clearer picture, pairwise comparisons are made between the effect of the simple partisan veto player index and each of the competing explanatory factors. The results of this pairwise comparison, presented in Table 5.7, confirm that the poverty level is not just positively influenced by many partisan veto players, a hegemonic social democratic government, and an open economy. In addition, a small number of constitutional veto players has a positive effect on the poverty rate. The national poverty level can thus be explained by using at least three different theoretical traditions: political-institutional theory, partisan theory, and globalization theory. In the case of globalization, however, it is not the thesis of convergence, predicting globalization would lead to a common process of underbidding or 'social dumping', that is confirmed. Rather, the positive relationship between the openness of the economy and the low poverty rate points instead much more to an effect Cameron (1978) first identified, whereby nations with open economies respond to economic uncertainty by expanding the role of government and by strengthening social welfare measures and guarantees. This result, that can be interpreted more as a confirmation of the opposite theory of divergence, is consistent with a number of studies that have reached similar conclusions (Garrett 1998; Rodrik 1998; Crepaz 2001). Among the control factors that were theoretically proposed, only the level of wealth appears to have no effect on the poverty rate.

An at least implicit basic premise of the new institutionalism or of political–institutional theory states that the effects of political institutions are stable over time. To examine this premise, the explanatory model was investigated for each of the four time periods in our study. The results, also displayed in Table 5.7, do not confirm the premise. For one, the simple partisan veto player index had a significant effect on the poverty rate only during the first (1974–9) and last (1990–5) time periods. For another, the effects of the other explanatory factors were not consistently statistically significant; the minimal governmental system index B, for example, only revealed a significant (negative) effect on the poverty rate for the last period. As for the most important determinant of the poverty rate, the informal structure (as measured by simple partisan veto player index), one can draw the conclusion from the results in Table 5.7 that, power dispersion in this dimension always has a positive influence on poverty, but that the effect is not statistically significant at all times. This also points to possible interactions between informal structure and other factors.

We then considered to what extent these results stemmed from the missing data on poverty that led to the extensive use of data estimation procedures. Data was completely missing for four nations (New Zealand, Greece, Portugal, and Japan) and all the values here had to be estimated. But running a multivariate regression without these nations yields results fundamentally no different than when one includes them.[8] One can thus assume that the results as to the determinants of poverty rates presented here are not an artefact of the data replacement procedures employed.

For the second performance dimension investigated here, namely for municipal waste consumption, we find the opposite pattern than for the

---

[8] The following coefficients were found for the remaining seventeen nations: simple partisan veto-player index = 7.58 (1.974); ideological orientation of the government = 11.29* (2.80); openness of the economy = 39.85* (2.603); constant = −8.039 (−0.52); adjusted R^2 = 0.57.

TABLE 5.7. *Determinants of poverty: comparing different models (multivariate regression analysis)*[a]

Independent variables	Poverty							
	Pairwise comparison of determinants				Time periods			
	1	2	3	4	1974–9	1980–4	1985–9	1990–5
Minimal governmental system index B (Fuchs)	—	-4.30 (1.901)	—	—	—	—	—	-4.50 (-1.891)
Simple partisan veto player index	11.26** (3.088)	11.59** (3.104)	11.64* (2.783)	7.37 (1.763)	13.04** (4.525)	—	—	10.22* (2.765)
Ideological orientation of the government (Schmidt)	9.05* (2.118)	—	—	—	8.64** (3.586)	7.38 (1.812)	—	—
Gross domestic product	—	—	-0.33 (-0.702)	—	—	—	—	—
Openness of the economy	—	—	—	31.32 (1.833)	—	47.59** (3.203)	43.11* (2.809)	—
Constant	14.28 (1.01)	17.67 (1.276)	47.65* (2.663)	26.18* (2.36)	12.49 (1.278)	16.61 (1.211)	35.37** (3.452)	16.84 (1.230)
Adjusted R^2	0.36	0.34	0.22	0.33	0.59	0.36	0.26	0.31

** $p < 0.01$; * $p < 0.05$ (two-tailed).
[a] Unstandardized regression coefficients (OLS-estimate) in the first and t-values in the second line; $N = 21$.

poverty rate. Here the multivariate analysis finds only the simple partisan veto player index and the national level of wealth to be relevant explanatory factors (see Table 5.6). Power-dispersing informal institutions on the one hand and a low national level of wealth on the other hand have positive effects on municipal waste production. The pairwise comparison presented in Table 5.8 found no additional explanatory factors. Here, too, only the simple partisan veto player index and GDP remain as significant explanatory factors with considerable explained variance. The analysis over the four time periods indicates that this is a robust explanatory model.

The various multivariate regression analyses presented here on the relationship between governing and opposition parties confirm, in principle, the positive influences of informal negotiation democracies that Lijphart argued they displayed in the non-economic policy areas ('kinder and gentler'). But there are two important caveats. Statistically significant effects of informal settings exist only for individual effectiveness dimensions, namely poverty, social policy in general and municipal waste production. This speaks more strongly for the competing 'Lijphart-critical' argument that sees the positive influence of informal negotiation democracies as limited to only a few areas. These effects of informal negotiation democracies are also not stable over time, varying in terms of their strength and their level of statistical significance. These caveats have implications for the theory on the impact of the political institutions on performance.

Stability of Policy-specific and General Effectiveness

The various approaches that are reflected in the hypotheses about the influence political institutions have on the stability or variability of policies and policy outcomes all rest on a basic premise of political decision-making theory: concentration of power is associated with variability, dispersion of power with stability. This premise is adopted in quite varied ways, however, and results in contradictory hypotheses. As to the governmental system, some authors expect greater variability for constitutional majoritarian democracies (Tsebelis 1995; Birchfield and Crepaz 1998), while others assume that variability in majoritarian democracies is dependent on the political preferences of the governing parties (Schmidt 1996). As to the relationship between governing and opposition parties, greater stability is predicted for informal negotiation than for informal majoritarian democracies (Tsebelis 1995), yet others expect greater variability among informal negotiation democracies (Birchfield and Crepaz 1998).

The coefficient of variation is used as a measure of stability or variability in political effectiveness, as it can be compared across varying distributions. For each nation and for each individual effectiveness dimension, the standard deviation over the entire 1974–95 period is divided by the mean value for

TABLE 5.8. *Determinants of municipal waste: comparing different models (multivariate regression analysis)*[a]

Independent variables	Municipal waste production							
	Pairwise comparison of determinants				Time periods			
	1	2	3	4	1974–9	1980–4	1985–9	1990–5
Minimal governmental system index B (Fuchs)	—	−3.76 (1.50)	—	—	—	—	—	—
Simple partisan veto player index	7.99 (1.831)	8.60 (2.075)	11.96** (3.968)	6.85 (1.411)	8.23* (2.483)	11.97** (4.365)	10.09** (3.917)	10.13* (2.813)
Ideological orientation of the government (Schmidt)	1.52 (0.298)	—	—	—	—	—	—	—
Gross domestic product	—	—	−1.61** (−4.795)	—	−2.83** (−4.09)	−1.74** (−5.194)	−1.42** (−5.303)	−0.93** (−3.166)
Openness of the economy	—	—	—	9.66 (0.487)	—	—	—	—
Constant	29.78 (1.761)	16.53 (1.077)	84.90** (6.583)	30.24 (2.347)	78.16** (7.105)	79.42** (7.214)	89.12** (7.604)	77.44** (4.259)
Adjusted R^2	0.07	0.17	0.59	0.07	0.46	0.65	0.61	0.37

$**p < 0.01$; $*p < 0.05$ (two-tailed).
[a] Unstandardized regression coefficients (OLS-estimate) in the first and t-values in the second line; $N = 21$.

this time period; the larger the coefficient, the larger the variability. The distribution of this nation-specific coefficient of variation for each of the effectiveness dimensions was given in Tables 4.2 to 4.15. While the national differences, taken overall, are relatively small, it is notable that one can find one country each time, in the majority of the effectiveness dimensions, which displays an above-average variability. The variability of the USA in the case of violent crimes (see Table 4.2), for example, is by far the highest, while in the case of property crimes it is the Netherlands (see Table 4.3). Given these distributions, the probability is high that some of the relationships between the veto player indices and the nation-specific coefficients of variation are caused by these outliers.

The influence of formal and informal institutional arrangements on the stability of the level of effectiveness is investigated on the basis of bivariate regressions. The dependent variables here are the nation-specific coefficients of variation, while the independent variables are the four constitutional and the four partisan veto player indices. As one can see from the results given in Table 5.9 (constitutional veto players) and Table 5.10 (partisan veto players), outliers with above-average variability distort the picture in the majority of the regression equations. The USA and Portugal are the two most frequent outliers, but the Netherlands, Spain, and Canada also play this role, each for a specific effectiveness dimension. These nations already drew our attention in the descriptive analysis of general effectiveness due to their deviant development. When we only consider those bivariate regressions that had no outliers, our analysis of the influence of political institutions on stability would be confined to only some effectiveness dimensions. Despite this considerable limitation, however, two clear patterns can be discerned.

As was the case in the previous analysis of the level of effectiveness, there are contradictory effects the *governmental system* exerts on stability. The results presented in Table 5.9 indicate that constitutional negotiation democracies, unlike constitutional majoritarian democracies, tend to show greater stability in economic policy. On the other hand, constitutional negotiation democracies show greater variability in their policies in the case of domestic security and in the quality of the environment. This inconsistent pattern can be observed equally in all four constitutional veto player indices (Lijphart's federal–unitary index, Schmidt's institutional constraints of central state government, Fuchs's minimal governmental system indices A and B), though only some of these bivariate regression coefficients are statistically significant. Indeed, the few statistically significant relationships almost always occur in conjunction with an outlier.

By contrast, a coherent pattern can be seen in the case of the *relationship between governing and opposition parties*. The regression coefficients presented in Table 5.10 are all negative, which means that informal negotiation democracies, unlike informal majoritarian democracies, tend to produce

TABLE 5.9. *Constitutional veto player indices and the stability of political effectiveness (bivariate regression analysis)*[a]

	Federal–unitary index (Lijphart 1999a)		Institutional constraints of central state government (Schmidt 1996)		Minimal governmental system index A (Fuchs 2000)		Minimal governmental system index B (Fuchs 2000)		
	b (t-value)	beta	b (t-value)	beta	b (t-value)	beta	b (t-value)	beta	Outlier
Domestic security policy	−0.03 (1.054)	0.24	0.01 (0.620)	0.14	0.02 (1.151)	0.26	0.02 (1.104)	0.25	—
(a) Violent crimes	−0.03 (1.659)	0.36	0.02 (1.656)	0.36	0.03 (1.681)	0.36	0.03* (2.288)	0.47*	USA
(b) Property crimes	−0.00 (−0.122)	−0.03	−0.01 (−0.644)	−0.15	−0.00 (−0.003)	−0.00	−0.01 (−0.491)	−0.11	The Netherl.
Economic policy	−0.02 (−1.139)	−0.25	−0.01 (−0.546)	−0.12	−0.02 (−1.113)	−0.25	−0.01 (−0.815)	−0.18	Portugal
(a) National income	−0.02 (−1.315)	−0.29	−0.01 (−0.707)	−0.16	−0.02 (−1.358)	−0.30	−0.02 (−1.503)	−0.33	—
(b) Misery	−0.03 (−1.488)	−0.32	−0.02 (−1.094)	−0.24	−0.03 (−1.481)	−0.32	−0.02 (−1.139)	−0.25	—
Unemployment	−0.02 (−0.691)	−0.16	−0.02 (−0.834)	−0.19	−0.01 (−0.441)	−0.10	−0.01 (−0.626)	−0.14	Spain
Inflation	−0.05** (−2.945)	−0.56***	−0.03 (−2.068)	−0.43	−0.03* (−2.298)	−0.47*	−0.02 (−1.902)	−0.40	Portugal
Social policy	−0.00 (−0.373)	−0.09	−0.01 (−0.362)	−0.08	−0.02 (−0.913)	−0.21	−0.01 (−0.694)	−0.16	Portugal
(a) Health	−0.00 (−0.317)	−0.07	−0.00 (−0.089)	−0.02	−0.00 (−0.401)	−0.09	−0.00 (−0.282)	−0.07	Portugal
(b) Poverty	−0.06 (1.613)	0.35	0.05 (1.828)	0.39	0.05 (1.70)	0.36	0.05* (2.308)	0.47*	USA
Environmental policy	0.04 (1.926)	0.40	0.03 (1.971)	0.41	0.03 (1.741)	0.37	0.03* (2.579)	0.51*	USA
(a) Environment	0.07* (2.725)	0.53*	0.04 (1.625)	0.35	0.05* (2.098)	0.43*	0.03 (1.647)	0.35	—
Sulphur oxides emissions	0.02 (0.941)	0.21	−0.00 (−0.03)	−0.01	0.00 (0.057)	0.01	−0.00 (−0.094)	−0.02	Canada
Municipal waste	0.01 (0.240)	0.06	0.02 (0.563)	0.13	0.02 (0.638)	0.15	0.02 (0.900)	0.20	—
(b) Resources	0.06* (2.370)	0.48*	0.04 (1.945)	0.41	0.04 (1.786)	0.38	0.04* (2.611)	0.51*	USA
General effectiveness	0.05* (2.155)	0.44*	0.03 (1.972)	0.41	0.03 (1.509)	0.33	0.03* (2.312)	0.47*	USA
General effectiveness without wealth	0.03 (1.549)	0.34	0.02 (1.392)	0.30	0.02 (1.163)	0.26	0.02 (1.921)	0.40	USA
General effectiveness without economy	0.03 (1.794)	0.38	0.02 (1.584)	0.34	0.02 (1.517)	0.33	0.03* (2.178)	0.45*	USA

**$p < 0.01$; * $p < 0.05$ (two-tailed).

[a] Measure for stability = coefficient of variation (low values indicate stability and high values variability); unstandardized (b) and standardized (beta) regression coefficients (OLS-estimate); beta equals Pearson's r; $N = 21$. Significant coefficients are in italics.

TABLE 5.10. *Partisan veto player indices and the stability of political effectiveness (bivariate regression analysis)*[a]

	Number of governing parties		Simple partisan veto player index		Veto players in the lower house (Schnapp 2004)		Effective number of parliamentary parties		
	b (t-value)	beta	b (t-value)	beta	b (t-value)	beta	b (t-value)	beta	Outlier
Domestic security policy	-0.02 (-0.764)	-0.17	-0.02 (-0.731)	-0.17	-0.02 (-0.704)	-0.16	-0.02 (-0.814)	-0.18	—
(a) Violent crimes	-0.02 (-1.017)	-0.23	-0.01 (-0.570)	-0.13	-0.01 (-0.667)	-0.15	-0.02 (-0.962)	-0.22	USA
(b) Property crimes	-0.00 (-0.018)	-0.00	-0.01 (-0.365)	-0.08	-0.01 (-0.245)	-0.06	0.00 (-0.097)	-0.02	The Netherlands
Economic policy	-0.01 (-0.447)	-0.10	-0.01 (-0.288)	-0.07	0.00 (0.128)	0.03	0.00 (-0.250)	-0.06	Portugal
(a) National income	-0.01 (-0.435)	-0.10	-0.01 (-0.51)	-0.12	0.00 (-0.315)	-0.07	-0.01 (-0.51)	-0.12	—
(b) Misery	-0.02 (-0.834)	-0.19	-0.02 (-0.73)	-0.17	-0.01 (-0.489)	-0.11	-0.01 (-0.567)	-0.13	—
Unemployment	-0.02 (-0.718)	-0.16	-0.02 (-0.568)	-0.13	-0.03 (-1.036)	-0.23	-0.01 (-0.401)	-0.09	Spain
Inflation	-0.02 (-1.013)	-0.23	-0.02 (-1.019)	-0.23	-0.02 (-0.746)	-0.17	-0.02 (-1.034)	-0.23	—
Social policy	-0.03 (-1.363)	-0.30	-0.03 (-1.475)	-0.32	-0.02 (-0.874)	-0.20	-0.03 (-1.375)	-0.30	Portugal
(a) Health	-0.01 (-0.649)	-0.15	-0.02 (-0.950)	-0.21	-0.01 (-0.428)	-0.10	-0.02 (-1.191)	-0.26	Portugal
(b) Poverty	-0.06 (-1.607)	-0.35	-0.04 (-1.232)	-0.27	-0.04 (-1.053)	-0.24	-0.06 (-1.854)	-0.39	USA
Environmental policy	-0.02 (-0.663)	-0.15	-0.01 (-0.284)	-0.07	-0.01 (-0.242)	-0.06	-0.02 (-0.944)	-0.21	USA
(a) Environment	-0.04 (-1.302)	-0.29	-0.05 (-1.446)	-0.32	-0.04 (-1.117)	-0.25	-0.04 (-1.414)	-0.31	—
Sulphur oxides emissions	-0.01 (-0.524)	-0.12	-0.01 (-0.587)	-0.13	-0.01 (-0.370)	-0.09	-0.01 (-0.499)	-0.11	Canada
Municipal waste	-0.06 (-1.655)	-0.36	-0.05 (-1.358)	-0.30	-0.05 (-1.247)	-0.28	-0.05 (-1.799)	-0.38	—
(b) Resources	-0.03 (-1.080)	-0.24	-0.02 (-0.727)	-0.17	-0.02 (-0.613)	-0.14	-0.03 (-1.297)	-0.29	USA
General effectiveness	-0.03 (-1.206)	-0.27	-0.02 (-0.794)	-0.18	-0.01 (-0.521)	-0.12	-0.03 (-1.287)	-0.28	USA
General effectiveness without wealth	-0.03 (-1.462)	-0.32	-0.02 (-1.140)	-0.25	-0.02 (-0.797)	-0.18	-0.02 (-1.544)	-0.33	USA
General effectiveness without economy	-0.03 (-1.446)	-0.32	-0.02 (-1.137)	-0.25	-0.02 (-0.912)	-0.21	-0.03 (-1.657)	-0.36	USA

** $p < 0.01$; * $p < 0.05$ (two-tailed).

[a] Measure for stability = coefficient of variation (low values indicate stability and high values variability); unstandardized (b) and standardized (beta) regression coefficients (OLS-estimate); beta equals Pearson's r; N = 21.

more stable levels of effectiveness. None of the regression coefficients are statistically significant. Given that all coefficients are negative, and that across all effectiveness dimensions and all four partisan veto player indices (number of governing parties, simple partisan veto player index, Schnapp's veto players in the lower house, effective number of parliamentary parties), makes it possible to assert that we are seeing a systematic, if weak, effect.

We can summarize these results by asserting that the basic premise of decision-making theory that power dispersion leads to higher degrees of policy stability can only be confirmed, and that only as a tendency, in the case of informal institutions. Among constitutional institutions, the effect of power dispersion differs by policy area. The empirical finding that constitutional and informal institutions have a different influence on the stability of effectiveness contradicts the veto player concept (Tsebelis 1995) that assumes both institutions have the same effects. Birchfeld and Crepaz (1998), in their concept of competitive and collective veto points, have argued for differing effects of constitutional and informal institutions—but they have assumed the exact opposite of what we have been able to find empirically. The first empirical result, following that power dispersion in the governmental system is dependent on the policy area and results either in variability or stability, seems to support Schmidt's interaction theory (1996) which holds that the effect of constitutional institutions is dependent on the policy preferences of the governing parties. The second empirical result, following that power dispersion in the relationship between governing and opposition parties leads to stability, supports a partial hypothesis in Tsebelis's veto player approach (1995). In sum: Policy stability does not necessarily come about just because there are many constitutionally-mandated institutions that need to approve a political decision, but it does come about when there are many actors (veto players) whose approval is needed *within* a decision-making body like a government.

Structure of Political Effectiveness (Policy Patterns)

Finally, we turn to the influence the institutional setting has on the structure of political effectiveness, or on the policy pattern. This dimension has been neglected until now in the comparative research on democracy. We derived two hypotheses out of the fundamental principles of constitutional and informal majoritarian and negotiation democracies in the theoretical part of our analysis. The first assumes that constitutional negotiation and constitutional majoritarian democracies do not systematically differ from one another with respect to the balance of their policy patterns. The second, by contrast, assumes that informal negotiation democracies are characterized by more balanced policy patterns than is the case in informal majoritarian democracies.

These hypotheses are investigated for the four most important policy patterns, on the one hand for the two propositions of conflict between economic and social policy as well as the economic and environmental policy, and on the other hand for the concept of sustainability, whose narrower version only includes economic, social, and environmental policies, but whose broader version also includes domestic security policy. The degree of balance or imbalance between these policy areas is measured as the absolute difference between the respective levels of effectiveness in individual policy areas per nation over the 1975–95 time period. Thus, in the case of conflicts between economic and social policy, the absolute difference between the levels of performance in economic policy and in social policy is calculated per nation. High values, or differences, indicate imbalance while a zero value indicates complete balance in the policy pattern. For sustainability, as it includes more than two policy areas, the mean of the absolute differences between all the respective policy areas is used as the measure of imbalance. These four difference measures for the two propositions of conflict and the two forms of sustainability constitute the dependent variable in the bivariate regression equations. The independent variables are the same as in the preceding analyses: the four constitutional veto player indices (federal–unitary index, institutional constraints of central state government, minimal governmental system indices A and B) and the four partisan veto player indices (number of governing parties, simple partisan veto player index, number of veto players in the lower house, effective number of parliamentary parties).

As one can see in Table 5.11, the results for the *governmental system* always show negative (with one exception) relationships with the measures of difference, which is to say that power dispersion co-varies with compatibility. However, the unstandardized regression coefficients and the *t*-values are all so low that one is forced to speak of a lack of relationship. The first hypothesis, that there is an absence of difference between constitutional majoritarian and constitutional negotiation democracies, is clearly supported by these regressions.

The *relationship between governing and opposition parties* shows a more complex structure of relations. Both narrow and broad sustainability policy patterns show consistently negative relationships (Table 5.12), and as with the governmental system, power dispersion co-varies with compatibility but at a very weak level. Yet, the picture is different for the proposition of conflict between the economy and the environment. Here the relationships are not just negative but also statistically significant in two cases. Balanced policy patterns between these two policy areas are thus characteristic of informal negotiation democracies but not of informal majoritarian democracies. Matters are also different in the proposition of conflict between economic and social policy, for here all the relationships are positive. That

TABLE 5.11. *Constitutional veto player indices and the imbalance of policy patterns (bivariate regression analysis)*[a]

Imbalance between...	Federal–unitary index (Lijphart 1999a)		Institutional constraints of central state government (Schmidt 1996)		Minimal governmental system index A (Fuchs 2000)		Minimal governmental system index B (Fuchs 2000)	
	b (t-value)	beta	b (t-value)	beta	b (t-value)	beta	b (t-value)	beta
Economic and social policy	-0.45 (-0.194)	-0.04	-0.74 (-0.407)	-0.09	-1.04 (-0.546)	-0.12	-0.165 (-0.105)	-0.02
Economic and environmental policy	-0.81 (-0.231)	-0.05	-0.43 (-0.158)	-0.04	-1.34 (-0.467)	-0.11	0.09 (0.039)	0.01
Economic, social and environmental policy	-0.64 (-0.335)	-0.08	-0.57 (-0.381)	-0.09	-1.21 (-0.776)	-0.18	-0.24 (-0.184)	-0.04
Economic, social, environmental and domestic security policy	-1.33 (-0.769)	-0.17	-1.06 (-0.781)	-0.18	-1.78 (-1.28)	-0.28	-0.79 (-0.673)	-0.15

$**p < 0.01$; $* p < 0.05$.

[a] Measure for imbalance = absolute difference between the levels of effectiveness in two policy areas (the mean of these differences in the case of more than two policy areas); unstandardized (b) and standardized (beta) regression coefficients (OLS-estimate); beta equals Pearson's r; $N = 21$.

TABLE 5.12. *Partisan veto player indices and the imbalance of policy patterns (bivariate regression analysis)*[a]

Imbalance between . . .	Number of governing parties		Simple partisan veto player index		Veto players in the lower house (Schnapp 2004)		Effective number of parliamentary parties	
	b (t-value)	beta	b (t-value)	beta	b (t-value)	beta	b (t-value)	beta
Economic and social policy	2.04 (0.801)	0.18	3.43 (1.394)	0.31	2.22 (0.909)	0.20	2.34 (1.186)	0.26
Economic and environmental policy	−8.08* (−2.367)	−0.48*	−6.77* (−1.903)	−0.40*	−6.64 (−1.938)	−0.41	−6.81* (−2.569)	−0.51*
Economic, social and environmental policy	−1.77 (−0.842)	−0.19	−1.27 (−0.598)	−0.14	−1.17 (−0.573)	−0.13	−1.48 (−0.895)	−0.20
Economic, social, environmental and domestic security policy	−1.40 (−0.729)	−0.17	−0.93 (−0.479)	−0.11	−0.77 (−0.412)	−0.09	−0.99 (−0.649)	−0.15

**$p < 0.01$; * $p < 0.05$.

[a] Measure for imbalance = absolute difference between the levels of effectiveness in two policy areas (the mean of these differences in the case of more than two policy areas); unstandardized (b) and standardized (beta) regression coefficients (OLS-estimate); beta equals Pearson's r; $N = 21$; significant coefficients are in italics.

means, and contrary to the hypothesis suggested above, informal negotiation democracies show more imbalanced than balanced policy patterns here. Still, none of the bivariate regressions are significant. Additional analyses, not documented here, were able to show that this imbalance is characterized by a higher level of effectiveness in social policy than in economic policy.

In sum we can state that, as expected, there are no differences between constitutional majoritarian and constitutional negotiation democracies with respect to the balance in policy patterns. However, against expectation, informal negotiation democracies do not a priori ensure a balance of policy patterns. Rather, such balance depends upon the respective policy pattern. This finding indicates that in addition to the formal features of informal institutional arrangements (number of partisan veto players), the political interests represented in the respective party system also play a role.

SUMMARY

In this second chapter of the empirical analysis, the hypotheses as to the influence of the formal and informal institutions on the level, stability, and structure of political effectiveness formulated in the theoretical part of the study have been examined. In addition, the validity of the various veto player indices is investigated.

A number of hypotheses as to the influence of political institutions on the level of political effectiveness have been suggested by Lijphart. He assumes that there are no differences, as a rule, between constitutional majoritarian and constitutional negotiation democracies, and that the latter shows greater effectiveness only in the case of the inflation rate. Our empirical analyses refute this hypothesis. On the one hand, when one holds competing explanatory factors constant, the effect of the constitutional settings on the inflation rate vanishes. On the other hand, other effects can be found, though they do not always favour the constitutional negotiation democracies. Lijphart also assumes that informal negotiation democracies generally show higher performance in non-economic policy areas than do informal majoritarian democracies. According to the empirical results presented here, power dispersion has a significant effect, in the case of informal institutions, only on poverty, social policy in general, and on the environmental dimension of municipal waste production. Thus there are some, albeit not very strong, indications that informal negotiation democracies show policy traits that Lijphart (1999a) calls 'kinder and gentler'.

A basic premise of decision-making theory holds that power dispersion is associated with stability and power concentration with variability or policy change, and this has led to differing hypotheses concerning the stability of policies and policy outcomes. The empirical analysis indicates that this thesis applies only to informal but not to formal institutions. The empirical fact that constitutional and informal arrangements have differing influences on the stability of effectiveness contradicts Tsebelis's veto player concept (1995) that expects the same effects in both arrangements. Birchfeld and Crepaz (1998) assume different influences of constitutional and informal institutions in their concept of competitive and collective veto points, but in a manner exactly opposite to what we found empirically. The first empirical finding, that power dispersion in the governmental system results either in variability or stability depending upon policy area, seems to speak for Schmidt's inter-action theory (1996) that assumes that the effect of constitutional institutions is dependent upon the policy preferences of the governing parties. The second empirical finding, that power dispersion in the relationship between governing and opposition parties tends to lead to stability, supports a partial hypothesis of Tsebelis's veto player approach (1995). The basic premise of political decision-making theory as to the connection between power dispersion and policy stability therefore only applies to power dispersion *within*, but not to power dispersion *between*, constitutional institutions.

As for the structure, or policy patterns, the hypothesis was derived from the basic principles of constitutional and informal majoritarian and negotiation democracies that constitutional negotiation and constitutional major-itarian democracies do not differ, but that informal negotiation democracies—unlike informal majoritarian democracies—are distinguished by more balanced policy patterns. Here only the first but not the second hypothesis could be empirically supported. Depending upon the policy patterns, informal negotiation democracies may display relatively balanced (economic vs. environmental policy, sustainability) or instead imbalanced (economic policy vs. social policy) policy patterns.

One significant result of this analysis is that it was possible to discern influences of the political institutions on the level, stability, and structure of political effectiveness. These were not general influences, however, but were limited instead to specific dimensions of effectiveness. It was also possible to show that mixed influences flowed from the constitutionally defined govern-mental system in particular. The position Lijphart (1999*a*) initially took, namely that power dispersion a priori positively influences performance, is thereby refuted. But the theory regarding the impact of political institutions that tried to explain differing effects of the governmental system and of the relationship between governing and opposition parties with differing forms of power distribution—both between and within institutions—is also inad-equate. It cannot sufficiently explain the empirically established, policy-specific and mixed effects of political institutions, and this result implies that political–institutional theory needs further development—a point to which we will return in Chapter 6.

Three methodological questions were also investigated. The first addressed Lijphart's executives–parties index which is not only a broad measure of informal structures but also a problematic instrument. A re-analysis showed that many of the positive effects of negotiation democracies that Lijphart found can be traced back to the inclusion of corporatism in this index, and that, beyond this, the inclusion of the party system in the measure is in part responsible for finding these positive relationships. The part of the index that measures the relationship between governing and opposition parties is based on two quite problematic indicators (government composition, executive dominance) that showed themselves to have no statistically significant relationships with the individual effectiveness dimensions. Based on the theoretical and empirical analyses presented here, one can therefore draw the conclusion that the executives–parties index is on the one hand too unspecific, in a theoretical sense, and on the other hand is of questionable quality in a methodological sense, at least with respect to specific components of the index.

The second methodological question addressed the validity of the three partisan veto player indices that were suggested as alternatives for the executives–parties index. All three—the number of governing parties, the simple partisan veto player index, and the number of veto players in the lower house—proved themselves both in the dimensional and in the causal analyses, so that one can assert that these are valid indicators for the relationship between governing and opposition parties. The index conceived of as a surrogate instrument that measures the power distribution in the party system, the effective number of parliamentary parties, can also be used as an instrument to measure the relationship between governing and opposition parties.

The third question was about the differences within the four partisan veto player indices on the one hand, and within the four constitutional veto player indices on the other hand. Overall, the differences among the respective partisan and constitutional indices are small, and that speaks for the generalizability of the empirical patterns found here. However, the analysis also demonstrated that the previously identified theoretical differences between the various indices also have empirical consequences. Minimal governmental system indices that only include primary structural characteristics such as bicameralism and federalism (as in Fuchs's minimal governmental system index A and B) behave somewhat differently than maximal governmental system indices that include secondary structural characteristics such as referenda or central bank autonomy (as in Lijphart's federal–unitary index and Schmidt's institutional constraints of central state government). Beyond this, there are also distinct differences between the two maximal governmental system indices of Lijphart and Schmidt; Schmidt's index not only measures more but more specific secondary characteristics than does Lijphart's. By the same token, it is decisive for the partisan veto player indices whether these indices are only based on the number of parties (as in the number of governing parties or effective number of parliamentary parties indices) or whether in addition the governmental type—majority or minority—is taken into account (as in the simple partisan veto player index or Schnapp's number of veto players in the lower house).

6

Conclusions

This study measures the performance of contemporary democracies, that is, the extent to which collective goals are realized. Two questions have guided the analyses: (a) Has the effectiveness of western democracies actually decreased and did conflict between important policy goals increase since the economic recession that followed the Oil Crisis in 1973? (b) Do democratic institutional arrangements have an impact on the level, the stability and the structure of political effectiveness?

The first question arose in the context of various crisis theories suggesting structural causes for effectiveness problems of western democracies since the mid-1970s. Nowadays, the assumption of a decreasing effectiveness has been picked up in globalization theories. They have specified it in the following way: In the course of growing international interdependence and competition between nation-states the scope of national governments will shrink and social and environmental policy standards will be lowered. These structural processes will lead to a continuous decline of the effectiveness of modern democracies resulting in a convergence of western democracies at a lower level of effectiveness. Furthermore, it will lead to an increasing incompatibility or trade-off between economic and other, social and environmental goals. The loss of effectiveness can have far-reaching negative consequences for democratic systems as a whole. It undermines the confidence of citizens in the democratic regime and could lead to a legitimation crisis which in the end is a threat to the persistence of democracies.

The second question derives from the oft-heard assertion in public and academic discourse that national democratic institutions determine and decisively influence the effectiveness of public policies. The interest in the performance of different types of democracies goes back to the emergence of the 'new institutionalism' in the early 1980s. Since that time, answering the question 'Do institutions matter?' has become a key concern in the comparative research on democracy. It has received increasing attention since the 1990s with the collapse of socialist systems of government in central and eastern Europe. With the demise of the most important rival system of government, more attention has been drawn to the differences within the community of democracies. Knowledge about the performance of specific institutional settings is not only of theoretical interest but also of great practical importance. Based on such information, recommendations can be made as to which kinds of constitutions should be implemented in new democracies (constitutional engineering) and what kind of institutional reforms should be conducted in established democracies to enhance political effectiveness.

Our study sought to provide theoretical and empirical clarity with respect to these two questions. We summarize the most important findings of our investigation and discuss them with respect to their theoretical and practical implications.

The Effectiveness of Liberal Democracies

Though the comparative research on democracy has devoted considerable attention to the evaluation of political systems in recent years, to this point no integrated research tradition has been able to establish itself. Our first task was therefore to develop a theoretical 'Model for Evaluating the Effectiveness of Liberal Democracies'. We defined political effectiveness as a specific dimension of performance referring to the realization of those policy goals that democracies, like other political orders, are expected to pursue for their societies. Starting from Almond and Powell's concept of political productivity (1978; Almond et al. 2003), we developed a list of five criteria for evaluating the effectiveness of democracies—international security, domestic security, wealth, socio-economic security and socio-economic equality, and environmental protection—all of which are so-called political goods (Pennock 1966: 420) that meet the needs of citizens and 'whose fulfillment makes the polity valuable to man, and gives it its justification.'

Our study examined all these criteria, with the exception of international security. It identified fourteen indicators to measure outcomes in the domestic security, economic, social, and environmental policy areas. We then took extensive stock of the effectiveness in western democracies for the time from 1974 until 1995.

Comprehensive stocktaking, as one characteristic of our study, enabled us to examine several important and controversial questions. First, we empirically investigated the trade-offs between policy goals. Though goal conflicts are a key aspect of political decisions and have found increasing interest in globalization theories, propositions about whether policy goals are in conflict or are compatible are not only rarely addressed in the literature, but also rarely empirically investigated. Second, we analysed and identified national types of political effectiveness or policy patterns that encompass the most important domestic policy areas. By doing so we were able to describe policy patterns of western democracies such as the ideologically defined libertarian, classical social democratic and sustainability models that take a prominent place in contemporary political theory but have been matched with empirical evidence only in part. And third, we analysed not only effectiveness in individual policy areas but also general effectiveness by means of a multi-policy measure that encompasses several policy areas. This enables us to test the central hypothesis about the *general* loss of the effectiveness of western democracies. The global index is capable of differentiating between levels of effectiveness among highly developed nations, which is not possible with the UNDP's well-known *Human Development Index* (1990).

A further characteristic of our study lies in the fact that we use outcome indicators throughout in order to measure effectiveness. This means that we are not measuring the actions or efforts needed to reach the goals but rather the actual results of political action. Most evaluations of democracies are based only on output indicators (see Putnam 1993) or a mixture of output and outcome indicators (see Scruggs 1999). By that they focus on means to reach goals rather than the accomplishment of the announced goal itself. This distinction is crucial because the same policy goals can be realized using different means.

The empirical results enable us to falsify a series of common assumptions about the effectiveness of western democracies. One of these referred to the development of effectiveness in western democracies since 1974. The notion, derived from theories of crisis, that western democracies as a whole would converge at a lower level of performance in the wake of the 1973 Oil Shock, could not be confirmed by the empirical analysis. It is true that performance decreased in the specific case of domestic security policy, but this develop-ment had already begun in the immediate post-war period and did not just start with the economic recession of the early 1970s. Other policy areas either showed an increase in effectiveness (economic policy, social policy), or remained stable (environmental policy). However, it is true that opposite trends lay behind this stable development of environmental policy; increases in performance among nations that were pioneers in environmental protec-tion (USA and Germany), and losses in environmental performance among economic latecomers (southern European nations and Ireland).

General effectiveness even increased between 1974 and 1995, though this was due primarily to a general increase in wealth over this time period. If one removes 'wealth' from this global measure, then one is merely left with the finding that general effectiveness has remained stable. The few empirical results that confirm the predicted negative trend are confined to a small number of indicators of performance, such as increasing levels of unemploy-ment or municipal waste production.

Therefore, there was no loss of general effectiveness among western dem-ocracies after 1974, as the crisis theories have asserted. On the other hand, there is also no empirical evidence for the opposite, namely a progressive development along the lines sometimes asserted in modernization theories. Such positive trends also exist but are limited to increasing national income and decreasing infant mortality, dimensions of performance usually accounted as part of socio-economic modernity. Still, there is an increase in effectiveness in at least one environmental policy indicator, namely the steady reduction in sulphur oxides emissions. This is the only far-reaching success that one can ascribe to the environmental policies practised in democracies since the 1970s.

The results of our investigation of conflicting policy goals also could not confirm the common assumption that there are trade-offs between economic and social policy as well as between economic and environmental policy. We could not discover a systematic and negative relationship between national income and poverty, nor between national income and the indicators of environmental performance. In fact, in the case of the other two economic dimensions, namely full employment and price stability, most of the relationships were positive, and that included complementary relationships with poverty and with the environment. Based on our analyses, therefore, one can draw the conclusion that the degree of conflict between policy goals is exaggerated both in public and in academic discourse. The reasons for such exaggeration likely include the human predilection to pay more attention to conflict than to harmony, as well as the prominence of the USA, a particular case which does, in fact, display an imbalanced policy pattern of this kind: economic policy is in conflict with social policy and with environmental policy (and additionally with domestic security policy). Our empirical analyses make clear that such incompatibilities, characteristic of the 'libertarian model', cannot be generalized. There are other nations, such as Switzerland, Japan, and Norway, that are able to realize all three policy goals at the same time, and at a high level.

The empirical findings about the trade-offs between economic and other policy goals are also revealing for another reason: the role of national income or wealth for national performance patterns. Wealth should not be taken as only a performance dimension but is also as an indication of the extent of financial resources available for realizing other policy goals, particularly in social or environmental policy. Yet, based on our empirical findings, this type of positive relationship exists only for the infant mortality indicator (health) that forms part of the social policy dimension. There is no systematic relationship between wealth and poverty rates, or between wealth and environment, and the relationship to domestic security is even negative. Therefore wealth does not play a central role in determining national policy patterns.

The comparatively weak factor of 'culture', by contrast, appears to play a much more significant role. We analysed its influence on political effectiveness using the concept of families of nations (Castles 1993, 1998a). This concept is based on the premise that nations with common cultural traditions develop similar political institutions and policy orientations, both among citizens and among politicians, and that these not only shape political decisions but also result in similar patterns of effectiveness. Our empirical analysis found systematic differences in effectiveness between the various families of nations.

The heart of the empirical investigation was the examination of general hypotheses about political effectiveness. Nevertheless, the analyses revealed interesting results for individual nations or families of nations that sometimes serve as positive or negative models in both public and academic discourse. The results for the Netherlands are particularly interesting as its economic and socio-political development since the 1980s has been praised as a 'miracle' (Visser and Hemerijck 1997). Our assessment of political effectiveness more sharply reveals the costs of the recent Dutch economic and social welfare reforms (dubbed the 'polder model'), particularly in the accompanying increase in the rate of poverty. It also draws attention to the continuous, radical increase in the national crime rate, though admittedly this trend began in the 1950s and was not a direct consequence of political reforms of the 1980s. Holland's negative trends show that if one examines all policy areas together, it is no longer possible to argue for the development of its performance as being extraordinarily positive. Quite the opposite: the Netherlands has slipped in the ranking of the democracies we examine from seventh position in 1974–9 to fifteenth position by 1990–5 (see Table 4.14).

A similar, if far smaller, correction is warranted in the case of the Scandinavian nations, long regarded as exemplary. Nordic welfare capitalism, even beyond its accomplishments in social policy, was judged in political discourse to display above-average performance. Based on the comparisons we drew between the families of nations, however, we were able to establish that the difference between the Scandinavian and the Continental Western European nations were limited to social policy. We could additionally show that there were special cases (Switzerland and Japan) of nations not under long social democratic rule that also showed above-average performance in the social policy dimension of health (infant mortality rates). This last result is a good example for the argument that it is not only social democratic welfare states that ensure a high level of social policy performance, but that the same degree of goal attainment can be achieved by the use of other policies or instruments as well.

Corrections are also warranted in the case of the negative model the USA provides. Overall, the USA has by far the lowest general level of effectiveness, but with the exception of social policy, it also always belongs to those nations that have most improved the level of their performance between 1974–9 and 1990–5. Quite clearly, the USA possesses an above-average ability to reform.

By contrast, the inability to reform has been a central theme on the political agenda in Germany during the 1990s. This assertion calls for correction at least in environmental policy, as Germany surpassed the USA as environmental pioneer during the 1990s. This is documented by the fact that between 1985–9 and 1990–5 German environmental policy performance, measured in terms of environmental quality, increased by 7.6 points, the largest increase among the nations studied (see Table 4.11). The one-sided picture of a German inability to reform, for which even the constitutional structures are sometimes blamed (Henkel 1997), thus clearly needs correcting. We were also able to show in this context that the increase in environmental performance led to an improvement in Germany's policy pattern that enabled it to move from the 'classical social democratic' type in the 1970s to the 'sustainability' type in the 1990s. This means that Germany not only shows above-average (when compared with other western democracies) economic and social policy performance, but also shows above-average environmental policy performance. The 'middle way' political style characteristic of German politics (Schmidt 1987, 2000*b*) has at the latest since the 1990s also included environmental policy.

It is widely accepted that the 'golden age of the post-war era' came to an end for western democracies in 1973, but based on our assessment of political effectiveness, we were not able to find the expected continual decline in the ensuing twenty years. In fact, we find instead a picture of stability across all policy areas. There is thus barely any empirical evidence at the moment that would support the 'newer' diagnoses of crisis (contained in globalization theories) that the already existing general losses of effectiveness in western democracies will become more serious as a consequence of increasing economic globalization. Based on our analysis, there are only indications of an increasing rate of unemployment and, with reservations, of a further rise in poverty. Both of these lead one to suspect that the processes of de-industrialization and the restructuring or dismantling of the welfare state will be the two structural processes that will continue to negatively affect the performance of western democracies in the future. De-industrialization is associated with a decline in the number of well-paid industrial workplaces for underqualified and unqualified workers. Given the continual restructuring and dismantling of welfare states since the 1970s, it is unlikely that welfare payments will be sufficiently comprehensive or generous enough to compensate for the poverty that is created by the economic changes.

However, despite these economic and social policy developments, there are indications of an improvement in domestic security during the 1990s. This positive trend, based on three measures of serious criminal offenses, contradicts the thesis of societal disintegration, one that has also been presumed as a consequence of the processes of economic globalization (Habermas 1998; Münch 1998).

Do Constitutional and Informal Institutions Matter?

Research on the influence of political institutions is largely based on two premises. One is that political institutions have an independent effect on the performance of democracies. The other is that individual institutional settings do not exert mixed but instead uniformly positive or uniformly negative effects on political performance. These premises are reflected in the practical conclusion Lijphart (1999*a*: 301–2) draws at the end of his *Patterns of Democracy* study:

> because the overall performance record of the consensus democracies is clearly superior to that of the majoritarian democracies, the consensus option is the more attractive option for countries designing their first democratic constitutions or contemplating democratic reform.

Research on the question 'Do institutions matter?' has a considerably longer tradition than research on the evaluation of political performance. But even here no consensus exists either on the definition of political institutions or on which effects on performance can be expected from which institutional arrangements.

Our task, therefore, was to first develop a theoretical 'Model for Explaining Performance of Liberal Democracies'. The first important theoretical decision concerned the term 'institution'. We selected a narrowed concept in our study that sees institutions as *complexes of rules for action* and that is limited to *political* institutions engaged in making and implementing collectively binding decisions. Thus, institutions of political economy such as corporatist arrangements are explicitly excluded from the analysis.

A second important theoretical decision was to determine the institutions of democratic governance, such as legislatures or cabinets, as those institutions that exert influence on performance. Institutions to select leaders, such as the electoral system, thus do not have a direct effect on performance. Their influence, instead, is mediated through the institutions of democratic governance. The institutions of democratic governance themselves can be analytically separated between those based on formal and those based on informal rules (Fuchs 2000). Formal rules are constitutionally set, while informal rules only develop through relatively lasting constellations of participating actors. The formal rule complexes, designated the 'governmental system', are defined by constitutional institutions (e.g. legislatures, state structure) and their relations. The informal rule complexes, by contrast, emerge from the 'relationship between governing and opposition parties' that is determined by the composition of government (one-party vs. coalition government) and the parliamentary support for the government. The actual form both rule complexes take—whether they concentrate or disperse power—determines the degree of autonomy a government has in making its decisions. Based on both dimensions four types of democracy could be differentiated: constitutional majoritarian, constitutional negotiation, informal majoritarian, and informal negotiation democracies.

A third important theoretical decision concerned the influence of the institutional settings. Until recently, the notion that formal and informal institutions exerted the same influence dominated the literature. Lijphart's (1994, 1999a) performance studies were originally based on the expectation that power dispersion in both types of institutions (the executives–parties and the federal–unitary dimensions), had the same, positive effects on performance. Tsebelis (1995) in turn assumed that the stability of policies and policy outcomes increases with increasing numbers of constitutional and partisan veto players (thus with power dispersion in formal and informal institutions). Taking later concepts into account (Armingeon 1996; Birchfield and Crepaz 1998) we instead began from the theoretical premise that constitutional and informal institutions exert differing influence on political performance because of different forms of power dispersion. Following these concepts, power in the 'governmental system' is separated *between* different constitutionally defined institutions that possess veto power over each other, which in turn implies that they can hinder or block decisions made by the government. Power dispersion regarding the 'relationship between governing and opposition parties', by contrast, means that power is divided *within* government and parliament between different actors (parties). These actors, who interact on a daily and direct manner with one another, are forced to engage in bargaining and to reach compromises if they want to ensure their ability to act and to survive politically.

The investigation of the various hypotheses regarding the influence of constitutional and informal institutions on political effectiveness stood at the centre of Chapter 5, the second empirical part of our study. The goals of the analysis can be described with respect to the most important reference study for our work, Lijphart's *Patterns of Democracy*. First, we investigated the impact political institutions have not only on the level but also on the stability and the structure of political effectiveness. Lijphart, by contrast, limited himself to analysing only the level of different dimensions of performance. Second, we examined effectiveness in central policy areas using pure outcome measures. Lijphart also examined a broad spectrum of policies, but measured performance not just with outcome but also with output indicators.

Third, we employed several indicators for measuring the constitutional and informal institutions. In the case of the constitutional 'governmental system', we used four constitutional veto player indices: Lijphart's federal–unitary index (1999a), Schmidt's institutional constraints of central state government (1996) and Fuchs's minimal governmental system indexes A and B (2000). To measure the 'relationship between governing and opposition parties', we developed two partisan veto player indices, a simple partisan veto player index, and a number of governing parties index; we also employed Schnapp's (2004) veto players in the lower house index, and as a surrogate measure, the effective number of parties. One result of our theoretical and empirical analyses of Lijphart's executives–parties index was to show that this index could not be used for measuring informal institutions due to its considerable conceptual and methodological deficiencies. Fourth, we controlled for the most important competing explanatory factors that have been identified—the ideological orientation of the government, the national level of wealth, and economic globalization—in the explanatory model. Lijphart limited himself to only controlling for the national level of economic development and population size.

The empirical analysis of the influence of political institutions on the level, stability and the structure of political effectiveness came to the following conclusions. Even after controlling for competing explanatory factors, the *governmental system* (measured by constitutional veto player indices) definitely exerts an influence on the level of at least some dimensions of effectiveness. However, these influences are uneven; constitutional negotiation democracies show both better and worse levels of effectiveness than constitutional majoritarian democracies in specific policy areas. The same contradictory patterns can be found for constitutional negotiation democracies in the case of stability. As for the balance of policy patterns, there are no differences between constitutional majoritarian and constitutional negotiation democracies.

Similarly, the *relationship between governing and opposition parties* (measured by partisan veto player indices) also shows an influence on the level of effectiveness, after controlling for competing explanatory factors. These are uniformly positive, that is, informal negotiation democracies consistently show higher levels of effectiveness than do informal majoritarian democracies. The only statistically significant effects, however, are on poverty, social policy as a whole, and on municipal waste production; and, as can be shown for poverty, this effect is not stable over time. Furthermore, informal negotiation democracies reveal generally greater stability in the levels of effectiveness than informal majoritarian democracies. No clear picture emerges for the policy patterns (economic vs. social policy, economic vs. environmental policy, sustainability). Sometimes it is the informal negotiation democracies and at other times it is the informal majoritarian democracies that show more balanced patterns.

Thus, the empirical analyses confirm first, that democratic institutions have an effect on political effectiveness, and second, that such influence differs between constitutional and informal institutions. Third, these influences are also inconsistent in part, with constitutional institutions exerting both positive and negative influences on the level and stability of political effectiveness, and the informal institutions likewise showing both positive and negative influences on the policy patterns. Fourth, we could see an effect of the political institutions only in a few, select policy areas and not in all areas; this effect varied over time.

The third and fourth findings about inconsistent and selective effects contradict several of the theoretical assumptions about the impact of political institutions that were suggested above. This raises the question of the theoretical implications of these empirical findings. For when one confronts theory with empirical findings, the facts make clear that the theory of the impact of political institutions must be made more complex. No clear predictions can be made solely on the basis of the character of rules (formal, informal) resulting in different forms of power dispersion (between and within constitutional institutions).

In Chapter 5 we suggested in which direction such a theory needs to be further developed. Beyond differing forms of power dispersion the theory needs to integrate additionally a substantive or *content* dimension, by which we primarily mean the interests or policy preferences of the actors who make their decisions in the context of the institutional settings. To develop such a theory we suggest starting from two different theses:

1. The theory of the impact of constitutional and informal institutions focuses on different forms of power dispersion (between and within constitutional institutions). Another important difference between both types of institutions, however, has been neglected, namely that political parties (the veto players in the case of informal institutions) are not only veto players like constitutional veto players (in the case of constitutional institutions) but also the representatives of societal interests and groups. Constitutional and informal institutions therefore differ not only in their forms of power dispersion but also by their degree to which they determine the breadth of representation of political interests.
2. In order to explain the actual effects of constitutional and informal institutions in specific policy areas, political interests or policy preferences of parties need to be taken into account in the theory of the impact of political institutions. This dimension of political interests would need to be integrated into the theory in different ways.

The first thesis on the *differing degree of determining the breadth of interest representation* argues that constitutional and informal institutions differ not just with respect to the form of power dispersion. The dimension of political interest is already part of informal institutions because partisan veto players (political parties) are also the representatives of societal interests and groups. Consequently, increasing numbers of partisan veto players means increasing representation of political interests in government and parliament. By contrast, constitutional institutions themselves are characterized by indeterminism with respect to political interests. It is only the actual party composition that sets the political interests of a constitutional veto player. Consequently, it is completely open whether a multiplicity of constitutional veto players will mean a narrow or a broad spectrum of interest representation.

We assume that at least some of the empirical findings can be explained with the help of these two features of differing forms of power dispersion and the differing degree of determining the breadth of interest representation. The interest indeterminism of the 'governmental system' can be made responsible for the fact that power dispersion exerts inconsistent influence on the level and stability of political effectiveness. The opposite is true for power dispersion in the 'relationship between governing and opposition parties'. The greater it is, the more broadly political interests are represented in this body, and thereby the greater the probability that minority interests will be represented. The range of political interests on the one hand, and the structural need to negotiate and find compromise in this body on the other hand, means the likelihood rises that minority interests are taken into account in political decisions. As a consequence, effectiveness is higher in those policy areas that are favoured by societal minorities (e.g. poverty or environmental protection), though it also means that policy changes become less likely.

Both features, the form of power dispersion and the degree of determining the breadth of interest representation, can help to explain the inconsistent influence of constitutional institutions as well as the uniformly positive influence of informal institutions on the level and stability of political effectiveness. Yet, the actual effects found for both types of institutions in specific policy areas cannot be explained or predicted with the help of these two characteristics alone. For example, one cannot predict, in the case of constitutional negotiation democracies, in which areas they will show higher or lower performance. The same is true for informal negotiation democracies: one cannot predict in which policy areas they will show higher performance or which policy patterns will be balanced or imbalanced. This is where the second thesis of *integrating political interests* of parties into the theory of the impact of political institutions can play a part.

This additional dimension needs to be introduced in different ways. In the case of 'governmental systems', political interests or policy preferences of parties need to be integrated as interacting factors. Schmidt (1996) formulated this idea as a fundamental element in his theory of the interaction between constitutional structures and governing parties. At the centre stands the government with very specific policy preferences. If a power-concentrating constitutional structure exists, then the government will be able to push through these preferences, and such preferences will lead to corresponding policy outcomes. Social policy in the Nordic nations can be taken as prototypical example of this kind of interaction between a power-concentrating constitutional structure and (long-) dominant social democratic government. This notion of interaction between governing parties and constitutional structures is very promising, but we have to keep in mind that in this case the explanatory power and prediction is limited to the effects of power-concentrating structures. The effects of power-dispersing constitutional structures cannot thereby be explained or predicted.

In the case of the 'relationship between governing and opposition parties' we can predict that informal negotiation democracies show higher effectiveness in policy areas of importance to minorities. Yet, from the empirical finding that power dispersion primarily had a positive effect on poverty (social policy) and municipal waste production (environmental policy), we can only conclude a posteriori that both policies represented minority interests in western democracies between 1974 and 1995. On the basis of the breadth of interest representation and the structural need to negotiate and come to agreement one cannot a priori assert in *which* individual policy areas informal negotiation democracies will show higher performance. To do so, one would need to include the policy preferences of the parties—which change relatively frequently—as an additional independent variable. The same consideration applies to the prediction of balanced policy patterns, the only aspect for which inconsistent influences could be found even for informal institutions. Only when the policy preferences of the government are known can one assert which particular policy patterns show balance or imbalance.

Such theses about the further development of the theory of political institution impacts marks a clear turning away from a unified or general theory on the influence of constitutional and informal institutions suggested by Lijphart (1984, 1999a). His theory of majoritarian and consensus democracy began with the notion of power distribution, and he assumed that democracies could be built on one of two basic principles, either 'rule by the majority of the people' or 'rule by as many people as possible'. All other dimensions, including the differentiation between formal and informal institutions, were accorded no independent theoretical significance. This theory may have been sufficient for describing the structure of democracies and developing a typology of democracies as presented in *Democracies* (1984). But for the analysis of political performance in *Patterns of Democracy* (Lijphart 1999a) it was not fruitful, and even in part misleading, because important differences between the constitutional (federal–unitary) and informal (executives–parties) institutions that are of decisive significance for questions about the effect of political institutions are thereby hidden. In our judgment, based on the theoretical and empirical analyses presented here, the type of structures—whether formal or informal—is an appropriate starting point to develop a theory of the impact of political institutions.

In the end, how can one answer the central research question about the influence of political institutions 'Do institutions matter?' In the wake of our theoretical and empirical findings, we can answer it affirmatively: institutions do have an influence on effectiveness—if, however, with reservations.

The nature and extent of the effect depends on the type of institution. The 'governmental system' does not primarily exert an independent influence on effectiveness; the performance in the end comes about as a result of the interaction with the policy preferences of the governing parties. By contrast, the 'relationship between governing and opposition parties' clearly exerts independent, albeit limited influences on effectiveness. Power dispersion in this dimension has the consequence that effectiveness is greater in those policy areas favoured by societal minorities, and levels of effectiveness are more stable over time. To summarize, informal institutions matter only sometimes and formal institutions only in interaction with policy preferences of governing parties; both matter only to a limited degree.

What are the implications of our study for the *practical* question whether political effectiveness can be improved through institutional reforms? On the one hand, the 'governmental system' has the advantage that it can be changed directly through constitutional reforms. By reducing the number of constitutional veto players, the decision-making ability of a government can be increased. The hindrance is, however, that the governmental system exerts no independent effect on the level of effectiveness but only in interaction with the party composition of the government.

On the other hand, the 'relationship between governing and opposition parties' exerts an independent influence on effectiveness. By increasing power dispersion in this dimension the likelihood increases that effectiveness in those policy areas favoured by societal minorities can be improved. The relationship between governing and opposition parties, however, cannot be directly changed because it is based on informal rules that emerge through the interaction between actors. The electoral laws can certainly be altered, but they do not directly affect the relationship between governing and opposition parties but only in interaction with societal factors. If one changed a majority-based voting system into a proportional representation system, there is no guarantee that the result would be many political parties. Furthermore, many parties in the government alone do not ensure that they could also work together and find compromises in such a manner that minority interests would be respected in political decisions. For that, additional helpful circumstances are necessary, such as elite consensus or an ideological distance between the governing parties that is not too great, and that makes cooperation between the representatives of different parties possible.

Hence, our analyses do not support the widely held assumption that fundamental political problems can be simply resolved through institutional reforms of liberal democracies.

Appendix

PERFORMANCE INDICATORS—DISTRIBUTION
OF THE ORIGINAL VARIABLES

The distribution of the original variables for the fourteen performance indicators, with the most important statistical indices, is given in the following Tables (A.1.1–A.1.14). The nations are grouped according to the five different families of nations suggested by Castles (1998*a*): English-speaking, Scandinavian (Nordic), Continental Western European, Southern European, and the special cases of Switzerland and Japan. Indications are given, where appropriate, to the data replacement procedures used and the nations to which they apply.

TABLE A.1.1 *Murder and manslaughter (per 100,000 residents) 1974–95*[a]

	Level (mean per period)					Growth rates (between periods)			
	1974–9	1980–4	1985–9	1990–5	1974–95	1974–84	1984–9	1989–95	1974–95
Australia	1.8	1.9	2.0	1.9	1.9	4.6	7.4	−5.3	6.4
Canada	2.5	2.3	2.1	2.0	2.2	−9.2	−10.4	−5.3	−23.0
Great Britain	1.4	0.9	0.9	0.9	1.0	−34.1	4.4	−2.5	−32.9
Ireland	0.8	0.9	0.8	0.7	0.8	25.3	−14.9	−18.5	−13.1
New Zealand	1.5	1.3	2.0	2.1	1.7	−9.7	50.7	2.3	39.3
USA	9.6	9.4	8.8	9.8	9.4	−2.4	−6.8	12.2	2.0
Denmark	0.7	1.2	1.2	1.3	1.1	68.6	3.4	3.8	80.9
Finland	3.0	2.9	2.9	3.2	3.0	−2.7	0.7	8.3	6.1
Norway	0.7	1.1	1.3	1.2	1.1	55.5	14.0	−11.4	57.1
Sweden	1.2	1.2	1.4	1.3	1.3	1.7	11.5	−5.6	6.9
Austria	1.4	1.5	1.3	1.3	1.4	8.6	−17.1	4.5	−6.0
Belgium	1.1	1.6	1.7	1.6	1.5	54.3	6.2	−5.2	55.3
France	1.0	1.1	1.1	1.1	1.1	15.9	0.0	−4.2	11.0
Germany	1.2	1.2	1.1	1.2	1.2	1.7	−8.2	4.2	−2.8
Italy	1.4	1.9	1.7	2.3	1.8	37.6	−9.6	35.1	68.0
The Netherlands	0.8	0.8	0.9	1.2	1.0	2.9	11.9	25.9	44.9
Greece	0.7	0.8	0.9	1.3	0.9	20.0	14.6	33.0	82.9
Portugal	1.6	1.4	1.4	1.6	1.5	−13.8	0.0	14.3	−1.5
Spain	0.9	1.0	1.0	1.0	1.0	8.9	6.1	−7.4	7.0
Switzerland	0.9	1.2	1.2	1.5	1.2	33.6	3.4	20.1	65.9
Japan	1.2	1.0	0.8	0.6	0.9	−20.0	−18.7	−22.5	−49.6
Mean	1.68	1.75	1.75	1.85	1.76	4.2	−0.3	5.7	9.8
Coefficient of variation	1.14	1.04	0.97	1.04	1.05				
Correlation with 1974–9		0.99	0.98	0.98					−0.23

[a] Portugal from 1976 and Spain from 1977.

Source: WHO, *World Health Statistics Annual* (with substitution of missing values through interpolation and extrapolation).

TABLE A.1.2. *Robbery (per 100,000 residents) 1974–95*[a]

	Level (mean per period)					Growth rates (between periods)			
	1974–9	1980–4	1985–9	1990–5	1974–95	1974–84	1984–9	1989–95	1974–95
Australia	40.3	63.3	60.2	77.6	60.3	57.0	−4.9	28.9	92.5
Canada[b]	99.0	102.8	92.0	109.1	101.0	3.9	−10.5	18.6	10.3
Great Britain	31.7	45.3	65.8	80.1	55.8	43.0	45.3	21.7	152.9
Ireland	38.2	49.0	45.2	63.9	49.3	28.3	−7.8	41.5	67.3
New Zealand	6.2	10.8	39.4	50.2	26.8	73.5	264.4	27.3	705.2
USA	203.6	225.3	220.0	251.3	225.3	10.7	−2.3	14.2	23.4
Denmark	20.3	30.2	38.6	66.5	39.3	48.9	27.6	72.5	227.5
Finland	41.7	38.2	37.2	48.3	41.7	−8.5	−2.5	29.7	15.8
Norway[c]	18.1	22.0	19.5	26.4	21.6	21.8	−11.5	35.5	46.1
Sweden	38.1	41.2	49.8	67.9	49.6	8.1	20.8	36.5	78.2
Austria	30.0	31.7	31.7	53.1	37.1	5.7	−0.2	67.7	76.9
Belgium	24.9	40.8	67.5	74.1	51.6	64.0	65.5	9.8	198.0
France	57.3	84.9	94.2	120.9	89.3	48.2	11.0	28.3	111.1
Germany	34.6	45.5	47.5	68.8	49.3	31.7	4.3	44.8	99.0
Italy	26.9	27.6	48.3	57.5	40.3	2.6	75.1	19.1	114.0
The Netherlands	31.9	43.0	72.9	106.6	64.1	35.1	69.4	46.3	234.7
Greece[d]	0.8	1.5	4.7	13.4	5.3	88.6	221.1	182.5	1610.9
Portugal	14.5	19.6	28.2	39.1	26.6	35.4	43.5	38.7	169.6
Spain	32.4	86.5	212.9	221.9	154.0	167.0	146.1	4.2	585.1
Switzerland[e]	22.2	24.4	22.1	30.6	24.9	10.3	−9.7	38.7	38.0
Japan	1.8	1.9	1.5	1.7	1.7	8.1	−23.3	19.7	−0.8
Means	38.77	49.32	61.86	77.58	57.84	27.2	25.4	25.4	100.1
Coefficient of variation	1.11	0.98	0.92	0.78	0.88				
Correlation with 1974–9		0.97	0.73	0.76					−0.31

[a] Portugal from 1976 and Spain from 1977.
[b] Starting point of the time-series 1980.
[c] Starting point of the time-series 1985.
[d] Missing values for 1974–6 were substituted through extrapolation based on the development from 1977 to 1981.
[e] Starting point of the time-series 1983.

Source: Interpol, *International Crime Statistics* (starting point of the time-series 1977; with substitution of missing values through interpolation and extrapolation).

TABLE A.1.3. *Burglary (per 100,000 residents) 1974–95^a*

	Level (mean per period)					Growth rates (between periods)			
	1974–9	1980–4	1985–9	1990–5	1974–95	1974–84	1984–9	1989–95	1974–95
Australia	1066.4	1441.1	1868.2	2071.5	1607.9	35.1	29.6	10.9	94.3
Canada[b]	1480.2	1485.6	1394.6	1468.0	1458.6	0.4	-6.1	5.3	-0.8
Great Britain	1230.4	1475.8	1791.8	2180.9	1673.0	19.9	21.4	21.7	77.2
Ireland	758.2	881.0	867.7	901.2	850.0	16.2	-1.5	3.9	18.9
New Zealand	1602.1	2031.3	2579.8	2662.1	2210.9	26.8	27.0	3.2	66.2
USA	1495.6	1455.4	1309.4	1130.8	1344.7	-2.7	-10.0	-13.6	-24.4
Denmark	1680.3	1991.5	2390.9	2263.3	2071.5	18.5	20.1	-5.3	34.7
Finland[c]	1877.2	1893.6	1908.5	1903.9	1895.3	0.9	0.8	-0.2	1.4
Norway[d]	120.1	110.8	112.9	94.8	109.4	-7.8	1.9	-16.0	-21.1
Sweden	1748.6	1676.1	1684.3	1737.8	1714.6	-4.1	0.5	3.2	-0.6
Austria	688.5	832.5	848.4	1169.1	888.6	20.9	1.9	37.8	69.8
Belgium	422.1	631.9	604.9	919.0	646.8	49.7	-4.3	51.9	117.7
France	450.8	660.9	715.3	783.1	649.3	46.6	8.2	9.5	73.7
Germany	1179.1	1409.5	1870.0	1900.7	1585.3	19.5	32.7	1.6	61.2
Italy[e]	749.1	1057.7	1345.6	1613.6	1190.6	41.2	27.2	19.9	115.4
The Netherlands	1005.0	1753.7	2689.3	3296.3	2182.9	74.5	53.3	22.6	228.0
Greece[f]	0.2	55.8	201.9	322.4	146.6	27450.8	261.5	59.7	158990.0
Portugal	76.6	89.0	73.2	108.2	88.3	16.2	-17.8	47.7	41.2
Spain	159.3	610.3	1224.6	948.2	807.4	283.1	100.7	-22.6	495.2
Switzerland[g]	1033.5	1023.2	1007.1	1019.1	1021.2	-1.0	-1.6	1.2	-1.4
Japan	269.8	251.8	224.4	190.8	233.8	-6.7	-10.9	-15.0	-29.3
Mean	909.2	1086.6	1272.0	1365.95	1160.8	19.5	17.1	7.4	50.2
Coefficient of variation	0.66	0.59	0.63	0.63	0.60				
Correlation with 1974–9		0.95	0.80	0.73	0.60				-0.35

[a] Portugal from 1976 and Spain from 1977.
[b] Starting point of the time-series 1980.
[c] Starting point of the time-series 1991.
[d] Starting point of the time-series 1985.
[e] Mean of the family of nation (Austria, Belgium, France, Germany, and the Netherlands).
[f] Missing values for 1974–8 were substituted through extrapolation based on the development from 1979 to 1980.
[g] Starting point of the time-series 1983.

Source: Interpol, *International Crime Statistics* (starting point of the time-series 1977; with substitution of missing values through interpolation and extrapolation).

TABLE A.1.4. *Gross domestic product in US dollars per capita (adjusted for price and purchasing power) 1974–95[a]*

	Level (mean per period)					Growth rates (between periods)			
	1974–9	1980–4	1985–9	1990–5	1974–95	1974–84	1984–9	1989–95	1974–95
Australia	6175	10040	13688	17585	11873	62.6	36.3	28.5	184.8
Canada	7129	11597	16025	19707	13597	62.7	38.2	23.0	176.4
Great Britain	5766	9271	13237	16843	11282	60.8	42.8	27.2	192.1
Ireland	3578	6159	8483	14211	8179	72.1	37.7	67.5	297.1
New Zealand	5796	9277	12064	14787	10464	60.1	30.0	22.6	155.1
USA	8719	13861	18909	24252	16440	59.0	36.4	28.3	178.2
Denmark	6460	10628	14836	19667	12913	64.5	39.6	32.6	204.5
Finland	5353	9459	13328	16150	11043	76.7	40.9	21.2	201.7
Norway	6023	10772	15161	20517	13132	78.8	40.8	35.3	240.6
Sweden	6583	10691	14514	17416	12274	62.4	35.8	20.0	164.6
Austria	5941	10144	13606	18859	12162	70.7	34.1	38.6	217.4
Belgium	6145	10243	13584	19187	12324	66.7	32.6	41.3	212.3
France	6623	10873	14341	18812	12667	64.2	31.9	31.2	184.0
Germany	5760	9682	13244	18441	11811	68.1	36.8	39.2	220.2
Italy	5605	9700	13354	17974	11670	73.1	37.7	34.6	220.7
The Netherlands	6248	9821	13088	17810	11768	57.2	33.3	36.1	185.1
Greece	3643	5990	7853	10848	7098	64.4	31.1	38.1	197.8
Portugal	3372	5234	7286	11454	7240	55.2	39.2	57.2	239.7
Spain	4845	6744	9298	13213	9159	39.2	37.9	42.1	172.7
Switzerland	8358	13467	17667	23154	15670	61.1	31.2	31.1	177.0
Japan	5509	9752	13958	20307	12429	77.0	43.1	45.5	268.6
Mean	5887	9686	13215	17676	11676	64.5	36.4	33.8	200.2
Coefficient of variation	0.23	0.23	0.22	0.19	0.20				
Correlation with 1974–9		0.98	0.96	0.89					−0.54

[a] Portugal from 1976 and Spain from 1977.

Source: OECD, *National Accounts* (no missing values).

TABLE A.1.5. *Unemployment rate (standardized) 1974–95*[a]

	Level (mean per period)					Growth rates (between periods)			
	1974–9	1980–4	1985–9	1990–5	1974–95	1974–84	1984–9	1989–95	1974–95
Australia	5.1	7.6	7.6	9.4	7.4	48.1	−0.5	24.5	83.5
Canada	7.2	9.9	8.8	10.2	9.0	36.4	−10.3	14.8	40.5
Great Britain	5.0	9.9	9.9	9.1	8.3	100.2	−0.04	−7.9	84.4
Ireland[b]	7.6	11.7	16.2	14.3	12.3	52.9	39.2	−11.8	87.7
New Zealand[c]	0.8	4.1	5.0	8.7	4.7	445.7	21.0	74.8	1054.6
USA	6.8	8.3	6.2	6.4	6.9	22.6	−25.1	3.1	−5.3
Denmark[d]	6.1	9.6	6.3	8.5	7.6	58.8	−34.2	34.3	40.4
Finland	4.4	5.2	5.0	11.9	6.8	17.4	−3.4	136.1	167.9
Norway	1.8	2.6	3.0	5.6	3.3	44.7	14.6	85.7	207.9
Sweden	1.9	3.0	2.2	6.3	3.4	57.2	−24.9	182.5	233.3
Austria[e]	1.8	3.2	3.4	3.7	3.0	77.2	8.9	6.8	106.1
Belgium	6.3	10.4	9.4	8.2	8.5	64.2	−9.3	−12.6	30.2
France	4.5	7.8	10.0	10.8	8.2	73.0	27.6	8.0	138.5
Germany	3.2	5.6	6.3	6.4	5.3	73.8	13.3	0.9	98.7
Italy	6.6	7.6	9.5	10.1	8.4	15.3	25.6	6.1	53.6
The Netherlands	4.9	8.3	7.8	6.4	6.7	70.1	−6.2	−18.5	30.0
Greece[f]	1.9	5.7	7.5	8.8	5.9	194.0	31.8	16.4	351.3
Portugal[g]	7.4	7.7	6.9	5.5	6.8	3.9	−11.0	−20.6	−26.6
Spain	6.8	15.6	20.0	20.1	16.8	130.5	28.5	0.4	197.3
Switzerland[h]	0.4	0.6	0.7	2.8	1.1	59.9	22.2	309.1	699.5
Japan	1.9	2.4	2.6	2.5	2.3	23.6	8.8	−4.4	28.5
Mean	4.4	6.99	7.36	8.36	6.8	58.8	5.4	13.6	90.0
Coefficient of variation	0.54	0.52	0.61	0.48	0.51				
Correlation with 1974–9		0.85	0.70	0.55					−0.65

[a] Portugal from 1976 and Spain from 1977.
[b] 1974–81 unstandardized values.
[c] 1974–85 unstandardized values.
[d] 1974–87 unstandardized values.
[e] 1986–90 unstandardized values.
[f] 1974–95 unstandardized values.
[g] 1976–82 unstandardized values.
[h] 1986–90 unstandardized values.

Source: OECD, *Main Economic Indicators* (with substitution of missing values through extrapolation).

TABLE A.1.6. *Inflation rate (consumer price index) 1974–95*[a]

	Level (mean per period)					Growth rates (between periods)			
	1974–9	1980–4	1985–9	1990–5	1974–95	1974–84	1984–9	1989–95	1974–95
Australia	12.2	9.0	7.8	3.3	8.0	−26.1	−13.1	−57.8	−72.9
Canada	9.2	8.7	4.3	2.7	6.2	−5.5	−50.5	−37.8	−71.0
Great Britain	15.7	9.6	5.3	4.4	8.9	−38.9	−45.1	−16.1	−71.9
Ireland	15.0	15.0	3.7	2.7	9.1	−0.1	−75.1	−28.8	−82.3
New Zealand	13.8	12.4	11.3	2.8	9.9	−10.0	−9.2	−75.6	−80.0
USA	8.6	7.5	3.6	3.5	5.8	−12.3	−52.0	−2.7	−59.0
Denmark	10.8	9.5	4.3	2.1	6.6	−12.0	−54.2	−52.1	−80.7
Finland	12.7	9.6	4.8	2.9	7.5	−24.5	−50.1	−39.2	−77.1
Norway	8.7	10.1	6.6	2.7	6.9	16.2	−35.1	−59.4	−69.4
Sweden	9.8	10.3	5.7	5.4	7.8	5.1	−44.5	−4.4	−44.2
Austria	6.2	5.5	2.2	3.2	4.3	−10.8	−60.7	49.8	−47.5
Belgium	8.4	7.4	2.4	2.6	5.2	−12.2	−67.6	9.0	−69.0
France	10.7	11.2	3.6	2.4	6.9	4.3	−68.1	−31.5	−77.2
Germany	4.6	4.5	1.2	3.5	3.5	−1.4	−72.5	176.7	−25.0
Italy	16.8	16.5	6.2	5.2	11.1	−1.7	−62.5	−15.4	−68.8
The Netherlands	7.2	5.0	0.7	2.7	4.0	−30.2	−86.3	287.4	−62.8
Greece	16.2	21.8	17.2	15.0	17.4	34.3	−21.0	−13.0	−7.7
Portugal	25.1	22.7	12.6	8.3	16.3	−9.8	−44.4	−34.4	−67.1
Spain	20.0	13.6	6.9	5.4	10.3	−32.0	−49.3	−21.4	−72.9
Switzerland	4.0	4.4	2.1	3.5	3.5	9.6	−51.7	66.2	−12.0
Japan	10.1	3.9	1.1	1.7	4.3	−61.1	−70.8	44.9	−83.5
Mean	11.7	10.39	5.41	4.09	7.8	−11.2	−47.9	−24.4	−65.0
Coefficient of variation	0.44	0.50	0.76	0.71	0.48				
Correlation with 1974–9		0.86	0.69	0.51					−0.32

[a] Portugal from 1976 and Spain from 1977.

Source: OECD, *Main Economic Indicators* (no missing values).

TABLE A.1.7. *Infant mortality (per 1,000 live births) 1974–95*[a]

	Level (mean per period)					Growth rates (between periods)			
	1974–9	1980–4	1985–9	1990–5	1974–95	1974–84	1984–9	1989–95	1974–95
Australia	13.4	10.0	8.8	6.7	9.7	−25.6	−11.4	−24.4	−50.2
Canada	13.0	9.1	7.5	6.4	9.1	−29.8	−17.9	−14.2	−50.6
Great Britain	14.6	10.8	9.1	6.7	10.3	−25.9	−15.9	−25.8	−53.8
Ireland	15.6	10.4	8.2	6.9	10.4	−33.2	−20.9	−16.9	−56.1
New Zealand	14.3	12.1	10.6	7.6	11.1	−15.4	−12.2	−28.6	−47.0
USA	14.8	11.6	10.2	8.5	11.3	−21.8	−12.2	−16.5	−42.7
Denmark	9.6	8.0	8.0	6.3	8.0	−16.9	0.3	−21.5	−34.5
Finland	9.1	6.6	6.1	4.9	6.7	−27.1	−7.9	−18.9	−45.5
Norway	9.8	8.0	8.2	5.6	7.9	−18.3	2.8	−31.7	−42.7
Sweden	8.3	6.8	6.1	5.1	6.6	−18.1	−10.9	−15.6	−38.4
Austria	18.1	12.6	9.5	6.8	11.8	−30.3	−24.4	−28.4	−62.3
Belgium	14.7	11.0	9.3	7.9	10.8	−24.9	−15.2	−15.8	−46.4
France	12.2	9.3	7.9	6.5	9.0	−23.4	−15.5	−18.1	−47.0
Germany	17.0	11.0	8.1	6.1	10.7	−35.3	−26.0	−24.7	−63.9
Italy	19.1	13.1	9.7	7.4	12.4	−31.5	−25.8	−23.9	−61.3
The Netherlands	10.1	8.4	7.4	6.2	8.0	−16.6	−12.1	−15.5	−38.1
Greece	21.5	15.6	11.7	8.6	14.4	−27.1	−24.9	−26.6	−59.9
Portugal	29.7	20.4	14.6	9.2	17.4	−31.4	−28.4	−37.0	−69.1
Spain	15.2	11.4	8.6	6.7	9.8	−25.3	−24.6	−21.7	−55.9
Switzerland	10.1	7.8	6.9	5.9	7.7	−22.8	−11.5	−15.5	−42.3
Japan	9.2	6.7	5.0	4.4	6.4	−27.5	−24.9	−12.7	−52.4
Mean	14.25	10.51	8.65	6.68	9.97	−26.3	−17.7	−22.7	−53.1
Coefficient of variation	0.35	0.31	0.24	0.18	0.27				
Correlation with 1974–9		0.98	0.89	0.81					−0.83

[a] Portugal from 1976 and Spain from 1977.

Source: OECD, *Health Data* (no missing data).

TABLE A.1.8. *Poverty rate (below 50% of the median of equivalent income) 1974–95*[a]

	Level (mean per period)					Growth rates (between periods)			
	1974–9	1980–4	1985–9	1990–5	1974–95	1974–84	1984–9	1989–95	1974–95
Australia[b]	11.9	11.7	12.0	13.6	12.4	-1.6	3.1	13.0	14.5
Canada	13.6	12.3	11.4	10.9	12.1	-9.8	-6.6	-4.3	-19.4
Great Britain	9.1	9.2	10.4	13.9	10.7	0.1	13.8	33.5	52.1
Ireland[c]	10.4	10.7	11.1	11.5	10.9	3.8	3.3	3.5	11.0
New Zealand[d]	12.2	12.1	12.5	13.5	12.6	-0.5	3.6	7.8	11.1
USA	15.9	16.7	17.7	17.6	16.9	5.1	6.1	-0.3	11.1
Denmark[e]	10.2	9.3	9.2	7.5	9.0	-9.0	-0.9	-18.1	-26.2
Finland[e]	5.6	5.5	5.5	5.5	5.5	-1.0	-0.7	0.1	-1.6
Norway	5.7	5.9	6.9	6.6	6.3	3.9	18.0	-4.4	17.2
Sweden	6.1	5.8	7.2	6.7	6.4	-4.7	24.3	-6.1	11.3
Austria[i]	5.9	6.3	6.7	7.1	6.5	7.2	6.1	6.3	21.0
Belgium[f]	4.5	4.7	4.6	5.1	4.7	4.8	-1.6	10.9	14.3
France	7.7	7.4	8.3	8.4	8.0	-3.8	11.7	1.1	8.6
Germany[g]	6.5	5.8	5.9	6.6	6.2	-11.2	2.3	12.6	2.2
Italy[g]	9.6	10.7	10.5	11.9	10.7	10.7	-1.4	12.9	23.3
The Netherlands[h]	4.5	4.9	4.8	7.2	5.4	7.8	-1.4	49.1	58.5
Greece[j]	11.9	11.8	10.7	9.9	11.0	-0.8	-8.9	-8.0	-16.8
Portugal[j]	11.7	11.8	10.7	9.9	10.9	0.3	-8.9	-8.0	-16.0
Spain[k]	11.7	11.8	10.7	9.9	10.9	0.8	-8.9	-8.0	-15.5
Switzerland[l]	7.8	7.9	8.5	9.2	8.3	1.9	6.9	8.9	18.6
Japan[m]	7.8	7.9	8.5	9.2	8.3	1.9	6.9	8.9	18.6
Mean	9.05	9.04	9.23	9.61	9.23	0.0	2.1	4.1	6.2
Coefficient of variation	0.35	0.35	0.34	0.33	0.33				
Correlation with 1974–79		0.99	0.95	0.83					-0.45

[a] Portugal from 1976 and Spain from 1977. [b] Starting point of the time-series 1981. [c] Only one time point available (1987). [d] Mean of the family of nation (Australia, Canada, Great Britain, Ireland, and the USA). [e] Starting point of the development in Australia, Canada, Great Britain, and the USA. [f] Starting point of the time-series 1985. [g] Starting point of the time-series 1986. [h] Starting point of the time-series 1987. [i] Only one time point available (1987). Missing values were substituted through extrapolation on the basis of the development of the family of nation (Belgium, France, Germany, Italy, and the Netherlands). [j] Spanish values. [k] Starting point of the time-series 1980. [l] Starting point of the time-series 1982. [m] Swiss values.

Source: Luxembourg Income Study (with substitution of missing values through interpolation and extrapolation; periods with missing original data are underlined).

TABLE A.1.9. *Emissions of sulphur oxides (kg per capita) 1974–95*[a]

	Level (mean per period)					Growth rates (between periods)			
	1974–9	1980–4	1985–9	1990–5	1974–95	1974–84	1984–9	1989–95	1974–95
Australia[b]	122.9	95.5	78.9	70.4	92.4	−22.3	−17.4	−10.8	−42.7
Canada	222.6	164.1	119.0	104.2	153.5	−26.3	−27.5	−12.4	−53.2
Great Britain	94.4	75.6	67.4	54.8	73.2	−19.9	−10.9	−18.7	−42.0
Ireland	60.7	48.2	44.7	47.7	50.7	−20.5	−7.2	6.6	−21.4
New Zealand[b]	122.9	95.5	78.9	70.4	92.4	−22.3	−17.4	−10.8	−42.7
USA	114.0	94.2	84.7	75.1	92.2	−17.3	−10.2	−11.3	−34.2
Denmark	85.6	69.8	51.0	34.6	60.2	−18.4	−27.0	−32.0	−59.5
Finland	116.4	97.1	64.4	30.8	76.8	−16.5	−33.7	−52.2	−73.6
Norway	34.5	28.0	18.5	9.3	22.5	−18.9	−33.7	−50.0	−73.1
Sweden	77.5	45.9	27.4	12.3	41.2	−40.7	−40.3	−55.0	−84.1
Austria[c]	37.8	39.6	19.4	9.3	26.3	4.6	−51.0	−51.8	−75.3
Belgium[c]	65.4	66.9	36.9	27.8	49.0	2.3	−44.8	−24.7	−57.5
France	62.6	44.8	23.3	19.5	37.9	−28.5	−48.1	−16.0	−68.8
Germany	53.4	46.4	28.3	35.6	41.2	−13.2	−39.0	25.7	−33.5
Italy	58.7	46.3	32.0	25.7	40.8	−21.0	−31.0	−19.7	−56.2
The Netherlands	33.4	27.7	16.9	11.2	22.3	−17.0	−38.8	−33.8	−66.4
Greece[d]	40.7	38.8	37.2	35.4	38.0	−4.5	−4.1	−4.8	−12.8
Portugal	23.2	28.1	22.0	29.5	26.0	21.2	−21.5	33.8	27.3
Spain[c]	62.6	65.2	49.6	53.9	57.1	4.1	−24.0	8.6	−14.0
Switzerland	17.6	16.5	9.6	5.3	12.2	−5.9	−41.9	−44.5	−69.7
Japan	19.8	9.5	7.1	4.9	10.5	−51.9	−25.4	−30.5	−75.1
Mean	72.69	59.24	43.68	36.57	53.16	−18.5	−26.3	−16.3	−49.7
Coefficient of variation	0.66	0.60	0.67	0.73	0.64				
Correlation with 1974–9		0.98	0.95	0.85					−0.04

[a] Portugal from 1976 and Spain from 1977.
[b] Mean of the family of nation (Canada, Great Britain, Ireland, and the USA).
[c] Starting point of the time-series 1980.
[d] Only two time points available (1980, 1983).

Source: OECD, *Environmental Data Compendium* (with substitution of missing values through interpolation and extrapolation).

TABLE A.1.10. *Emissions of nitrogen oxides (kg per capita) 1974–95*[a]

	Level (mean per period)					Growth rate (between periods)			
	1974–9	1980–4	1985–9	1990–5	1974–95	1974–84	1984–9	1989–95	1974–95
Australia[b]	134.7	129.9	129.1	123.9	129.4	−3.5	−0.7	−4.0	−7.9
Canada	78.3	77.5	80.7	70.8	76.6	−0.9	4.1	−12.4	−9.6
Great Britain	41.0	43.1	46.7	45.0	43.9	5.2	8.2	−3.6	9.7
Ireland[c]	25.3	24.1	31.1	33.6	28.6	−4.5	28.7	8.0	32.8
New Zealand[d]	74.6	73.0	74.6	70.8	73.2	−2.1	2.2	−5.1	−5.1
USA	93.8	90.3	85.5	80.9	87.6	−3.7	−5.4	−5.3	−13.8
Denmark	45.6	50.6	58.7	54.1	52.0	11.1	16.0	−8.0	18.6
Finland	45.2	52.1	58.1	56.1	52.7	15.3	11.6	−3.5	24.2
Norway	45.3	45.9	56.5	51.9	49.8	1.3	23.1	−8.2	14.5
Sweden	43.0	53.5	51.6	44.4	47.7	24.3	−3.6	−13.8	3.3
Austria[c]	32.6	32.2	30.7	24.6	29.9	−1.2	−4.7	−19.8	−24.4
Belgium[c]	39.8	40.1	33.9	34.6	37.1	0.9	−15.5	2.0	−13.1
France	30.4	28.3	25.7	27.3	28.0	−6.8	−9.3	6.3	−10.2
Germany	41.5	42.1	39.0	29.5	37.8	1.5	−7.2	−24.4	−28.8
Italy	27.4	27.5	31.2	35.4	30.5	0.2	13.4	13.7	29.3
The Netherlands	37.3	39.9	40.3	36.7	38.4	7.1	1.0	−8.9	−1.4
Greece[c]	24.6	25.9	32.0	33.7	29.1	5.1	23.5	5.4	36.8
Portugal	14.0	17.3	12.3	23.7	17.3	23.2	−28.9	92.9	69.1
Spain[c]	24.5	23.9	25.3	31.5	26.8	−2.4	5.9	24.6	28.8
Switzerland	25.8	27.2	26.5	21.8	25.2	5.4	−2.4	−17.8	−15.4
Japan	15.2	12.3	11.1	11.7	12.7	−19.0	−10.1	5.8	−23.0
Mean	44.75	45.56	46.7	44.86	45.44	1.8	2.5	−3.9	0.3
Coefficient of variation	0.64	0.61	0.59	0.57	0.60				
Correlation with 1974–9		0.99	0.98	0.97	0.60				−0.34

[a] Portugal from 1976 and Spain from 1977.
[b] Starting point of the time-series 1988.
[c] Starting point of the time-series 1980.
[d] Mean of the family of nation (Australia, Canada, Great Britain, Ireland, and the USA).

Source: OECD, *Environmental Data Compendium* (with substitution of missing values through interpolation and extrapolation).

TABLE A.1.11. *Emissions of carbon dioxide (kg per capita) 1974–95*[a]

	Level (mean per period)					Growth rates (between periods)			
	1974–9	1980–4	1985–9	1990–5	1974–95	1974–84	1984–9	1989–95	1974–95
Australia	14.0	14.4	14.6	15.6	14.7	2.8	1.4	6.9	11.4
Canada	17.8	16.8	16.1	15.5	16.5	-5.4	-4.3	-3.8	-12.9
Great Britain	10.8	10.0	10.1	9.9	10.2	-7.9	1.7	-2.3	-8.6
Ireland	7.3	7.7	8.5	9.5	8.3	6.0	10.6	10.8	29.9
New Zealand	6.0	5.9	7.1	7.9	6.7	-2.3	21.8	10.3	31.2
USA	20.8	19.6	19.8	19.7	20.0	-5.6	0.8	-0.4	-5.3
Denmark	11.5	10.9	11.6	11.5	11.4	-5.4	6.3	-0.9	-0.4
Finland	10.7	9.8	11.2	10.9	10.7	-8.5	13.5	-2.6	1.1
Norway	7.2	7.0	7.5	7.6	7.3	-2.6	7.1	1.9	6.2
Sweden	9.9	7.7	7.1	6.2	7.8	-21.8	-8.4	-13.0	-37.6
Austria	7.3	7.3	7.3	7.5	7.4	1.0	0.3	1.7	3.0
Belgium	13.2	11.5	10.8	11.4	11.8	-12.9	-5.8	5.9	-13.1
France	8.8	7.9	6.7	6.5	7.5	-10.9	-15.1	-3.6	-27.1
Germany	12.1	12.0	11.7	11.2	11.7	-0.5	-2.7	-4.0	-7.1
Italy	6.3	6.4	6.6	7.2	6.7	1.6	3.4	8.8	14.4
The Netherlands	12.3	10.3	10.6	11.2	11.2	-15.7	2.6	5.7	-8.6
Greece	4.5	5.2	6.3	7.2	5.8	13.4	21.4	15.5	59.1
Portugal	2.5	2.8	3.2	4.7	3.4	10.2	17.7	43.3	85.8
Spain	5.0	5.2	5.0	5.9	5.3	2.8	-2.7	16.8	16.7
Switzerland	6.3	6.3	6.4	6.4	6.4	0.7	1.8	-1.2	1.3
Japan	8.0	7.6	7.7	8.9	8.1	-5.7	2.1	14.5	10.3
Mean	9.64	9.16	9.34	9.63	9.46	-5.0	2.0	3.1	-0.9
Coefficient of variation	0.46	0.44	0.42	0.39	0.42				
Correlation with 1974–9		0.99	0.96	0.93					-0.60

[a] Portugal from 1976 and Spain from 1977.

Source: OECD, *Environmental Data Compendium* (with substitution of missing values through interpolation and extrapolation).

TABLE A.1.12. Municipal waste production (kg per capita) 1974–95[a]

	Level (mean per period)					Growth rates (between periods)			
	1974–9	1980–4	1985–9	1990–5	1974–95	1974–84	1984–9	1989–95	1974–95
Australia[b]	684.5	686.5	700.2	704.6	694.0	0.3	2.0	0.6	2.9
Canada[b]	569.1	556.8	623.3	629.3	595.1	-2.2	12.0	1.0	10.6
Great Britain[c]	491.4	523.4	577.4	623.3	554.2	6.5	10.3	7.9	26.8
Ireland	174.5	236.9	336.6	404.0	288.1	35.7	42.1	20.0	131.5
New Zealand	466.9	525.1	566.3	662.8	556.2	12.5	7.8	17.1	42.0
USA	562.1	611.8	660.5	715.6	637.6	8.8	8.0	8.3	27.3
Denmark[b]	431.5	430.0	488.1	520.8	468.4	-0.3	13.5	6.7	20.7
Finland[d]	295.7	304.7	350.5	399.3	338.4	3.1	15.0	13.9	35.1
Norway	414.4	432.5	484.3	565.2	475.5	4.4	12.0	16.7	36.4
Sweden	290.3	308.3	374.3	448.5	356.6	6.2	21.4	19.8	54.5
Austria[e]	424.5	440.9	455.9	449.4	442.2	3.9	3.4	-1.4	5.9
Belgium	298.8	321.3	341.3	400.9	341.4	7.5	6.2	17.5	34.2
France[e]	461.8	467.9	473.5	471.6	468.5	1.3	1.2	-0.4	2.1
Germany	339.5	335.2	340.6	315.4	332.2	-1.3	1.6	-7.4	-7.1
Italy	243.6	254.5	296.4	411.3	303.8	4.5	16.5	38.8	68.9
The Netherlands[b]	456.6	473.9	462.6	537.9	484.1	3.8	-2.4	16.3	17.8
Greece[b]	280.8	276.9	301.2	300.0	289.8	-1.4	8.8	-0.4	6.8
Portugal[b]	215.9	214.2	261.5	328.6	260.7	-0.8	22.1	25.7	52.2
Spain	252.1	271.4	294.0	343.6	297.1	7.7	8.3	16.9	36.3
Switzerland	325.1	378.6	417.8	405.8	380.3	16.5	10.3	-2.9	24.8
Japan	374.9	369.3	379.1	404.4	382.6	-1.5	2.6	6.7	7.9
Mean	383.52	400.96	437.41	478.22	426.04	4.5	9.1	9.3	24.7
Coefficient of variation	0.34	0.32	0.29	0.27	0.30				
Correlation with 1974–9		0.99	0.95	0.87	0.30				-0.58

[a] Portugal from 1976 and Spain from 1977.
[b] Starting point of the time-series 1980.
[c] Mean of the family of nation (Australia, Canada, Ireland, New Zealand, and the USA).
[d] Only one time point available (1995). Missing values were substituted through extrapolation on the basis of the development of the family of nations (Denmark, Norway, and Sweden).
[e] Only two time points available (1990, 1995).

Source: OECD, Environmental Data Compendium (with substitution of missing values through interpolation and extrapolation).

TABLE A.1.13. *Fertilizer use (tons per square kilometer) 1974–95*[a]

	Level (mean per period)					Growth rates (between periods)			
	1974–9	1980–4	1985–9	1990–5	1974–95	1974–84	1984–9	1989–95	1974–95
Australia	0.1	0.2	0.2	0.2	0.2	33.2	11.9	8.5	61.7
Canada	0.2	0.2	0.2	0.2	0.2	39.9	4.6	3.2	50.9
Great Britain	7.8	9.9	10.3	9.1	9.2	27.4	4.3	−11.8	17.1
Ireland	6.9	9.0	9.6	10.1	8.9	29.7	6.7	4.8	45.0
New Zealand	1.8	1.8	1.4	1.9	1.7	−1.1	−25.4	38.2	2.0
USA	2.1	2.1	1.9	2.0	2.0	−1.5	−7.8	6.1	−3.6
Denmark	14.7	15.1	14.6	12.5	14.2	2.6	−3.2	−14.6	−15.2
Finland	1.5	1.5	1.5	1.1	1.4	0.6	−0.3	−26.3	−26.1
Norway	0.7	0.8	0.7	0.6	0.7	7.6	−11.7	−9.7	−14.2
Sweden	1.1	1.1	0.9	0.7	0.9	−6.6	−16.7	−21.9	−39.2
Austria	4.1	4.6	4.0	3.3	4.0	10.9	−13.4	−16.5	−19.8
Belgium	14.8	14.1	13.7	11.3	13.4	−4.9	−2.9	−17.5	−23.8
France	9.1	10.4	10.7	9.2	9.8	13.6	3.3	−13.7	1.3
Germany	10.5	10.1	9.4	7.7	9.4	−4.1	−7.3	−17.8	−26.9
Italy	5.6	6.9	6.9	6.5	6.4	22.1	0.4	−5.7	15.6
The Netherlands	15.9	16.6	16.0	13.5	15.4	4.0	−3.4	−15.8	−15.4
Greece	3.6	4.5	5.0	4.7	4.4	24.9	10.1	−7.0	27.9
Portugal	2.7	2.7	3.0	2.8	2.8	−2.0	10.0	−6.4	0.9
Spain	3.1	3.0	3.9	3.7	3.5	−2.2	28.0	−3.9	20.3
Switzerland	3.8	4.2	4.3	3.8	4.0	12.6	0.9	−10.6	1.5
Japan	4.9	5.3	5.3	4.8	5.0	8.8	0.1	−9.6	−1.5
Mean	5.49	5.90	5.87	5.22	5.60	7.6	−0.5	−11.1	−4.9
Coefficient of variation	0.90	0.86	0.85	0.82	0.85				
Correlation with 1974–9		0.99	0.98	0.96					−0.33

[a] Portugal from 1976 and Spain from 1977.

Source: OECD, *Environmental Data Compendium* (with substitution of missing values through interpolation).

TABLE A.1.14. *Water consumption (cubic meters per capita) 1974–95*[a]

	Level (mean per period)					Growth rates (between periods)			
	1974–9	1980–4	1985–9	1990–5	1974–95	1974–84	1984–9	1989–95	1974–95
Australia[b]	840.8	816.3	902.7	850.5	852.0	-2.9	10.6	-5.8	1.2
Canada	1345.4	1608.5	1654.9	1694.1	1570.6	19.6	2.9	2.4	25.9
Great Britain[b]	229.5	225.7	205.9	184.2	210.9	-1.7	-8.8	-10.5	-19.7
Ireland[b]	312.6	316.2	317.8	323.4	317.6	1.1	0.5	1.8	3.5
New Zealand	354.0	466.2	586.1	573.1	492.0	31.7	25.7	-2.2	61.9
USA	2221.3	2144.3	1926.6	1911.3	2052.3	-3.5	-10.2	-0.8	-14.0
Denmark	233.9	234.2	230.8	198.9	223.7	0.1	-1.5	-13.8	-15.0
Finland	759.2	791.0	677.3	473.6	669.9	4.2	-14.4	-30.1	-37.6
Norway	575.6	518.1	516.5	496.7	527.6	-10.0	-0.3	-3.8	-13.7
Sweden	500.9	438.7	353.1	327.5	405.9	-12.4	-19.5	-7.3	-34.6
Austria	322.2	286.0	291.8	291.1	298.6	-11.2	2.0	-0.2	-9.6
Belgium[c]	916.7	901.4	898.2	902.5	905.1	-1.7	-0.3	0.5	-1.6
France	557.4	643.3	651.4	686.5	633.5	15.4	1.3	5.4	23.2
Germany	590.0	680.1	713.1	744.7	680.6	15.3	4.9	4.4	26.2
Italy[b]	917.0	962.0	936.1	961.8	943.8	4.9	-2.7	2.7	4.9
The Netherlands	885.9	646.3	614.1	537.6	674.7	-27.1	-5.0	-12.5	-39.3
Greece	600.5	585.3	573.1	539.0	574.0	-2.5	-2.1	-6.0	-10.2
Portugal[d]	796.2	835.2	819.7	704.9	784.4	4.9	-1.9	-14.0	-11.5
Spain	1043.8	1118.2	1098.8	898.7	1032.0	7.1	-1.7	-18.2	-13.9
Switzerland	254.1	409.1	405.0	381.7	358.4	61.0	-1.0	-5.8	50.2
Japan	771.9	745.3	730.5	724.9	743.6	-3.4	-2.0	-0.8	-6.1
Mean	715.66	731.97	719.22	686.02	711.97	2.3	-1.7	-4.6	-4.1
Coefficient of variation	0.64	0.63	0.60	0.64	0.62				
Correlation with 1974–9		0.98	0.95	0.93					-0.17

[a] Portugal from 1976 and Spain from 1977.
[b] Starting point of the time-series 1980.
[c] Only one time point available (1980). Missing values were substituted through extrapolation on the basis of the development of the family of nation (Austria, France, Germany, Italy, and the Netherlands).
[d] Only one time point available (1990). Missing values were substituted through extrapolation on the basis of the development of the family of nation (Greece and Spain).

Source: OECD, *Environmental Data Compendium* (with substitution of missing values through interpolation and extrapolation).

References

Aberbach, Joel D., and Bert A. Rockman (1992). 'Does Governance Matter—And if So, How? Process, Performance, and Outcomes', *Governance*, 5, 135–53.

Abrams, Burton A. (1999). 'The Effect of Government Size on the Unemployment Rate', *Public Choice*, 99, 395–401.

Addison, John T. (1997). 'The U.S. Labor Market: Structure and Performance', in Horst Siebert (ed.), *Structural Change and Labor Market Flexibility: Experience in Selected OECD Countries*. Tübingen, Germany: Mohr Siebeck, pp. 187–222.

Alber, Jens (1988). 'Continuities and Changes in the Idea of the Welfare State', *Politics and Society*, 16, 451–68.

—— and Guy Standing (2000). 'Social Dumping, Catch-up, or Convergence? Europe in a Comparative Global Context', *Journal of European Social Policy*, 10, 99–119.

Alesina, Alberto, and Dani Rodrik (1994). 'Distributive Politics and Economic Growth', *The Quarterly Journal of Economics*, 109, 465–90.

Almond, Gabriel A. (1956). 'Comparative Political Systems', *Journal of Politics*, 18, 391–409.

—— and G. Bingham Powell (1978). *Comparative Politics: System, Process, and Policy* (1st edn. 1966). Boston, MA: Little, Brown & Company.

—— and Sidney Verba (1963). *The Civic Culture: Political Attitudes and Democracy in Five Nations*. Princeton, NJ: Princeton University Press.

—— G. Bingham Powell Jr., Kaare Strøm, and Russell J. Dalton (eds.) (2003). *Comparative Politics Today: A World View*, updated 7th edn. New York: Longman.

Alvarez, R. Michael, Geoffrey Garrett, and Peter Lange (1991). 'Government Partisanship, Labor Organization, and Macroeconomic Performance', *American Political Science Review*, 85, 539–56.

Amenta, Edwin, and Theda Skocpol (1989). 'Taking Exception: Explaining the Distinctiveness of American Public Policies in the Last Century', in Francis G. Castles (ed.), *The Comparative History of Public Policy*. Oxford: Oxford University Press, pp. 292–333.

Anderson, Liam (2001). 'The Implications of Institutional Design for Macroeconomic Performance: Reassessing the Claims of Consensus Democracy', *Comparative Political Studies*, 34, 429–52.

Andrews, Frank M. (1981). 'Subjective Social Indicators, Objective Social Indicators, and Social Accounting Systems', in F. Thomas Juster and Kenneth C. Land (eds.), *Social Accounting Systems: Essays on the State of the Art*. New York: Academic Press, pp. 377–419.

Andrews, Richard N. L. (1997). 'United States', in Martin Jänicke and Helmut Weidner (eds.), *National Environmental Policies: A Comparative Study of Capacity-Building*. Berlin: Springer, pp. 25–71.

Armingeon, Klaus (1996). 'Konkordanzzwänge und Nebenregierungen als Handlungshindernisse?', *Schweizerische Zeitschrift für Politische Wissenschaft*, 2, 277–303.

—— (1999). 'Politische Reaktionen auf steigende Arbeitslosigkeit', in Andreas Busch and Thomas Plümper (eds.), *Nationaler Staat und internationale Wirtschaft: Anmerkungen zum Thema Globalisierung*. Baden-Baden: Nomos, pp. 169–96.

—— (2002). 'The Effects of Negotiation Democracy: A Comparative Analysis', *European Journal of Political Research*, 41, 81–105.

—— Michelle Beyeler, Markus Freitag, and Martin Senti (1999). 'Comparative Political Data Set 1960–96', University of Bern, Institute of Political Science.

Arrow, Kenneth, Bert Bolin, Robert Costanza, Partha Dasgupta, Carl Folke, C. S. Holling, Bengt-Owe Jansson, Simon Levin, Karl-Göran Mäler, Charles Perrings, and David Pimentel (1995). 'Economic Growth, Carrying Capacity, and the Environment', *Science*, 268, 520–1.

Atkinson, Anthony B. (1995). 'The Welfare State and Economic Performance', *National Tax Journal*, 48, 171–98.

—— (1996). 'Seeking to Explain the Distribution of Income', in John Hills (ed.), *New Inequalities: The Changing Distribution of Income and Wealth in the United Kingdom*. Cambridge: Cambridge University Press, pp. 19–48.

—— Lee Rainwater and Timothy M. Smeeding (1995). *Income Distribution in OECD Countries: Evidence from the Luxembourg Income Study*. Paris: Organisation for Economic Co-operation and Development.

Barrell, Ray, Melanie Lansbury, Nigel Pain, and Julian Morgan (1996). *US Labour Markets—The Process of Job Creation*. National Institute of Economic and Social Research, Research Studies RS 47, London: The Stationary Office.

Barro, Robert J. (1999). Inequality, Growth, and Investment, *NBER Working Paper* 7038. Cambridge, MA: National Bureau of Economic Research.

—— and Jong-Wha Lee (1993). 'International Comparisons of Educational Attainment', *Journal of Monetary Economics*, 32, 363–94.

Beck, Nathaniel, and Jonathan N. Katz (1995). 'What to Do (and Not to Do) with Time-Series Cross-Section Data', *American Political Science Review*, 89, 634–47.

—— and Jonathan N. Katz (1996). 'Nuisance vs. Substance: Specifying and Estimating Time-Series Cross-Section Models', *Political Analysis*, 6, 1–36.

Beck, Ulrich (ed.) (1998). *Politik der Globalisierung*. Frankfurt a. M.: Suhrkamp.

Becker, Uwe (1998). 'Beschäftigungswunderland Niederlande', *Aus Politik und Zeitgeschichte. Beilage zur Wochenzeitung 'Das Parlament'*. B11/98, 12–21.

Beisheim, Marianne, and Gregor Walter (1997). ' "Globalisierung"—Kinderkrankheiten eines Konzeptes', *Zeitschrift für internationale Beziehungen*, 4, 153–80.

—— Sabine Dreher, Gregor Walter, Bernhard Zangl, and Michael Zürn (1999). *Im Zeitalter der Globalisierung? Thesen und Daten zur gesellschaftlichen und politischen Denationalisierung*. Baden-Baden, Germany: Nomos.

Bennett, Richard R., and James P. Lynch (1990). 'Does a Difference Make a Difference? Comparing Cross-national Crime Indicators', *Criminology*, 28, 153–82.

Berelson, Bernhard R., Paul F. Lazarsfeld, and William N. McPhee (1954). *Voting: A Study of Opinion Formation in a Presidential Campaign*. Chicago, IL: The University of Chicago Press.

Bernecker, Walther L. (1990). 'Spanien und Portugal zwischen Regime-Übergang und stabilisierter Demokratie', *Aus Politik und Zeitgeschichte. Beilage zur Wochenzeitung 'Das Parlament'*. B51/90, 15–38.

Berry, William D., and Stanley Feldman (1985). *Multiple Regression in Practice*. Newbury Park, CA: Sage.

Binder, Manfred (1996). 'Die Operationalisierung umweltpolitischen Erfolges: Probleme und Lösungsansätze', in Martin Jänicke (ed.), *Umweltpolitik der Industrieländer: Entwicklung–Bilanz–Erfolgsbedingungen*. Berlin: edition sigma, pp. 133–52.

Birchfield, Vicki, and Markus M. L. Crepaz (1998). 'The Impact of Constitutional Structures and Collective and Competitive Veto Points on Income Equality in Industrialized Democracies', *European Journal of Political Research*, 34, 175–200.

Blank, Rebecca M., David Card, and Philip K. Robins (1999). Financial Incentives for Increasing Work and Income Among Low-Income Families, *NBER Working Paper* 6998. Cambridge, MA: National Bureau of Economic Research.

Blau, Judith R., and Peter M. Blau (1982). 'The Cost of Inequality: Metropolitan Structure and Violent Crime', *American Sociological Review*, 47, 114–29.

Bobbio, Norberto (1987). *The Future of Democracy. A Defence of the Rules of the Game*. Minneapolis, MN: University of Minnesota Press (Orig.: Il Futuro della democraczia 1984).

Bok, Derek (1996). *The State of the Nation: Government and the Quest for a Better Society*. Cambridge, MA: Harvard University Press.

Bollen, Kenneth (1980). 'Issues in the Comparative Measurement of Political Democracy', *American Sociological Review*, 45, 370–90.

Bonoli, Guilano (1997). 'Classifying Welfare States: A Two-Dimension Approach', *Journal of Social Policy*, 26, 351–72.

Brettschneider, Frank (1995). *Öffentliche Meinung und Politik: Eine empirische Studie zur Responsivität des deutschen Bundestages zwischen 1949 und 1990*. Opladen: Westdeutscher Verlag.

Brockhaus (1993). *Enzyklopädie Band 20*, 19th edn. Mannheim: Brockhaus.

Buchanan, James M., Robert D. Tollison, and Gordon Tullock (1980). *Toward a Theory of the Rent-seeking Society*. Texas, TX: College Station.

—— and Gordon Tullock (1962). *The Calculus of Consent: Logical Foundations of Constitutional Democracy*. Ann Arbor, MI: The University of Michigan Press.

Budge, Ian, Hans-Dieter Klingemann, Andrea Volkens, Judith Bara, and Eric Tannenbaum (2001). *Mapping Policy Preferences: Estimates for Parties, Electors and Governments, 1945–1998*. Oxford: Oxford University Press.

Burniaux, Jean-Marc, Thai-Thanh Dang, Douglas Fore, Michael Förster, Marco Mira d'Ercole, and Howard Oxley (1998a). Income Distribution and Poverty in Selected OECD Countries, *OECD Economics Department Working Papers* No. 189. Paris: Organisation for Economic Co-operation and Development.

—— (1998b). Income Distribution and Poverty in Selected OECD Countries. Annex 3. Main Trends in Income Distribution and Poverty: Evidence From Recent

Studies, *OECD Economics Department Working Papers* No. 189. Paris: Organisation for Economic Co-operation and Development.

Busch, Andreas and Thomas Plümper (eds.) (1999). *Nationaler Staat und internationale Wirtschaft*. Baden-Baden, Germany: Nomos.

Cameron, David R. (1978). 'The Expansion of the Public Economy: A Comparative Perspective', *American Political Science Review*, 72, 1243–61.

Carley, Michael (1981). *Social Measurement and Social Indicators: Issues of Policy and Theory*. London: Allen and Unwin.

Castles, Francis G. (ed.) (1982). *The Impact of Parties: Politics and Policies in Democratic Capitalist States*. Beverly Hills, CA: Sage.

—— (ed.) (1993). *Families of Nations: Patterns of Public Policy in Western Democracies*. Aldershot: Dartmouth.

—— (1998*a*). *Comparative Public Policy: Patterns of Post-War Transformation*. Cheltenham: Edward Elgar.

—— (1998*b*). 'The Really Big Trade-Off: Home Ownership and the Welfare State in the New World and the Old', *Acta Politica*, 33, 5–19.

—— (2002). 'Policy Performance in the Democratic State: An Emergent Field of Study', in Hans Keman (ed.), *Comparative Democratic Politics. A Guide to Contemporary Theory and Research*. London: Sage, pp. 215–32.

—— and Steve Dowrick (1990). 'The Impact of Government Spending Levels on Medium-Term Economic Growth on the OECD, 1960–85', *Journal of Theoretical Politics*, 2, 173–204.

—— and Peter Mair (1984). 'Left-Right Political Scales: Some "Expert" Judgements', *European Journal of Political Research*, 12, 73–88.

—— and Robert D. McKinlay (1979). 'Does Politics Matter: An Analysis of the Public Welfare Commitment in Advanced Democratic States', *European Journal of Political Research*, 7, 169–86.

—— (1997). 'Reflections: Does Politics Matter? Increasing Complexity and Renewed Challenges', *European Journal of Political Research*, 31, 102–7.

—— and Deborah Mitchell (1992). 'Identifying Welfare State Regimes: The Links between Politics, Instruments and Outcomes', *Governance*, 5, 1–26.

Clayton, Richard and Jonas Pontusson (1998). 'Welfare-State Retrenchment Revisited: Entitlement Cuts, Public Sector Restructuring, and Inegalitarian Trends in Advanced Capitalist Societies', *World Politics*, 51, 67–98.

Cohen, Lawrence E., and Marcus Felson (1979). 'Social Change and Crime Rate Trends: A Routine Activity Approach', *American Sociological Review*, 44, 588–608.

Collier, David (1993). 'The Comparative Method', in Ada W. Finifter (ed.), *Political Science: The State of the Discipline II*. Washington, DC: The American Political Science Association, 105–19.

Collins Cobuild (1987). *English Language Dictionary*. London: Collins.

Colomer, Joseph M. (ed.) (1996). *Political Institutions in Europe*. London: Routledge.

Coppedge, Michael, and Wolfgang H. Reinicke (1991). 'Measuring Polyarchy', in Alex Inkeles (ed.), *On Measuring Democracy: Its Consequences and Concomitants*. New Brunswick, NJ: Transaction Publisher, pp. 47–68.

Crepaz, Martin M. L. (1995). 'Explaining National Variations of Air Pollution Levels: Political Institutions and Their Impact on Environmental Policy-Making', *Environmental Politics*, 4, 391–414.

—— (1996). 'Consensus versus Majoritarian Democracy: Political Institutions and their Impact on Macroeconomic Performance and Industrial Disputes', *Comparative Political Studies*, 29, 4–26.

—— (1998). 'Inclusion vs. Exclusion: Political Institutions and Welfare Expenditures', *Comparative Politics*, 31, 61–80.

—— (2001). 'Veto Players, Globalization and the Redistributive Capacity of the State: A Panel Study of 15 OECD Countries', *Journal of Public Policy*, 21, 1–22.

Crozier, Michel J., Samuel P. Huntington, and Joji Watanuki (1975). *The Crisis of Democracy: Report on the Governability of Democracies to the Trilateral Commission*. New York: New York University Press.

Cusack, Thomas R. (1995). Politics and Macroeconomic Performance in the OECD Countries, *WZB Discussion Paper* FS I 95–315. Berlin: Wissenschaftszentrum Berlin für Sozialforschung.

Czada, Roland and Manfred G. Schmidt (eds.) (1993). *Verhandlungsdemokratie, Interessenvermittlung, Regierbarkeit: Festschrift für Gerhard Lehmbruch*. Opladen, Germany: Westdeutscher Verlag.

Dahl, Robert A. (1967). 'The Evaluation of Political Systems', in Ithiel de Sola Pool (ed.), *Contemporary Political Science: Toward Empirical Theory*. New York: McGraw-Hill, pp. 166–81.

—— (1971). *Polyarchy. Participation and Opposition*. New Haven, CT: Yale University Press.

—— (1989). *Democracy and its Critics*. New Haven, CT: Yale University Press.

Dahrendorf, Ralf (1996). 'Die Quadratur des Kreises: Ökonomie, sozialer Zusammenhalt und Demokratie im Zeitalter der Globalisierung. Ein "Blätter"-Gespräch mit Ralf Dahrendorf', *Blätter für deutsche und internationale Politik*, 9, 1060–71.

Diamond, Larry (1999). *Developing Democracy. Toward Consolidation*. Baltimore, MD: The Johns Hopkins University Press.

Diener, Ed (1995). 'A Value Based Index for Measuring National Quality of Life', *Social Indicators Research*, 36, 107–27.

Dijk, Jan van, and John van Kesteren (1996). 'The Prevalence of Perceived Seriousness of Victimization by Crime: Some Results of the International Crime Victims Survey', *European Journal of Crime, Criminal Law and Criminal Justice*, 4, 48–70.

—— Pat Mayhew, and Martin Killias (1990). *Experiences of Crime Across the World: Key Findings of the 1989 International Crime Survey*. Deventer, The Netherlands: Kluwer Law and Taxation.

Di Palma, Giuseppe (1977). *Surviving Without Governing. The Italian Parties in Parliament*. Berkeley, CA: University of California Press.

Easton, David (1990). *The Analysis of Political Structure*. New York: Routledge.

Ebbinghaus, Bernhard (1998). 'Europe through the Looking-Glass: Comparative and Multi-Level Perspectives', *Acta Sociologica*. 41, 301–13.

Eckstein, Harry (1971). *The Evaluation of Political Performance: Problems and Dimensions*. Beverly Hills, CA: Sage.

Elkins, Paul (1994). 'The Environmental Sustainability of Economic Processes: A Framework for Analysis', in Jeroen van den Bergh and Jan van der Straaten (eds.), *Toward Sustainable Development: Concepts, Methods and Policy*. Washington, DC: Island Press, pp. 25–55.

Elster, Jon (1979). *Ulysses and the Sirens: Studies in Rationality and Irrationality*. Cambridge: Cambridge University Press.

Esping-Andersen, Gøsta (1990). *The Three Worlds of Welfare Capitalism*. Cambridge: Polity Press.

Esser, Hartmut (1987). 'Warum die Routine nicht weiterhilft: Überlegungen zur Kritik an der "Variablen"-Soziologie', in Norbert Müller and Herbert Stachowiak (eds.), *Problemlösungsoperator Sozialwissenschaft: Anwendungsorientierte Modelle der Sozial- und Planungswissenschaften in ihrer Wirksamkeitsproblematik, Vol. 1*. Stuttgart: Ferdinand Enke, pp. 230–45.

Eurostat (1997). *Living Conditions in Europe—Selected Indicators*. Luxembourg: European Communities.

Flora, Peter and Arnold J. Heidenheimer (eds.) (1981). *The Development of Welfare States in Europe and America*. New Brunswick, NJ: Transaction Books.

—— Jens Alber, and Jürgen Kohl (1977). 'Zur Entwicklung der westeuropäischen Wohlfahrtsstaaten', *Politische Vierteljahresschrift*, 18, 707–72.

Förster, Michael (1994). *Measurement of Low Incomes and Poverty in a Perspective of International Comparisons*, OECD Labour Market and Social Policy Occasional Papers, No. 14. Paris: Organisation for Economic Co-operation and Development.

Foweraker, Joe (2001). 'Democratic Performance', in Paul Barry Clarke and Joe Foweraker (eds.), *Encyclopedia of Democratic Thought*. London: Routledge, pp. 202–7.

—— and Roman Krznaric (2000). 'Differentiating the Democratic Performance of the West', *European Journal of Political Research*, 42, 313–40.

Franz, Peter (1986). 'Der "Constraint Choice"—Ansatz als gemeinsamer Nenner individualistischer Ansätze in der Soziologie', *Kölner Zeitschrift für Soziologie und Sozialpsychologie*, 38, 32–54.

Freedom House (1990). *Freedom in the World: The Annual Survey of Political Rights and Civil Liberties 1989–*. New York.

Friedman, Milton (1962). *Capitalism and Freedom*. Chicago, IL: University of Chicago Press.

Friedrichs, Jürgen (1997). 'Globalisierung—Begriff und grundlegende Annahmen', *Aus Politik und Zeitgeschichte. Beilage zur Wochenzeitung 'Das Parlament'*, B33–34/97, 3–11.

Fuchs, Dieter (1989). *Die Unterstützung des politischen Systems der Bundesrepublik Deutschland*. Opladen: Westdeutscher Verlag.

—— (1993). A Metatheory of the Democratic Process, *WZB Discussion Paper* FS III 93–203. Berlin: Wissenschaftszentrum Berlin für Sozialforschung (WZB).

—— (1998). 'Kriterien demokratischer Performanz in Liberalen Demokratien', in Michael Greven (ed.), *Demokratie—eine Kultur des Westens? 20. Wissenschaftlicher Kongreß der Deutschen Vereinigung für Politische Wissenschaft*. Opladen: Leske + Budrich, 152–79.

—— (1999). 'Soziale Integration und politische Institutionen in modernen Gesellschaften', in Jürgen Friedrichs and Wolfgang Jagodzinski (eds.), *Soziale Integration, Special Issue 39 of Kölner Zeitschrift für Soziologie und Sozialpsychologie*. Opladen, Germany: Westdeutscher Verlag, pp. 147–78.

—— (2000). 'Typen und Indizes demokratischer Regime. Eine Analyse des Präsidentialismus und des Veto-Spieler-Ansatzes', in Hans-Joachim Lauth, Gert Pickel, and Christian Welzel (eds.), *Empirische Demokratiemessung*. Opladen, Germany: Westdeutscher Verlag, pp. 27–48.

—— and Hans-Dieter Klingemann (2002). 'Eastward Enlargement of the European Union and the Identity of Europe', *West European Politics*, 25, 19–54.

Gabler (1997). *Wirtschaftslexikon, CD-ROM*, 14th edn. Wiesbaden: Gabler.

Gallagher, Michael (1991). 'Proportionality, Disproportionality and Electoral Systems', *Electoral Studies*, 10, 33–51.

Garrett, Geoffrey (1998). *Partisan Politics in the Global Economy*. Cambridge: Cambridge University Press.

Gebhardt, Thomas, and Herbert Jacobs (1997). 'Amerikanische Verhältnisse? Sozialhilfe in den USA und Deutschland: Ein Vergleich aus historischer, institutioneller und rechtlicher Perspektive', *Zeitschrift für Sozialreform*, 43, 597–634.

Giddens, Anthony (1998). *The Third Way. The Renewal of Social Democracy*. Cambridge: Polity Press.

—— (2000). *The Third Way and its Critics*. Cambridge: Polity Press.

Göhler, Gerhard (1994). 'Politische Institutionen und ihr Kontext: Begriffliche und konzeptionelle Überlegungen zur Theorie politischer Institutionen', in Gerhard Göhler (ed.), *Die Eigenart der Institutionen: Zum Profil politischer Institutionentheorie*. Baden-Baden: Nomos, pp. 19–46.

Goodin, Robert E. (1996). 'Institutionalizing the Public Interest: The Defense of Deadlock and Beyond', *American Political Science Review*, 90, 331–43.

—— Bruce Heady, Ruud Muffels, and Henk-Jan Dirven (1999). *The Real Worlds of Welfare Capitalism*. Cambridge: Cambridge University Press.

Gottschalk, Peter, and Timothy M. Smeeding (1997). 'Cross-National Comparisons of Earnings and Income Inequality', *Journal of Economic Literature*, 35, 633–86.

—— (2000). 'Empirical Evidence on Income Inequality in Industrialized Countries', in Anthony B. Atkinson and François Bourguignon (eds.), *Handbook of Income Distribution*, Vol. 1. Amsterdam: Elsevier, pp. 261–307.

Gottschalk, Peter, Björn Gustafsson, and Edward Palmer (1997). 'What's Behind the Increase in Inequality? An Introduction', in Peter Gottschalk, Björn Gustafsson, and Edward Palmer (eds.), *Changing Patterns in the Distribution of Economic Welfare: An International Perspective*. Cambridge: Cambridge University Press, pp. 1–11.

Grimm, Dieter (ed.) (1996). *Staatsaufgaben*. Frankfurt a. M.: Suhrkamp.

Grossman, Gene M., and Alan B. Krueger (1993). 'Economic Growth and the Environment', *The Quarterly Journal of Economics*, 110, 353–77.

Gurr, Ted Robert (1972). *Politimetrics: An Introduction to Quantitative Macropolitics*. Englewood Cliffs, NJ: Prentice-Hall.

—— (1977). 'Crime Trends in Modern Democracies since 1945', *International Annals of Criminology*, 16, 41–86.

Gurr, Ted Robert (1979). 'On the History of Violent Crime in Europe and America', in Hugh Davis Graham and Ted Robert Gurr (eds.), *Violence in America: Historical and Comparative Perspectives*. Beverly Hills, CA: Sage, pp. 353–74.

—— (ed.), (1980). *Handbook of Political Conflict: Theory and Research*. New York: Free Press.

—— (1989). 'Historical Trends in Violent Crime: Europe and the United States', in Ted Robert Gurr (ed.), *Violence in America. Vol. 1, The History of Crime*. Newbury Park, CA: Sage, pp. 11–54.

—— and Mark Irving Lichbach (1986). 'Forecasting Internal Conflict: A Competitive Evaluation of Empirical Theories', *Comparative Political Studies*, 19, 3–38.

—— and Muriel McClelland (1971). *Political Performance: A Twelve-Nation Study*. Beverly Hills, CA: Sage.

—— Keith Jaggers, and Will H. Moore (1990). 'The Transformation of the Western State: The Growth of Democracy, Autocracy, and State Power since 1800', *Studies in Comparative International Development*, 25, 73–108.

Gustafsson, Björn, and Mats Johansson (1999). 'In Search of Smoking Guns: What Makes Income Inequality Vary Over Time in Different Countries', *American Sociological Review*, 64, 585–605.

Habermas, Jürgen (1988). *Legitimation Crisis*. Cambridge: Polity Press (Orig.: Legitimationsprobleme im Spätkapitalismus 1973).

—— (1998). 'Jenseits des Nationalstaats? Bemerkungen zu Folgeproblemen der wirtschaftlichen Globalisierung', in Ulrich Beck (ed.), *Politik der Globalisierung*. Frankfurt a. M.: Suhrkamp, pp. 67–84.

Hagerty, Micheal R., Robert Cummins, Abbott L. Ferriss, Kenneth Land, Alex C. Michalos, Mark Peterson, Andrew Sharpe, Joseph Sirgy, and Joachim Vogel (2000). *Quality of Life Indexes for National Policy: Review and Agenda for Research*, Report of the Committee for Societal QOL Indexes, ISQOLS-International Society for the Quality of Life, http://www.gsm.ucdavis.edu/mrhagert/papers/working_paper.html.

Hall, Peter A. (1986). *Governing the Economy: The Politics of State Intervention in Britain and France*. Cambridge: Polity Press.

—— and Rosemary C. R. Taylor (1996). 'Political Science and the Three New Institutionalisms', *Political Studies*, 44, 952–73.

Hayek, Friedrich August von (1960). *The Constitution of Liberty*. Chicago, IL: University of Chicago Press.

Heidenheimer, Arnold J. (1981). 'Education and Social Security: Entitlements in Europe and America', in Peter Flora and Arnold J. Heidenheimer (eds.), *The Development of Welfare States in Europe and America*. New Brunswick, NJ: Transaction Books, pp. 269–304.

Heinze, Rolf G., Josef Schmid, and Christoph Strünck (1999). *Vom Wohlfahrtsstaat zum Wettbewerbsstaat: Arbeitsmarkt- und Sozialpolitik in den 90er Jahren*. Opladen: Leske + Budrich.

Held, David, Anthony McGrew, David Goldblatt, and Jonathan Perraton (1999). *Global Transformations. Politics, Economics and Culture*. Stanford, CA: Stanford University Press.

Henkel, Hans-Olaf (1997). 'Für eine Reform des politischen Systems', in Manfred Bissinger (ed.), *Stimmen gegen den Stillstand: Roman Herzogs 'Berliner Rede' und 33 Antworten*, Hamburg: Hoffmann & Campe, pp. 87–90.

Hibbs, Douglas A. Jr. (1977). 'Political Parties and Macroeconomic Policy', *American Political Science Review*, 71, 1467–87.

Hicks, Alexander M. (1994). 'Introduction to Pooling', in Thomas Janoski and Alexander M. Hicks (eds.), *The Comparative Political Economy of the Welfare State*. Cambridge: Cambridge University Press, pp. 169–88.

—— and Lane Kenworthy (1998). 'Cooperation and Political Economic Performance in Affluent Democratic Capitalism', *American Journal of Sociology*, 103, 1631–72.

Hinterberger, Friedrich, Markus Hofreither, Philipp Schepelmann, Dietmar Kanatschnig, Joachim Spangenberg, Petra Schmutz, and Bernhard Burdick (1998). Integration von Umwelt-, Wirtschafts- und Sozialpolitik, *EU Policy Paper* No. 1. Wuppertal: Wuppertal-Institut für Klima, Umwelt, Energie; Vienna: Österreichisches Institut für Nachhaltige Entwicklung.

Hirst, Paul, and Grahame Thompson (1999). *Globalization in Question. The International Economy and the Possibilities of Governance*, 2nd edn. Cambridge: Polity Press.

Hoffmann-Riem, Wolfgang (1997). 'Tendenzen in der Verwaltungsrechtsentwicklung', *Die Öffentliche Verwaltung*, 50, 433–42.

Huang, Wei-Sung Wilson and Charles F. Wellford (1989). 'Assessing Indicators of Crime among International Crime Data Series', *Criminal Justice Policy Review*, 3, 28–47.

Huber, Evelyne, Charles Ragin, and John D. Stephens (1993). 'Social Democracy, Christian Democracy, Constitutional Structure, and the Welfare State', *American Journal of Sociology*, 99, 711–49.

Huber, John, and Ronald Inglehart (1995). 'Expert Interpretations of Party Space and Party Locations in 42 Societies', *Party Politics*, 1, 73–111.

Hucke, Jochen (1992). 'Umweltschutzpolitik', in Manfred G. Schmidt (ed.), *Die westlichen Länder, Band 3 des Lexikons der Politik edited by Dieter Nohlen*. Munich: C. H. Beck, pp. 440–7.

Huntington, Samuel P. (1996). *The Clash of Civilizations and the Remaking of World Order*. New York: Simon & Schuster.

Immergut, Ellen M. (1992). *Health Politics: Interests and Institutions in Western Europe*. Cambridge: Cambridge University Press.

Inglehart, Ronald, Miguel Basañez, and Alejandro Moreno (1998). *Human Values and Beliefs: A Cross-cultural Sourcebook: Political, Religious, Sexual, and Economic Norms in 43 Societies: Findings From the 1990–93 World Values Survey*. Ann Arbor, MI: The University of Michigan Press.

Interpol (International Criminal Police Organization). *International Crime Statistics 1977–*. Paris.

Iversen, Torben, and Thomas R. Cusack (2000). 'The Causes of Welfare State Expansion: Deindustrialization or Globalization?', *World Politics*, 52, 313–49.

Jackman, Robert W., and Ross A. Miller (1995). 'Voter Turnout in the Industrial Democracies during the 1980s', *Comparative Political Studies*, 27, 467–92.

Jänicke, Martin (1992). 'Conditions for Environmental Policy Success: An International Comparison', *The Environmentalist*, 12, 47–58.

—— and Helmut Weidner (1997). 'Zum aktuellen Stand der Umweltpolitik im internationalen Vergleich–Tendenzen zu einer globalen Konvergenz?', *Aus Politik und Zeitgeschichte. Beilage zur Wochenzeitung 'Das Parlament'*, B27/97, 15–24.

—— Harald Mönch, and Manfred Binder (1996a). 'Getting Rich–Getting Clean? Umweltindikatorenprofile im Industrieländervergleich', *Zeitschrift für angewandte Umweltforschung*, 9, 41–55.

—— (1996b). 'Umweltindikatorenprofile im Industrieländervergleich: Wohlstandsniveau und Problemstruktur', in Martin Jänicke (ed.), *Umweltpolitik der Industrieländer: Entwicklung–Bilanz–Erfolgsbedingungen*. Berlin: edition sigma, pp. 114–31.

Jaggers, Keith, and Ted Robert Gurr (1995). 'Tracking Democracy's Third Wave with Polity III', *Journal of Peace Research*, 32, 469–82.

Jahn, Detlef (1998). 'Environmental Performance and Policy Regimes: Explaining Variations in 18 OECD-Countries', *Policy Sciences*, 31, 107–31.

Jakobeit, Cord (1997). *Internationale Institutionen in den ökonomischen und ökologischen Nord-Süd-Beziehungen: Kooperation als Ausweg aus den Irrwegen der Entwicklungs- und Umweltpolitik in der 'Einen Welt'?*. University of Hamburg: Habilitationsschrift.

Jöhr, Walter A., and Hans W. Singer (1955). *The Role of the Economist as Official Adviser*. London: Allen & Unwin

Jörgens, Helge (1996). 'Die Institutionalisierung von Umweltpolitik im internationalen Vergleich', in Martin Jänicke (ed.), *Umweltpolitik der Industrieländer: Entwicklung–Bilanz–Erfolgsbedingungen*. Berlin: edition sigma, pp. 59–111.

Kaase, Max (1995). 'Demokratie im Spannungsfeld von politischer Kultur und politischer Struktur', *Jahrbuch für Politik*, 5, 199–220.

Kaiser, André (1997). 'Types of Democracy: From Classical to New Institutionalism', *Journal of Theoretical Politics*, 9, 419–44.

Kalish, Carol B. (1988). *International Crime Rates: U.S. Department of Justice, Bureau of Justice Statistics, Special Report*. Washington, DC: Bureau of Justice Statistics.

Kamp, Matthias (2000). 'Grund zur Unruhe', *Wirtschaftswoche*, No. 6, 2nd March 2000, 38–40.

Katzenstein, Peter J. (1985). *Small States in World Markets: Industrial Policy in Europe*. Ithaca, NY: Cornell University Press.

Kaufmann, Franz-Xaver (1996). 'Diskurse über Staatsaufgaben', in Dieter Grimm (ed.), *Staatsaufgaben*. Frankfurt a. M.: Suhrkamp, pp. 15–41.

Keesing's Contemporary Archives/Keesing's Record of World Events 1960. Cambridge: Keesing's Worldwide.

Kenworthy, Lane (1995). *In Search of National Economic Success: Balancing Competition and Cooperation*. Thousand Oaks, CA: Sage.

Kern, Kristine, and Stefan Bratzel (1996). 'Umweltpolitischer Erfolg im internationalen Vergleich: Zum Stand der Forschung', in Martin Jänicke (ed.), *Umweltpolitik der Industrieländer: Entwicklung–Bilanz–Erfolgsbedingungen*. Berlin: edition sigma, pp. 29–58.

Kesteren, John van, Pat Mayhew, and Paul Nieuwbeerta (2000). *Criminal Victimisation in Seventeen Industrialised Countries: Key Findings from the 2000 International Crime Victims Survey*. The Hague: Wetenschappelijk Onderzoek- en Documentatiecentrum.

King, Anthony (1973). 'Ideas, Institutions and the Policies of Governments: A Comparative Analysis', *British Journal of Political Science*, 3, Part I and II, 293–313; Part III, 409–23.

—— (1975). 'Overload: Problems of Governing in the 1970s', in *Political Studies*, 23, 284–96.

King, Gary, James Honaker, Anne Joseph, and Kenneth Scheve (2001). 'Analyzing Incomplete Political Science Data: An Alternative Algorithm for Multiple Imputation', *American Political Science Review*, 95, 49–69.

Kirschen, Etienne S., J. Benard, H. Besters, F. Blackaby, O. Eckstein, J. Faaland, F. Hartog, L. Morissens, and E. Tosco (1964). *Economic Policy in Our Time, Vol. I: General Theory*. Amsterdam: North-Holland.

Kitschelt, Herbert, Peter Lange, Gary Marks, and John D. Stephens (Hrsg.), (1999). *Continuity and Change in Contemporary Capitalism*. Cambridge: Cambridge University Press.

Kittel, Bernhard (1999). 'Sense and Sensitiveness in Pooled Analysis of Political Data', *European Journal of Political Research*, 35, 225–53.

Klingemann, Hans-Dieter, Richard I. Hofferbert, and Ian Budge (1994). *Parties, Policies, and Democracy*. Boulder, CO: Westview.

Kluckhohn, Clyde (1962). 'Values and Value-Orientation in the Theory of Action: An Exploration in Definition and Classification', in Talcott Parsons and Edward A. Shils (eds.), *Toward a General Theory of Action*. New York: Harper & Row, pp. 388–433.

Knoepfel, Peter, and Helmut Weidner (1985). *Luftreinhaltepolitik (stationäre Quellen) im internationalen Vergleich*. Berlin: edition sigma.

Koelble, Thomas A. (1995). 'The New Institutionalism in Political Science and Sociology', *Comparative Politics*, 37, 231–43.

Kohl, Jürgen (1992). 'Armut im internationalen Vergleich: Methodische Probleme und empirische Ergebnisse', in Stephan Leibfried and Wolfgang Voges (eds.), *Armut im modernen Wohlfahrtsstaat, Special Issue 32 of Kölner Zeitschrift für Soziologie und Sozialpsychologie*. Opladen, Germany: Westdeutscher Verlag, 272–99.

—— (1999). 'Leistungsprofil wohlfahrtsstaatlicher Regimetypen', in Peter Flora and Heinz-Herbert Noll (eds.), *Sozialberichterstattung und Sozialstaatsbeobachtung: Individuelle Wohlfahrt und wohlfahrtsstaatliche Institutionen im Spiegel empirischer Analysen*. Frankfurt a. M.: Campus, pp. 111–39.

Korpi, Walter (1985). 'Economic Growth and the Welfare State: Leaky Bucket or Irrigation System?', *European Sociological Review*, 1, 97–118.

—— and Joakim Palme (1998). 'The Paradox of Redistribution and Strategies of Equality: Welfare State Institutions, Inequality, and Poverty in the Western Countries', *American Sociological Review*, 63, 661–87.

Kühnel, Steffen M., and Dagmar Krebs (2001). *Statistik für die Sozialwissenschaften: Grundlagen, Methoden, Anwendungen*. Reinbek bei Hamburg: Rowohlt.

Kuznets, Simon (1955). 'Economic Growth and Income Inequality', *American Economic Review*, 45, 1–28.

—— (1966). *Modern Economic Growth: Rate, Structure and Spread*. New Haven, CT: Yale University Press.

Laakso, Markku, and Rein Taagepera (1979). ' "Effective" Number of Parties: A Measure with Application to West Europe', *Comparative Political Studies*, 12, 3–27.

Land, Kenneth (2000). 'Social Indicators', in Edgar F. Borgatta and Rhonda J. V. Montgomery (eds.), *Encyclopedia of Sociology*, 2nd edn. New York: Macmillan, pp. 2682–90.

Landau, Daniel L. (1985). 'Government Expenditure and Economic Growth in the Developed Countries: 1952–76', *Public Choice*, 47, 459–77.

Lane, Jan Erik, and Svante Ersson (1994). *Comparative Politics: An Introduction and a New Approach*. Cambridge: Polity Press.

Lasswell, Harold D. (1960). *Psychopathology and Politics*. New York: Viking Press.

Lauvaux, Philippe (1990). *Les grandes démocraties contemporaines*. Paris: Presses Universitaires de France.

Laver, Michael J., and Ian Budge (1992). *Party Policy and Government Coalitions*. New York: St. Martin's.

Lehmbruch, Gerhard (1967). *Proporzdemokratie: Politisches System und politische Kultur in der Schweiz und in Österreich*. Tübingen: J.C.B. Mohr (Paul Siebeck).

—— (1992). 'Konkordanzdemokratie', in Manfred G. Schmidt (ed.), *Die westlichen Länder, Band 3 des Lexikon der Politik ed. by Dieter Nohlen*. Munich: Beck, 206–11.

Leibfried, Stephan (1992). 'Towards a European Welfare State? On Integrating Poverty Regimes into the European Community', in Zsuzsa Ferge and John Eivind Kolberg (eds.), *Social Policy in a Changing Europe*. Frankfurt a. M.: Campus, 245–79.

Lijphart, Arend (1968). *The Politics of Accommodation: Pluralism and Democracy in the Netherlands*, 2nd edn. Berkeley, CA: University of California Press.

—— (1971). 'Comparative Politics and Comparative Method', *American Political Science Review*, 65, 682–93.

—— (1984). *Democracies: Patterns of Majoritarian and Consensus Government in Twenty-one Countries*, New Haven, CT: Yale University Press.

—— (1989). 'Democratic Political Systems: Types, Cases, Causes and Consequences', *Journal of Theoretical Politics*, 1, 33–48.

—— (1994). 'Democracies: Forms, Performance, and Constitutional Engineering', *European Journal of Political Research*, 25, 1–17.

—— (1997). 'About Peripheries, Centres and Other Autobiographical Reflections', in Hans Daalder (ed.), *Comparative European Politics: The Story of a Profession*. London: Pinter, pp. 241–52.

—— (1999*a*). *Patterns of Democracy: Government Forms and Performance in Thirty-Six Countries*. New Haven, CT: Yale University Press.

—— (1999*b*). 'Power-Sharing and Group Autonomy in the 1990s and the 21st Century', Paper delivered at the Conference 'Constitutional Design 2000', December 9–11, 1999, Kellogg Institute for International Studies, University of Notre Dame.

―― (2002). 'Negotiation Democracy versus Consensus Democracy: Parallel Conclusions and Recommendations', *European Journal of Political Research*, 41, 107–13.

―― and Markus M. L. Crepaz (1991). 'Corporatism and Consensus Democracy in Eighteen Countries: Conceptual and Empirical Linkages', *British Journal of Political Science*, 21, 235–46.

Lindert, Peter H., and Jeffrey G. Williamson (1985). 'Growth, Equality and History', *Explorations in Economic History*, 22, 341–77.

Linz, Juan J. (1978). *The Breakdown of Democratic Regimes: Crisis, Breakdown, and Reequilibration*. Baltimore, MD: The Johns Hopkins University Press.

Lipset, Seymour Martin (1981). *Political Man: The Social Bases of Politics*, 2nd edn. Baltimore, MD: The Johns Hopkins University Press.

―― (1990). *Continental Divide: The Values and Institutions of the United States and Canada*, New York: Routledge.

―― (1996). *American Exceptionalism: A Double-Edged Sword*. New York: W. W. Norton.

LIS—Luxembourg Income Study (2000). http://www.lis.ceps.lu/.

Loewenstein, Karl (1957). *Political Power and the Governmental Process*. Chicago, IL: The University of Chicago Press.

Loske, Reinhard, and Raimund Bleischwitz (1996). *Zukunftsfähiges Deutschland: Ein Beitrag zu einer global nachhaltigen Entwicklung: Studie des Wuppertal Instituts für Klima, Umwelt, Energie GmbH*, ed. by BUND (Bund für Umwelt und Naturschutz in Deutschland) and Misereor. Basil: Birkhäuser.

Lynch, James (1995). 'Crime in International Perspective', in James Q. Wilson and Joan Petersilia (eds.), *Crime: Twenty-eight Leading Experts Look at the Most Pressing Problems of Our Time*. San Francisco: ICS Press, pp. 11–38.

Mackie, Thomas T., and Richard Rose (1991). *The International Almanac of Electoral History*, 3rd edn. New York: The Free Press.

Maddison, Angus (1991). *Dynamic Forces in Capitalist Development: A Long-Run Comparative View*. Oxford: Oxford University Press.

―― (1995). *Monitoring the World Economy 1820–1992*. Paris: Organisation for Economic Co-operation and Development.

Maier, Matthias Leonard (1999). 'The Role of Ideas in the Politics of Sustainable Development' (Florence: The European University Institute, unpublished manuscript).

Mair, Peter (1996). 'Comparative Politics: An Overview', in Robert E. Goodin and Hans-Dieter Klingemann (eds.), *A New Handbook of Political Science*. Oxford: Oxford University Press, pp. 309–35.

Maravall, José Maria (1993). 'Politics and Policy: Economic Reforms in Southern Europe', in Luiz Carlos Bresser Pereira, José Maria Maravall, and Adam Przeworski, *Economic Reforms in New Democracies: A Social-Democratic Approach*. Cambridge: Cambridge University Press, pp. 77–131.

March, James G., and Johan P. Olsen (1984). 'The New Institutionalism: Organizational Factors in Political Life', *American Political Science Review*, 78, 734–49.

Maslow, Abraham H. (1938). *Motivation and Personality*. Oxford: Oxford University Press.

Mayntz, Renate, and Fritz W. Scharpf (eds.) (1995). *Gesellschaftliche Selbstregulierung und politische Steuerung*. Frankfurt a. M.: Campus.

McClintock, Brent (1998). 'Whatever Happened to New Zealand? The Great Capitalist Restoration Reconsidered', *Journal of Economic Issues*, 32, 497–503.

Meadows, Dennis, Donella Meadows, Jørgen Randers, and William W. Behrens III (1972). *The Limits to Growth: A Report for the Club of Rome's Project on the Predicament of Mankind*. New York: Universe Books.

Merriam, Charles E. (1962). *Systematic Politics*. Chicago, IL: University of Chicago Press.

Messner, Steven F. (1989). 'Economic Discrimination and Societal Homicide Rates: Further Evidence on the Cost of Inequality', *American Sociological Review*, 54, 597–611.

Milanovic, Branko (1994). Determinants of Cross-Country Income Inequality. An 'Augmented' Kuznets' Hypothesis, *Policy Research Working Paper* No. 1246. Washington: The World Bank, Policy Research Department, Transition Economics Division.

Morris, David (1979). *Measuring the Condition of the World's Poor: the Physical Quality of Life Index*. New York: Pergamon Press.

Mosley, Hugh, and Christopher Engelmann (2000). 'Methodological Issues of Radar Work Charts as a Benchmarking Tool in European Employment Policy (Draft final report, Part II), Report prepared for European Commission, Directorate-General Employment, and Social Affairs (DG V/A2)'. Berlin: Wissenschaftszentrum Berlin für Sozialforschung (June 2000).

—— and Antje Mayer (1999). Benchmarking National Labour Market Performance: A Radar Chart Approach, *WZB Discussion Paper* FS I 99–202. Berlin: Wissenschaftszentrum Berlin für Sozialforschung.

Mueller, Dennis C. (1996). *Constitutional Democracy*. New York: Oxford University Press.

Münch, Richard (1998). *Globale Dynamik, lokale Lebenswelten: Der schwierige Weg in die Weltgesellschaft*. Frankfurt a. M.: Suhrkamp.

Nie, Norman H., C. Hadlai Hull, Jean G. Jenkins, Karin Steinbrenner, and Dale H. Bent (1975). *SPSS: Statistical Package for the Social Sciences*, 2nd edn. New York: McGraw-Hill.

Niedermayer, Oskar (1996). 'Zur systematischen Analyse der Entwicklung von Parteiensystemen', in Oscar W. Gabriel and Jürgen W. Falter (eds.), *Wahlen und politische Einstellungen in westlichen Demokratien*. Frankfurt a. M: Peter Lang, pp. 19–49.

Noll, Heinz-Herbert, and Wolfgang Zapf (1994). 'Social Indicators Research: Societal Monitoring and Social Reporting', in Ingwer Borg and Peter P. Mohler (eds.), *Trends and Perspectives in Empirical Social Research*. Berlin: Walter de Gruyter, pp. 1–16.

Norström, Thor (1988) . 'Theft Criminality and Economic Growth', *Social Science Research*, 17, 48–65.

Obinger, Herbert, and Uwe Wagschal (2001). 'Families of Nation and Public Policy', *West European Politics*, 24, 99–114.

OECD (1985). *OECD Environmental Data Compendium 1985*. Paris: Organisation for Economic Co-operation and Development.

—— (1986*a*). *Living Conditions in OECD Countries: A Compendium of Social Indicators*. Paris: Organisation for Economic Co-operation and Development.

—— (1986*b*). *Economic Outlook*. December 1986. Paris: Organisation for Economic Co-operation and Development.

—— (1987). *Economic Outlook*. June 1987, Paris: Organisation for Economic Co-operation and Development.

—— (1992). *Education at a Glance: OECD Indicators*. Paris: Organisation for Economic Co-operation and Development.

—— (1993). *OECD Environmental Data Compendium 1993*. Paris: Organisation for Economic Co-operation and Development.

—— (1994). *Environmental Indicators: OECD Core Set*. Paris: Organisation for Economic Co-operation and Development.

—— (1995*a*). *Income Distribution in OECD Countries. Evidence from the Luxembourg Income Study*, Prepared by Anthony B. Atkinson, Lee Rainwater, and Timothy M. Smeeding. Paris: Organisation for Economic Co-operation and Development.

—— (1995*b*). *OECD Environmental Data Compendium 1995*. Paris: Organisation for Economic Co-operation and Development.

—— (1995*c*). *Historical Statistics 1960–94 on Diskette*. Paris: Organisation for Economic Co-operation and Development.

—— (1997). *OECD Environmental Data Compendium 1997*. Paris: Organisation for Economic Co-operation and Development.

—— (1998*a*). *Education at a Glance: OECD Indicators*. Paris: Organisation for Economic Co-operation and Development.

—— (1998*b*). *OECD Work on Sustainable Development: A Discussion Paper on Work to be Undertaken over the Period 1998–2001*. Paris: Organisation for Economic Co-operation and Development, http://www.oecd.org/subject/sustdev/oecdwork.htm.

—— (1998*c*). *Health Data 98* (CD-ROM).

—— (1998*d*). Income Distribution and Poverty in Selected OECD Countries, Annex 2: Sensitivity of Results to Equivalence Scales, Annex 3: Main Trends in Income Distribution and Poverty: Evidence from Recent Studies, *Economics Department Working Papers* No. 189, by Jean-Marc Burniaux, Thai-Thanh Dang, Douglas Fore, Michael Förster, Marco Mira d'Ercole, and Howard Oxley. Paris: Organisation for Economic Co-Operation and Development.

—— (1999*a*). *OECD Statistical Compendium*, Edition 01#1999 (CD-ROM).

—— (1999*b*). 'Standardised Unemployment Rates', *Quarterly Labour Force Statistics*, No. 2, 133–35.

—— (2000). *Issues Concerning the Analysis of Prices Changes*, www.oecd.org/std/CPIANALY.htm.

Okun, Arthur M. (1975). *Equality and Efficiency: The Big Tradeoff*. Washington, DC: The Brookings Institution.

Olson, Mancur (1982). *The Rise and Decline of Nations*. New Haven, CT: Yale University Press.

Osberg, Lars, Sadettin Erksoy, and Shelley Phipps (1997). 'Unemployment, Unemployment Insurance and the Distribution of Income in Canada in the 1990s', in Peter Gottschalk, Björn Gustafsson, and Edward Palmer (eds.), *Changing*

Patterns in the Distribution of Economic Welfare: An International Perspective.
Cambridge: Cambridge University Press, pp. 84–107.

Ostrom, Elinor (1995). 'New Horizons in Institutional Analysis', *American Political Science Review*, 89, 174–78.

Palmer, Monte (1997). *Political Development: Dilemmas and Challenges*. Itasca, IL: Peacock.

Parsons, Talcott (1971). *The System of Modern Societies*. Englewood Cliffs, NJ: Prentice Hall.

Pearce, David W, and Jeremy J. Warford (1993). *World without End: Economics, Environment and Sustainable Development*. Oxford: Oxford University Press (Published for the World Bank).

Pennings, Paul, Hans Keman, and Jan Kleinnijenhuis (1999). *Doing Research in Political Science: An Introduction to Comparative Methods and Statistics*. London: Sage.

Pennock, Roland J. (1966). 'Political Development, Political System, and Political Goods', *World Politics*, 18, 415–34.

—— (1979). *Democratic Political Theory*. Princeton, NJ: Princeton University Press.

Persson, Torsten, and Guido Tabellini (1994). 'Is Inequality Harmful for Growth?', *American Economic Review*, 84, 600–21.

Peters, Guy (1999). *Institutional Theory in Political Science: The 'New Institutionalism'*. London: Continuum.

Pfaller, Alfred, with Ian Gough (1991). 'The Competitiveness of Industrialized Welfare States: A Cross-Country Survey', in Alfred Pfaller, Ian Gough, and Göran Therborn (eds.), *Can the Welfare State Compete? A Comparative Study of Five Advanced Capitalist Countries*. Houndsmills, UK: Macmillan, pp. 15–43.

Phillips, Alban W. (1958). 'The Relationship between Unemployment and the Rate of Change of Money: Wage Rates in the United Kingdom 1861–1957', *Economica*, 34, 283–99.

Pierson, Paul (1996). 'The New Politics of the Welfare State', *World Politics*, 48, 143–79.

—— (1999). 'Coping with Permanent Austerity: Welfare State Restructuring in Affluent Societies', European University Institute, European Forum, Centre for Advanced Studies, 1998–9; Project directed by Maurizio Ferrera and Martin Rhodes 'Recasting the European Welfare State: Options, Constraints, Actors', Florence, June 21–22, 1999.

Pocock, John G. A. (1975). *The Machiavellian Moment: Florentine Political Thought and the Atlantic Republican Tradition*. Princeton, NJ: Princeton University Press.

Powell, G. Bingham, Jr. (1982). *Contemporary Democracies: Participation, Stability and Violence*. Cambridge, MA: Harvard University Press.

—— (1990). 'Holding Governments Accountable: How Constitutional Arrangements and Party Systems Affect Clarity of Responsibility for Policy in Contemporary Democracies', Paper Delivered to the Annual Meeting of the American Political Science Association, San Francisco, California, August 1990.

—— (1992). 'Liberal Democracies', in Mary Hawkesworth and Maurice Kogan (eds.), *Encyclopedia of Government and Politics*, Vol. I. London: Routledge, pp. 195–214.

Powell, Elwin H. (1966). 'Crime as a Function of Anomie', *The Journal of Criminal Law, Criminology, and Police Science*, 57, 161–71.

Przeworski, Adam and Henry Teune (1970). *The Logic of Comparative Social Inquiry*. New York: John Wiley.

—— Susan C. Stokes, and Bernard Manin (eds.) (1999). *Democracy, Accountability, and Representation*. Cambridge: Cambridge University Press.

Putnam, Robert D., with Robert Leonardi and Raffaella Y. Nanetti (1993). *Making Democracy Work: Civic Traditions in Modern Italy*. Princeton, NJ: Princeton University Press.

Ricken, Christian (1995). 'Nationaler Politikstil, Netzwerkstrukturen sowie ökonomischer Entwicklungsstand als Determinanten einer effektiven Umweltpolitik: Ein empirischer Industrieländervergleich', *Zeitschrift für Umweltpolitik und Umweltrecht*, 18, 481–501.

Riker, William H. (1962). *The Theory of Political Coalitions*. New Haven, CT: Yale University Press.

Ringquist, Evan J. (1995). 'Evaluating Environmental Policy Outcomes', in James P. Lester (ed.), *Environmental Politics & Policy: Theories and Evidence*, 2nd edn. Durham and London: Duke University Press, pp. 303–27.

Ritchie, Ella (1992). 'Law and Order', in Martin Harrop (ed.), *Power and Policy in Liberal Democracies*. Cambridge: Cambridge University Press, pp. 195–217.

Roberts, J. Timmons, and Peter E. Grimes (1997). 'Carbon Intensity and Economic Development 1962–91: A Brief Exploration of the Environmental Kuznets Curve', *World Development*, 25, 191–98.

Rodrik, Dani (1998). 'Why Do More Open Economies Have Bigger Governments?', *Journal of Political Economy*, 106, 997–1032.

Rokeach, Milton (1973). *The Nature of Human Values*. New York: The Free Press.

Roller, Edeltraud (1991). Ein analytisches Schema zur Klassifikation von Politikinhalten, *WZB Discussion Paper* FS III 91–201. Berlin: Wissenschaftszentrum Berlin für Sozialforschung (WZB).

—— (1992). *Einstellungen der Bürger zum Wohlfahrtsstaat der Bundesrepublik Deutschland*, Opladen, Germany: Westdeutscher Verlag.

—— (1995). 'Political Agendas and Beliefs about the Scope of Government', in Ole Borre (ed.), *The Scope of Government*. Oxford: Oxford University Press, pp. 55–86.

—— (1998). 'Positions- und performanzbasierte Sachfragenorientierungen und Wahlentscheidung: Eine theoretische und empirische Analyse aus Anlass der Bundestagswahl 1994', in Max Kaase and Hans-Dieter Klingemann (eds.), *Wahlen und Wähler: Analysen aus Anlass der Bundestagswahl 1994*. Opladen: Westdeutscher Verlag, pp. 173–219.

—— (2000). 'Ende des sozialstaatlichen Konsenses? Zum Aufbrechen traditioneller und zur Entstehung neuer Konfliktstrukturen in Deutschland', in Oskar Niedermayer and Bettina Westle (eds.), *Demokratie und Partizipation*. Opladen: Westdeutscher Verlag, pp. 88–114.

Rose, Richard (1976). 'On the Priorities of Government: A Developmental Analysis of Public Policies', *European Journal of Political Research*, 4, 247–89.

Rossi, Peter H. and Howard E. Freeman (1989). *Evaluation: A Systematic Approach*, 4th edn. Newbury Park, CA: Sage.

Rostow, Walt W. (1971). *Politics and the Stages of Growth*. Cambridge: Cambridge University Press.

Samuelson, Paul A., and William D. Nordhaus (1995). *Economics*. New York: McGraw-Hill.

Sangmeister, Hartmut (1994). 'Soziale Indikatoren', in Jürgen Kriz, Dieter Nohlen, and Rainer-Olaf Schultze (eds.), *Politikwissenschaftliche Methoden, Band 2 des Lexikon der Politik edited by Dieter Nohlen*, Munich: C. H. Beck, pp. 422–6.

Sartori, Giovanni (1976). *Parties and Party Systems: A Framework for Analysis*. Cambridge: Cambridge University Press.

—— (1987). *The Theory of Democracy Revisited*. Chatham, NY: Chatham House Publishers.

—— (1994). *Comparative Constitutional Engineering: An Inquiry into Structures, Incentives and Outcomes*. Houndsmills, UK: Macmillan.

Saunders, Peter (1986). 'What Can We Learn from International Comparison of Public Sector Size and Economic Performance?', *European Sociological Review*, 2, 52–60.

Schafer, J. L. (2000). *Analysis of Incomplete Multivariate Data*. London: Chapman & Hall.

Scharpf, Fritz W. (1989). 'Decision Rules, Decision Styles, and Policy Choices', *Journal of Theoretical Politics*, 1, 149–76.

—— (1991). *Crisis and Choice in European Social Democracy*. Ithaca, NY: Cornell University Press (Orig.: Sozialdemokratische Krisenpolitik in Europa 1987).

—— (1997). Employment and the Welfare State: A Continental Dilemma, *MPIfG Working Paper* 97/7. Cologne: Max-Planck-Institut für Gesellschaftsforschung.

—— (1998). 'Demokratische Politik in der internationalisierten Ökonomie', in Michael Greven (ed.), *Demokratie—eine Kultur des Westens? 20. Wissenschaftlicher Kongreß der Deutschen Vereinigung für Politische Wissenschaft*. Opladen: Leske & Budrich, pp. 81–103.

—— (1999). The Viability of Advanced Welfare States in the International Economy: Vulnerabilities and Options, *MPIfG Working Paper* 99/9. Cologne: Max-Planck-Institut für Gesellschaftsforschung.

Schmid, Günther (1998). 'Können wir von den Niederlanden lernen? Ein Vergleich des niederländischen und deutschen Beschäftigungssystems', in Bernd Müller (ed.), *Vorbild Niederlande?*. Münster: Agenda, pp. 97–113.

—— Holger Schütz, and Stefan Speckesser (1999). 'Broadening the Scope of Benchmarking. Radar Charts and Employment Systems', *Labour*, 13, 879–99.

Schmidt, Manfred G. (1982). *Wohlfahrtsstaatliche Politik unter bürgerlichen und sozialdemokratischen Regierungen: Ein internationaler Vergleich*. Frankfurt a. M.: Campus.

—— (1987). 'West Germany: The Policy of the Middle Way', *Journal of Public Policy*, 7, 135–77.

—— (1989). 'Learning from Catastrophes—West Germany's Public Policy', in Francis G. Castles (ed.), *The Comparative History of Public Policy*. New York: Oxford University Press, pp. 56–99.

—— (1992*a*). 'Arbeitslosigkeit und Vollbeschäftigung', in Manfred G. Schmidt (ed.), *Die westlichen Länder, Band 3 des Lexikon der Politik edited by Dieter Nohlen*. Munich: C. H. Beck, pp. 27–34.

—— (1992*b*). 'Regierungen: Parteipolitische Zusammensetzung', in Manfred G. Schmidt (ed.), *Die westlichen Länder, Band 3 des Lexikon der Politik edited by Dieter Nohlen*. Munich: C. H. Beck, pp. 393–400.

—— (1993). 'Theorien in der international vergleichenden Staatstätigkeitsforschung', in Adrienne Héritier (ed.), *Policy-Forschung: Kritik und Neuorientierung. Special Issue 24 of Politische Vierteljahresschrift*. Opladen: Westdeutscher Verlag, pp. 371–93.

—— (1995). *Wörterbuch zur Politik*. Stuttgart: Alfred Kröner.

—— (1996). 'When Parties Matter: A Review of Possibilities and Limits of Partisan Influence on Public Policy', *European Journal of Political Research*, 30, 155–83.

—— (1997*a*). 'Policy-Analyse', in Arno Mohr (ed.), *Grundzüge der Politikwissenschaft*, 2nd edn., Munich: R. Oldenbourg, pp. 567–604.

—— (1997*b*). 'Determinants of Social Expenditure in Liberal Democracies. The Post World War II Experience', *Acta Politica*, 32, 153–73.

—— (1998*a*). 'Das politische Leistungsprofil der Demokratien', in Michael Greven (ed.), *Demokratie—eine Kultur des Westens? 20. Wissenschaftlicher Kongreß der Deutschen Vereinigung für Politische Wissenschaft*. Opladen: Leske + Budrich, pp. 181–99.

—— (1998*b*). 'Wohlfahrtsstaatliche Regime: Politische Grundlagen und politisch-ökonomisches Leistungsvermögen', in Stephan Lessenich and Ilona Ostner (eds.), *Welten des Wohlfahrtkapitalismus: Der Sozialstaat in vergleichender Perspektive*. Frankfurt a. M.: Campus, pp. 179–200.

—— (2000*a*). *Demokratietheorien: Eine Einführung*, 3rd edn. (1st edn., 1995). Opladen: Leske + Budrich.

—— (2000*b*). 'Immer noch auf dem "mittleren Weg"? Deutschlands Politische Ökonomie am Ende des 20. Jahrhunderts', in Roland Czada and Hellmut Wollmann (eds.), *Von der Bonner zur Berliner Republik: 10 Jahre Deutsche Einheit, Special Issue 19/1999 of Leviathan*. Opladen, Germany: Westdeutscher Verlag, pp. 491–513.

—— (2002). 'Political Performance and Types of Democracy: Findings from Comparative Analysis', *European Journal of Political Research*, 41, 147–63.

Schmitter, Philippe C. (1993). 'Comparative Politics', in Joel Krieger (ed.), *The Oxford Companion to Politics of the World*. New York: Oxford University Press, pp. 171–77.

Schnapp, Kai-Uwe (2004). *Ministerialbürokratien in westlichen Demokratien. Eine vergleichende Analyse*. Opladen, Germany: Leske + Budrich.

Schröder, Dieter, together with Konrad Roester, and Gotthold Zubeil (1971). *Wachstum und Gesellschaftspolitik: Gesellschaftliche Grundlagen der längerfristigen Sicherung des wirtschaftlichen Wachstums*. Stuttgart, Germany: Kohlhammer.

Schütz, Holger, Stefan Speckesser, and Günther Schmid (1998). Benchmarking Labour Market Performance and Labour Market Policies: Theoretical Foundations and Applications, *WZB Discussion Paper* FS I 98–205. Berlin: Wissenschaftszentrum Berlin für Sozialforschung (WZB).

SCP (The Dutch Social and Cultural Planning Office) (1998). *Social and Cultural Report 1998: 25 Years of Social Change*. Rijswijk: Sociaal en Cultureel Planbureau.

Scruggs, Lyle A. (1999). 'Institutions and Environmental Performance in Seventeen Western Democracies', *British Journal of Political Science*, 29, 1–31.

—— (2003). *Sustaining Abundance. Environmental Performance in Industrial Democracies*. Cambridge: Cambridge University Press.

Shafik, Nemat (1994). 'Economic Development and Environmental Quality: An Econometric Analysis', *Oxford Economic Papers*, 46 (Supp.), 757–73.

—— and Sushenjit Bandyopadhyay (1992). Economic Growth and Environmental Quality: Time-Series and Cross-Country Evidence, *Working Paper for the World Development Report WPS* 904. Washington, DC: The World Bank.

Shalev, Michael (1998). 'Limits of and Alternatives to Multiple Regression in Macro-Comparative Research', Paper prepared for presentation at the second conference on The Welfare State at the Crossroads, Stockholm, June 12–14, 1998.

Shepsle, Kenneth A. (1988). 'Representation and Governance: The Great Legislative Trade-Off', *Political Science Quarterly*, 103, 461–84.

Shugart, Matthew Soberg, and John M. Carey (1992). *Presidents and Assemblies: Constitutional Design and Electoral Dynamics*. Cambridge: Cambridge University Press.

Siaroff, Alan (1999). 'Corporatism in 24 Industrial Democracies: Meaning and Measurement', *European Journal of Political Research*, 36, 175–205.

Sigmund, Paul E. (1971). *Natural Law in Political Thought*. Cambridge, MA: Winthrop Publishers.

Simon, Herbert A. (1987). 'Bounded Rationality', in John Eatwell, Murray Milgate, and Peter Newman (eds.), *The New Palgrave: A Dictionary of Economics*, Vol. I. London: The Macmillan Press, pp. 266–8.

Smeeding, Timothy M. (1997). Financial Poverty in Developed Countries. The Evidence from LIS. Final Report to the UNDP, *LIS Working Paper* No. 155, 1997.

—— Michael O'Higgins, and Lee Rainwater (eds.) (1990). *Poverty, Inequality and Income Distribution in Comparative Perspective: The Luxemburg Income Study (LIS)*. New York: Harvester Wheatsheaf.

Spelthahn, Sabine (1994). 'Umweltschutz als Wettbewerbsvorteil?', in Eberhardt Schmidt and Sabine Spelthahn (eds.), *Umweltpolitik in der Defensive: Umweltpolitik trotz Wirtschaftskrise*. Frankfurt a. M.: Fischer, pp. 57–69.

Steffani, Winfried (1979). *Parlamentarische und präsidentielle Demokratie. Strukturelle Aspekte westlicher Demokratien*. Opladen, Germany: Westdeutscher Verlag.

Stephens, John D., Evelyne Huber, and Leonard Ray (1999). 'The Welfare State in Hard Times', in Herbert Kitschelt, Peter Lange, Gary Marks, and John D. Stephens (eds.), *Continuity and Change in Contemporary Capitalism*. Cambridge: Cambridge University Press, pp. 164–93.

Stern, David I., Michael S. Common, and Edward B. Barbier (1996). 'Economic Growth and Environmental Degradation: The Environmental Kuznets Curve and Sustainable Development', *World Development*, 24, 1151–60.

Stimson, James A., Michael B. MacKuen, and Robert S. Erikson (1995). 'Dynamic Representation', *American Political Science Review*, 89, 543–65.

Stokes, Donald E. (1963). 'Spatial Models of Party Competition', *American Political Science Review*, 57, 368–77.

Streit, Manfred (2000). *Theorie der Wirtschaftspolitik*, 5th edn. Düsseldorf: Werner.

Strøm, Kaare, Wolfgang C. Müller, and Torbjörn Bergmann (eds.) (2003). *Delegation and Accountability in Parliamentary Democracies*. Oxford: Oxford University Press.

Summers, Robert and Alan Heston (1991). 'The Penn World Table (Mark 5). An Expanded Set of International Comparisons, 1950–1988', *Quarterly Journal of Economics*, 106, 327–68.

Swank, Duane (2002). *Global Capital, Political Institutions, and Policy Change in Developed Welfare States*. Cambridge: Cambridge University Press.

Taagepera, Rein (1997). 'Effective Number of Parties for Incomplete Data', *Electoral Studies*, 16, 145–51.

Taylor, Charles Lewis, and David A. Jodice (1983). *World Handbook of Political Indicators*, 3rd edn. New Haven, CT: Yale University Press.

Tronti, Leonello (1998). 'Benchmarking Labour Market Performances and Policies', *Labour*, 12, 489–513.

Tsebelis, George (1995). 'Decision Making in Political Systems: Veto Players in Presidentialism, Parliamentarism, Multicameralism, and Multipartyism', *British Journal of Political Science*, 25, 289–325.

—— (1999). 'Veto Players and Law Production in Parliamentary Democracies: An Empirical Analysis', *American Political Science Review*, 93, 591–608.

—— (2000). 'Veto Players and Institutional Analysis', *Governance*, 13, 441–74.

—— (2002). *Veto Players. How Political Institutions Work*. Princeton, NJ: Princeton University Press.

Tuchtfeldt, Egon (1982). 'Wirtschaftspolitik', in Willi Albers et al. (eds.), *Handwörterbuch der Wirtschaftswissenschaft (HdWW)*, Vol. 9. Stuttgart: Gustav Fischer, pp. 178–206.

UN (United Nations, Department of International Economic and Social Affairs). (1969–97) *Demographic Yearbook 1969–1997*. New York.

—— (ed.) (1989). *Handbook on Social Indicators*. New York.

UN-DPCSD (United Nations, Department for Policy Coordination and Sustainable Development) (1996–97). *Indicators of Sustainable Development: Framework and Methodologies*, gopher://gopher.un.org:70/00/esc/cn17/1996–97/indicators/.

UNDP (United Nations Development Programme) (1990). *Human Development Report 1990*. New York: UNDP.

UNDP (United Nations Development Programme) (1995). *Human Development Report 1995*. New York: Oxford University Press.

UNDP (United Nations Development Programme) (1998). *Human Development Report 1998*. New York: Oxford University Press.

UNESCO. *Statistics*. http://unescostat.unesco.org/.

Uusitalo, Hannu (1985). 'Redistribution and Equality in the Welfare State: An Effort to Interpret the Major Findings of Research on the Redistributive Effects of the Welfare State', *European Sociological Review*, 1, 163–76.

Vanhanen, Tatu (1984). *The Emergence of Democracy: A Comparative Study of 119 States, 1850–1979*. Helsinki: Finnish Society of Sciences and Letters.

Visser, Jelle, and Anton Hemerijck (1997). *A Dutch Miracle: Job Growth, Welfare Reform and Corporatism in the Netherlands*. Amsterdam: Amsterdam University Press.

Vogel, David (1993). 'Representing Diffuse Interests in Environmental Policymaking', in Kent R. Weaver and Bert A. Rockman (eds.), *Do Institutions Matter? Government Capabilities in the United States and Abroad*. Washington, DC: The Brookings Institutions, pp. 237–71.

—— and Veronica Kun (1987). 'The Comparative Study of Environmental Policy: A Review of the Literature', in Meinold Dierkes, Hans N. Weiler, and Ariane Berthoin Antal (eds.), *Comparative Policy Research: Learning from Experience*. Aldershot: Gower, pp. 99–170.

Vogel, Joachim (1998). 'The European "Welfare Mix": Institutional Configuration and Distributive Outcome in Sweden and the European Union: A Longitudinal and Comparative Perspective', *Social Indicators Research*, 48, 245–97.

Wagschal, Uwe (1999a). 'Schranken staatlicher Steuerungspolitik: Warum Steuerreformen scheitern können', in Andreas Busch and Thomas Plümper (eds.), *Nationaler Staat und internationale Wirtschaft: Anmerkungen zum Thema Globalisierung*. Baden-Baden, Germany: Nomos, pp. 223–47.

—— (1999b). *Statistik für Politikwissenschaftler*. Munich: R. Oldenbourg.

WCED (World Commission on Environment and Development) (1987). *Our Common Future*. Oxford: Oxford University Press.

Weaver, Kent R., and Bert A. Rockman (eds.) (1993). *Do Institutions Matter? Government Capabilities in the United States and Abroad*. Washington, DC: The Brookings Institutions.

Weede, Erich (1984). 'Demokratie, schleichender Sozialismus und ideologischer Sozialismus als Determinanten des Wirtschaftswachstums: Eine international vergleichende Studie zur "rent-seeking-society" ', *Zeitschrift für Politik*, 31, 408–24.

—— (1991). 'The Impact of State Power on Economic Growth Rates in OECD Countries', *Quality and Quantity*, 25, 421–38.

Weidner, Helmut, and Peter Knoepfel (1983). 'Innovation durch international vergleichende Politikanalyse dargestellt am Beispiel der Luftreinhaltepolitik', in Renate Mayntz (ed.), *Implementation politischer Programme II: Ansätze zur Theoriebildung*. Opladen: Westdeutscher Verlag, pp. 221–55.

Weingast, Barry R. (1996). 'Political Institutions: Rational Choice Perspectives', in Robert E. Goodin and Hans-Dieter Klingemann (eds.), *A New Handbook of Political Science*. Oxford: Oxford University Press, pp. 167–90.

Weiss, Carol H. (1972). *Evaluation Research: Methods of Assessing Program Effectiveness*. Englewood Cliffs, NJ: Prentice Hall.

Wessels, Bernhard (1991). *Erosion des Wachstumsparadigmas: Neue Konfliktstrukturen im politischen System der Bundesrepublik?* Opladen: Westdeutscher Verlag.

WHO (World Health Organization). *World Health Statistics Annual 1962–*. Geneva.

Wicke, Lutz, together with Wilfried Franke (1991). *Umweltökonomie: Eine praxisorientierte Einführung*, 3rd edn. Munich: Franz Vahlen.

Wilensky, Harold L. (1975). *The Welfare State and Equality: Structural and Ideological Roots of Public Expenditures*. Berkeley, CA: University of California Press.

Windhoff-Héritier, Adrienne (1991). 'Institutions, Interests and Political Choice', in Roland Czada and Adrienne Windhoff-Héritier (eds.), *Political Choice: Institutions, Rules, and the Limits of Rationality*. Frankfurt a. M.: Campus, pp. 27–52.

Woldendorp, Jaap, Hans Keman, and Ian Budge (eds.) (1993). 'Special Issue: Political Data 1945–1990: Party Government in 20 Democracies', *European Journal of Political Research*, 24, 1–119.

—— (1998). 'Party Government in 20 Democracies: An Update (1990–1995)', *European Journal of Political Research*, 33, 125–64.

World Economic Forum (1999). 'Wake up Europe! Europe 2050 Initiative: A Call by European GLTs [European Global Leaders for Tomorrow] for Visionary Leadership'. Davos.

Webster Dictionary. *Merriam-Webster*. http://www.m-w.com/.

Zapf, Wolfgang (1977). 'Soziale Indikatoren—Eine Zwischenbilanz', in Hans-Jürgen Krupp and Wolfgang Zapf, *Sozialpolitik und Sozialberichterstattung*. Frankfurt a. M.: Campus, pp. 231–46.

—— (1979). 'Modernization and Welfare Development: The Case of Germany', *Social Science Information*, 18, 219–46.

Zentralarchiv für Empirische Sozialforschung (1999). *ISSP 1996: Role of Government III: Codebook: ZA Study 2900*. Cologne: Zentralarchiv für Empirische Sozialforschung.

Zimmermann, Gunter E. (1998). 'Armut', in Bernhard Schäfers and Wolfgang Zapf (eds.), *Handwörterbuch zur Gesellschaft Deutschlands*. Opladen: Leske + Budrich, pp. 35–49.

Zimmermann, Horst (1973). 'Die Ausgabenintensität der öffentlichen Aufgabenerfüllung', *Finanzarchiv*, 32, 1–20.

—— (1996). *Wohlfahrtsstaat zwischen Wachstum und Verteilung: Zu einem grundlegenden Konflikt in Hocheinkommensländern*. Munich: Franz Vahlen.

Zukunftskommission der Friederich-Ebert-Stiftung (1998). *Wirtschaftliche Leistungsfähigkeit, sozialer Zusammenhalt, ökologische Nachhaltigkeit: Drei Ziele—ein Weg*. Bonn: Dietz.

Zürn, Michael (1998). *Regieren jenseits des Nationalstaates*. Frankfurt a. M.: Suhrkamp.

Author Index

Subject Index

Note: t indicates a table or a figure